Contemporary
Religious Issues

42-63

WADSWORTH CONTINUING EDUCATION SERIES
Leonard Freedman, General Editor

ARMAMENT AND DISARMAMENT: THE CONTINUING DISPUTE
edited by Walter R. Fisher
University of Southern California
and Richard D. Burns
California State College, Los Angeles

CONTEMPORARY COMMUNISM
edited by Howard R. Swearer
and Richard Longaker
University of California, Los Angeles

CONTEMPORARY LABOR ISSUES
edited by Walter R. Fogel
and Archie Kleingartner
University of California, Los Angeles

CONTEMPORARY MORAL ISSUES, Second Edition
edited by Harry K. Girvetz
University of California, Santa Barbara

CONTEMPORARY RELIGIOUS ISSUES
edited by Donald E. Hartsock
University of California, Los Angeles

ISSUES OF THE SEVENTIES
edited by Leonard Freedman
University of California, Los Angeles

METROPOLIS: VALUES IN CONFLICT
edited by C. E. Elias, Jr.
Fresno State College
James Gillies
York University
and Svend Riemer
University of California, Los Angeles

THE NEW TECHNOLOGY AND HUMAN VALUES
edited by John G. Burke
University of California, Los Angeles

POVERTY: AMERICAN STYLE
edited by Herman P. Miller
U.S. Bureau of the Census

PROBLEMS AND PROSPECTS OF THE NEGRO MOVEMENT
edited by Raymond J. Murphy
University of Rochester
and Howard Elinson
University of California, Los Angeles

TENSION AREAS IN WORLD AFFAIRS
edited by Arthur C. Turner
University of California, Riverside
and Leonard Freedman
University of California, Los Angeles

TWENTIETH CENTURY: THE GREAT ISSUES
edited by William R. Hitchcock
University of California, Santa Cruz

Contemporary
Religious Issues

*BTQ
128
H37*

*BL
25
H33*

Edited by
Donald E. Hartsock
University of California, Los Angeles

Wadsworth Publishing Company, Inc., Belmont, California

3 4 5 6 7 8 9 10   74 73 72 71

L. C. Cat. Card No.: 68–29159
Printed in the United States of America

Preface

The nineteenth century announced the death of God; the twentieth century has laid God to rest. Dostoevsky's lament has become contemporary man's anthem: "Everything is now permissible for man."

Yet a closer reading of our times, with all its sloganeering and cliché thinking, reveals that while nineteenth-century concepts of God have died, a new vitality has been born within religious thought. The accelerated evolution of our world into a technological, urbanized, increasingly crowded "spaceship" has forced traditional religion to come to grips with the uneasy modern feeling that "everything that was nailed down is coming loose."

The traditional answers to the timeless questions of man—Who is man? What is his situation? What is his destiny?—are being challenged. Questions with which men have wrestled in all ages are becoming increasingly urgent in the revolutionary twentieth century. The tenaciousness of these questions and the memory of their traditionally accepted answers may restrain many men from entering fully into the spirit of this new permissive age. But many others have taken new hope from what they see as the downfall of religious "tyranny." Although they may discard the old answers, however, they cannot elude the questions themselves.

This book will examine the questions confronting man in the twentieth century and the premises, expectations, and actions he brings to bear on them. The bulk of the book's materials reflects Western roots and perspectives, but the increasingly critical confrontation of Western with non-Western views, religious and nonreligious, is not ignored.

Part One poses what I judge to be basic religious questions whose answers form the foundation of a culture, the authoritative norm of a society: Who is man? What is man's situation? What is man's destiny? Is God necessary for modern man? The first three questions are implicit in all past cultural systems. The fourth is offered because it is the crucial question for this modern, "secularized" age.

Part Two presents issues with which modern man is faced. Our responses to the questions of Part One offer clues as to how we might approach these issues.

The role of religion is not to wrestle only with the issues of the past, nor to counter change with the promise of a return to greener pastures or of shelter or crusade against the paradoxical world. As Part Three demonstrates, religion is becoming revolutionary because it is going back to the roots of its heritage, recovering a sense of faith in facing the future, and inviting men to participate in shaping their destiny. By responding to a rapidly changing world, by recovering its heritage in response to today's questions and issues, religion has become a participant in the affairs of the twentieth century.

I wish to thank the authors and publishers who have allowed their material to be reprinted in this collection of readings and to acknowledge the assistance of others who helped to make this book possible: Dr. Leonard Freedman, friend, counselor, and general editor of this series; Claudine Guest, my faithful and patient secretary; and my wife, Jo, whose wit and charm are evidence that grace is not solely a religious issue for me.

Donald E. Hartsock

Contents

part one
Religious Questions

1
Introduction

This chapter introduces the situation in which traditional religion finds itself in the modern world. The issues touched on here will be explored more fully in subsequent chapters.

In the first selection, William Hamilton conveys the tone of the religious ferment characteristic of the twentieth century in his discussion of the century's pivotal religious event, the "death" of God. Hamilton's premise is that, for more men than established religion is willing to admit, God has truly died; and if religion is to be relevant in the modern world, it must accept that fact. Neither its fundamental doctrines nor its role in the world can any longer be taken for granted. A growing realization of this is, perhaps, responsible for the energy with which basic religious questions and answers are currently being re-examined.

The way in which the condition of religion reflects the condition of culture is described by John Turnbull in his analysis of American religion. Insofar as American culture is "confusing, self-contradictory, and ambiguous," Turnbull remarks, so is American religion. On the other hand, as Mircea Eliade's article points out, the condition of culture also reflects the condition of religion. Eliade explores the difficulties and self-contradictions encountered in a culture in which both religion and myth have been discarded. In such a culture, those facets of human experience previously interpreted and thus controlled through religion and myth are now interpreted through a patchwork of ultimately unfulfilling pseudo-religions and pseudo-myths.

The last two articles in this chapter reflect the kind of attitudes and thought required for an understanding of the growing involvement of world cultures one with another and the probable intermeshing of future civilizations. Karl Reischaurer's analysis of world religions demonstrates that different concepts of God can be seen as a continuum in which areas of overlap become possibilities for religious synthesis. Huston Smith foresees the emergence of one world civilization, arising from an amalgam of the three great surviving cultures—the Western, the Chinese, and the Indian. Each of these cultures, says Smith, has accented one of man's three basic and inescapable conflicts: his conflict with nature, his conflict with his fellow men, and his conflict with himself. Smith warns that in a world civilization, man will be required to cope with all three conflicts simultaneously. Now is the time, he suggests, for each culture to begin looking to the others for guidance.

Since the focus of Western culture has always been on man's conflict with nature, we have produced a technological society in which man's conflicts with his fellow men and with himself are aggravated. It is not an exaggeration to say that the survival of Western culture is contingent on its success in relieving these aggravations. Therefore, the question implicit in this book is whether Western religion will play a part in this all-important task. Or is religion even relevant in the context of the contemporary world? The essays gathered together here will help to provide an answer.

William Hamilton

The Death of God

> *Have you ever heard of the madman who on a bright morning lighted a lantern and ran to the market place calling out unceasingly: "I seek God! I seek God!"—As there were many people standing about who did not believe in God, he caused a great deal of amusement. Why! is he lost? said one. Has he strayed away like a child? said another. Or does he keep himself hidden? Is he afraid of us? Has he taken a sea-voyage? Has he emigrated?—the people cried out laughingly, all in a hubbub. The insane man jumped into their midst and transfixed them with his glances. "Where is God gone?" he called out. "I mean to tell you! <u>We have killed</u> him—you and I! We are all his murderers! . . .*
>
> *"Do we not smell the divine putrefaction?—for even Gods putrefy! God is dead! God remains dead! And we have killed him! How shall we console ourselves, the most murderous of all murderers? . . . Is not the magnitude of this deed too great for us? Shall we not ourselves have to become Gods, merely to seem worthy of it? There never was a greater event—and on account of it, all who are born after us belong to a higher history than any history hitherto!"—Here the madman was silent and looked again at his hearers: they also were silent and looked at him in surprise. At last he threw his lantern on the ground, so that it broke in pieces and was extinguished. "I come too early," he then said, "I am not yet at the right time. This prodigious event is still on its way, and is traveling—it has not yet reached men's ears . . ."*

These wild and lovely words, written by Friedrich Nietzsche toward the close of the last century, have recently broken loose from the obscurity of lecture, textbook and monograph, into the incomprehending

From *Playboy Magazine*, Vol. 13, No. 8, August 1966. Copyright © 1966 by HMH Publishing Co., Inc. Reprinted by permission of the author and the publisher.

William Hamilton, Professor of Theology at Colgate-Rochester Divinity School, is coauthor of *Radical Theology and the Death of God* with W. J. J. Altizer.

world of cocktail party, newsmagazine with intellectual pretensions and television. Why? What has happened? Is there really an event properly called "the death of God"? Or is the current chatter enveloping the phrase simply another of the many non-events afflicting our time?

No. The death of God *has* happened. To those of us with gods, and to those without. To the indifferent, the cynical and the fanatical. God is dead, whatever that means. To some, this is an event of terror, warranting tears and the writing of requiems. In the above passage, Nietzsche seems to reflect some of this cosmic horror. But to others, the event is one of great liberation and joy; an event not keeping one from something, but making something newly possible, in this case the Christian faith. In another connection, Nietzsche knew this joy as well.

> *In fact, we . . . feel ourselves irradiated as by a new dawn by the the report that the "old God is dead"; our hearts overflow with gratitude, astonishment, presentiment and expectation. At last the horizon seems open once more, granting even that it is not bright; our ships can at last put out to sea in face of every danger; every hazard is again permitted to the discerner; the sea, our sea, again lies open before us; perhaps never before did such an "open sea" exist.*

I am a Christian theologian by profession; I have recently been involved in the death-of-God fuss, and I am, as well, committed to the death of God as a theological and human event.

It is hard to know just exactly why the furor started last fall. I had been defending the death of God, off and on for years, on C.B.S. television programs, coast to coast, as the saying goes. But this was in the decent obscurity of the Sunday-morning cultural ghetto, and no one really listens to the words people say on television anyhow. What matters is if you are sincere, like Hugh Downs. A book or two came out in 1963, and in 1964 and 1965 a few articles began to appear indicating a common interest in doing Christianity without God. Three or four of us seemed to be working similar lines, and critics—both fearful and interested—began to call us a movement, and we looked around and decided that perhaps they were right. This was the first decisive alteration in Protestant theology to take place since the communications explosion of the early Fifties, and no one was prepared for the rapidity of information passing when the snowball really started to pick up momentum. A handful of articles, commissioned by a bland weekly Protestant journal (which in turn is earnestly monitored by the religion editors of the weekly newsmagazines), provided perhaps the real trigger last fall. An excellent analysis by a young *New York Times* reporter was syndicated quite widely, and a rather ineffectual and tired piece in *Time* made the kind of mark that ineffectual and tired pieces in *Time* often do. A confused *New*

Yorker series on the "new theology" added words without sense to the scene, and, at last, the religion-desk people in wire services, local chains and papers moved in and rewrote the rewritten work of others. By about Christmas, the non-events and the events were thoroughly mixed together; hostile reactions were being recorded to words never uttered, institutions were upset, trustees perplexed, colleagues bewildered and hostile, and in general the reaction to the news and publicity was becoming part of the news and publicity, which in turn engendered more reaction, and so on. For a while it looked as if the reaction had become the event, and otherwise sensible Christian critics decided to reject the death-of-God theology on the grounds that it was faddish and beginning to turn up at cocktail parties. As time went on, and cooler heads prevailed, it was apparently decided that mention at cocktail parties is evidence for neither the truth nor falsity of an idea.

One of the consequences of the mishmash character of the intellectual life of our day is that it makes clarity and precision difficult to obtain. "Death of God" is a difficult, complex, rather mysterious idea, and I'd like to set down some of the meanings that it seems to me to have today.

There is no question about it: "death of God" is a striking, rhetorical and offensive phrase. We death-of-God theologians do not call ourselves that in order to give offense. We mean "death." Traditional religious thought has spoken about the "disappearance" or "absence" or "eclipse" or "silence" of God. It means, by these words, that men do not permanently enjoy the experience of faith or the presence of God. The presence is, from time to time, withdrawn, and men cannot count on the timing or character of its return. This is a common enough religious affirmation in our time, but it is not what we death-of-God people are talking about. We are talking about a real loss, a real doing without, and—whatever we do expect of the future—we do not expect the return of the Christian God, open or disguised.

"Death of God" sounds not only offensive, it sounds arrogant. It seems to suggest not only that this experience has happened to us, but that it has, or ought to have, happened to everybody. "Death" seems to legislate for you as well as to illuminate for me. This is, however, not as great a problem as first appears. We death-of-God theologians, along with a good many others today, accept without reservation the relativistic intellectual and spiritual climate of our time. We may fight passionately for what we hold. But we have given up believing that there is something about Christians that makes our views inevitable or necessary or (by definition) better than alternatives. We merely represent one of the possible intellectual options today. We expect to be listened to, if we say anything honest and clear, and we expect to listen. Given this relativism, the arrogant sound to the declaration of God's death is partly overcome.

There is, incidentally, a practical advantage in the shocking character of the phrase "death of God." It is just not something that conventional religious people or bishops or officials can pick up and use in their own way, saying, "Why, we've been saying that all along." There are those who feature this kind of complacency, but it is tough to do it with "death of God." The phrase is, you might say, nonsoluble in holy water, even when uttered with extreme unction.

The affirmation of the death of God is Christian in two senses. It is, for the most part, made by Christian theologians. (Not entirely, however, and a dialog between Christians and Jews around this idea is coming into being that seems most promising and exciting.) And it is made by us in order to affirm the possibility of thinking and living as Christians. To say "death of God," then, is somehow to move toward and not away from Christianity. Thus it should be clear that we theologians are not trying to reduce the Christian faith to a bland and noncontroversial minimum so that it can be accepted by scientists, rationalists and freethinkers. We are not particularly anxious about relevance or communication. It is not because we long to slip something into the mind of "modern man" that we do what we do. It is because something has happened to us, and because we suspect that it may have happened to others, that we are talking about the death of God.

But let's move beyond introductory matters. Just what does the phrase "death of God" mean as we "radical" theologians use it? And how is this related to other possible and historical uses of the phrase? The best way to start this answer is to indicate that there are perhaps ten possible meanings for the phrase "death of God" in use today:

1. It might mean that there is no God and that there never has been. This position is traditional atheism of the old-fashioned kind, and it does seem hard to see how it could be combined, except very unstably, with Christianity or any of the Western religions.

2. It might mean that there once was a God to whom adoration, praise and trust were appropriate, possible and even necessary, but that there is now no such God. This is the position of the death-of-God or radical theology. It is an atheist position, but with a difference. If there was a God, and if there now isn't, it should be possible to indicate why this change took place, when it took place and who was responsible for it. I will be returning to questions like this.

3. It might mean that the idea of God and the word God itself both are in need of radical reformulation. Perhaps totally new words are needed; perhaps a decent silence about God should be observed; but

ultimately, a new treatment of the idea and the word can be expected, however unexpected and surprising it may turn out to be.

4. It might mean that our traditional liturgical and theological language needs a thorough overhaul; the reality abides, but classical modes of thought and forms of language may well have had it.

5. It might mean that the Christian story is no longer a saving or healing story. It may manage to stay on as merely illuminating or instructing or guiding, but it no longer performs its classical functions of salvation or redemption. In this new form, it might help us cope with the demons, but it cannot abolish them.

6. It might mean that certain concepts of God, often in the past confused with the classical Christian doctrine of God, must be destroyed: for example, God as problem solver, absolute power, necessary being, the object of ultimate concern.

7. It might mean that men do not today experience God except as hidden, absent, silent. We live, so to speak, in the time of the death of God, though that time will doubtless pass.

8. It might mean that the gods men make, in their thought and action (false gods or idols, in other words), must always die so that the true object of thought and action, the true God, might emerge, come to life, be born anew.

9. It might have a mystical meaning: God must die in the world so that he can be born in us. In many forms of mysticism the death of Jesus on the cross is the time of that worldly death. This is a medieval idea that influenced Martin Luther, and it is probably this complex of ideas that lies behind the German chorale *God Himself Is Dead* that may well be the historical source for our modern use of "death of God."

10. Finally, it might mean that our language about God is always inadequate and imperfect.

I want to go back to the second meaning of the phrase. If there was once a God and there is now not one, when did this change take place? There are a number of paths toward an answer. In one sense, God is always dying, giving himself to the world and to men, as in the fall of the primitive sky gods into animism. In a more decisive sense for Christians, the coming and the death of Jesus (the Incarnation, to use the technical term) stand for a kind of death of God. Here God, Christians have always said, takes on sin and suffering. Can it not also be said that God takes on mortality, that the coming of Jesus is the beginning of the death of God, and that because of this coming, men no longer need gods in the old religious sense? The New Testament perhaps comes closest to this in the saying, "He who abides in love abides in God."

But the "when" question has to be answered not only in terms of Jesus, but in terms of the nineteenth century. If Jesus makes the death of God a possible experience for men, the nineteenth century lives that reality and instructs us to do the same. A whole series of themes in the nineteenth century deals, directly or indirectly, with the collapse of God into the world, and thus with the death of God. Goethe and the romantics spoke of the movement from transcendence to nature, and even Protestants were invited by some of their spokesmen at the beginning of the century to fling themselves on the bosom of nature in order to recapture a lost divinity. William Blake is singing mysteriously of the death of the transcendent God at the close of the eighteenth century, and in the French Revolution itself we can perceive the close connection between regicide and deicide. Hegel, as early as 1807, speaks elliptically of God's death, and the left-wing Hegelians like Strauss and Feuerbach make it much clearer—the attributes of God must be transmuted into concrete human values. Karl Marx's own Marxism is in one sense an attempt to recover for the human community the values previously ascribed to God.

Ibsen and Strindberg knew the death of God, as did Victorian England. George Eliot found God and immortality impossible, duty alone irresistible, while the young Matthew Arnold's *Dover Beach* sang a song for a whole generation.

> The Sea of Faith
> Was once, too, at the full, and round earth's shore
> Lay like the folds of a bright girdle furl'd.
> But now I only hear
> Its melancholy, long, withdrawing roar,
> Retreating, to the breath
> Of the night-wind, down the vast edges drear
> And naked shingles of the world.

And on our side of the Atlantic, Hawthorne rather quietly, and Melville with unforgettable force, laid the God of the Puritan tradition to rest. Perhaps the most unforgettable image of the dying God in our language is that of Ahab finally fixing his harpoon in Moby Dick's side, as the two of them sink together, both of them God, both of them evil.

Cryptically, but not entirely falsely, in Europe and America between the French Revolution and the start of World War One, the Christian God is dying. The coming and death of Jesus makes God's death possible; the nineteenth century makes it real. And today, it is our turn to understand and to accept.

Thus, "When did it happen?" gets a three-part answer. In one sense with Jesus and the cross. In another sense in the Europe and

America of the last century. In a final sense, today, just now. Just what is there about our time that has led us to see and to grasp this event?

Every man must answer for himself the question "What is the special quality of your experience of the death of God?" In one sense, I don't think one can or should try to persuade anyone else of the reality of the death of God. When I talk or write about it, I don't try to place a new thing into another's head, I try to remind him of what he already knows. If there is no answer, no recognition, I can be of no further use to him except as an example of the way he should not go. For me, the death of God is not a consequence of a simple experience like the discovery of, say, the scientific method that automatically rules out God. It is an emotional event, in the guts. It is made up of a number of things, modest in themselves, but overwhelming when taken together. It is for me partly the disappearance of the idea of God as a meeter of needs and a solver of problems. For much of its history, classical Christianity felt that while men, by their own hands, could solve many of the problems of life, there was always a dimension where man was powerless and which had to be ascribed to God. In this sense the longing for God was said to be common to all. Our hearts are restless, Saint Augustine said, until they come to rest in God. Today we must say some hearts are and some hearts aren't. Men may not need God, just as they may not need a single ultimate loyalty. Needs and problems are for the world to meet, and if it cannot meet them, nothing else can. This is one strand in the experience of the death of God for me.

Another has to do with the problem of suffering. If for you there is nothing special about the twentieth century's experience of suffering, then this line of argument will not persuade. There has always been unmerited suffering in the world, and it has always been a problem for the heart and the head to hold to the reality of suffering and to the goodness and power of God at the same time. It has always been hard, I am saying, and now it is impossible; for the terrible burden of suffering our time has witnessed can be ascribed to God only by turning him into a monster. The problem of Job, of Ivan Karamazov, of Albert Camus has fallen on our heads. It was *Christians* who did the work at Auschwitz, and their God became impossible after they had finished. Ernest Hemingway, whom we do not ordinarily think of as having been moved by these problems, has a touching scene on this point in *For Whom the Bell Tolls:* Anselmo is speaking to Jordan about his hopes when the war is over.

> "But if I live later, I will try to live in such a way, doing no harm to any one, that it will be forgiven."

"By whom?"

"Who knows? Since we do not have God here any more, neither His Son nor the Holy Ghost, who forgives? I do not know."

"You have not God any more?"

"No. Man. Certainly not. If there were God, never would He have permitted what I have seen with my eyes. Let *them* have God."

"They claim Him."

"Clearly I miss Him, having been brought up in religion. But now a man must be responsible to himself."

"Then it is thyself who will forgive thee for killing."

"I believe so," Anselmo said.

Let me put this in another way. The death of God means two closely related things: that some of the human experiences to which men have traditionally given the name of God must be redescribed and renamed, and also that some of those experiences are no longer ours. For example, religious men have often pointed to experiences of dependence, awe, reverence, wonder, mystery, tragedy as signs of the incalculable and mysterious character of life, saying of these experiences taken together, "Something like this is what we mean by God." There are, of course, such things about us, and the only point I wish to make here is that one needn't give any of them the name of God. They are real facts of our life, we have human sciences and arts to clarify them, and they point to mystery and wonder, but not to God.

But a second thing is just as true. There are experiences that men have had in the past and which they have traditionally understood as pointing to God that are simply not available to us in the same way today. Take the experiences of dependence, especially in the presence of nature. Listen to a research biologist or a doctor or a physicist or a space scientist talk about his work. He is talking about mastery, control and power; not about a sense of his smallness before the universe. This is true of our kids as well. The other night I was out in the back yard with one of my children, who had to identify some constellations for his science homework. When I was young and used to stand under the starry sky, I recall being filled with all the things you were supposed to be filled with: awe, a sense of my own smallness, dependence. But my son is a full citizen of the modern world, and said to me, after he had located the required constellations, "Which are the ones we put up there, Dad?" He was more interested in what he could do up there than in what he could feel down here. He had become a technological man, and this means something religiously. Are there other traditional religious experiences that we're losing touch with? The death of God lives in this kind of world.

It is quite foolish to say that the death-of-God theology wants to reduce life to the scientifically knowable or the immediately relevant. It has no special interest in relevance or in being acceptable to that non-existent chimera, "modern man." In no sense does it wish to turn its back on the mysterious, the sacred, the holy or the transcendent. It simply will not call such things by the name of God. As a matter of fact, it might be very interesting to work out a way of talking about godless forms of the sacred—ideas and experiences of the sacred that need not include the experience of God. It is doubtless true that some roads to the sacred are ruled out for many of us in our rationalized and technological culture. There probably cannot be, for example, any way to the sacred via holy men, holy books or holy gestures in the usual sense. But even if our way to God is cut off, need it be the çase for our experience of the sacred? Can the experience of sex become a way to the sacred for some? Not just sex as intercourse, but as total affirmation of one's sexuality in the midst of the human community. What would it mean to say that sex can become a new kind of sacred space? What would sacred mean in such a statement?

Perhaps death can also become a sacred event in our time of the death of God. Not, of course, our experience of our own death, but at least the experience of its coming, of mortality, and a facing up to death, our own and others, so as to befriend it and deprive it of its ability to hurt and surprise us. What meaning would "sacred" have if we tried to say that death may become a way to a godless form of the sacred today?

Some examples might make this point a bit less bewildering. In the Gettysburg Address, Lincoln was offering what seems to me a moving example of death as a human, godless form of the sacred. He said, you'll recall, that they had met to dedicate a portion of the battlefield. Then he went on:

> But, in a larger sense, we cannot dedicate—we cannot consecrate—we cannot hallow—this ground.

You might have expected him to make the pious point here and to say that we mortals cannot consecrate anything because that is God's prerogative alone. But he didn't say that:

> The brave men, living and dead, who struggled here, have consecrated it, far above our poor power to add or detract.

Not just the "right" side, but all those who fought, are the consecrators. Suffering and dying men, he suggests, have the power to make holy or sacred what was ordinary and profane before.

It would be easy to find a contemporary example of sex as a sacred event. Such a view is common rhetoric in our modern sentimental panegyrics to sex, both Christian and secular. So I would rather turn to another source, to Puritan New England, as a matter of fact. This is from

Nathaniel Hawthorne's *The Scarlet Letter,* and Dimmesdale is speaking to Hester about their adulterous love.

> "We are not, Hester, the worst sinners in the world. There is one worse than even the polluted priest! That old man's revenge has been blacker than my sin. [He is referring to Chillingworth's diabolical attack on him.] He has violated, in cold blood, the sanctity of a human heart. Thou and I, Hester, never did so!"
>
> "Never, never," whispered she. "What we did had a consecration of its own. We felt it so! We said so to each other! Hast thou forgotten it?"

Here is not only sex, but nonmarital sex, and in the heart of Puritanism, affirmed as a form of the sacred. Along such lines as these, I think, a conception of the sacred without God might be worked out.

I want to raise one final question about the idea of the death of God. If God is dead, as we say, what do we put in his place? What does the work in this godless Christian vision that God used to do in the classical tradition? Have we, it might be asked, taken the full measure of the terrible cry of Ivan Karamazov, If there is no God, then everything is permitted? Are people really strong enough to lose not only the fear of hell and the consolations of the next life, but also the reality of God?

There are two answers, or two forms of the same answer, to the question about the replacement of God. In one sense the answer must be "the human community" and in another sense it must be "Jesus." Let us distinguish between two kinds of meaning or function classically ascribed to God. If by God you mean the means by which forgiveness is mediated, or consolation in time of sorrow or despair, or judge of my arrogance and my idolatry—then we say that these functions, as central for us as they ever were in classical Christianity, must be taken over by the human community. We must learn to forgive each other with the radical un-conditioned grace men used to ascribe to God. (Recall the touching words between Anselmo and Jordan quoted above.) We must learn to comfort each other, and we must learn to judge, check and rebuke one another in the communities within which we are wounded and in which we are healed. If these things cannot now be done by the human com-munities in the world, then these communities must be altered until they can perform these tasks and whatever others, once ascribed to God, that need to be done in this new context. In this sense the death of God leads to politics, to social change, and even to the foolishness of utopias.

But it would be misleading to pass over to what we are calling the human community every task once given to God. There is another kind of meaning attached to the classical idea of God that needs another kind of surrogate. If by God you mean the focus of obedience, the object of trust and loyalty, the meaning I give to love, my center, my meaning—

then these meanings are given not to men in general but to Jesus, the *man*, in his life, his way with others and his death. We death-of-God theologians thus stake out a claim to be able to make it as Christians not merely because we speak of the death of the Christian God, but because we see as the center of the Christian faith a relation of obedience and trust directed to Jesus. Something like this is placed on the lips of Uncle Nikolai by Boris Pasternak in *Doctor Zhivago:*

> "As I was saying, one must be true to Christ. I'll explain. What you don't understand is that it is possible to be an atheist, it is possible not to know whether God exists, or why, and yet believe that man does not live in a state of nature but in history, and that history as we know it now began with Christ, and that Christ's Gospel is its foundation. Now what is history? It is the centuries of systematic explorations of the riddle of death, with a view to overcoming death. That's why people discover mathematical infinity and electromagnetic waves, that's why they write symphonies. Now, you can't advance in this direction without a certain faith. You can't make such discoveries without spiritual equipment. And the basic elements of this equipment are in the Gospels. What are they? To begin with, love of one's neighbor, which is the supreme form of vital energy. Once it fills the heart of man it has to overflow and spend itself. And then the two basic ideals of modern man—without them he is unthinkable—the idea of free personality and the idea of life as sacrifice."

The human community in general—not as it is, but as it might be altered to become—and that particular instance of the human community, Jesus of Nazareth, thus take over the work, the action, the deeds, once ascribed to the Christian God. Thus the death of God is the least abstract event one can imagine. It moves straight into politics, revolutionary change, and the tragedies and delights of this world.

At the start of this article, the question was posed whether the death of God might be a non-event, fashioned by nothing more substantial than the eager and empty publicity mills of our day. We radical theologians have found, I think, that it is something more. It is a real event; it is a joyous event; it is a liberating event, removing everything that might stand between man and the relief of suffering, man and the love of his neighbor. It is a real event making possible a Christian form of faith for many today. It is even making possible church and ministry in our world.

John W. Turnbull

Some Notes on Religious America

The impious presumption of legislators and rulers, civil as well as ecclesiastical, who being themselves but fallible and uninspired men, have assumed dominion over the faith of others, setting up their own opinions and modes of thinking as the only true and infallible, and as such endeavoring to impose them on others, hath established and maintained false religions over the greatest part of the world, and through all time.

> Thomas Jefferson, *The Virginia*
> *Statute of Religious Liberty* (1786)

I believe in an America that is officially neither Catholic, Protestant, nor Jewish, where no public official either requests or accepts instructions on public policy from the Pope, the National Council of Churches, or any other ecclesiastical source, where no religious body seeks to impose its will directly or indirectly upon the general populace or the public acts of its officials, and where religious liberty is so indivisible that an act against one church is treated as an act against all.

> John F. Kennedy, *Address to the*
> *Ministerial Association of Greater*
> *Houston* (1960)

The reader of the above quotations and the thoughtful observer of American history might conclude that our religious passion is never more fervent than when it is aroused against the excessive claims of religion itself. Such a conclusion would, I submit, not be wide of the mark, and I would submit further that this fact is one of the keys to the understanding of that bewildering and paradoxical phenomenon which is American religion.

Reprinted from *Student World*, No. 4, 1962, pp. 415–426; published by the World Student Federation. Reprinted by permission.

John W. Turnbull is Associate Professor of Christian Ethics, Episcopal Theological Seminary of the Southwest, Austin, Texas.

The purpose of this article is to suggest how a few of the mysteries of American religion may be illuminated if they are considered as manifestations of this, if you will, radically protestant religious impulse. The suggestions offered represent mostly new and unproved ideas, even to the author, and they are therefore offered in a tentative and preliminary way, for the reader's consideration and criticism.

I ought to state at the outset that while I have not come to praise American religion, neither have I come to bury it: however they may sound to others, and however questionable they may be even to me, the characteristics of American religion which I am about to describe do not, to me at any rate, constitute *ipso facto* its condemnation. Since it is impossible to think without bias, I choose here to make an American bias quite explicit (though I hope not wholly uncriticized), and I would urge the reader to try to share with me this bias at least temporarily, if for no other reason than to get a better sight on the target which he may wish later to demolish.

American Religion and the Church

Consider first the typical American attitude towards the Church itself. The first observation might well be that the American characteristically does not think much about "the Church" at all, or have any very well-defined attitude towards it. For one thing, more conspicuously than in any other nation with a large Christian population, what is presented to the American is not "the Church" but "churches." This is true not only because of the mere fact of the unparalleled multiplicity of sects (or, to use a more American term, denominations) in our land, but also because throughout the greater part of our history this multiplicity has been regarded as not an abnormal but the normal pattern of ecclesiastical life. Here there is not, and never has been, any one dominant, much less established, national church. The idea of the Church as the universal community of believers remains a very dim one to us because, unlike any other nation in the Christian west, we have never had a body which, however pretentious its claim and however imperfect its performance, even attempted to represent such a reality. This fact has obvious consequences for our attitudes on the question of Christian unity: it accounts at least in part for the fact that the separation of the churches honestly just does not seem as "scandalous" in America as it does in western Europe, and that our movements towards unity are not characterized by the same religious and theological passion that they seem to be there.

Again, the American does not think much in terms of "the Church" because even when "the churches" present themselves to him, they do not do so as clear entities; they are fuzzy around the edges and perhaps even at the heart. Each denomination (at least within main-stream Protestantism) is in the first place imperfectly distinguished from the others. A vast majority of Americans think of themselves as associated in one way or another with one of the denominational forms of American religion. (Clergy are often, and often rightly, accused of padding church membership rolls; it is therefore particularly interesting to note that, according to statistics quoted by Will Herberg, there were in 1952 some ten million or more adult Americans who considered themselves church members but whose names were not in fact carried on the lists of any church.) But even most "good church members" are very unclear, and probably even less concerned, about the historical, doctrinal, liturgical, or political distinctiveness of their own denomination. Thus they are sustained, or burdened, as the case may be, by remarkably little "denominational loyalty," and tend to regard questions of comparative ecclesiology more as interesting curiosities than as serious issues.

In the second place, "church" as such is imperfectly distinguished from "not-church." Perhaps just because no important segment of the American people identifies itself as being outside the churches, neither do those who identify themselves as being inside them have any firm idea of what that identification signifies. And rare indeed is the American whose primary form of self-identification is his church affiliation; rather this formal religious identification is only one among many—social, political, economic, familial, ethnic—and by no means necessarily the controlling one. These self-identifications overlap, conflict, reinforce, or challenge one another in an endless variety of ways, and the typical American does not hold any one of them in clear focus for very long. Even as a priest in one of the "churchier" of the American religious bodies, I find it very difficult to locate myself in discussions about "the Church" in relation to "the world." The Church and the world are so difficult for the American Christian to distinguish either sociologically or psychologically that the distinction itself seems to have little relevance to his situation.

What then are we to make of these curious facts—that while America is probably the greatest church-belonging and church-going nation in the world, the American typically has no vivid sense of the Church, either as catholic or as denominational or even as distinguished from the world? I would offer the following line of thought as not, of course, a complete, but perhaps a partial, explanation.

The American is first of all a very religious man. Because he is religious, he is a hearty supporter of the churches, since they are the representative agencies of religion. (They represent, to be exact, what we like to call "organized religion"—perhaps a typically American expression, and if so a very revealing one.) But the churches are, of course, secondary in his concern to religion itself; they are important only insofar as they faithfully serve religion's cause. The fact is that, in the American's mind, they often have not served and often do not serve that cause faithfully. America has therefore created for itself a culture in which no church or combination of churches is permitted to make too large a claim upon any man or upon society as a whole. Hence our cultural and religious pluralism, which seems to us not just an historical accident or even a regrettable necessity, but rather a positive virtue, yes, even a religious virtue. The fact we have noted—that the Church remains an indistinct reality in the American mind—may be understood as both requisite for, and consequent upon, the limitation that we desire to impose upon the churches' claim.

I would stress again that this limitation is not just an expression of American "secularism." (On many counts, the word probably ought in any case to be banished from theological discussion.) It is also, and I believe perhaps even more importantly, the expression precisely of the distinctive shape of the American religious mentality. It is the limitation upon the religious institution imposed by religion itself, and the assertion of the freedom of religion to express itself through other means. So we support the churches with enthusiasm, but the Church is really not one of the articles of our faith.

Let me offer an illustration of the way American religion works: the current protest movement against racial discrimination, especially in the south. (I had better confess that I chose this illustration partly to elicit your favorable judgment upon American religion; we can all think of others less gratifying.) The protest movement has been rightly characterized as a religious movement. Persons of religious conviction are prominent among both its leaders and its rank and file. It uses religious, even specifically Christian-inspired, ideas, symbols, motivations, and methods in its work. It is bursting with that combination of religious and American idealism which has characterized so many of our social reform movements, and it has aroused the social passion of Christian students and student organizations as no cause has in the past twenty years.

But while it is a religious movement in these and doubtless other senses, it is also a movement of protest not only against racial discrimination itself but also, implicitly if not explicitly, against the failure of the churches ("organized religion") to make a clear witness in word and deed in what is felt to be a matter of elemental Christian and human dignity. It is a para-ecclesiastical movement which by its very existence protests against the faithlessness of the Church itself. In such a movement, one speaks not of the doctrines of a universal Church but simply of those of a universal brotherhood; not of obedience to a confessional tradition but of fidelity to a universal Father; not of distinguishing oneself from the world but of affirming one's part in its struggle for justice. In sum, just because of their religious passion, the people involved in this movement think very little about the Church.

Church and State, Religion and Public Life

The First Amendment to the Constitution of the United States begins with the following momentous words: "Congress shall make no law respecting an establishment of religion, or prohibiting the free exercise thereof." Upon the interpretation of these words has hung a long series of sometimes bitter arguments and often apparently conflicting judgments throughout the course of American history. The meaning of the constitutional separation of Church and State has again become a bone of contention . . . as a result of the Supreme Court's decision declaring the reading in public schools of a prayer recommended by the Board of Regents of the State of New York to be a violation of the no-establishment clause of the First Amendment. (The prohibition placed upon Congress in the First Amendment is extended to the states in the Fourteenth.)

I do not wish to enter into the discussion of the merits and demerits of the decision except to observe that, whatever its constitutional rationale and whatever its implications for the future status of religion in American public life, it is surely consistent with the impulse which Jefferson expressed in the Virginia Statute of Religious Liberty and which continually reasserts itself in the American tradition, to guard with all possible vigor against the association of the State with any kind of "official religion." Mr. Justice Black is squarely within this tradition when he judges in his majority opinion that the Regents' prayer "officially establishes" the religious beliefs which are embodied in it (however "denominationally neutral" it may be), and goes on to say:

> When the power, prestige, and financial support of government is placed behind a particular religious belief, the indirect coercive pressure upon religious minorities to conform to the prevailing officially approved religion is plain.

It was Jefferson's opinion, and it is also that of Justice Black, that to make any form of religion official is to degrade religion itself. A part at least of the justification for the Supreme Court's decision, which on the face of it appears to thwart the influence of religion in public life, is the conviction that right religion must be protected against the excessive claims of a possibly false official one:

> Religion is too personal, too sacred, too holy, to permit its "unhallowed perversion" by a civil magistrate.

American church leaders insist, and have been quick to observe . . . that the separation of Church and State was not intended by the writers of the Constitution to deprive religion of its influence in public life. That assertion is perfectly correct; but unfortunately it is not very helpful, because it overlooks precisely that somewhat unclear but very important distinction which the American consciousness makes between those forms of religious influence and expression in public life which are salutary both to religion and to the body politic, and those which are destructive of either or both.

That distinction is roughly and partially indicated by the presumed opposition, which Justice Black's opinion reflects, between "personal," "voluntary" religious expressions on the one hand, and "official," "imposed" ones on the other. America permits, encourages, indeed very nearly requires that "personal" religion be operative in every area of public life; for example, we like our public officials to show it in large measure. But America opposes vigorously the suggestion of any "official" religion, whether of civil or ecclesiastical inspiration. The distinction, as I have said, may not be very clear, and it may of course be open to all manner of objection; but be it unclear or objectionable or both, it is still there and cannot be ignored. It means at least that the separation of Church and State is not only a matter of the legal relations between government and the churches; it is also a symbol of a far deeper instinct, an instinct which in the name of (personal, voluntary) religion will protest against what is felt to be an improper role of (official, imposed) religion in public life. The distinction between the two itself represents one of our most deeply held religious convictions; it is indeed for us a way of indicating the difference between true religion and idolatry.

Do Americans Have Any Theology?

I remember vividly a theological discussion in which I participated here in America some years ago. There was a particular subject which we had set ourselves to discuss, but by the time we had got warmed up most of us had forgotten what it was and were having what seemed to me at any rate to be an entertaining and sufficiently constructive session, ranging widely over a cluster of topics whose connection with one another was less a matter of logic than of corporate stream-of-consciousness. Suddenly a European member of the group, who for some time had been brooding silently over the scholarly biblical apparatus he had brought with him, looked up and announced rather testily that our talk had degenerated into "theological gossip" and that it was time we got back to business.

We American theologians are a badly educated and badly disciplined lot, and I sometimes wonder why our Continental brethren haven't long since given us up altogether. But our attitude towards, and our way of doing, theology are not just the result of these deficiencies; they are also manifestations of the American religious temperament. We are, to tell the truth, ambivalent about the theological enterprise, and therefore we engage in it in a curiously roundabout way.

As Americans we fear and resist the inhibition of our religious impulses and insights by the strictures of theological systems; the very word "dogmatic" is an almost unequivocally pejorative term with us. We doubt the competence of theology alone to illuminate, much less to judge, all aspects of religious reality, not to mention those aspects of reality which we regard as other than religious—politics, art, labor-management relations, or sex, for example. Thus our most influential religious thinkers are characteristically part theologian and part something else—a sufficient example may be Reinhold Niebuhr, who has been declared, both by others (as a kind of accusation) and by himself (almost as a boast), to be no theologian at all.

If even our theologians have this anti-theological streak, then it is not surprising that the American layman is even more doubtful of the prerogatives of theology. No right-thinking American will hesitate to reject out of hand, either in detail or as a whole, the theology of even a St. Thomas or a Karl Barth simply on the ground that it does not accord with his own experiences. If this attitude seems to you to manifest unspeakable arrogance, then I only beg you to remember in all charity that a kind of arrogance in the face of authority is one of the qualities which, for better or worse, got our nation going and brought it where it is. We believe that no one has the last word to say on any subject, including, indeed especially, religion, since it is in our view so personal a matter. Our theology is therefore modest, provisional, disorderly, careless of tradition, and subject to continual invasion and modification by other forms of thought and experience. If it were anything else, it would be struck down as destructive of religion itself.

When theologians or church leaders move out of their proper sphere—reflection upon and guidance of the religious life—and attempt to speak about or influence, say, political or economic matters, then their position is even more vulnerable. For as long as I can remember, theologians and church leaders have been laboring mightily to bring forth some convincing theological justification for the seemingly obvious proposition that the Church and Christian people ought to be concerned with, and involved in, the social order, and to enunciate the principles which ought to shape that concern and involvement. I have nearly concluded that this effort will in the nature of the case always be self-frustrating in America. I will not say that it is impossible, but it is certainly very difficult to persuade the American religious temperament that theological considerations have any relevance to other than religious matters. It is not that Americans do not believe that "the gospel speaks to the whole of life," or that "Christian discipleship must be exercised in all our relationships," and the like. They do believe those things, and they are very earnest in their hope that their religious leaders can somehow assist them to make their faith "relevant to daily life." But they prefer that this assistance be in personal religious terms. They really do not know what it means when (to quote the title of a pamphlet recently distributed by my own denomination) *The Church Speaks* on these matters; for, as we have already noted, they do not have any very clear sense of what "the Church" is. They do not feel themselves identified with the individuals or bodies who make these statements, and if they disagree with their contents they will say so, not just because they are perverse and prejudiced, but in the name of their own religious integrity. Efforts to explain to them by what authority "the Church speaks" on these matters do not relieve their uneasiness but if anything add to it, for they make the whole thing sound more like that kind of "official" religion of which they are particularly suspicious by instinct. Like Mr. Kennedy, they do not want any "religious body" to "seek to impose its will directly or indirectly" upon them. They hold the Church and the clergy in great respect and affection, but since (as they suppose) they do not attempt to instruct them in their business, religion, they do not expect instructions from them concerning their business, the affairs of the world.

In addition, however, and quite apart from the question of the authority of the Church to speak for or to them, Americans do not see that competence in theology or religious matters carries with it any special competence in non-theological or non-religious matters. They do not find theological analyses of, for example, the nature of the state or the economic order very illuminating. In the first place, they are not accustomed to thinking in such abstract terms anyway. In the second place, they feel, at least subsconsciously, that when political or economic questions are treated theologically they are being introduced into a realm where they do not belong, and are therefore being misunderstood. We have an unusually earnest concern to maintain what we take to be the relative independence of various realms of human life and thought. Such a concern is, I guess, a fair characterization of "the secular mind." If so, so be it, and Americans will rejoice in being "secularists." But I would submit that it is in our case also the expression of a religious concern to limit the claims of religion upon man's most precious possessions, his mind and his will.

The Acculturation of American Religion

Let us look at one more characteristic of American religion, namely, the apparent ease with which it accommodates itself to, indeed nearly identifies itself with, American cultural values. This accommodation is the source of great dismay to both American and foreign observers. We are appalled to hear religion recommended in both the pulpit and the market place as the means to overcome every threat to our security from communism to insomnia. We are horrified at the identification of the eternal gospel with various palpably relative and perhaps even false human values, whether they be those of a constricting personal morality (by some fundamentalists) or those of bourgeois liberalism (by some middle- and upper-class Protestants). We are alarmed at the ease with which all of us emasculate religion of its mystery, its terror, and its transcendence, and transform it into a *mélange* of useful advice, pious sentiment, and respectable good works. We wonder what on earth the "moral and spiritual values" to which our politicians pay tribute have to do with the faith of Abraham, Isaac, and Jacob. We remember with shame our persistent tendency to identify the Kingdom of God with fallible human programs for either the destruction or the protection of the social *status quo*.

A preliminary remark is in order. It is salutary to remember that there is no such thing as a religion which is not a culture-religion. Every religion must find some way of living with other powers, ideas, values, and institutions which constitute culture. Since religion can seldom if ever capture them completely, its living with them is a matter of give-and-take, or, if you like, of accommodation. Furthermore, every religion is in part a product of culture, and of a particular culture. If some cultures seem, on the one hand, more compatible than others with a particular religion, and if some forms of religion seem, on the other hand, more distorted than others by their cultural affiliations, then that is partly because some cultures and some religious forms have grown up together and have taken on each other's coloring, and others have not.

To be specific, what we now know as Christianity in the West did a large part of its growing up and took much of its characteristic ideological, liturgical, and institutional shape along with western European culture. When both were transplanted to North America, both began to grow in forms measurably different from those of their European originals. American religion thus cannot be judged solely by the criteria of western European Christianity any more than American culture can be judged solely by the criteria of western European culture; unless, indeed, one judges in advance that the American version of each is in fact a perversion of its true European form.

American religion reflects American culture just as European religion reflects European culture. Just because it is American and not European, it tends to espouse and articulate American values, such as pragmatism, democracy, optimism, individual initiative, informality—the list could be endless. It is useless to "accuse" American religion of these propensities, just as it is useless for the American to "accuse" European religion of what can look to him like its dogmatism, authoritarianism, pessimism, constraint, ceremoniousness, and the rest. If there is something wrong with American culture-religion, then the difficulty is not that American religion has adjusted itself to its culture. That is not a bad thing; it is a necessary and inevitable thing. The difficulty must be that the cultural values and ideals to which religion has adjusted itself are themselves, some of them at any rate, erroneous or inadequate. But their error or inadequacy must be argued; they cannot be assumed *a priori*. And the religion which espouses them cannot be dismissed out of hand as "cultural" and therefore distorted.

When all has been said, however, it must still be admitted that American religion seems remarkably weak in its sense of distinction from culture and therefore in its capacity for criticizing and reforming culture. Not only are we captive to the frivolous, insipid, and even destructive forces in our culture: we are woefully fatuous and unreflective in our espousal of the serious and creative ones. While Dale Carnegie is preached from one pulpit, Tennessee Williams is preached from another; while one group finds the hope of the world in the resurgence of American nationalism, another finds it in the United Nations. We too readily identify provisional social and personal programs and proximate social and personal goals with the "will of God."

These foibles are in part, however, the reflection of the characteristic American refusal to limit religious fervor to religious causes. American religion will not be bound, and interestingly enough it will sooner or later and somewhere or other rise up in wrath even against its own excesses. It will, if necessary, deny and rebel against the claim of every idea, institution, and symbol in order to assert and express its fervor. But in our history it has seldom been necessary for religion to deny or rebel against these possible restraints; rather it has been strong enough to capture and shape them to the service of all manner of personal and social purposes. It has thereby transformed them from restraints into instruments. It has made "organized religion" serve the ends of that much deeper reality, the American religious spirit itself. That many dangers beset such a religious spirit, no one can deny, and the obvious absurdities and corruptions of American religion amply testify. But the dangers must be countered in full recognition of the fact that they are the dangers inherent in that very dynamic which gives American religion its peculiar vitality and authenticity.

A Footnote

As I have reread and reworked these pages, I have become vividly aware of their many defects. I fear that many of my compatriots will fail altogether to recognize themselves or even their neighbors in the characterizations I have made. To them I can only say that American religion is, like America itself, an immensely varied phenomenon, and that I tried to select some characteristics which, while certainly not universal, are perhaps typical of American religion especially in contrast to European. In particular, they are doubtless truer to mainstream American Protestantism than to the other major American religious traditions— fundamentalist sectarianism, Catholicism, and Judaism—although I would suggest that manifestations of the same tendencies can be found in those groups as well.

I fear that many non-Americans will find the presentation confused and full of inner contradictions and ambiguities. To them I would say that American religion just is, like America itself, confusing, self-contradictory, and ambiguous. In particular, the ambiguity of both denotation and connotation of the word "religion" itself is very striking. Perhaps some confusion would have been avoided by developing and trying to use consistently different terminology to indicate the different meanings of the word. The trouble is that, especially in America, these different meanings are not distinct but overlapping. The greater clarity, if it could be achieved, might therefore be deceptive rather than illuminating. I elected, at any rate, to use the word and the idea with something of the very ambiguity with which, as it seems to me, Americans typically use it.

In any case, if the reader finds that the presentation only heightens his uncertainties about American religion and leaves many questions unanswered, I will only say that it has done the same for me.

Mircea Eliade

Archaic Myth and Historical Man

It would be hard to find a definition of myth that would be acceptable to all scholars and at the same time intelligible to nonspecialists. Myth is an extremely complex cultural reality, which can be approached and interpreted from various and complementary viewpoints. The definition that seems least inadequate because most embracing is this. Myth narrates a sacred history: it relates an event that took place in primordial time, the fabled time of the "beginnings." In other words, myth tells how, through the deeds of Supernatural Beings, a reality came into existence, be it the whole of reality, the Cosmos, or only a fragment of reality—an island, a species of plant, a particular kind of human behavior, an institution. Myth, then, is always an account of a "creation"; it relates how something was produced, began to be.

Myth tells only of that which *really happened*, which manifested itself *completely*. The actors in myths are Supernatural Beings. They are known primarily by what they did in the times of the "beginnings." Hence myths disclose their creative activity and reveal the sacredness (or simply the "supernaturalness") of their works. In short, myths describe the various and sometimes dramatic breakthroughs of the sacred that really establishes the world and makes it what it is today. Furthermore, it is as a result of the intervention of Supernatural Beings that man himself is what he is today, a mortal, sexed, and cultural being. The myth is regarded as a sacred story, and hence a "true history," because it always

Reprinted from *McCormick Quarterly*, January 1965, pp. 23–36 (McCormick Theological Seminary, Chicago), by permission of the publisher and the author.

Mircea Eliade is Sewell L. Avery Distinguished Service Professor at the University of Chicago.

deals with realities. The cosmogonic myth is "true" because the existence of the World is there to prove it; the myth of the origin of death is equally true because man's mortality proves it, and so on.

Because myth relates the *gesta* of Supernatural Beings and the manifestation of their sacred powers, it becomes the *exemplary model* for all significant human activities. When the missionary and ethnologist, G. Strehlow asked the Australian Arunta why they performed certain ceremonies, the answer was always: "Because the ancestors so commanded it." The Kai of New Guinea refused to change their way of living and working, and they explained: "It was thus that the Nemu (the Mythical Ancestors) did, and we do likewise." Asked the reason for a particular detail in a ceremony, a Navaho chanter answered: "Because the Holy People did it that way in the first place." The same justification is alleged by the Hindu theologians and ritualists. "We must do what the gods did in the beginning" (*Satapatha Brāhmana*, VII, 2, 1, 4). "Thus the gods did: thus men do" (*Taittiriya Brāhmana*, I, 5, 9, 4). In summary, the foremost function of myth is to reveal the exemplary models for all human rites and all significant human activities—alimentation or marriage, work or education, art or wisdom, and so on.

We might add that in societies where myth is still alive the natives carefully distinguish myths—"true stories"—from fables or tales, which they call "false stories." . . .

The distinction made by natives between "true stories" and "false stories" is significant. Both categories of narratives present "histories," that is, relate a series of events that took place in a distant and fabulous past. Although the actors in myths are usually Gods and Supernatural Beings, while those in tales are heroes or miraculous animals, all the actors share the common trait that they do not belong to the everyday world. Nevertheless, the natives have felt that the two kinds of "stories" are basically different. For everything that the myths relate concerns them directly, while the tales and fables refer to events that, even when they have caused changes in the world (such as the anatomical or physiological peculiarities of certain animals), have not altered the human condition as such.

Myths narrate not only the origin of the World, of animals, plants, and of man, but also all the primordial events in consequence of which man became what he is today—mortal, sexed, organized in a society, obliged to work in order to live, and working in accordance with certain rules. If the World exists, if man exists, it is because Supernatural Beings exercised creative powers in the "beginning." But after the cosmogony and the creation of man other events occurred, and man as he is today is the direct result of those mythical events; he is constituted by those events. He is mortal because something happened in the mythical time. If that thing had not happened, man would not be mortal—he would have gone on existing indefinitely, like rocks; or he might have changed his skin periodically like snakes, and hence would have been able to renew his life, that is, begin it over again indefinitely. But the myth of the origin of death narrates what happened *in illo tempore*, and, in telling the incident, explains why man is mortal.

Similarly, a certain tribe lives by fishing—because in mythical times a Supernatural Being taught their ancestors to catch and cook fish. The myth tells the story of the first fishery, and, in so doing, at once reveals a superhuman act, teaches men how to perform it, and finally, explains why this particular tribe must procure their food in this way.

It would be easy to multiply examples. But those already given show why, for archaic man, myth is a matter of primary importance, while tales and fables are not. Myth teaches him the primordial "stories" that have constituted him existentially; and everything connected with his existence and his legitimate mode of existence in the Cosmos concerns him directly. However, what happened *ab origine* can be repeated by the power of rites. For the man of archaic societies, it is essential to know the myths. By recollecting the myths, by re-enacting them, he is able to repeat what the Gods, the Heroes, or the Ancestors did *ab origine*. To know the myths is to learn the secret of the origin of things. In other words, one learns not only how things came into existence but also where to find them and how to make them reappear . . .

In most cases it is not enough to know the origin myth; it must also be recited. This, in a sense, is a proclamation of one's knowledge, a display of it. But this is not all. He who recites or performs the origin myth is thereby steeped in the sacred atmosphere in which these miraculous events took place. The mythical time of origins is a "strong" time because it was transfigured by the active, creative presence of the Supernatural Beings. By reciting the myths one reconstitutes that fabulous time and hence in some way becomes "contemporary" with the events described; one is in the presence of the Gods or Heroes. As a summary formula, we might say that by "living" the myths one emerges from profane, chronological time and enters a time that is of a different quality, a "sacred" Time at once primordial and indefinitely recoverable.

In general it can be said that myth, as experienced by archaic societies, 1) constitutes the history of the acts of the Supernaturals; 2) that this history is considered to be absolutely *true* (because it is concerned with realities) and *sacred* (because it is the work of the Supernaturals); 3) that myth is always related to a "creation"; it tells *how something came into existence*, or how a pattern of behavior, an institution, a manner of working were established (this is why myths *constitute the paradigms for all significant human acts*); 4) that by knowing the

myth one knows the "origin" of things and hence can control and manipu-
late them at will (this is not an "external," "abstract" knowledge but a
knowledge that one "experiences" ritually, either by ceremonially recount-
ing the myth or by performing the ritual for which it is the justification);
5) that in one way or another one "lives" the myth, in the sense that one
is seized by the sacred, exalting power of the events re-collected or re-
enacted.

"Living" a myth, then, implies a genuinely religious experience,
since it differs from the ordinary experience of everyday life. The "re-
ligiousness" of this experience is due to the fact that one re-enacts
fabulous, exalting, significant events, one again witnesses the creative
works of the Supernaturals; one ceases to exist in the everyday world and
enters a transfigured, auroral world impregnated with the Supernaturals'
presence. What is involved *is not a commemoration of mythical events
but a reiteration of them.* The protagonists of the myth are made present;
one becomes their contemporary. This also implies that one is no longer
living in chronological time, but in the primordial Time, the Time when
the event took place. This is why we can use the term the "strong time" of
myth; it is the prodigious, "sacred" time when something new, strong,
and significant was manifested. To re-experience that time, to re-enact it
as often as possible, to witness again the spectacle of the divine works, to
meet with the Supernaturals and relearn their creative lesson is the desire
that runs like a pattern through all the ritual reiterations of myths. In
short, myths reveal that the World, man and life have a supernatural
origin and history, and that this history is significant, precious, and
exemplary.

Every mythical account of the origin of anything presupposes
and continues the cosmogony. From the structural point of view, origin
myths can be homologized with the cosmogonic myth. The creation of the
World being the pre-eminent instance of creation, the cosmogony becomes the exemplary model for "creation" of every kind. This does not
mean that the origin myth imitates or copies the cosmogonic model, for
no concerted or systematic reflection is involved. But every new appearance—an animal, a plant, an institution—implies the existence of a
World. Every origin myth narrates and justifies a "new situation"—new in
the sense that it did not exist from the beginning of the World. Origin
myths continue and complete the cosmogonic myth; they tell how the
world was changed, made richer or poorer.

This is why some origin myths begin by outlining a cosmogony.
The history of the great families and dynasties of Tibet opens by re-
hearsing the birth of the Cosmos from an Egg. The Polynesian genealogical chants begin in the same way. Such ritual genealogical chants are

composed by the bards when the princess is pregnant, and they are communicated to the *hula* dancers to be learned by heart. The dancers, men and women, dance and recite the chant continuously until the child is born. It is as if the embryological development of the future chief were accompanied by a recapitulation of the cosmogony, the history of the World, and the history of the tribe. The gestation of a chief is the occasion for a symbolic "recreation" of the World. The recapitulation is at once a reminder and a ritual reactualization, through song and dance, of the essential mythical events that have taken place since the Creation.

The close connection between the cosmogonic myth, the myth of the origin of sickness and its remedy, and the ritual of magical healing is clearly exemplified in, for example, the Ancient Near East or among the Tibetans. Sometimes a solemn recitation of the cosmogonic myth is enough to cure certain sicknesses or imperfections. As the exemplary model for all "creation," the cosmogonic myth can help the patient to make a "new beginning" of his life. The return to origins gives the hopes of a rebirth. . . .

A contemporary Polynesian, Hare Hongi, puts it this way:

> The words by which Io fashioned the Universe—that is to say, by which it was implanted and caused to produce a world of light—the same words are used in the ritual for implanting a child in a barren womb. The words by which Io caused light to shine in the darkness are used in rituals for cheering a gloomy and despondent heart, the feeble aged, the decrepit; for shedding light into secret places and matters, for inspiration in song—composing and in many other affairs, affecting men to despair in times of adverse war. For all such the ritual includes the words (used by Io) to overcome and dispel darkness. (E. S. C. Handy, *Polynesian Religion* [Honolulu, 1927], pp. 10–11.)

This remarkable text presents direct and incontrovertible testimony concerning the function of the cosmogonic myth in a traditional society. As we have just seen, this myth serves as the model for every kind of "creation"—the procreation of a child as well as the reestablishment of a military situation in jeopardy or of a psychic equilibrium threatened by melancholy and despair. . . .

All this is clearly apparent from the many ritual applications of the Polynesian cosmogonic myth. According to this myth, in the beginning there were only the Waters and Darkness. Io, the Supreme God, separated the Waters by the power of thought and of his words, and created the Sky and the Earth. He said: "Let the Waters be separated, let the Heavens be formed, let the Earth be!" These cosmogonic words of Io's, by virtue of which the world came into existence, are creative words, charged with sacred power. Hence men utter them when there is something to do, to create. They are repeated during the rite for making a suckling drink water or eat solid food. The child is ritually projected into the time of "origin" when milk, water, and grains first appeared on earth. The idea implicit in this belief is that it is *the first manifestation of a thing which is significant and valid*, and not its successive epiphanies.

Through the reactualization of his myths, the man of primitive societies attempts to approach the gods and to participate in *being;* the imitation of paradigmatic divine models expresses at once his desire for sanctity and his ontological nostalgia.

In the primitive and archaic religions the eternal repetition of divine exploits is justified as an *imitatio dei.* The sacred calendar annually repeats the same festivals, repeats, that is, the reactualizations of the same mythical events. Strictly speaking, the sacred calendar proves to be the "eternal return" of a limited number of divine *gesta* and this is true not only for primitive religions but for all others. The festal calendar everywhere constitutes a periodical return of the same primordial situations and hence a reactualization of the same sacred time. For religious man, reactualization of the same mythical events constitutes his greatest hopes, for with each reactualization he again has the opportunity to transfigure his existence, to make it like its divine model. In short, for religious man of the primitive and archaic societies, the eternal repetition of paradigmatic gestures and the eternal recovery of the same mythical time of origin, sanctified by the gods, in no sense implies a pessimistic vision of life. On the contrary, for him it is by virtue of this eternal return to the sources of the sacred and the real that human existence appears to be saved from nothingness and death.

The perspective changes completely when the sense of the *sacrality of the Cosmos becomes lost.* This is what occurs when, in certain more highly evolved societies, the intellectual élites progressively detach themselves from the patterns of the traditional religion. The religious meaning of the repetition of paradigmatic gestures is forgotten. But *repetition emptied of its religious content necessarily leads to a pessimistic vision of existence.* When it is no longer a vehicle for reintegrating a primordial situation, and hence for recovering the mysterious presence of the gods, that is, *when it is desacralized*, the mythical time becomes terrifying; it is seen as a circle forever turning on itself, repeating itself to infinity.

This is what happened in India, where the doctrine of cosmic cycles (*yugas*) was elaborately developed. To Indian thought, time was homologized to the cosmic illusion (*mâyâ*) and the eternal return to existence signified indefinite prolongation of suffering and slavery. In the view of these religious and philosophical élites, the only hope was non-return-to-existence, the abolition of *karma;* in other words, final deliverance (*mokska*) implying a transcendence of the cosmos. Greece, too, knew the myth of the eternal return, and the Greek philosophers of the late period carried the conception of circular time to its furthest limits.

Compared with the archaic and palaeo-oriental religions, as well as with the mythic-philosophical conception of the eternal return, as they were elaborated in India and Greece, Judaism presents an innovation of the first importance. For Judaism, time has a beginning and will have an end. The idea of cyclic time is left behind. Yahweh no longer manifests himself in *mythical time* (like the gods of other religions) but in a *historical time,* which is irreversible. Each new manifestation of Yahweh in history is no longer reducible to an earlier manifestation. The fall of Jerusalem expresses Yahweh's wrath against his people, but it is no longer the same wrath that Yahweh expressed by the fall of Samaria. His gestures are *personal* interventions in history and reveal their deep meaning *only for his people,* the people that Yahweh had *chosen.* Hence, the historical event acquires a new dimension; it becomes a theophany.

Christianity tried to go even further in valorizing *historical time.* The Christian Fathers insisted on the historicity of the life of Jesus and attempted to substantiate all the historical testimonies. Justin, for example, held that the Nativity could be proved by the "tax declarations submitted under the procurator Quirinus and available at Rome a century later." Origen thinks that the earthquake and the darkness can be confirmed by the historical narrative of Phlegon of Tralles. The Last Supper is a historical event that can be dated with absolute precision. Origen admits that the Gospels contain episodes that are not "authentic" historically though they are "true" on the spiritual plane. But in answering Celsus' criticisms, he also admits the difficulty of proving the historicity of a historical event. He writes: "An attempt to substantiate the truth of almost any story as historical fact, even if the story is true, and to produce complete certainty about it, is one of the most difficult tasks and in some cases impossible" (*Contra Celsum* I, 42).

Though he does not doubt the historicity of the life, passion, and resurrection of Jesus Christ, Origen is more concerned with the spiritual, nonhistorical meaning of the Gospel text. The true meaning is "beyond history." The exegetist must be able to "free himself from the historical materials," for these are only a "steppingstone." To overstress the historicity of Jesus and neglect the deeper meaning of his life and message is, in fact, to mutilate Christianity. "People marvel at Jesus," he writes in his *Commentary on the Gospel of John,* "when they look into the history about him, but they no longer believe when the deeper meaning is disclosed to them; instead they suppose it to be false."

In proclaiming the Incarnation, Resurrection, and Ascension of the Word, the Christian Fathers were sure that they were not putting forth a new myth. Actually, they were employing the categories of mythical thought. Obviously they could not recognize this mythical thought in the desacralized mythologies of the pagan scholars who were their contemporaries. But it is clear that for Christians of all creeds the center of religious life is constituted by the drama of Jesus Christ. Although played out in History, this drama first established the possibility of salvation; hence there is only one way to gain salvation—to reiterate this exemplary drama ritually and to imitate the supreme model revealed by the life and teaching of Jesus. Now, this type of religious behavior is bound up with genuine mythical thought.

It must at once be added that, by the *very fact that it is a religion*, Christianity had to keep at least one mythical aspect—liturgical Time, that is, the periodical recovery of the *illud tempus* of the "beginnings." The religious experience of the Christian is based upon an *imitation* of the Christ as *exemplary pattern*, upon the liturgical repetition of the life, death, and resurrection of the Lord, and upon the *contemporaneity* of the Christian with *illud tempus* which begins with the Nativity at Bethlehem and ends with the Ascension. Now, as we have seen, the imitation of a transhuman model, the repetition of an exemplary scenario and the breakaway from profane time through a moment which opens out into the Great Time, are the essential marks of "mythical behavior"— that is, the behavior of the man of the archaic societies, who finds the very source of his existence in the myth.

Ultimately, Christianity arrives, not at a *philosophy*, but at a *theology* of history. For God's intervention in history, and above all his incarnation in the historical person of Jesus the Christ, have a transhistorical purpose—the *salvation* of man.

Hegel takes over the Judaeo-Christian ideology and applies it to universal history in its totality: the universal spirit *continually* manifests itself in historical events and manifests itself *only* in historical events. Thus *the whole* of history becomes a theophany; everything that has happened in history *had to happen as it did,* because the universal Spirit so willed it. The road is thus opened to the various forms of twentieth-century historicistic philosophies. Yet we must add that historicism arises as a decomposition product of Christianity; it accords decisive importance to the historical event (which is an idea whose origin is Christian), but to the *historical event as such,* that is, by denying it any possibility of revealing a transhistorical, soteriological intent.

The modern, nonreligious, "historical" man can be considered the result of a radical secularization of the Hegelian understanding of

History. The nonreligious man refuses transcendence, accepts the relativity of "reality," and may even come to doubt the meaning of existence. The great cultures of the past too have not been entirely without nonreligious men. But it is only in the modern western societies that nonreligious man has developed fully. Modern nonreligious man assumes a new existential situation; he regards himself solely as the subject and agent of history, and he refuses all appeal to transcendence. In other words, he accepts no model for humanity outside the human condition as it can be seen in the various historical situations. Man *makes himself,* and he only makes himself completely in proportion as he desacralized himself and the world. The sacred is the prime obstacle to his freedom. He will become himself only when he is totally demystified. He will not be truly free until he has killed the last god.

The modern nonreligious man assumes a tragic existence and his existential choice is not without its greatness. But this nonreligious man descends from *homo religiosus* and, whether he likes it or not, he is also the work of religious man. In short, he is the result of a desacralization of human existence. But this means that nonreligious man has been formed by opposing his predecessor, by attempting to "empty" himself of all religion and all transhuman meanings. He recognizes himself in proportion as he "frees" and "purifies" himself from the "superstitions" of his ancestors. In other words, profane man cannot help preserving some vestiges of the behavior of religious man, though they are emptied of religious meaning. Do what he will, he is an inheritor. He cannot utterly abolish his past, since he is himself the product of his past. He forms himself by a series of denials and refusals, but he continues to be haunted by the realities that he has refused and denied. To acquire a world of his own, he has desacralized the world in which his ancestors lived; but to do so he has been obliged to adopt the opposite of an earlier type of behavior, and that behavior is still emotionally present to him, in one form or another, ready to be reactualized in his deepest being.

The nonreligious man *in the pure state* is a comparatively rare phenomenon, even in the most desacralized of modern societies. The majority of the "irreligious" still behave religiously, even though they are not aware of the fact. We refer not only to the modern man's many "superstitions" and "taboos," all of them magico-religious in structure. But the modern man who feels and claims that he is nonreligious still retains a large stock of camouflaged myths and degenerated rituals. The festivities that go with the New Year or with taking up residence in a new house, still exhibit the structures of a ritual of renewal.

A whole volume could well be written on the myths of modern man, on the mythologies camouflaged in the plays that he enjoys, in the books that he reads. The cinema, that "dream factory," takes over and employs countless mythical motifs—the fight between hero and monster, initiatory combats and ordeals, paradigmatic figures and images (the Maiden, the Hero, the Paradisal Landscape, Hell, and so on). Even reading includes a mythological function, not only because it replaces the recitation of myths in archaic societies and the oral literature that still lives in the rural communities of Europe, but particularly because through reading the modern man succeeds in obtaining an "escape from time" comparable to the "emergence from Time" effected by myths.

Strictly speaking, the great majority of the irreligious are not liberated from religious behavior, from theologies and mythologies. They sometimes stagger under a whole magico-religious paraphernalia, which, however, has degenerated to the point of caricature and hence is hard to recognize for what it is. We do not refer to the countless "little religions" that proliferate in all modern cities, to the pseudo-occult, neo-spiritualistic, or so-called hermetic churches, sects or movements; for all these phenomena still belong to the sphere of religion, even if they almost always present the aberrant aspects of pseudo-morphs. Nor do we allude to the various political movements and social utopianisms whose mythological structure and religious fanaticism are visible at a glance. For but one example we need only refer to the mythological structure of communism and its eschatological content. Marx takes over and continues one of the great eschatological myths of the Asian Mediterranean world— the redeeming role of the Just (the "chosen," the "anointed," the "innocent"; in our day, the proletariat), whose sufferings are destined to change the ontological status of the world. In fact, Marx's classless society and the consequent disappearance of historical tensions find their closest precedent in the myth of the Golden Age that many traditions put at the beginning and the end of history. Marx enriched this venerable myth by a whole Judaeo-Christian messianic ideology: on the one hand, the prophetic role and soteriological function that he attributes to the proletariat; on the other, the final battle between Good and Evil, which is easily comparable to the apocalyptic battle between Christ and Antichrist, followed by the total victory of the former.

But it is not only in the "little religions" or in the political mystiques that we find degenerated or camouflaged religious and mythical behavior. It is no less to be seen in movements that openly avow themselves to be secular or even antireligious. Examples are of nudism or the movements for complete sexual freedom, ideologies in which we can discern traces of the "nostalgia for Eden," the desire to reestablish the paradisal state before the Fall, when sin did not exist.

Then, too, it is interesting to observe to what an extent the scenarios of initiation still persist in the modern world—for instance, in psychoanalysis. The patient is asked to descend deeply into himself, to make his past live, to confront his traumatic experience again; structurally, this dangerous operation resembles initiatory descents into hell, the realm of ghosts, and combats with monsters. Just as the initiate was expected to emerge from his ordeals victorious—so the patient undergoing analysis today must confront his own unconscious, haunted by ghosts and monsters, in order to find psychic health and integrity and hence the world of cultural values.

In short, the majority of men "without religion" and "without myths" still hold to pseudo religions and degenerated mythologies. There is nothing surprising in this, for as we saw, profane man is the descendant *homo religiosus* and he cannot wipe out his own history—that is, the behavior of his religious ancestors which has made him what he is today. This is all the more true because a great part of his existence is fed by impulses that come to him from the depths of his being, from the unconscious. Now, the contents and structures of the unconscious exhibit astonishing similarities to mythological images and figures. We do not mean to say that mythologies are the "product" of the unconscious, for the mode of being of the myth is precisely that it *reveals itself as myth*. That is, it announces that something *has been manifested in a paradigmatic manner*. A myth is "produced" by the unconscious in the same sense in which we could say that *Madame Bovary* is the "product" of an adultery.

Yet the contents and structures of the unconscious are the results of immemorial existential situations, especially of critical situations, and this is why the unconscious has a religious aura. Thus, the nonreligious man of modern societies is still nourished and aided by the activity of his unconscious, but without thereby attaining to a properly religious experience and vision of the world. From one point of view, it could almost be said that in the case of those moderns who proclaim that they are nonreligious, religion and mythology are "eclipsed" in the darkness of their unconscious. Or, from the Christian point of view, it could also be said that nonreligion is equivalent to a new "fall" of man—in other words, that nonreligious man has lost the capacity to live religion consciously, and hence to understand and assume it; but that, in his deepest being, he still retains a memory of it, as, after the first "fall," his ancestor, the primordial man, retained intelligence enough to enable him to rediscover the traces of God that are visible in the world. After the first "fall," the religious sense descended to the level of the "divided consciousness"; now, after the second, it has fallen even further, into the depths of the unconscious; it has been "forgotten."

August Karl Reischauer

A Summary Statement of God-Concept

The conception of the Divine in the major religions of mankind is rather varied. While there are areas in which there is substantial agreement, there are also real differences. Even within what is nominally one and the same religion that God-concept is sometimes far from uniform. This is especially true in Indian religions and in the religions of East Asia with their characteristic tolerance of widely differing views even in the great essentials of religion such as the conception of the Divine.

Now this bewildering array of the God-concept can, perhaps, be more or less systematized and made less confusing by taking the personalistic God-concept of the great monotheistic faiths as a provisional norm. To be sure, there are some differences in the conception of the Divine even among these great monotheistic faiths but there is nevertheless a wide area of agreement. Furthermore, in other great religions which differ more or less in their conception of the Divine from the great monotheistic faiths, there are definite trends towards a theistic view, as . . . in later Hinduism, in certain Branches of Mahāyāna Buddhism and also in other East Asian religions. In a summary way one might say

From *Nature and Truth of the Great Religions* by August Karl Reischauer (Rutland, Vt.: Charles E. Tuttle Co., Inc., 1966) pp. 78–86. Reprinted by permission of the publisher.

Karl Reischauer was formerly Professor of History of Religion at Union Theological Seminary and was an educational missionary to Japan for thirty-five years.

that the theistic view as held by the great monotheistic faiths is flanked on either side with God-concepts that differ from it more or less widely. On one side are the views found in the more primitive religions and which may well be designated as Pre-theistic views because they often tend to evolve in the direction of the theistic God-concept, especially when there is a rising level of intelligence among the adherents of such faiths. On the other side of the theistic God-concept are various views of the Divine which tend to move away from the theistic concept in search of what is felt to be a more adequate view and which therefore may be summarily spoken of as Post-theistic conceptions.

In the Pre-theistic conceptions of the Divine . . . in the religions of India and East Asia there is a wide range of views. On the lower levels there is the worship of certain natural phenomena and innumerable spirits, both semi-personalized nature spirits and deified humans. This belief in innumerable spirits and deities often evolves into a sort of organized polytheism or so-called Monarchical Polytheism according to which the lesser deities and spirits are seen as subordinated to some major deity though each lesser deity still retains control over its own limited sphere. This stage of development in the God-concept often evolves into a sort of pantheism according to which the lesser deities which formerly were seen as controlling their own limited sphere now become just so many local manifestations of the Divine. These local manifestations of the Divine are seen in more or less personalistic terms, while the all-inclusive Divine Being or Reality is not further defined. Or again, the evolution of the God-concept may result in what is virtually a theistic conception according to which the Divine is seen in ideal personalistic terms; and what were formerly lesser deities become mere messengers or possibly temporary incarnations of the One Supreme Being.

It should, however, be observed that in Indian and East Asian religions, even when the God-concept becomes virtually theistic, so that man turns to One Supreme Being conceived of in personalistic terms for help, such a Supreme Being is seldom if ever regarded as One who creates, sustains and controls all things in any such way as one finds in the great monotheistic faiths. Indian and East Asian religions, rather, accept the universe as a given fact; or if they attempt to account for its origin, and as being under the power or control of the Divine, they think of the Divine in terms which are best designated as Post-theistic just because they reject the theistic view as being philosophically inadequate however much it may be most satisfying to the common believer who needs a person-to-person relationship between himself and his deity.

Now it is these Post-theistic conceptions of the Divine that need further elucidation than we have given them, for they represent a continuing problem in religion, particularly for those who think seriously about "the Divine Mystery."

There are really two major types of the Post-theistic God-concept or mode of the God-consciousness, namely, various types of mysticism and various forms of pantheism or cosmotheism.

In mysticism one can hardly speak of a God-concept, for the typical mystic holds that "the Divine Mystery" in its full being forever transcends all human concepts. It is therefore more correct to speak of "the mode of the God-consciousness." What the mystic experiences in his awareness of the Divine can be known, according to the mystic, only to those who have had the mystical experience. However, when the mystic seeks to communicate to others the content of his mystical experience, he must inevitably resort to concepts derived from man's ordinary spiritual experience.

There can be little doubt but that the typical mystic's approach to the Divine Mystery is psycho-centric. It is away from the things of sense and the outer world and seeks to penetrate to the inner nature of man's own spiritual being in the hope of finding in it a depth of being which is at the same time beyond the merely human, the depth where the human becomes the divine, or at least the fore-court of the divine. "Sit in the center of thyself and thou seest what is and shall be," says a Sufi mystic. And Catherine of Sienna, though a Christian who presumably accepted as valid God's revelation of himself in Jesus Christ, wrote, "If thou wouldst arrive at a perfect knowledge of Me, the Eternal Truth, never go outside thyself."

While the typical mystic usually seeks the true and Ulimate Reality within his own spiritual being rather than in the outer world and while virtually all mystics insist that the Divine Mystery in its full nature is beyond all human concepts, one can, nevertheless, say that there are really two major types of mysticism, namely personal mysticism and impersonal mysticism.

In personal mysticism as exemplified by most Christian mystics, the mode of the God-consciousness does not run counter to the personalistic conception of the Divine. Its major emphasis is rather on man's direct awareness of and ecstatic communion with God. To be sure, even Christian mystics characteristically insist that God is infinitely more than what can be expressed by any personalistic concepts or what man experiences on the highest levels of spiritual insight. But this "infinitely more" which the mystic experiences in his ecstatic visions is rather in the direction of an all-comprehensive truth, an all-compelling purity and goodness, and a loveliness of spirit which lifts the human personality above its ordinary experiences and limitations. This type of mysticism would never reject the personalistic conception of the Divine in favor of any impersonal or sub-personal concept. Even when there is at times a tendency to flirt, as it were, with the irrational, this is largely a way of saying that man cannot comprehend the full nature of God even with his highest and noblest conceptions rather than that the irrational is the key. And certainly no Christian mystic has suggested that God is to be seen better in the non-moral or the immoral than in the moral, for the words of Jesus, "Blessed are the pure in heart for they shall see God" have always been normative for the most pronounced Christian mystic. And if Christian art is to be trusted it would seem that the beautiful rather than the grotesque or the ugly has ever been regarded as appropriately associated with the Divine. These external expressions of the beautiful are seen as having their full purpose only as they help man in his quest for "the beauty of holiness."

Thus it should be clear that in characteristic Christian mysticism, and we might add, in the mysticism associated with the other great theistic faiths, there is little that runs counter to a worthy personalistic God-concept. It is rather a way of stressing the possibility of the finite human being coming into a close and intimate relationship with his God. However close this relationship may become in the mystic's ecstatic experience it apparently never quite obliterates the distinction between the experiencing human self and the Divine and Eternal Self.

There is, however, another type of mysticism, namely, impersonal mysticism, which rejects the personalistic God-concept as being too limiting or cast too much in man's own little image to express adequately the true nature of the Divine Mystery. While this type of mysticism is equally psychocentric with personal mysticism, it nevertheless attempts to pass through this center to a reality beyond, which is so wholly other in its true nature that it cannot be defined in personalistic terms. Impersonal mysticism does not reject the personalistic God-concept on grounds that the physical cosmos is also an aspect of reality, as is the case with pantheism, which we shall consider below, for impersonal mysticism is as psychocentric as personal mysticism is and the outer world is the first obstacle to be overcome in the quest for the Divine and the ultimately real. All sense experience and concepts built up from sense perception must be disposed of as much as possible largely by reducing the concrete details of actual sense contacts to abstractions and vague universals thus freeing the mind from all limiting distractions. In man's moral experience, likewise, man must pass beyond what in his personal relations with his fellow-men is the right and the good to what is Absolute and which as such is really "beyond good and evil." Whether in the realm of the true, the good or the beautiful this type of mystic may use man's ordinary experience in these fields as a sort of ladder on which he climbs upward and then from the upper rung he leaps with ecstatic vision into the realm of the Divine and experiences what is so wholly other from man's ordinary experience that it cannot be expressed in terms of the latter. However, when this type of mystic does attempt to communicate to others who have not had this experience, he must naturally resort to concepts that have meaning to them even though such concepts do not adequately express what he has found in his mystical experience. He, therefore, resorts to a terminology which though comprehensive in meaning is also quite vague. The Divine is, therefore, spoken of as "Being" and without any qualifying adjectives such as "Personal" or even "Supreme." Even the term "Being" is often regarded as too limiting and so the Divine Mystery is spoken of as both "Being and Non-Being," or by other terms of affirmation and negation. It might seem that such terms cancel each other and it must be admitted that at times the negation seems like a flat contradiction of what is contained in the affirmation. Usually, however, the negation is intended to convey "the much more" or "the wholly other" than what is conveyed in the affirmation about the full nature of the Divine as the Absolute and Ultimate Reality.

Now this type of mysticism finds its best representatives in certain phases of Hinduism and also in the Dyāna School of Mahāyāna Buddhism . . . But it is interesting to note that one finds even among Christian theologians some who speak of God in similar terminology. They too seem to feel that personalistic concepts are too anthropomorphic and hence too limiting to convey adequately what God is in his full being, and so they speak of the Divine as "Being Itself," "Pure Being," "Being as Such" or simply as "Being" and without any qualifying adjectives. And since even the term "Being" may be too definitive and limiting they speak of God as "Being and Non-Being." We are not here discussing what we regard as the most adequate terminology in speaking of God or "the Divine Mystery" but only pointing out that when Christian theologians resort to the above terminology, they are only repeating what oriental philosophers have said about "the Divine Mystery" for upward of two thousand years. And we might add that this vague terminology has not been very helpful to the common believer who needs a person-to-person relationship with his god, however much the philosopher may feel that in using such terminology he expresses more adequately what "the Divine Mystery" is.

There is another form of impersonal mysticism which we must mention briefly, namely, what we have called nature mysticism and which has its best representative in certain phases of Taoist philosophy. We said above that all types of mysticism are psycho-centric. This type of mysticism seems to belie this and to be rather cosmo-centric, for it is definitely a feeling of man's oneness with Nature. But even though there is here such an awareness of the external world, it nevertheless remains psycho-centric in that it is rather an emotional reaction towards Nature or a mood which reads into external nature much that is purely spiritual or subjective, rather than being a truer understanding of the physical cosmos as such. It might be said that this nature mysticism is a sort of connecting link between impersonal mysticism and the pantheism or cosmotheism which we speak of next.

Pantheism or cosmotheism is seen best in certain phases of Upanishad philosophy, especially in the Vedānta interpretation of the Upanishads, and in certain branches of Mahāyāna Buddhism. Like impersonal mysticism, it rejects the personalistic conception of the Divine as being too limiting, but it differs from the latter in what it regards as a more adequate conception. Where impersonal mysticism, like all forms of mysticism, tends to eliminate the things of the outer world as obstacles to man's communion with the Divine, pantheism or cosmotheism frankly accepts the things of the outer world as being just as truly an aspect of the Divine or Ultimate Reality as is man's own psychic and spiritual nature. However, it would add that the pluralistic world of the ordinary man's experience, i.e., the world as seen by the unenlightened, is not what it seems to be but is largely illusory. The real world as seen by the fully enlightened is a glorious and harmonious Unity. Back of the multiplicity of the phenomenal world is the all-inclusive Oneness of the noumenal world or the world of Ultimate Reality; back of the ever changing and the temporal is the Changeless and the Eternal.

Now while such concepts and terminology may satisfy the philosopher with his quest for the unitary ground of all finite existence, it is all too vague in meaning to be of much help in solving man's practical problems of life. It is for this reason that the pantheistic or cosmotheistic conception of the Divine seldom, if ever, stands by itself in actual religion, even in the religion of the philosopher. It is almost always linked with conceptions of the Divine that are cast in rather personalistic terms, as in . . . Hinduism and Mahāyāna Buddhism. Thus the outstanding Vedānta philosopher, Sankara, with all his monistic interpretation of Brahman as the Ultimate Reality, had to speak of a "lower Brahma" cast in personalistic concepts. And Mahāyāna Buddhism has its *Trikaya,* "Three Bodies" doctrine, namely, *Dharmakaya,* "Law Body" or "Cosmic Body" standing for the all-inclusive Absolute which in its full nature is beyond all human concepts; *Sambhogakaya,* "Compensation Body" or Buddha conceived in terms of ideal personality; and *Nirmanakaya,* "Accommodated Body" or Buddha seen as a historic human being.

In short, the pantheist or cosmotheist rejects the personalistic God-concept as being too limiting to stand for the Divine as the Ultimate Reality or the Unitary Ground of all existence, but he is nevertheless compelled to resort to personalistic concepts when he would speak of the

Divine in a way that can have any real meaning or be helpful in meeting man's religious needs. In fact, as . . . with both Hinduism and Mahāyāna Buddhism, the pantheist or cosmotheist tends at times to speak of the Divine in terms that are all too much patterned after man's own little image. And this suggests that the very attempt on the part of the philosopher to pass beyond even the most worthy personalistic God-concept to a conception which is more adequate and all-inclusive results all too often in a conception of the Divine which is really sub-personal rather than super-personal in meaning.

A third form of the Post-theistic conception of the Divine finds its expression in what might be best designated as "reverent agnosticism." Although we speak of it as an agnosticism, it is not the blatantly anti-religious agnosticism which is really a concealed materialism holding that the Divine which the man of religion seeks to know is unknowable for the simple reason that it does not exist. Reverent agnosticism is almost the direct opposite of this. Where the former would explain all psychic and spiritual aspects of existence as mere epiphenomena or reduce everything to mere "matter and motion," the latter holds that we do not know enough about the nature of Ultimate Reality, call it the Divine or whatever term you care to use, to say much about it. Even our best understanding of physical nature and our deepest insights into the spiritual aspects of existence, though true enough as far as they go, are only fragmentary bits of truth and far from what is the true and full nature of Ultimate Reality or the Divine Mystery. In fact, says the reverently agnostic philosopher, the larger the sphere of the known becomes, the greater is our contact with the Unknown. How, then, can one be so dogmatic in making affirmations about the Divine Mystery as some men of religion are?

Now this spirit of reverent agnosticism has found expression in various ways in connection with the major religions of mankind. Thus, for example, in Indian religions the Buddha felt that the philosophers of his day were talking rather glibly about the Brahman as the Ultimate Reality, while the gods of the common masses were seen too much in terms of finite man to be worthy of respect and worship. While the Buddha was not an atheist, as some western scholars have maintained, it is true that he was reluctant to speak about metaphysical realities. Even when pressed by his disciples to answer their questions he usually said that such speculations were unprofitable and really were a hindrance in solving problems nearer at hand, namely the problem of conquering one's lower passions and achieving a truly ethical personality. When he did refer to what lies beyond this life and to what is ultimately real he used the term *Nirvana*, "the Void," as some translate it. *Nirvana* is not an absolute Void, but a reality so wholly other from the world of the unenlightened man's experience that it cannot be expressed in terms of that experience. One might, therefore, regard the Buddha as one who was reverently agnostic regarding the nature of Ultimate Reality or the Divine Mystery. Even if it be maintained that he claimed that the fully enlightened understood, it must be admitted that such understanding could not be formulated in any definite concepts that are intelligible to the average human mind. This hesitancy on the part of the Buddha to say anything more definite on this matter left his followers in a position where they had to work out their own answers as best they could. . . . The Buddhist masses usually worshipped gods patterned after man's own nature, while the philosophers gave widely differing answers ranging from a definitely personalistic conception of the Divine to one which is so wholly transcendental in nature that it can be spoken of only in paradoxes or in an endless series of affirmations and negations but in which series the negation had the last word over the affirmation; and with some the last word about the Divine Mystery was no word at all but rather "the White Silence of Truth"; or as Nagaryuna felt it, "Silence is the ultimate truth for the wise."

Another way in which this reverently agnostic mood found expression, especially in Mahāyāna Buddhism, was in its theory of knowledge with its emphasis on the relativity of all human truth or what was called "Accommodated Truth." All human truth must be accommodated to the varying levels of human intelligence, and especially is that the case in dealing with the Divine. This emphasis, as we saw, resulted in a generous tolerance of widely differing conceptions of the Divine and other essentials of religion, but it also led at times towards an out and out agnosticism, while with the more deeply religious it never went beyond a "reverent agnosticism."

One might include also certain aspects of Vedānta philosophy as being reverently agnostic towards the nature of the Divine Mystery. Vedānta looks upon the world of man's ordinary experience as largely illusory, for what seems to be a multiplicity of differing and conflicting realities, when seen in their true nature, are but aspects of an all-inclusive Unity and Oneness. However, the Vedānta philosopher with all his assurance about the Unity of what is Ultimately Real never gets very far beyond this monistic affirmation and so leaves virtually unanswered the question as to the real nature of the Divine Mystery.

In Confucianism and in typical Chinese thought one can find this spirit of reverent agnosticism expressing itself, though it differs somewhat from the typical Indian form. The Chinese mind usually accepts the world of man's ordinary experience as real rather than as being largely illusory. While it is realized that this very real world has its cause or grounding in Ultimate Reality, call this Heaven, the *Tao* or what not, it is felt that man's first task is to master and understand better the things that are nearest at hand rather than speculate too much about the full nature of Ultimate Reality. Frequently in Chinese thought, this emphasis on the immediate practical, even when it includes ethical and spiritual values and meanings, is carried to the point where it virtually ignores what is beyond the human sphere and so becomes what amounts to an out and out agnosticism. However, with some, and especially with those who have been influenced by Buddhist thought, it is more of what we have been calling a mood of "reverent agnosticism" towards the "Divine Mystery."

The great monotheistic faiths usually state the God-concept in definitely personalistic and positive terms. There are, however, passages in the sacred scriptures of these faiths which also seem to endorse an attitude of "reverent agnosticism" when speaking of the Divine. "Canst thou by searching find God? Canst thou find out the Almighty to perfection?" (Job II. 7). And Isaiah writes: "For my thoughts are not your thoughts, neither are my ways your ways, saith the Lord. For as the heavens are higher than the earth so are my ways higher than your ways, and my thoughts higher than your thoughts." God is one who "dwells in thick darkness," says the psalmist, "clouds and darkness are around him." Paul also warns that man's knowledge of things spiritual is quite limited, for "now we see in a mirror dimly" . . . "now we know [only] in part." God, he says, is One "dwelling in the light which no man can approach unto; whom no man hath seen, or can see." These and similar passages would seem to suggest that man be somewhat hesitant in what he says about God and that an attitude of "reverent agnosticism towards the Divine Mystery" might be more fitting. Undoubtedly there is in these and similar passages in the Bible a warning not to think of God, the Infinite and Eternal, all too much in terms of man's own finite nature. Men of religion need to be reminded that "the high and lofty One who inhabiteth eternity whose name is Holy" dwells "with him who is of a contrite and humble spirit." But while there is this warning it does not mean that the last word about the Divine can only be one that is cast in the language of a "reverent agnosticism." However true it is that God in his full being forever transcends man's comprehension, Christianity and the other great monotheistic faiths maintain with good reason that man can and does have some real knowledge of the "Divine Mystery" and that the most adequate concept of the Divine is in terms of man's highest experience as a personal being. . . .

Huston Smith

Toward a World Civilization

About the middle of the century, Arnold Toynbee predicted that for another hundred years historians would still be interested primarily in the continuing impact of the West upon Asia, but that two hundred years down the line they would be more involved with the answering impact of Asia upon the West; and two thousand years down the line (only Toynbee could venture to look that far ahead) historians would look back on the twentieth century as the one in which mankind took its first concerted steps toward the creation of a genuine world civilization.

Of course, it is too early to anticipate in any detail what the contours of this emerging world civilization will be, but not too early, I think, to ask what the great enduring civilizations have to contribute to it.

I take as my basic assumption that man is inescapably engaged in three basic conflicts: 1) with nature, 2) with his fellow men, and 3) with himself. Roughly, these may be identified as man's natural, social, and psychological problems. The great surviving cultural civilizations are also three—the Chinese, the Indian, and the Western. It helps us to understand and relate the unique perspectives of these three civilizations if we think of each as accenting one of man's basic problems. For, generally speaking, the West has attended more assiduously and with higher expectations to the problem with nature, China with the social, and India with the psychological.

Beginning with the West, I think what distinguishes Western civilization has been its conviction that human fulfillment is to be sought naturalistically. By this is meant not only *in* nature but *through* nature.

Reprinted from *Center Diary: 17,* pp. 45–49. Published by the Center for the Study of Democratic Institutions. © 1967 by the Fund for the Republic, Inc. By permission of the publisher.

Huston Smith teaches philosophy at Massachusetts Institute of Technology.

Three ideas arose indigenously in the West and nowhere else: the individual, faith in historical progress, and modern science. Each of these is related to one of nature's three components: space, time, and matter. If anything has no location in space, or cannot be identified in time, or has no material component, then we are inclined in the West to say that if it exists, it is not part of nature; it is supernatural.

There is a connection between each of the great discoveries of the West and each of the components of nature. Science bears an obvious correlation with matter. Scrutinize the material world carefully enough and sooner or later the patterns of connection and correlation begin to emerge, and one finds the way to modern science. The idea of progress bears an obvious connection to time. Ponder the mystery of time long enough and one notices the novelty that time introduces, and then one realizes that what is new may be better; and thus one finds the way to progress. Lastly, the individual bears a correlation with space, perhaps not so obvious, but I think real. The reason, in the end, that I am an individual distinct from my neighbor is that I occupy a different body and thereby a different region of space.

Why the West turned in the direction of nature we shall never fully know, for its origins, like all origins, are veiled in the twilight of early history. But its basic interest in and high regard for nature seem traceable to the hospitality of its cradle environment, significantly christened the "Fertile Crescent." Here nature almost coaxes inquiry and certainly rewards advances. Western man accepted her overtures; from the first, his primary curiosity was directed outward, toward nature. His growing feeling was that everything is orderly, exact, measurable, impartial.

Perhaps the most important factor, however, was not geography but theology. For, of the three great civilizations, the West is the only one that regarded nature or the cosmos as the deliberate creation of a being perfect both in will and in power. The very first verse of the West's Bible proclaims that "in the beginning God created the heaven *and the earth*," and when at the close of the chapter he looks upon "every thing that he had made," earth included, "behold it was very good." Furthermore, the goodness of the earth lies not only in beholding it but in working with it: man is commissioned to "have dominion over . . . the earth." The incarnation pays matter its highest conceivable compliment—it can become divine. The Kingdom of Heaven, from Jewish and early Christian revelation down to the social gospel, is to come on earth. Even in death, the West will not desert the body. If there is to be life after death, it, too, must be in some sense physical: "I believe . . . in the resurrection of the body." All of this, then, invests the natural world with a dignity not really to be found to the same extent in the attitudes of other civilizations.

What gave the West its interest in time, or progress—here we are clearest—is that one of its major components, namely the Hebraic perspective, arose through the concrete historical event of the exodus. The exodus gathered the milling tribe together and gave them a sense of peoplehood and destiny. One looks in vain in either Indian history or Chinese history for a single historical event that initiated a perspective comparable to the exodus. But there is another point about time in the West. The West is the only civilization whose perspective continues to be molded by a people—the Jews—who in their formative period were for the most part either displaced or oppressed persons. This experience made of the Jews a people in waiting. The Jews were always waiting for something—to cross over into Jordan, to get back to the Promised Land, to throw off the yoke of the oppressor. This waiting quality gives to the Jewish mind a future orientation which eventuates in the idea of the prophet. The idea's specifically Jewish form is messianism, its Christian form is the Second Coming, its secular form is the idea of historical progress, and its heretical form is the Marxist dream of a classless society.

Finally, in tracing the development of the interest of the West in the individual we are again on tenuous ground, but there is this much to point out: For the individual to be encouraged to express his full potential, it may be that it is necessary for a good bit of fate to be available; otherwise there is the danger that if the individual expresses himself to the maximum, he might rub too harshly against another individual. Perhaps this is why Western man needed to be spread out more, rather than living in tightly packed wall cities as in China. The point is enshrined in the notion of the frontier as being the breeding ground of individualism. Of the three great civilizations, the Western is the one that has been historically the frontier civilization, moving first from the eastern shores of the Mediterranean around towards the western shores and then up into the largely uninhabited swamps and marshes of Europe, and finally skipping across the ocean to the New World.

Now let us swing across the huge Eurasian land mass over into China. To do so means to move across the greatest barrier to man's mobility on the earth, that mammoth mountainous range beginning in the Himalayas and focusing in Tibet whose average altitude is the highest of any country in the world, and then sweeping down in that immense mountainous chain into Southeast Asia. Even today, this range is cut only by two narrow-gauge railroads and by a few paths precariously maneuverable by jeeps. In historic times it constituted the greatest barrier to man's free movement on the face of this planet; even the oceans were not as formidable. I point this out merely to remind us that the civilization which developed behind that barrier was unique, *sui generis*. It had a different racial stock, the Mongolian; a different mode of eating, chopsticks instead of fingers as in Southeast Asia or utensils as in Europe. But those are surface features. What is interesting is the distinctive fundamental option of these people in their search for human fulfillment.

I think that the Chinese option was to build the good life through building the good society. Nature, for some reason, never appeared to the Chinese mind as lending itself to alteration for improvement. Against nature the most that could be hoped was a holding operation. It never occurred to the Chinese mind that life could be improved by changing the basic relationship between man and nature. So they turned toward society, where they had a wonderful opportunity. They were a homogeneous racial stock, because Mongolians were all very much alike, and so these black-haired sons of Khan set theselves to perfecting human relationships. Their basic technique was to identify those values they felt would be most worth developing in human relations and then to turn all the powers of education, formal and informal, toward internalizing these values in every Chinese citizen.

One of the most important principles that guided the Chinese in their social relations was that the group had priority over the individual. Whereas in the West we think of the individual as the basic unit of social reality and of groups as relations into which individuals enter and out of which they may pass, the Chinese turn this around. For them the basic unit of social reality is the group. For certain purposes individuals may be abstracted in thought but these abstractions have no reality apart from the concrete whole. The individual has no more viability in his own rights than an eye when plucked out of its orbit.

When the Chinese went on to ask which group is most important, they didn't hesitate to answer "the family." To move beyond the family to society, they thought it had to be a class society—this, of course, is traditional China, not the China of the last seventeen years—but the lines between the classes should be perforated to allow for mobility between classes. There never was great mobility in any of the historical civilizations, but the Chinese achieved a social system that allowed more movement than any other civilization over a comparable period in history. What chance was there of a serf in medieval Europe passing on to be a lord? But with the examination system in China it was not altogether outlandish for a peasant woman in some remote province to hold out the hope that if her son had real talent and drive, he might go right through the provincial examination to the Imperial examination and conceivably become prime minister.

When the Chinese asked how the classes should be layered in regard to prestige and emoluments, they put the scholar-administrator at the top; he was the most valuable person because he orchestrates, as it were, the human resources. The West, of course, has the ideal of the philosopher-king, but it has not made as concerted an effort as China did to realize that ideal—not that it was fully realized in China either, but it was at least more of a practical working ideal than it has been in the West.

Following in the order, next, were the producers, first the farmers and then the artisans, and under them the merchants. This meant that production was more important than distribution. In the West, since industrialization, this has not been so; hence, the sales force in our modern corporation occupies an importance at least equal to that of the production force: We can produce as much as we want to—the problem is to get it distributed. But in traditional China the ever-present problem was to get enough, not how to get it around.

Last in the class scale was the soldier; the man of violence seems to be necessary somewhere, but his role is never really creative. Part of all this was the belief that education was central in the social system, and the heart of education was not merely intellectual education but moral education.

Turning last to the third great civilization—the Indian—we find neither the natural nor the social environment looking promising to her. India's natural environment is different from but no more friendly than China's. The tropical region of the Ganges with its thick vegetation, unbearable humidity, and burning heat, the parching dryness of other regions, where for ten months of the year there is nothing but the nightly dew to quench the thirst of the ground—the Indian environment is one of fierce extremes. Discouraged by the overpowering forces of nature, Indian man surrendered his initiative and turned away from nature. His outlook became unrealistic in the technical sense. The desert, particularly, must have discouraged him. Facing nature in this form, gaunt, bleak, desiccated, dangling its haunting mirages—no wonder the Indian began to think: Nature is ungovernable and, in some strange way, unreal. She is shadowy, ever-shifting, mysterious, horrible if you will, but what is the use of trying to find out her laws. It is all *maya*. It is all magic, a trick, the play of a mysterious cosmic illusion.

Faced with a seemingly intractable nature, China turned her attention to society. But in this area India found herself facing the most devilish of social problems—a color-culture barrier. The distinction between Aryan and Dravidian was clear, and to this day—3500 years later—the line persists. No Indian ingenuity was adequate to break this curse. Caste tried to do so, but instead of caste's remedying the evil, in the end the evil took over caste, turning it into a device for perpetuating social distance. Relatively early, then, India lost hope of solving life's problems on the social frontier. Instead, she turned inward, centering her attention on the psychological problem. If we could only understand who we truly are we might win an inner freedom beyond the opposites that block both nature and society.

Thus, the Indians became introspective psychologists, perhaps the world's greatest. One evidence of India's preoccupation with psychology is found in the elaborateness of her psychological vocabulary. Coomaraswamy used to say that for every psychological term in English there are four in Greek and forty in Sanskrit. What India actually developed of continuing worth in psychology is a moot question, but it is remarkable to contemplate how certain insights considered very contemporary today were discovered and explored in detail by Indians over two thousand years ago: that our consciousness is not all on the surface but includes layers of subconsciousness (compare Freud, the whole psychoanalytic movement, and age regression under hypnosis); that the human being is a psycho-physical whole with interaction between its two aspects far more subtle than most people suppose (compare the mind-body connections that have come to light in hypnosis and psychosomatic medicine); that with respect to the mind we must distinguish between *manas* and *buddhi*, i.e., between rational, critical, analytical thought and what Radhakrishnan calls integral thought (compare the distinctiveness of the hypothecating faculty as described, for example, by Descartes, by Hamilton, and by Poincaré); that what we see is not a simple mirroring of the external world but in part a function or projection of the perceiving organism (compare the doctrine of *maya*—defined not as illusion but as psychological construct—with most contemporary theories of perception); that most life is dislocated or out of joint (*duhkha*) and that the cause of this is *tanha,* the will for private existence or individual fulfillment (compare the Buddha's Four Noble Truths with contemporary psychotherapy generally).

There is one point that Indians have seen far more clearly than we have: that the subconscious, besides being pathological, can also be healthy. When it is, it works for us beyond the powers of the conscious mind, balancing to a degree the damage it can do if it is pathologic. The West has tended to forget that doctors deal with sick patients; as a doctor, Freud dealt mainly with sick subconscious minds and he gave us a brilliant typology of the ways in which the pathological subconscious can create trouble. But what is equally true, that the subconscious can work in our behalf when it is healthy, perhaps only the frontier scientist and the really creative artist in the West understand.

Indian psychology can also teach us that there is no general criterion of objectivity or reality; that is, every criterion of reality derives from the purposes for which the epistemology was developed. In the West, since our epistemology is derived basically from science, it is, therefore, a correlate of the objectives of science, which come down, centrally, to the idea of control. If we happen to think that science is adequate for human life, that it will save us, then the epistemology that science sponsors is equally adequate. I happen to think that science cannot save us; it can benefit us, but it does not deliver fulfillment by itself. Hence, there is room for an alternative epistemology derived from different purposes. Gordon Allport of Harvard has noted that Indian psychology is alive to four goals of life: pleasure, worldly success, duty, and liberation. Allport goes on to say that Western psychology has a lot on the first goal—pleasure for pleasure's sake. The psychology of worldly success we also know pretty well; we are able to motivate people toward worldly achievement. But when it comes to duty, the West has only a nickel's worth in its concept of the super-ego. And with regard to liberation, virtually nothing in Western psychology speaks profoundly to that goal.

How well the patterns of civilization of India, China, and the West have succeeded, history testifies. Qualitatively, it is impossible to rank the three civilizations; there is just too much material and, anyway, one's biases are certain to enter. Quantitatively, there is a measure: The Chinese Empire lasted under a succession of dynasties for over two thousand years, making the empires of Alexander, Caesar, and Napoleon seem ephemeral by comparison. It constituted a social order which, if the number of years it lasted is multiplied by the number of people it encompassed, emerges as the greatest social institution that man has created.

Each of the three great civilizations has achieved notable results with one of man's basic problems, but each also has been brought to the brink of ruin by not attending sufficiently to the other two problems. The obvious conclusion is that an adequate world civilization must strike all three notes as a chord. History shows that whenever two civilizations have lived in proximity and rubbed shoulders, something always rubs off on each other.

Today the three great civilizations are rubbing shoulders to a degree unprecedented in history, and they will continue to do so if we can desist from blowing ourselves up. Although we cannot move bits and pieces mechanically from one civilization into another and thereby produce a world civilization, because civilizations are organic rather than machine-like, things will continue to rub off from each onto the other. The task is to keep ourselves open to what is best in our own and other civilizations. In the centuries ahead the best possible mix may then come about.

2
Who Is Man?

The concern of this chapter is with the *identity* of man, not merely with the descriptions of his attributes that preoccupy most contemporary social scientists. "Who is man?" not "What is man?" The question of man's identity must be resolved before an adequate response to the issues of this or any other age can be made; for man's view of the world and his behavior in it are predicated on how he identifies himself, how he thinks of himself.

Reinhold Niebuhr's survey of classical and Biblical views of man compares the way man has thought of himself in the past to the way he thinks of himself in the present. Niebuhr concludes that contemporary man's view of himself, a mixture of remnants of classical and Biblical conceptions with peculiarly modern conceptions, has led to confusion and contradiction. Abraham Heschel, on the other hand, suggests that man's conception of himself is only too clear, that his recognition of his own "dangerous greatness" has inspired in him a shameful and potentially catastrophic presumptuousness. He has forgotten his identity as "a witness to God": religion has failed "to keep alive the image of God in the face of man."

Man as creation in the image of God is a conception which, in the Judeo-Christian tradition, implies that "doing" as well as "being" is an attribute of human identity. The image of "man the doer" is deeply rooted in Western culture, whether religious or nonreligious. Although a spokesman for a nonreligious ideology, Milan Machovec implicitly testifies for the image of "man the doer" in his argument that "The only question is man and human society . . . and the struggle to make their living conditions more human." The question of what is more, or less, human is, of course, the question, what is man? Machovec's essay may be read as a nonreligious reply, one that poses a challenge for contemporary religion.

The remaining essays in this chapter contain other replies, either explicit or implicit. A currently popular American view of man, criticized here by Bernard Suran, is conveyed in the image of the playboy, "who . . . can live life to the hilt." The playboy conceives of human identity as self-reflexive—discernible in an individual man apart from all others, and best expressed through self-concern and spontaneity. Essentially, then, the playboy seeks fulfillment in dedication to subjective values. However, Victor Frankl, whose ideas are reviewed by Robert Leslie, asserts that fulfillment for man is to be found only in commitment to objective values. Frankl identifies man as a seeker for meaning in life. Man will find meaning only if he assumes responsibility for the circumstances of life and trusts in absolute values.

One of the circumstances of human life is that man lives in the world with others. Maurice Merleau-Ponty affirms that human identity is inextricably involved in the phenomenon of common experience: ". . . we live with other people; we are the image which they have of us." Pope Paul VI takes the next logical step: having in common an identity, a world, and the human experience, man must achieve cooperation with man if he is to attain fulfillment. "Unless he relates himself to others he can neither live nor develop his potential."

Reinhold Niebuhr

Man as a Problem to Himself

The Classical View of Man

Though man has always been a problem to himself, modern man has aggravated that problem by his too simple and premature solutions. Modern man, whether idealist or naturalist, whether rationalist or romantic, is characterized by his simple certainties about himself. He has aggravated the problem of understanding himself because these certainties are either in contradiction with each other or in contradiction with the obvious facts of history, more particularly of contemporary history; and either they have been controverted by that history or they are held in defiance of its known facts. It is not unfair to affirm that modern culture, that is, our culture since the Renaissance, is to be credited with the greatest advances in the understanding of nature and with the greatest confusion in the understanding of man. Perhaps this credit and debit are logically related to each other.

Fully to appreciate the modern conflicts in regard to human nature, it is necessary to place the characteristically modern doctrines of man in their historic relation to the traditional views of human nature which have informed western culture. All modern views of human nature are adaptations, transformations and varying compounds of primarily two distinctive views of man: (*a*) The view of classical antiquity, that is of the Græco-Roman world, and (*b*) the Biblical view. It is important to remember that while these two views are distinct and partly incompati-

This excerpt is reprinted with the permission of Charles Scribner's Sons from Volume I, pp. 4–25, of *The Nature and Destiny of Man* by Reinhold Niebuhr. Copyright 1941, 1943 Charles Scribner's Sons.

Reinhold Niebuhr is a leading Protestant theologian, one of the founders of *Christianity and Crisis,* and a retired professor at Union Theological Seminary.

ble, they were actually merged in the thought of medieval Catholicism. (The perfect expression of this union is to be found in the Thomistic synthesis of Augustinian and Aristotelian thought.) The history of modern culture really begins with the destruction of this synthesis, foreshadowed in nominalism, and completed in the Renaissance and Reformation. In the dissolution of the synthesis, the Renaissance distilled the classical elements out of the synthesis and the Reformation sought to free the Biblical from the classical elements. Liberal Protestantism is an effort (on the whole an abortive one) to reunite the two elements. There is, in fact, little that is common between them. What was common in the two views was almost completely lost after modern thought had reinterpreted and transmuted the classical view of man in the direction of a greater naturalism. Modern culture has thus been a battleground of two opposing views of human nature. This conflict could not be resolved. It ended in the more or less complete triumph of the modernized classical view of man, a triumph which in this latter day is imperilled not by any external foe but by confusion within its own household. To validate this analysis of the matter requires at least a brief preliminary analysis of the classical and the Christian views of human nature.

The classical view of man, comprised primarily of Platonic, Aristotelian and Stoic conceptions of human nature, contains, of course, varying emphases but it may be regarded as one in its common conviction that man is to be understood primarily from the standpoint of the uniqueness of his rational faculties. What is unique in man is his νοῦς. Νοῦς may be translated as "spirit" but the primary emphasis lies upon the capacity for thought and reason. In Aristotle the *nous* is the vehicle of purely intellectual activity and is a universal and immortal principle which enters man from without. . . .

In Plato the *nous* or *logistikon* is not as sharply distinguished from the soul as in Aristotle. It is, rather, the highest element in the soul, the other two being the spirited element (θυμοειδές) and the appetitive element (ἐπιθυμητικόν). In both Plato and Aristotle "mind" is sharply distinguished from the body. It is the unifying and ordering principle, the organ of *logos*, which brings harmony into the life of the soul, as *logos* is the creative and forming principle of the world. Greek metaphysical presuppositions are naturally determinative for the doctrine of man; and since Parmenides Greek philosophy had assumed an identity between being and reason on the one hand and on the other had presupposed that reason works upon some formless or unformed stuff which is never completely tractable. . . .

Plato and Aristotle thus share a common rationalism; and also a common dualism which is explicit in the case of Plato and implicit and covert in the case of Aristotle. The effect of this rationalism and dualism has been determinative for the classical doctrine of man and for all modern doctrines which are borrowed from it. The consequences are: (a) The rationalism practically identifies rational man (who is essential man) with the divine; for reason is, as the creative principle, identical with God. Individuality is no significant concept, for it rests only upon the particularity of the body. In the thought of Aristotle only the active *nous,* precisely the mind which is not involved in the soul, is immortal; and for Plato the immutability of ideas is regarded as a proof of the immortality of the spirit. (b) The dualism has the consequence for the doctrine of man of identifying the body with evil and of assuming the essential goodness of mind or spirit. This body-mind dualism and the value judgments passed upon both body and mind stand in sharpest contrast to the Biblical view of man and achieve a fateful influence in all subsequent theories of human nature. The Bible knows nothing of a good mind and an evil body.

     . . . The Stoic reason is more immanent in both the world process and in the soul and body of man than in Platonism; yet man is essentially reason. Even the dualism is not completely lacking. For while Stoicism is not always certain whether the reason which governs man must persuade him to emulate nature as he finds it outside of his reason or whether it, being a special spark of the divine reason, must set him against the impulses of nature, it arrives on the whole at convictions which do not qualify the classical concepts essentially. . . .

     Obviously, the Platonic, Aristotelian and Stoic conceptions which define the "classical" view of man do not exhaust Greek speculations about human nature. Modern vitalism and romanticism have their antecedents in the earlier Dionysian religion, in Heraclitus' conception of ultimate reality as Flux and Fire and more particularly in the development of the Dionysian theme in Greek tragedy. Subsequent mysticism is anticipated in Orphism and Pythagoreanism. Even more significant for developments in contemporary culture, Democritus and Epicurus interpreted man, in accordance with their naturalism and materialism, not as standing outside of nature by the quality of his unique reason, but as wholly a part of nature. This Greek materialism was no less rationalistic than Platonism or Aristotelianism but it reduced the immanental reason in the world to mechanical necessity and sought to understand man in terms of this mechanism. It was by combining Stoic with Democritan and Epicurean naturalism that modern culture arrived at concepts which were to express some of its most characteristic interpretations of man, as primarily a child of nature.

     It must be observed that while the classical view of human virtue is optimistic when compared with the Christian view (for it finds no defect in the centre of human personality) and while it has perfect confidence in the virtue of the rational man, it does not share the confidence of the moderns in the ability of all men to be either virtuous or happy. Thus an air of melancholy hangs over Greek life which stands in sharpest contrast to the all-pervasive optimism of the now dying bourgeois culture, despite the assumption of the latter that it had merely restored the classical world view and the Greek view of man. "There is nothing, methinks, more piteous than a man, of all things that creep and breathe upon the earth," declares Zeus in the *Iliad*, and that note runs as a consistent strain through Greek thought from Homer to the Hellenistic age. Primarily it was the brevity of life and the mortality of man which tempted the Greeks to melancholy. They were not dissuaded from this mood either by Plato's assurance of immortality nor yet by Epicurus' counsel that death need not be feared, since there was nothing on the other side of the grave. . . .

Neither Greek nor Roman classicists had any conception of a meaning in human history. History was a series of cycles, a realm of endless recurrences. Aristotle maintained that the arts and sciences were lost and found again not once but an infinite number of times. Zeno envisaged the end of the world as a huge conflagration which would destroy the world's body. This pessimism about both man and his history is the natural consequence of the mind-body dualism which characterizes Greek thought far beyond the limits of Platonism. It culminated invariably in the conviction that the body is a tomb, a conviction which makes neo-Platonism the logical consummation of Greek thought.

The pessimism of Greek tragedy is somewhat different from that of the philosophers and most nearly approaches the Christian interpretation of life. But, unlike Christian thought, it has no answer for the problem it presents. In Æschylus and Sophocles the capricious jealousy of Zeus against mortal men of Homeric legend had been transmuted into the justified jealousy of the ultimate principle of law and order against the lawlessness of human passions. But, unlike the philosophers, the dramatists see human passions as something more than mere impulses of the body. The principle of order and measure, represented by Zeus, is constantly defied by vitalities in human life which are creative as well as destructive. The tragedy of human history consists precisely in the fact that human life cannot be creative without being destructive, that biological urges are enhanced and sublimated by dæmonic spirit and that this spirit cannot express itself without committing the sin of pride. The heroes of Greek tragedy are always being counselled to remember their mortality and to escape νέμεσις by observing a proper restraint. But the ὕβρις which offends Zeus is an inevitable concomitant of their creative action in history. The tragic heroes are heroes precisely because they disregard this prudent advice of moderation. In that sense Greek tragedy is an explication of Nietzsche's observation: "Every doer loves his deed much more than it deserves to be loved; and the best deeds are born out of such an excess of love that they could not be worthy of it, even though their worth be very great." (*Kritik und Zukunft der Kultur*, Ch. IV, Par. 13). The various vitalities of human history are moreover not only in conflict with Zeus but in conflict with each other. There is no simple resolution of the conflict between the state and the family, usually symbolized as a conflict between man and woman, the latter representing the community of blood and family in contrast to the political community (as in *Iphigenia at Aulis* and in *Antigone*). The conflict in Greek tragedy is, in short, between Gods, between Zeus and Dionysus; and not between God and the devil, nor between spirit and matter. The spirit of man expresses itself in his vital energies as well as in the harmonizing force of mind; and while the latter, as the rational principle of order, is the more ultimate (here the dramatists remain typically Greek) there can be creativity in human affairs only at the price of disturbing this order.

Thus life is at war with itself, according to Greek tragedy. There is no solution, or only a tragic solution for the conflict between the vitalities of life and the principle of measure. Zeus remains God. But one is prompted to both admiration and pity toward those who defy him. It is significant that this profound problem, posed by Greek tragedy, was never sensed by the moderns who revived classicism and ostensibly built their view of man upon Greek thought. They may have understood or misunderstood Plato and Aristotle: but the message of Æschylus and Sophocles was neither understood nor misunderstood. It was simply neglected, except as the minor romantic note in modern culture appreciated and partly misunderstood it.

The Christian View of Man

. . . As the classical view is determined by Greek metaphysical presuppositions, so the Christian view is determined by the ultimate presuppositions of Christian faith. The Christian faith in God as Creator of the world transcends the canons and antinomies of rationality, particularly the antinomy between mind and matter, between consciousness and extension. God is not merely mind who forms a previously given formless stuff. God is both vitality and form and the source of all existence. He creates the world. This world is not God; but it is not evil because it is not God. Being God's creation, it is good.

The consequence of this conception of the world upon the view of human nature in Christian thought is to allow an appreciation of the unity of body and soul in human personality which idealists and naturalists have sought in vain. Furthermore it prevents the idealistic error of regarding the mind as essentially good or essentially eternal and the body as essentially evil. But it also obviates the romantic error of seeking for the good in man-as-nature and for evil in man-as-spirit or as reason. Man is, according to the Biblical view, a created and finite existence in both body and spirit. . . .

The Biblical view of the unity of man as body and soul has often seemed to be no more than the consequence of primitive Hebraic psychology. In Hebrew thought the soul of man resides in his blood and the concept of an immortal mind in a mortal body remains unknown to the end. It is true that certain distinctions are gradually made. At first both *ruach* and *nephesh* mean little more than "breath"; but they are gradually distinguished and *ruach* becomes roughly synonymous with spirit or *nous* and *nephesh* with soul or *psyche*. But, unlike Greek thought, this distinction does not lead to dualistic consequences. The monism of the Biblical view is something other than the failure to differentiate *physis, psyche* and *nous*, which characterized Greek thought before Anaxagoras; nor is it merely the consequence of an undeveloped psychology. It is ultimately derived from the Biblical view of God as the Creator and of the Biblical faith in the goodness of creation.

The second important characteristic of the Christian view of man is that he is understood primarily from the standpoint of God, rather than the uniqueness of his rational faculties or his relation to nature. He is made in the "image of God." It has been the mistake of many Christian rationalists to assume that this term is no more than a religious-pictorial expression of what philosophy intends when it defines man as a rational animal. We have previously alluded to the fact that the human spirit has the special capacity of standing continually outside itself in terms of indefinite regression. Consciousness is a capacity for surveying the world and determining action from a governing centre. Self-consciousness represents a further degree of transcendence in which the self makes itself its own object in such a way that the ego is finally always subject and not object. The rational capacity of surveying the world, of forming general concepts and analysing the order of the world is thus but one aspect of what Christianity knows as "spirit." The self knows the world, insofar as it knows the world, because it stands outside both itself and the world, which means that it cannot understand itself except as it is understood from beyond itself and the world.

This essential homelessness of the human spirit is the ground of all religion; for the self which stands outside itself and the world cannot find the meaning of life in itself or the world. It cannot identify meaning with causality in nature; for its freedom is obviously something different from the necessary causal links of nature. Nor can it identify the principle of meaning with rationality, since it transcends its own rational processes, so that it may, for instance, ask the question whether there is a relevance between its rational forms and the recurrences and forms of nature. It is this capacity of freedom which finally prompts great cultures and philosophies to transcend rationalism and to seek for the meaning of life in an unconditioned ground of existence. But from the standpoint of human thought this unconditioned ground of existence, this God, can be defined only negatively. This is why mystic religions in general, and particularly the neo-Platonic tradition in western culture, have one interesting similarity with Christianity and one important difference in their estimate of human nature. In common with Christianity they measure the depth of the human spirit in terms of its capacity of self-transcendence. . . . Mysticism and Christianity agree in understanding man from the standpoint of the eternal. But since mysticism leads to an undifferentiated ultimate reality, it is bound to regard particularity, including individuality, as essentially evil. All mystic religions therefore have the characteristic of accentuating individuality inasfar as individuality is inherent in the capacity for self-consciousness emphasized in mysticism and is something more than mere bodily particularity; but all mystic philosophies ultimately lose the very individuality which they first emphasize, because they sink finite particularity in a distinctionless divine ground of existence.

God as will and personality, in concepts of Christian faith, is thus the only possible ground of real individuality, though not the only possible presupposition of self-consciousness. But faith in God as will and personality depends upon faith in His power to reveal Himself. The Christian faith in God's self-disclosure, culminating in the revelation of Christ, is thus the basis of the Christian concept of personality and individuality. In terms of this faith man can understand himself as a unity of will which finds its end in the will of God . . . To understand himself truly means to begin with a faith that he is understood from beyond himself, that he is known and loved of God and must find himself in terms of obedience to the divine will. This relation of the divine to the human will makes it possible for man to relate himself to God without pretending to be God; and to accept his distance from God as a created thing, without believing that the evil of his nature is caused by this finiteness. Man's finite existence in the body and in history can be essentially affirmed, as naturalism wants to affirm it. Yet the uniqueness of man's spirit can be appreciated even more than idealism appreciates it, though always preserving a proper distinction between the human and divine. Also the unity of spirit and body can be emphasized in terms of its relation to a Creator and Redeemer who created both mind and body. These are the ultra-rational foundations and presuppositions of Christian wisdom about man.

This conception of man's stature is not, however, the complete

Christian picture of man. The high estimate of the human stature implied in the concept of "image of God" stands in paradoxical juxtaposition to the low estimate of human virtue in Christian thought. Man is a sinner. His sin is defined as rebellion against God. The Christian estimate of human evil is so serious precisely because it places evil at the very centre of human personality: in the will. This evil cannot be regarded complacently as the inevitable consequence of his finiteness or the fruit of his involvement in the contingencies and necessities of nature. Sin is occasioned precisely by the fact that man refuses to admit his "creatureliness" and to acknowledge himself as merely a member of a total unity of life. He pretends to be more than he is. Nor can he, as in both rationalistic and mystic dualism, dismiss his sins as residing in that part of himself which is not his true self, that is, that part of himself which is involved in physical necessity. In Christianity it is not the eternal man who judges the finite man; but the eternal and holy God who judges sinful man. Nor is redemption in the power of the eternal man who gradually sloughs off finite man. Man is not divided against himself so that the essential man can be extricated from the nonessential. Man contradicts himself within the terms of his true essence. His essence is free self-determination. His sin is the wrong use of his freedom and its consequent destruction.

Man is an individual but he is not self-sufficing. The law of his nature is love, a harmonious relation of life to life in obedience to the divine centre and source of his life. This law is violated when man seeks to make himself the centre and source of his own life. His sin is therefore spiritual and not carnal, though the infection of rebellion spreads from the spirit to the body and disturbs its harmonies also. Man, in other words, is a sinner not because he is one limited individual within a whole but rather because he is betrayed by his very ability to survey the whole to imagine himself the whole. . . .

The essence of man is his freedom. Sin is committed in that freedom. Sin can therefore not be attributed to a defect in his essence. It can only be understood as a self-contradiction, made possible by the fact of his freedom but not following necessarily from it. . . .

The Christian view of human nature is involved in the paradox of claiming a higher stature for man and of taking a more serious view of his evil than other anthropology.

The Modern View of Man

The modern view of man is informed partly by classical, partly by Christian and partly by distinctively modern motifs. The classical element tends to slip from the typical classical, Platonic and Aristotelian rationalism to a more naturalistic rationalism. That is, the Epicurean and

Democritan naturalism, which remained subordinate in the classical period of Greek thought, becomes dominant in the modern period. This modern naturalism is in accord with the Christian concept of man as "creature" but it contradicts the Christian concept of man as "image of God" which the early Renaissance emphasized in opposition to the Christian idea of man as creature and man as sinner. The curious compound of classical, Christian and distinctively modern conceptions of human nature, involved in modern anthropology, leads to various difficulties and confusions which may be briefly summarized as follows: (a) The inner contradictions in modern conceptions of human nature between idealistic and naturalistic rationalists; and between rationalists, whether idealistic or naturalistic, and vitalists and romanticists. (b) The certainties about human nature in modern culture which modern history dissipates, particularly the certainty about individuality. (c) The certainties about human nature, particularly the certainty about the goodness of man, which stands in contradiction to the known facts of history.

(a) One of the unresolved antinomies in modern culture is the contradictory emphasis of the idealists and the naturalists. The former are inclined to protest against Christian humility and to disavow both the doctrine of man's creatureliness and the doctrine of his sinfulness. This was the mood of the Renaissance, the thought of which upon this issue was determined by Platonic, neo-Platonic and Stoic conceptions. . . .

In terms of social history, this course of modern thought from an idealistic protest against the Christian conception of man as creature and as sinner to the naturalistic protest against man as the "image of God" may be interpreted as the anti-climactic history of bourgeois man. The middle-class world begins with a tremendous sense of the power of the human mind over nature. But having destroyed the ultimate reference by which medieval man transcended nature spiritually, even while acknowledging his dependence practically, the bourgeois and technical world ends by seeking asylum in nature's dependabilities and serenities. Modern capitalism really expresses both attitudes at the same time. The spirit of capitalism is the spirit of an irreverent exploitation of nature, conceived as a treasure-house of riches which will guarantee everything which might be regarded as the good life. Man masters nature. But the social organization of capitalism at least theoretically rests upon the naive faith that nature masters man and that her pre-established harmonies will prevent the human enterprise from involving itself in any serious catastrophes (physiocratic theory).

The conflict between idealistic and naturalistic rationalists is complicated by a further factor: the protest of the romantic naturalists who interpret man as primarily vitality and who find neither a pale reason nor a mechanical nature an adequate key to man's true essence. This romantic interpretation of man is in some respects the newest element in modern anthropological doctrines, for it is only partially foreshadowed in either classical or Christian thought. Its bitterest fruit is modern fascism. Marxist thought complicates the pattern further; for it interprets man, as he is, primarily in vitalistic terms and rightly discounts the pretenses of rational man who does not know his own finiteness; but the man who is to be will build a society which will be governed by the most remarkable rational coherence of life with life and interest with interest. The conflict between rationalists and romanticists has become one of the most fateful issues of our day, with every possible religious and political implication. Modern man, in short, cannot determine whether he shall understand himself primarily from the standpoint of the uniqueness of his reason or from the standpoint of his affinity with nature; and if the latter whether it is the harmless order and peace of nature or her vitality which is the real clue to his essence. Thus some of the certainties of modern man are in contradiction with one another; and it may be questioned whether the conflict can be resolved within terms of the presuppositions with which modern culture approaches the issues.

(b) The concept of individuality in modern culture belongs to that class of certainties of modern man about himself which his own history has gradually dissipated. The tremendous emphasis upon individuality in the Renaissance is clearly a flower which could have grown only on Christian soil, since the classical culture, to which the Renaissance is an ostensible return, lacked this emphasis completely. The Italian Renaissance avails itself primarily of neo-Platonic conceptions to establish its idea of the dignity and the liberty of man. But these conceptions would not yield the idea of individuality if Christian ideas were not presupposed. The Renaissance is particularly intent upon establishing the freedom of the human spirit in opposition to Christian doctrines of divine predestination.

Pico della Mirandola extols the freedom of the human spirit in concepts drawn from Platonism. God said to man, according to Pico: "You alone are not bound by any restraint, unless you will adopt it by the will which we have given you. I have placed you in the centre of the world that you may the easier look about and behold all that is in it. I created you a creature, neither earthly nor heavenly, neither mortal nor immortal, so that you could be your own creator and choose whatever form you may assume for yourself."

While classical thought was used by the Renaissance to challenge the Christian idea of man's dependence and weakness, by emphasis upon his uniqueness and the freedom of his spirit, classicism was obviously not able to suggest the concept of individuality which the Renaissance held so dear. This idea must be regarded as partly a Christian inheritance and partly a consequence of the emergence of the bourgeois individual from the historical and traditional cohesions, patterns and restraints of the medieval world. This bourgeois individual felt himself the master of his own destiny and was impatient with both the religious and the political solidarities which characterized both classical and medieval life. Speaking in social terms one may say that he lost this individuality immediately after establishing it by his destruction of the medieval solidarities. He found himself the artificer of a technical civilization which creates more enslaving mechanical interdependencies and collectivities than anything known in an agrarian world. Furthermore no one can be as completely and discreetly an individual as bourgeois individualism supposes, whether in the organic forms of an agrarian or the more mechanical forms of a technical society.

Considered in terms of philosophical issues bourgeois individualism had an insecure foundation, not only in the Platonism and neo-Platonism in which it first expressed itself but also in the later naturalism of the eighteenth and nineteenth centuries. Idealism begins by emphasizing man's freedom and transcendence over nature but ends by losing the individual in the universalities of rational concepts and ultimately in the undifferentiated totality of the divine. Naturalism begins by emphasizing natural variety and particularity. . . . As the idealists lose individuality in the absolute mind, so the naturalists lose it in "streams of consciousness" when dealing with the matter psychologically, and in "laws of motion" when thinking sociologically. Thus the individualism of the Renaissance and of the eighteenth century is dissipated culturally, just as bourgeois liberatarian idealism disintegrates politically and succumbs to fascist and Marxist collectivism. A genuine individuality can be maintained only in terms of religious presuppositions which can do justice to the immediate involvement of human individuality in all the organic forms and social tensions of history, while yet appreciating its ultimate transcendence over every social and historical situation in the highest reaches of its self-transcendence. The paradox of man as creature and man as child of God is a necessary presupposition of a concept of individuality, strong enough to maintain itself against the pressures of history, and realistic enough to do justice to the organic cohesions of social life.

(c) The final certainty of modern anthropology is its optimistic treatment of the problem of evil. Modern man has an essentially easy conscience; and nothing gives the diverse and discordant notes of modern culture so much harmony as the unanimous opposition of modern man to

Christian conceptions of the sinfulness of man. The idea that man is sinful at the very centre of his personality, that is in his will, is universally rejected. It is this rejection which has seemed to make the Christian gospel simply irrelevant to modern man, a fact which is of much more importance than any conviction about its incredibility. If modern culture conceives man primarily in terms of the uniqueness of his rational faculties, it finds the root of his evil in his involvement in natural impulses and natural necessities from which it hopes to free him by the increase of his rational faculties. This essentially Platonic idea manages to creep into many social and educational theories, even when they are ostensibly naturalistic and not Platonic. On the other hand, if it conceives of man primarily in terms of his relation to nature, it hopes to rescue man from the dæmonic chaos in which his spiritual life is involved by beguiling him back to the harmony, serenity and harmless unity of nature. In this the mechanistic rationalist and the Rousseauistic romantic of the French enlightenment seem to stand on common ground. Either the rational man or the natural man is conceived as essentially good, and it is only necessary for man either to rise from the chaos of nature to the harmony of mind or to descend from the chaos of spirit to the harmony of nature in order to be saved. The very fact that the strategies of redemption are in such complete contradiction to each other proves how far modern man is from solving the problem of evil in his life.

A further consequence of modern optimism is a philosophy of history expressed in the idea of progress. . . . The idea of progress is possible only upon the ground of a Christian culture. It is a secularized version of Biblical apocalypse and of the Hebraic sense of a meaningful history, in contrast to the meaningless history of the Greeks. But since the Christian doctrine of the sinfulness of man is eliminated, a complicating factor in the Christian philosophy is removed and the way is open for simple interpretations of history, which relate historical process as closely as possible to biological process and which fail to do justice either to the unique freedom of man or to the dæmonic misuse which he may make of that freedom.

There are of course pessimistic reactions to this optimism about both the individual and the total human enterprise. In the mechanistic naturalism of Hobbes and the romantic naturalism of Nietzsche a thoroughgoing pessimism is elaborated. One of the modern fruits of Nietzschean thought is Freudian pessimism. Here we have no good opinion about human nature; yet there is no uneasy conscience in this pessimism. The egotism and the will-to-power which Christian thought regards as the quintessence of sin and which, in the view of bourgeois liberalism, is a defect to be sloughed off by a new education or a new social organization, is regarded as normal and normative. Hobbes accepts and Nietzsche glorifies the will-to-power. In Hobbes a political vantage point against individual egotism is gained but none against the collective egotism, embodied in the state. In Nietzsche's transvaluation of values, the characteristics of human life which make for conflict between life and life are raised to the eminence of the ideal. The fateful consequences in contemporary political life of Hobbes's cynicism and Nietzsche's nihilism are everywhere apparent. . . .

Abraham Heschel

Sacred Image of Man

. . . There are many questions about man which have often been raised. What is his nature? Why is he mortal? None of these issues is central biblical thinking.

The problem that challenged the biblical mind was not the obscurity of man's nature but the paradox of his existence. The starting point was not a question about man but the distinction of man; not the state of ignorance about the nature of man but rather a state of amazement at what we know about man, namely: Why is man so significant in spite of his insignificance? Not the question, Why is man mortal? But the question, Why is he so distinguished?

The problem that challenged the biblical mind was not man in and by himself. Man is never seen in isolation but always in relation to God who is the Creator, the King, and the Judge of all beings. The problem of man revolved around God's relation to man.

Reprinted from *The Insecurity of Freedom*, by Abraham Heschel, by permission of Farrar, Straus & Giroux, Inc. Copyright © 1959, 1960, 1963, 1964, 1966 by Abraham Joshua Heschel.

Abraham Heschel is Professor of Ethics and Mysticism at the Jewish Theological Seminary of America.

Lord, what is man, that thou takest knowledge of him?
Or the son of man, that thou makest account of him?
Man is like unto a breath;
His days are as a shadow that passeth away.

Psalm 144:3–4

When I behold Thy heavens,
The work of Thy fingers,
The moon and the stars
Which Thou hast established—
What is man
That Thou shouldst be mindful of him?
And the son of man
That Thou shouldst think of him?
And make him
But a little lower than the Divine,
And crown him with glory and honour,
And make him rule over the works of Thy hands?
Thou hast put all things under his feet:
Sheep and oxen, all of them,
Yea, and the beasts of the field;
The fowl of the air, and the fish of the sea,
That pass through the paths of the seas.

Psalm 8:2–9

The insignificance of man compared with the grandeur of God underscores the paradox of God's concern for him. Neither Job nor the psalmist offers an answer to the overwhelming enigma which thus remains the central mystery of human existence. Yet the acceptance of the fact of divine concern established the biblical approach to the existence of man. It is from the perspective of that concern that the quest for an understanding of man begins.

Today the realization of the dangerous greatness of man, of his immense power and ability to destroy all life on earth, may help us to intuit man's relevance in the divine scheme. If this great world of ours is not a trifle in the eyes of God, if the creator is at all concerned with His creation, then man—who has the power to devise both culture and crime, but who is also able to be a proxy for divine justice—is important enough to be the object of divine concern.

Nowhere in Plato's Socratic dialogues do we find a direct solution to the problem, "What is man?" There is only an indirect answer, "Man is declared to be that creature who is constantly in search of himself—a creature who in every moment of his existence must examine and scrutinize the conditions of his existence."* He is a being in search of meaning.

* Ernst Cassirer, *An Essay on Man* (New Haven: Yale University Press, 1944) p. 5.

The Greek approach must be contrasted with the biblical contention that "unless the lord builds the house, those who build it labor in
vain" (Psalm 127:1). The pursuit of meaning is meaningless unless there
is a meaning in pursuit of man.

To the biblical mind man is not only a creature who is constantly
in search of himself but also *a creature God is constantly in search of.*
Man is a creature in search of meaning because there is a meaning in
search of him, because there is God's beseeching question, "Where art
thou?"

Man is prone to ignore this chief question of his existence as long
as he finds tranquillity in the ivory tower of petty presumption. But when
the tower begins to totter, when death wipes away that which seemed
mighty and independent, when in evil days the delights of success are
replaced by the nightmare of futility, he becomes conscious of the peril of
evasiveness, of the emptiness of small objectives. His apprehension lest in
winning small prizes he would gamble his life away, throws his soul open
to questions he was trying to avoid.

But what is man's answer to God's plea, "Where art thou?"

> Thus says the Lord:
> Why, when I came was there no man?
> When I called, was there no one to answer?
>
> Isaiah 50:2a.

Man not only refuses to answer; he often sets out to defy and to
blaspheme. Abundant are the references in the Bible not only to man's
callousness, but also to his rebellion. The human species is capable of
producing saints and prophets, but also scoundrels and "enemies of
God." The idea of the divine image of man offers no explanation to the
dreadful mystery of the evil urge in the heart of man.

> The heart is deceitful above all things and desperately corrupt;
> Who can understand it?
>
> Jeremiah 17:9

Because of the tension of "the good urge" and "the evil urge,"
human life is full of perils. The only safeguard against constant danger is
constant vigilance, constant guidance. If human nature were all we had,
there would be little reason to be hopeful. Yet we also have the word of
God, the commandment, the *mitzvah.* The central biblical fact is Sinai.
Sinai was superimposed on the failure of Adam. It initiated an order of
living, an answer to the question, How should man, a being created in the
image of God, think, act and feel?

Ugly and somber is the world to the prophetic eye; drunk with lust for power, infatuated with war, driven by envy and greed. Man has become a nightmare. History is being made by "guilty men, whose own might is their god" (Habakkuk 1:11).

The meaning of having been created in the image of God is veiled in an enigma. But perhaps we may surmise the intention was for man to be *a witness for God,* a symbol of God. Looking at man one should sense the presence of God. But instead of living as a witness, he became an imposter; instead of being a symbol, he became an idol. In his bristling presumption he developed *a false sense of sovereignty* which fills the world with terror.

We are proud of the achievements of our technological civilization. But our pride may result in our supreme humiliation. The pride in maintaining, "My own power and the might of my own hand have won this wealth for me" (Deuteronomy 8:17), will cause us to say "Our god" to the work of our hands (Hosea 14:4).

One shudders to think that involved in our civilization is a demonic force trying to exact vengeance on God.

After having eaten the forbidden fruit, the Lord sent forth man from Paradise, to till the ground from which he was taken. But man, who is more subtle than any other creature that God has made, what did he do? He undertook to build a Paradise by his own might, and he is driving God from his Paradise. For generations all looked well. But now we have discovered that our Paradise is built upon the top of a volcano. The Paradise we have built may turn out to be a vast camp for the extermination of man.

This is a time to cry out. One is ashamed to be human. One is embarrassed to be called religious in the face of religion's failure to keep alive the image of God in the face of man. We see the writing on the wall but are too illiterate to understand what it says. There are no easy solutions to grave problems. All we can honestly preach is a *theology of dismay.* We have imprisoned God in our temples and slogans, and now the word of God is dying on our lips. We have ceased to be symbols. There is darkness in the East, and smugness in the West. What of the night? What of the night?

What is history? Wars, victories, and wars. So many dead. So many tears. So little regret. So many fears. And who could sit in judgment over the victims of cruelty whose horror turns to hatred? Is it easy to keep the horror of wickedness from turning into a hatred of the wicked? The world is drenched in blood, and the guilt is endless. Should not all hope be abandoned?

What saved the prophets from despair was their messianic vision and the idea of man's capacity for repentance. That vision and that idea affected their understanding of history.

History is not a blind alley, and guilt is not an abyss. There is always a way that leads out of guilt: repentance or turning to God. The prophet is a person who living in dismay has the power to transcend his dismay. Over all the darkness of experience hovers the vision of a different day.

Egypt and Assyria are locked in deadly wars. Hating each other, they are both the enemies of Israel. Abominable are their idolatries, and frightful are their crimes. How does Isaiah, the son of a people which cherishes the privilege of being called by the Lord "My people," "the work of My hands" (Isaiah 60:21), feel about Egypt and Assyria?

> In that day there shall be a highway from Egypt to Assyria; the Assyrian will come to Egypt, and the Egyptian into Assyria, and the Egyptians will worship with the Assyrians.
> In that day Israel shall be a third with Egypt and Assyria, a blessing in the midst of the earth which the Lord of hosts has blessed, saying.
> Blessed be My People Egypt,
> and Assyria, the work of My hands,
> and Israel, My inheritance
>
> Isaiah 19:23–25

Our God is also the God of our enemies, without their knowing Him and despite their defying Him. The enmity between the nations will turn to friendship. They will live together when they will worship together. All three will be equally God's chosen people.

Milan Machovec

Marxism and Christianity—A Marxist View

The West Looks at the Communist World

. . . The history of Marxism over the past one hundred years has been the history of the question, "Who is man?" You may find this difficult to understand because of all you have heard about those of us who live in the so-called Communist countries, of us who try to live as communists. Here are some of the things the West says about us:

1. The world of communism is a world of uniformity, of monolithic order, the opposite of the free Western world with its diversity, its sense of individuality, and its opposing viewpoints. It is a world of dogmatism, of medieval Catholicism without God.

2. The world of communism can be very successful. It is famous for its scientific and technological achievements, achievements which have been bought too dearly at the cost of untold sacrifices and neglect of man's personal needs. It is therefore an inhuman world whose every success makes it a great danger to Western civilization.

3. The world of communism is governed by a bureaucracy. It is a world from which all true joys, all creative initiative, and all individual human personality are absent, a world which either does not recognize the values of Western culture or has lost them, these values of democratic community life, mutual respect, and Christian love.

4. The world of communism is one in which people's lives are

Reprinted from *Student World.* No. 1, 1963, by World Student Christian Federation, Geneva. © 1963. By permission of the publisher. The selection is an extract from an address. Translated from the German by Elizabeth Adler.

Milan Machovec is Professor of Philosophy, Charles University, Prague, Czechoslovakia.

governed by the values of gross materialism. It is a world which is enslaved by the cult of cheap entertainment and interests, one which is alienated from the higher values of honour and the ideals of piety and faith, and which persecutes and suppresses them by every possible means.

A Marxist Looks at Communism

It would be easy and cheap to say that all these are lies and slander, and I do not think you would accept this from me. Indeed, it is not so easy. The truth is that these impressions have not been manufactured out of whole cloth, but are caricatures of certain realities. I say quite frankly that there is in communism something of a monolithic unity, or better, an unceasing struggle for it. There is strict discipline and authority; there is something of human self-denial, and an anti-religious attitude does exist. All this is basic to the system.

Uniformity and totalitarianism do indeed sound negative, but the picture changes when we see behind these a great effort to achieve maximum human dignity, and both liberty and cultural enrichment for all men without distinction of nationality, race, sex, or religion, an effort to lift up the masses of the people who until recently vegetated in spiritual and material poverty.

With regard to the cult of personality, dogmatism, and intolerance, our movement has sinned, particularly in the Stalinist era, but we must not forget that, even then, there was always in the background a firm belief in truth and an effort to live according to scientific principles and to enable all men to build their lives on a foundation of truth. And what about the untold sacrifices and the devotion which have produced such great achievements? The West despises collectivism, but it forgets that it presupposes great enthusiasm, readiness for sacrifice, boldness, and self-denial.

And now we come to the essential. It is not to be found in the first place in certain methods or attitudes, because as time passes these can be corrected, but in the fundamental aim of the communist movement, the reason for which it has come into the world and has taught individuals to live and to work. We should not be surprised that the communist appears to the average Western intellectual with whom he has a superficial encounter as a fanatic and a dogmatist, as a man who follows the cult of authority. Do you really believe that people with such characteristics would have been able to bring communism into being and to develop it? Do you think that this movement would have been able to survive and to overcome the mistakes of the Stalinist methods, if there had not been something beyond this, something much more profound than this alleged uniformity, this cult of authority, this fanaticism? If this were not the case, the communist movement would long since have broken down.

The Roots of Communism

If you want to evaluate the communist movement correctly, you must realize that it came into being out of the humanist pathos of the nineteenth century, not only the intellectual pathos, not only the cult of aesthetic ideals and justice, but also the practical effort to prepare for millions of suffering men a life of human dignity. You can understand the roots of the communist movement if you consider the condition of European workers and farmers in the nineteenth century. These roots are also to be found in the work of such humanists as Kant, Hegel, and Feuerbach. Marx and Engels were their direct descendants; they started from their humanism and anthropocentrism. The essential contribution of Marx and Engels was that they showed how to put humanism into practice. Marx has shown it is possible to give help to millions of people. Feuerbach, in his *Religion of Man,* states that the heart of theology is anthropology. He has an important place in the genesis of the problem of so-called secularization. But he also has an important place in the history of the development of Marxism. The anthropocentrism of Feuerbach was prepared for by Lessing, Herder, Kant, and Hegel. For these thinkers, God and man were abstract ideas. They talked about the theoretical relationship between "the idea God" and "the idea man." This is taken up in the subsequent development of Protestant theories by Barth, Bonhoeffer, and others. Their thought seems strange to the Marxist, and yet not so strange: strange because in his scheme of things God does not exist; not so strange in the sense of its continuity and relationship with the past. We are convinced that Marxism is a logical continuation from the point where Feuerbach left off, and to a certain extent from Bonhoeffer. For a Marxist the only question is man and human society: not only man as such, or "the idea man," but the real destiny of living human beings and the struggle to make their living conditions more human.

Some of you may perhaps object that this is an obsolete and also a questionable theory of the nineteenth century, which has been put into practice only in backward countries and even there with great difficulty and with many inconsistencies. Don't be misled by outward appearances: even if Marxism is perhaps not the whole truth, today it is an historical fact and the primary reality in the lives of several hundred million people. You should not overlook this, even if (as some of you, in contrast to us, may believe) it should be true that there are better roads than this to progress. Certainly you cannot prove that these hundreds of millions of people do not think, feel, carry on the struggle to live, and seek for the deeper things of human life. Do you really believe that these people can live without asking questions about the meaning of life, about morality, about the voice of conscience, about the role of the individual and his relation to society and the time in which they live?

The Communist Answer to the Question "Who Is Man?"

The disciples of Karl Marx do not believe that it is possible for anyone in any era to arrive at a definitive and exhaustive answer to the question "Who is man?" through rational reflection. The Indian, Greek, and Roman philosophers, Kant and Hegel and many others have already struggled with this question. The answer of Marxism would be along these lines. Basic to the search for an answer to "Who is man?" is first of all the full development of man's faculties. We cannot find an answer by speculation, but by striving for a deeper and fuller expression of the life of millions of human beings. We Marxists understand the struggle for communism as a struggle, on the one hand, for the maximum development of man's scientific and productive powers and abilities and, on the other, for maximum recognition of each individual and the harmonious development of his emotional and intellectual faculties. The meaning and aim of all our efforts is man, not only his well-being but especially the complete fulfilment of his life. We see the solution of this historical riddle, of this question, "Who is man?" in the establishment of a communist society, which means in the full deployment of all human powers and faculties. We regard the world of the past, the world of class differences, of want, war, and oppression, of material and spiritual backwardness, as a world without human dignity, as a period of transition from the animal world to a truly human world, to an era of the full flowering of man.

We know that it appears to some that Marxists neglect man as a moral and spiritual being, that we are concerned only with the material life and its organization, with economics, production, and politics, and nothing else. But this is only the outward appearance. Do not be blinded by it. To put into practice the communist way of life requires in the first period a certain emphasis upon the material side which is a prerequisite of full human life. This results in an emphasis upon economic, political, and organizational questions. In this period, however, the fundamental objective must be maintained. Of course, there are those among us who become caught up in the means and lose sight of the ends. We must not write off those who are as yet unable to rise to the higher values of life, but try to help them. Furthermore, as the years go by and our movement develops, these people will be unmasked and be revealed as strangers to the spirit of the communist society and the principles for which we are striving. They will be forced to learn to live a fuller and less superficial life. If they do not manage to do this, they will be left behind as history moves ahead carrying other people with it.

You know very well that, mainly in the era of the Stalinist cult of personality, this blindness had tragic consequences. However, let us not forget that we have been taught a hard lesson: there were many mistakes, much evil, and also great humiliation, but also severe self-criticism and attempts to bring about change and to rediscover the true meaning of the communist movement. The international communist movement is now entering, of course not without difficulties and many set-backs, an era of great renaissance, with a return to its original aims and the fundamental meaning of communism. It now has at its disposal all the scientific and technological conditions which did not exist in the twenties and thirties. Therefore we have the possibility today of concentrating on educational, cultural, and ethical matters.

A Marxist Looks at Christianity

What is the relationship between the ideals of Marxists and those of Christians? Why are we not Christians? First of all, because we believe that the fundamental theses of Christianity are wrong. History and the results of research in all scientific fields, even if these are still somewhat confused, point today to the fact that faith belongs in the realm of human illusions which developed at a certain stage in the emancipation of man and which have now been replaced by a true understanding of nature, society, and man. We are of the opinion that Christianity originated under certain historical conditions and has spread mainly because of the longing of millions of people for a better life, for redemption at a time when they saw no means to achieve it. Therefore a mysterious "redeemer" was necessary. We know that the teachings of the Bible, in spite of the ideal of love for one's neighbour, have been used to suppress man, to encourage his passive acceptance of want and exploitation. The communist appreciates the ideals of forgiveness, mercy, and patience, but only in a situation where all men have equal rights, and not where these ideals mean a call to patience, humility, obedience, and acceptance of the privileges of the authorities, a call to a passive waiting for one's reward in eternity. The noble ideals of the Bible and the boldness and inner sincerity of Christians throughout history are for us typical human expressions. We have no reason to see in them "the word of God" or God coming to men. We seek the essence of morality in something unreligious—the responsibility of men for one another. We regard faith in a higher justice as a deformation of human morality which leads to passivity, to reliance upon higher powers, and to the conviction that the organization of human life and relationships is insignificant and that the preparation for eternal life is more important. This is what Marx meant when he spoke about "opium for the people."

Our criticisms of Christianity are of an historical nature. Christianity did not bring its best ideals to fulfilment. In the course of its expansion nothing fundamental has changed in human life. For two thousand years the Bible has called for change, and for love to one another, but is there today in our world more love, more peace, more forgiveness than two thousand years ago? From the Marxist point of view, experience with Christianity in history has shown that we must build on different principles if we want to remain faithful to our ideals, which we do. Honestly, for me the most relevant words in the whole Bible are those in Revelation: "Behold, I make all things new" (Rev. 21:5), for this is what matters in today's world.

We certainly do not want to take from man his faith, leaving him with an empty heart in the misery of his daily life. First of all we want to give him faith, a faith in humanity, in his future, in the extension of the values of knowledge and morality. We regard religiosity as an expression of unbelief in man and unbelief in this world. We do not want atheism at all costs, atheism of any kind. There are many forms of atheism which we reject indignantly, especially those which are combined with cynicism, individualism, and gross materialism. We reject atheism which ignores the highest human values.

We are able to respect Christians though we fight against Christianity. We know how to distinguish between the two. We appreciate in the efforts of Christians everything that is "human," everything that is in accordance with what we consider good. Many things which you regard as biblical or even of God, we regard as very human. . . . We do not believe that there is a basic difference between the essence of religion and the so-called biblical message, but we can appreciate that some people who hold this belief do so in rejection of bourgeois self-satisfaction. We follow therefore with great interest all efforts, like those of Dietrich Bonhoeffer, to formulate a so-called nonreligious interpretation of Christianity. For this reason we also appreciate the program of your conference, which deals with the complex problem of secularization. Secularization—well and good! However, the definition of this term is important. It would be unfortunate if you were to deal with it in terms of seeking a strategy by which you can better oppose us. However, it is entirely different if you have a sincere desire for mutual understanding.

I wish that in the future we might struggle to surpass one another in readiness for sacrifice, in creative work, in the development of the classical values of true humanity. We are convinced that the greatest task in human history, the building up of a communist society, contributes to the development of the highest human qualities. We cannot wait until non-communists trust us. Therefore may a sincere, fair struggle decide who wins the prize, in other words, who first gets close to man and stands up for him.

Bernard Suran

The Playboy in Profile

The age of the playboy is upon us. Hipsters, jaguars, the Jet Set and Joe College are still holding their own, but contemporary playtime is more and more being dominated by the playboys. They are but of yesterday, and already they fill our recreational arenas. Young men see visions and old men dream dreams, and the dapper-looking rabbit with the long ears and formal tux is rapidly becoming part and parcel of the manifest content of much of today's dreaming-visioning. Playboys may soon be "out" but at the moment they are definitely "in."

The Advent of the Playboy

In a few short years the playboy has become an institution on the American socio-sexual scene. His rise to prominence is an amazing success story, in the very best tradition of amazing success stories. A scant dozen years ago, an undistinguished University of Illinois graduate, one Hugh Hefner, borrowed enough money to purchase a set of photographic plates of the famous Marilyn Monroe calendar nude. Miss Monroe's *au naturel derrière* was the main feature of the first publication

Reprinted from *Listening: Current Studies in Dialog*, Winter 1966, Vol. 1 (Aquinas Institute, Dubuque, Iowa). © 1966. By permission of the publishers.

Bernard Suran is on the editorial staff of *Listening*.

of *Playboy* magazine, and Monroe in the raw titillated the fantasies of the American buying public, young male variety, to the tune of 55,000 copies. No mean titillating!

The following issue featured the first official "Playmate of the Month," a title which has since become famous for the buxom femininity of its many stalwart holders. *Playboy's* playmate quickly established herself as the "symbol *par excellence* of recreational sex," in subsequent issues broadening out to a multi-color, three-page fold-out which occasioned Mort Sahl's quip about girls that fold in two places and wear staples in their navels.

From these modest beginnings—modest in the sense of inauspicious—*Playboy* gradually grew in wisdom and in stature. It was not just another girlie book catering to peep show tastes. Hefner made a determined effort to combine sex with culture, and he succeded in creating a very sophisticated men's magazine. . . .

Of course, all has not been sweetness and light in the *Playboy* camp. As the magazine achieved greater and greater success, a few perceptive individuals began to sense that it was more than a mere vehicle for displaying the undraped female form. *Playboy* seemed to possess an attitude toward life, a viewpoint concerning sex and morals that distinguished it from the run-of-the-mill voyeuristic offerings that fill many newsstands. Voices of dissent began to raise the hue and cry. A Protestant theologian named Harvey Cox wrote a particularly intelligent article in which, among other things, he accused *Playboy* of being basically antisexual. Not just antisexual, but *basically* antisexual.

Well, Hefner was considerably miffed. What's more, he was downright indignant about the antisexual charge. After all, in his own right he had become quite an authority on sexual matters, and he didn't feel that he was antisexual in the least; much less *basically* antisexual. The evident confusion concerning the *Playboy* viewpoint prompted him to take a rather firm stand: "I would rather be damned for what I believe than what I don't believe." At any rate, the *Playboy* editor began spelling out his convictions in a series of editorials entitled "The Playboy Philosophy." To date, twenty-odd installments have appeared, unwieldy and repetitive, but written with much gusto. Hefner has enunciated his ideas with eloquence, aplomb, wit, occasional insight, considerable electicism, and a cunning use of truth and half truth. While no one will ever accuse him of originality, he does write entertainingly, lampooning Puritanism and censorship, rallying the American dream of freedom-creativity-individuality, often blending his natural aptitude for persuasion with impeccable logic. Always the emphasis is on permissive sexuality. He admits that his "thought" is still developing, progressing in print from a few germinal convictions to a rather elaborate statement of the sexual nature of man, or rather the nature of sexual man. He senses that he is the apostle of the movement known as the American Sexual Revolution, and he wears the mantle of leadership well, a fact that gives him a confidence that is ostensibly unbounded. . . .

The Playboy and His Philosophy

The verbiage of "The Playboy Philosophy" can easily give one the mistaken impression that the playboy in the abstract is a very complicated phenomenon. The playboy in the flesh may very well be a complex personality (especially if he falls short of the ideal), but the ideal described by Hefner is not the type of fellow that would keep you awake nights puzzling over the intricacies of his personality. He's a simple, uncomplicated person, rather easily described. This is always the case with any description of the Abstract Man, and Hefner should not be faulted if the Abstract Playboy doesn't have very much zip. I'm sure the flesh and blood varieties are much more interesting!

The playboy has a number of distinct characteristics that recommend him for a not too difficult analysis. In the first place, he has a ready-made definition of himself. Secondly, he possesses a frame of reference, a few solid principles that constitute his *Weltanschauung*. Thirdly, he has a few concrete goals or aims in life (sex and money, in that order) that also aid him in exploring and establishing his identity and individuality. Fourthly, he is armed with a rather well-developed psychology of sex that also serves as a very handy rationalization for his genital exploits if, by some quirk of fate, his well-trained superego should ever step out of line. Lastly, the playboy has a few pet peeves (Puritanism, overbearing religious bodies, censorship, anti-sex laws). I am led to believe that the peeves exist for the express purpose of occupying his mind when he can't get his fat little hands on one of those seductive little playmates.

In an age when personal identity and self-definition are major problems on the road to personal growth and fulfillment, the playboy has no difficulty identifying and defining himself. "Moses" Hefner has a canned answer to the problem of the "who," and he is far from reticent in descending the heights of Sinai to aid his fledgling apprentices in their respective quests for selfhood. Before defining the playboy, however, an erroneous notion must be dispelled. The world of the playboy is rife with prejudice and he is often misunderstood. He is definitely not the *La Dolce Vita* type, the functionless pleasure-seeker whose joyless diligence along the road of self-destruction is "more deserving of sympathy than righteous condemnation." Is our playboy simply a wastrel, a ne'er do well, a fashionable bum?

Far from it: He can be a sharp-minded young business executive, a worker in the arts, a university professor, an architect or engineer. He can be many things provided he possesses a *certain point of view*. He must see life not as a vale of tears, but as a happy time; he must take joy in his work, without regarding it as the end and all of living; he must be an alert man, an aware man, a man of taste, a man sensitive to pleasure, a man who—without acquiring the stigma of the voluptuary or dilettante—can live life to the hilt. This is the sort of man we mean when we use the word *playboy* ("The Playboy Philosophy," I).

. . . The playboy's philosophy hinges, in great measure, upon his concept of the individual. He is for the individual, and so am I. In this sense, I am for the playboy. His is a needed emphasis in a society where conformity, security, and the deification of the Common Man have reaped a heavy toll, although I suspect that I am more respectful of the common man than he is. Our bone of contention concerns the way in which a man best serves and nurtures his individuality.

Take the matter of aspiration. *Playboy* has another ready principle: "A man's reach should exceed his grasp, else what's a heaven for." The playboy has adopted this principle as part of his orientation toward life. I would like to respect him for his courage because a life lived according to high ideals requires great courage. And yet, I find that our respective interpretations of Browning's dictum are at considerable odds. His interpretation is primarily in terms of ambition, acquisition, and concession to his sex drive. "*Playboy's* entire editorial personality and point of view stress the positive aspects of affluence and serve as motivation to try to achieve these things" (XIX). The playboy seems to think of himself as a kind of trophy case in which are displayed souvenirs of his various conquests and all the insignia of affluence. He is motivated to be affluent so that he can learn to appreciate. But his mode of appreciation seems to be limited to the material possessions he has acquired: fine clothes, food and wines, sports cars, etc.

In fact, the playboy has no true ideals. He has goals, and these are concrete enough. Too concrete! He seems to think that all the important values are material. He respects the man with spiritual values but has none of his own. Now I would not indict a man simply because he's too materialistic. He has his viewpoint and I have mine; the gulf is too inseparable to be easily bridged here. In the context of his materialistic individualism, however, he will have difficulty convincing me that he is an idealist. I don't see how he is really "living life to the hilt" or how his "reach is exceeding his grasp." . . .

We have arrived, I think, at a root problem in any individualistic ethics. Hefner does not raise the issue, so I will raise it for him. The basic question, as I see it, is the question of self-love.

Perhaps the most constantly recurring theme in the history of human thought and endeavor is the theme of love. Throughout the ages, the heart and mind of man have consumed themselves with an unequalled zeal in a never-ending attempt to unravel the arcane mysteries of this elusive enigma. Love has been scrutinized from almost every conceivable vantage point. The lofty and ecstatic probings of the mystics, the sensitive and ethereal analyses of the poets, the penetrating indagations of the philosophers, the earthy descriptions of the novelists—all these are heraldic witnesses to the fact that love is man's most compelling theme; indeed, that it is the sacrament of eternity. . . .

True self-love cannot possibly be a restrictive phenomenon. A person can love himself truly only when he loves other selves. Only when drawn into communion with other persons is his own personality confirmed in being and his own love equal to the excellence to which it aspires. Self-love is the very antithesis of egoism, the very egoism which the playboy so heartily embraces. The playboy ego is an emasculated one because *Playboy* is the id from which that ego has emerged. Again, I do not doubt *Playboy's* sincerity; I simply question the competence of the psychology which it expounds. The playboy may pay occasional lip service to openness and self-fulfillment, but the entire thrust of his approach to life is selfish, self-centered, and self-gratifying. He is a beautifully embalmed corpse in the mausoleum of forfeited selfhood, so fascinated by the glitter of his coffin that he doesn't even know he is dead as a person.

The Playboy's Sexual Credo: "Virgins Need Not Apply"

For ourselves, any doctrine is evil if it teaches that . . . self-denial is preferable to self-gratification.

Chastity is just another word for repression (XIII, VIII).

A man's reach should exceed his grasp, else what's a heaven for.

Nowhere is the playboy's idealism and moral fibre more evident than in the benign attitude he takes toward his own genitals. Lesser men can only marvel at his perpetual tumescence! For the playboy, "virgin" is a term that is properly predicated of forests, and "pregnant" is a word that is meaningful only in terms of his own idea content. He shudders at any other connotation! Sailing his ship of sex gingerly between the Scylla of intelligent continence and the Charybdis of involvement and commitment, life is a merry-go-round of beds, sofas, rugs and any other convenience that will comfortably accommodate a prone position for two.

It would be unfair, however, to write off the playboy as an unimaginative roué. He has thought long and hard over his own sexuality and has tested his thinking in the arena of experience. What's more, he strives diligently to maintain a balanced position regarding his sexual indulgence. It would be an injustice to treat his sterling conclusions too blithely. We must give his conclusions due consideration for we are touching upon the very core of the playboy. Sex is his cause.

His cause is not an uninteresting one. Emphasizing the pleasures of sex rather than the responsibilities of sex, he sees no good reason for limiting sex to marriage and procreation. The main thrust of his argument is directed toward the adult premarital period. He contends that organized religion in America has failed to supply any sexual morality for the unmarried adult other than "Don't!" By denying sexual outlets to the single man and woman, religion has fostered unhappiness, disappointment, and various sexual perversions and anomalies. Violating the principle of church-state separation, the moral codes of organized religion have infiltrated civil law itself, a fact which is evidenced by various censorship and anti-sex laws which exist as statues in many states. Consequently, society has tended to look askance at extramarital sex play. The playboy seeks to root puritanism out of contemporary sexual codes and establish a more "reasonable" and permissive sexual morality. He advocates nonmarital but responsible, adult, nonprocreative, boy-girl sexual relations as a natural, normal phenomenon which should be accepted without censure in a free, rational, humane society.

Officially, the playboy does not endorse promiscuity or any sexual relationship that is entirely self-oriented. He is opposed to wholly selfish sex, but sees no reason for opposing merely impersonal sex, "unless it is irresponsible, exploitive, coercive, or in some way hurts one of the individuals involved" (XIX). Permissiveness, with or without affection, but, with or without affection, permissiveness! Ideally, the playboy sees himself as a kind of altruistic self-loving bee, coloring many flowers, yet storing up a little honey of his own. Sex is an end in itself, but it is also a means, even when taken in sporadic doses and with different partners, for developing one's self-esteem, exploring one's individuality, and establishing one's identity.

Having limned the sexual credo of the playboy, I think we can justly conclude that he poses for the man in the modern world a problem of no mean proportions: should a man or a woman, provided that the proper precautions are taken, enter into a nonmarital sexual relationship (i.e., sexual intercourse) or a series of nonmarital sexual relationships with a member or members of the opposite sex? The problem is, of course, not unique in the history of human thought and endeavor. Today, however, the problem is more pressing than at any other moment in man's history. I need not point out that much of its urgency is due to the fact that *Playboy* is posing the question to 16,000,000 monthly.

In the context of his philosophy of aspiration, we have seen how the playboy argues for an almost unqualified concession to man's sexual drive. To the casual observer, the argument may well appear almost convincing. I detect, however, a number of logical inconsistencies, and I think it would be helpful to point out a few of these logical improbities to some of the romantics in the audience.

The playboy's sexual exploits are motivated by a supposedly Freudian rule-of-thumb: repressed sex is bad sex; expressed sex is good sex. "We reject as totally without foundation the premise of the prude, who would have us believe that man would be healthier and happier if he were somehow able to curb these natural desires" (VIII). *I reject as totally without foundation the premise of the playboy, who would have us believe that any man who attempts to control his sexual appetite is a prude.*

According to Freud, impotence, fears, anomalies, and perversions in the adult sexual sphere can be traced primarily to parental and societal taboos against infantile masturbation. In the Freudian schema, infantile genital exploration is a natural activity in the growth of the child, but when parents discourage such activity, primary repression occurs, the child unconsciously developing a generalized fear of sexual matters. Thus, these instinctual processes are permanently forbidden entry into consciousness. The child becomes, as it were, prejudiced against sex. In the adult life of the psychologically impotent or perverted, secondary repression is operative: the person represses anything that would remind him of the excluded contents of primary expression. The sexual drive is still operative, but the person's generalized fear of sex causes the drive to be expressed aberrantly. The Freudian insights into the dynamics of repression and unconscious activity have been accepted, in the main, as basically sound psychology and constitute a part of any introductory course in psychology. The playboy gets an "A" in introductory psychology.

He fares considerably worse in the upper-division courses! Using this fundamental Freudian insight as his springboard, the playboy has made an inductive leap: "Don't suppress what is unsuppressible!" You'll notice the progression from repression to suppression.

Now the playboy is well aware of the fact that "imprecise language leads to imprecise thought." I might add that, for the playboy, imprecise thought leads to some interesting consequences in the behavioral field. Be that as it may, we are concerned with the confusion of the concepts of repression and suppression. The playboy would perhaps like to use them interchangeably. Such merry confusion would make for a neater rationalization of permissive sexuality. Nevertheless, repression and suppression refer to distinct psychological functions.

Repression is a largely unconscious process by which specific psychological activities or contents are excluded from conscious awareness. Our Freudian baby is a good example of the untoward effects that repressive processes can have on behavior. As an unconscious process, repression can wreak havoc with other psychological functions.

Suppression, on the other hand, is conscious control of behavior, a form of self-control in which impulses, instinctual drives, or disapproved desires are kept from direct expression. Let us illustrate the point. Suppose that our playboy friend zeroes in, as playboys are wont to do, on a playboy party, and meets there the beautiful and curvaceous wife of a professional football tackle. Being a model playboy, he may well be stimulated to spirit her off to some dark corner and explain to her the intricacies of his philosophy. Among other things! And yet, wily fellow that he is, he knows full well that, were he to do so, said football tackle husband might easily be tempted to rearrange the structure of his nose for him. The playboy consciously says to himself: "If I make a pass at this dame, her husband is going to mutilate me." Therefore, he suppresses his sexual drive. Very healthy behavior for a playboy!

The point is that suppression, or self-control or self-denial, unlike repression, is not a guilt-based unconscious inhibition and does *not* result "in perversion of the sexual impulse, general intellectual dulling, sado-masochistic inclinations, unreasonable (paranoid) suspiciousness, and a long list of neurotic and psychotic defense reactions with unmistakeable sexual content or overtone" (VI).

The playboy, for all his enthusiasm, has fallen error to a logical fallacy. His argument against traditional sexual morality is as precarious as his four-termed syllogism. At the risk of embarrassing the playboy, permit me to state his argument in precise syllogistic terms.

> Guilt-based *repression* of the sexual appetite leads to perversion of the sexual impulse, general intellectual dulling, etc.
> But, traditional morality has fostered *suppression* of the sexual appetite.
> Therefore, traditional morality has fostered perversion of the sexual impulse, general intellectual dulling, etc.

Sorry, playboy. *Non sequitur!*

Suppression is a factor that must be operative in all men all their lives. It is the very fundament of their continued existence. Civilization is based on the not so tenuous condition that man can and will control his various appetites. The playboy knows this; he is opposed to anarchy, license, and promiscuity. Obviously he must advocate some measure of self-denial and self-control. I am led to believe that his inability to master his own passions causes him to opt for permissive sexuality, with or without affection. He who does not want to dominate himself will not be able to do so.

Which brings us to another point of confusion in the playboy philosophy. The playboy frames his advocacy of sexual indulgence in the context of personal responsibility, establishment of identity, and exploration of personality. He is opposed to promiscuity. After all, promiscuity sounds like a good thing to be opposed to. Here's the rub. If one is going to use his sexual appetite as a vehicle for exploring his personality, it would logically follow that the promiscuous person is the person who has explored his personality to the fullest. He has pulled out all the stops and has completely negated "self-denial" and "self-control," those dirty words which the playboy so thoroughly despises.

My point is this: the playboy never defines for us what he means by responsibility and promiscuity. He's for responsibility, and for motherhood and democracy and stuff like that. He's opposed to promiscuity, and to crime and communism and stuff like that. But he never tells us what he means by promiscuity. I suppose that we would all agree that a man who engaged in sexual relations with a different woman every night would be promiscuous. If he did so only every other night he would probably be just a playboy. But what about all those areas of his personality that are left unexplored on his off nights! Of course there's always the possibility that the playboy may graduate and establish his identity to the fullest.

Responsibility is a word that gives a certain aura of respectability to the playboy's mellifluous language of the stud farm. But there is no responsibility in his system. He is a man who is hellbent on self-gratification, and the only responsibility he knows is to be the slave of the promptings of his over-sexed personality.

In the same way, the playboy is for freedom. "We believe that man was born free, that freedom should be his most cherished birthright, and that it should be society's function to see that his freedom is preserved" (VI). Nonsense! Man is not *born* free. No one who has ever seen a newborn babe would be tempted to wax eloquent about his freedom. Freedom is not given; it is an achievement. But freedom for the playboy simply means doing what he pleases!

I too am for freedom, and I think that I have some appreciation of what freedom means. Freedom and responsibility are opposite sides of the same coin. A man is free to the extent that he is able to initiate, guide and control his own behavior. The playboy's understanding of freedom is physical freedom, freedom from external restrictions and limitations. This is a *conditio sine qua non,* but it is not the essence of personal freedom. Society could guarantee a man all the safeguards of physical freedom, and that man might never be free. That man might never achieve the fullness of personal freedom. That man is the playboy, for he is a slave to himself.

Personal freedom is the achievement of a lifetime of dedication, and it is localized within the depths of the person himself. In the growth of the human person, his various powers and appetites pass through several stages of organization. At the beginning of his life, the infant lives a purely sensitive existence, determined solely by pleasure. He is limited by an organic determination. As the child grows and his powers become further organized, he is still determined by the external injunctions of his parents, teachers and guardians. He becomes socially determined. If a man is to become free, there must be a final organization of his powers imposed by the person himself. His will, his faculty for freedom, must concur with the demands of his rational nature, of which it is the loving faculty. This is a self-determination culminating in human freedom. If a person has not succeeded in integrating his powers and energies in the direction of self-determination and self-transcendence, then he remains a human dwarf. His life is restricted by pleasure (the organically determined infant) or by others (the socially dependent child). Such, I think, is the playboy.

I cannot help but conclude that the playboy has really missed the point of Freud's theory of sexuality. He has simply failed to master his infantile sexuality and is continually playing out the tragic drama of an unresolved Oedipal complex. As Dr. Karl Menninger, no mean Freudian in his own right, has averred:

> It is an axiom in psychiatry that a plurality of direct sexual outlets indicates the opposite of what it is popularly assumed to indicate. Dividing the sexual interest into several objectives diminishes the total sexual gratification, and men whose need for love drives them to the risks and efforts necessary to maintain sexual relationships with more than one woman show a deficiency rather than an excess in their masculine capacities (*Love Against Hate* [1942], pp. 72–73).

Dr. Menninger states very well the essence of my own complaint against the playboy. Playboyism, despite all its sundry attempts to project a masculine image, is really a travesty of man, an exaggeration of a caricature. Man is more than an appendage to the area below his mid-section. The playboy has created a dream world in which man's sexuality is reduced to the pleasurable excitation of his nervous system.

The Contribution of Playboy

I would like very much to extricate the issues that the playboy raises from the fantasy world in which he lives. The playboy as critic raises genuine problems that are in urgent need of discussion in the public forum. What is the relationship of the person to society? What is the role of pleasure in the life of the person? How does affluence contribute to human autonomy? How can we formulate a rational basis for evaluating premarital sex in a secular society? Where is the balance between selfishness and selflessness? What is the ultimate meaning of human sexuality?

The critical function of *Playboy* and its editor Hugh Hefner has brought these problems to the fore. They must be faced honestly and dispassionately by both playboy and non-playboy alike. I have no ready-made answers to the problems of man and his sexuality. The playboy may think that he has; he proposes facile solutions and pontificates freely. We should not mistake the courage of his convictions for their correctness.

Mutual openness and sincere dialog are the only hope for a satisfying solution to the problems which the playboy poses.

For myself, I recognize the fact that Hefner is driving home a fundamental truth concerning human nature. Human sexuality is always a crucial dimension in the human potential. It lies at the very core of the human person. It defines him and delimits him and proves to him that he is not a god.

But I believe that the gods must die so that man may live. I react strongly against the playboy because I think that he is molding both sex and self into idols. Man has fabricated many idols. He has deified the winds and the earth and has become a slave to superstition. He has deified honor and wealth and has become the servant of pride. He has deified his appetites and has become the lackey of his own passion. Will man serve his sexuality or will his sexuality serve him? Each man must choose for himself.

Robert Leslie

Frankl's New Concept of Man

There have been hints for some years of a growing dissatisfaction with the psychoanalytic view which sees man as caught in the trauma of the past, as bound by unresolved childhood experiences. The whole existentialist mood, in questioning the adequacy of the categories of psychoanalysis for interpreting man's needs in the current hour, has focused attention less on what has happened to one in the past than on what one can do with his life in the present. Among the existentialist voices that have insisted on seeing man as "becoming" rather than solely as "conditioned," Viktor Frankl's stands out prominently. Chosen to write the lead articles for two new contemporary journals in the field of existentialist psychology, Frankl is an acknowledged leader in what Gordon Allport calls "the most significant psychological movement of our day." In America Frankl is known especially for his writing about "the defiant power of the human spirit" as he saw it exhibited and as he lived it himself during two and a half years in four different concentration camps.

Frankl's distinctive emphasis is conveyed even in the term which he has coined to describe his work: logotherapy. The Greek word *logos* is translated neither as "word" (as in John's Gospel) nor as "speech" in the sense of logic, but rather as "spirit" and "meaning." The key word is "meaning." Frankl's view of man is that man seeks primarily neither pleasure (cf. Freud) nor power (cf. Adler) but *meaning*.

The obvious implication for therapy here is that any therapeutic approach which does not take into account man's search for meaning, his meaning-orientation in life, is not adequate to meet man's needs. Frankl designates a sense of meaninglessness as an "existential frustration"

Reprinted from *Motive* (March 1962) by permission.

Robert Leslie is Professor of Pastoral Psychology and Counseling at Pacific School of Religion, Berkeley, California.

leading to a "spiritual vacuum" which then becomes easy breeding ground for any one of many kinds of neuroses. He is convinced that the neurotic problems of our age are more concerned with a life orientation, a lack of sense of personal meaning in life, than with the more familiar defense mechanisms developed, according to the psychoanalytic approach, in the search for pleasure or for power. He finds patients today complaining less about specific symptoms and more about a feeling of inner emptiness, of absence of purpose, of lack of direction.

It is obvious that Frankl believes there *is* meaning in life. His major criticism of existentialism as a philosophy is that, whereas it rightfully stresses man's subjective experience in the midst of life, it tends to ignore the objective reality of values. Whereas Jean Paul Sartre, for example, stresses man's *freedom from* the circumstances of life, Frankl would add a *responsibility to* the world of objective value. All values are relative—not in the presence of the person making the value judgment but in the presence of the absolute value which is God. Imperfection points to perfection, finitude points to the infinite.

It is not enough to assert that there is objective meaning in the world, stemming out of absolute value (God). Man finds a meaning for his own personal life only as he acts in a responsible way, as he commits himself to the search for his personal niche in life, with a basic sense of trust in absolute Being. To find pesonal meaning in life calls for an action based on commitment rather than on any armchair, intellectual search. Thus to a 17-year-old girl who is confused about life because of her inability to find clear-cut answers, and whose spiritual vacuum is filled with somatic symptoms (heart disorder), Frankl asserts:

> Dedicate your self to the here and now, to the given situation and the present hour, and the meaning will dawn on you. . . . If you cannot grasp it intellectually, then you must believe in it emotionally. As long as I haven't found the supra-meaning and have only an inkling about it, I cannot wait until I am 80 years of age and only then dedicate myself to it, but must rely on my vague inkling and commit my heart in serving it. . . . Intellectual achievement is preceded by existential commitment. Trust in the wisdom of your heart, a wisdom which is deeper than the insight of your brain.

Frankl does more, however, than simply to assert that life has a meaning and that each person can find the specific meaning which life holds in store for him. This personal meaning can be found in one of three ways: through creative values, through experiential values, and through attitudinal values. Although most people find meaning through creative accomplishment, this pathway may be denied to some through illness, disability, age, or other circumstances. In this case, the second pathway is open, the realization of value through experiencing beauty or truth or sympathy and through encounter with other persons. Whenever this pathway is denied, values can still be realized through the attitudes that are adopted toward unavoidable circumstances. How one handles his inescapable fate, how one endures his unavoidable suffering, can create values and hence give meaning to life. Frankl describes how these three pathways were experienced by a young professional man who was paralyzed by an inoperable spinal tumor, and hence denied the opportunity to realize any further creative values.

> But even in this state the realm of experiential values remained open to him. He passed the time in stimulating conversations with other patients—entertaining them, also encouraging and consoling them. He devoted himself to reading good books, and especially to listening to good music on the radio. One day, however, he could no longer bear the pressure of the earphones, and his hands had become so paralyzed that he could no longer hold a book. Now his life took another turn; while before he had been compelled to withdraw from creative values to experiential values, he was forced now to make the further retreat to attitudinal values. How else shall we interpret his behavior—for he now set himself the role of advisor to his fellow sufferers, and in every way strove to be an exemplar to them. He bore his own suffering bravely (The Doctor and the Soul, Knopf, 1955, pp. 51–52).

Frankl does not hesitate to point out that there is always opportunity for realizing value, regardless of the conditions of life. It becomes clear that such an approach is a major departure from conventional psychoanalysis. Frankl would agree that repression is often at work in neurotic illness but he would say that what is repressed is the patient's unconscious spiritual needs rather than any kind of instinctual drives. In order to help him to realize his spiritual needs, to fill the spiritual vacuum in his life, Frankl sets about in a direct way to help the patient find his particular meaning in life, correcting, if need be, any erroneous outlook. His approach is implemented by two specific procedures: dereflection and paradoxical intention.

Dereflection is the process of deflecting the patient's attention away from his symptoms by refocusing them on his specific mission in life. Turning attention away from the symptoms, and from an obsessive preoccupation with them, is accomplished as a side effect of finding the personal meaning in life. Whereas most therapeutic procedures center attention on the symptoms, on uncovering their origin in the past or on revealing the extent to which they operate in a person's life in the present, logotherapy reorients the patient toward his life task with the consequence that the symptom becomes an unimportant detail. Symptoms, therefore, are dealt with as indications of failure to measure up to the responsibility of undertaking one's personal mission in life.

To assist in handling symptoms so that they do not occupy the center of attention, Frankl has developed the specific method called "paradoxical intention." This method aims at a change of attitude toward symptoms, at developing a sense of detachment from the symptoms by treating them humorously. The patient is encouraged to intend, paradoxically, that which he has hithertofore feared. Instead of fighting symptoms (as the obsessive-compulsive patient tends to do), or of fleeing from symptoms (as the phobic patient tends to do), the patient is encouraged consciously to exaggerate the symptoms. Recognizing that anticipation of anxiety increases anxiety (as in the fear of blushing), the patient is encouraged to wish exactly what he anticipates might happen (e.g., desire to blush) with the result that the wind is taken out of the sails of the anxiety. The patient who fears he will not be able to sleep, who fights sleeplessness is encouraged to try to stay awake, with the result that he becomes very sleepy. The patient who is compulsively neurotic about keeping things clean and orderly is encouraged to become as dirty and disorderly as he possibly can, thus making a joke of his obsessive traits.

The capacity for self-detachment from symptoms is a specifically human trait. It is a part of the human being's capacity for "psychonoetic antagonism," for exercising the defiant power of the human spirit. There is no symptom so severe, no situation so extreme, that the human person cannot take a stand against it. Even in psychosis the patient can stand over against his symptoms, can detach himself from them.

Frankl frequently combines paradoxical intention with drug therapy, using tranquilizers to quiet anxiety and energizers to mobilize the defiant power of the spirit. Indeed, his major critique of contemporary approaches in psychotherapy is that they do not take into account the full dimensions of human life: the somatic, the psychic and the spiritual. In order to make clear the spiritual dimension within the meaning-orientation dimension (but not necessarily a religious approach to life), Frankl uses the term "noetic"; thus the three dimensions of human life are the somatic, the psychic, and the noetic. Even though any one of these three dimensions may be responsible for a neurotic problem, all three need to be reckoned with in treatment. Frankl points out the fallacy of looking at human behavior as *nothing but* a psychic problem or as *purely* a somatic illness or as *solely* a question of meaning or values. In his own therapeutic practice he employs all three approaches. For example, in the case of a teacher with recurring depressions, Frankl prescribed a drug to deal with a somatic condition, employed psychotherapy to deal with her low self-esteem, and drew on logotherapy to help her to see her depressions as a challenge for her.

> *Here was a case where logotherapeutic treatment was necessary. It was the doctor's business to show the patient that her very affliction—these fated recurrent depressions—posed a challenge for her. Since men are free to take a rational position on psychic processes, she was free to take a positive attitude toward it. Her destiny should direct her to the conscious and responsible shaping of her life in spite of the inner difficulties that shadowed it—or, in other words, to the actualization of what we have called attitudinal values.*

Frankl goes on to say that "in time the patient learned to see her life as full of personal tasks in spite of her state of dejection." She eventually wrote to him: "I was not a human being until you made me one" (*The Doctor and the Soul*, p. 104).

It is apparent that Frankl reaches out in direct and genuine ways to his patients. Convinced that everyone can be helped, either by recovery from illness or by learning to live with unavoidable suffering, he dares to issue a challenge to live heroically. Making responsible commitment a cardinal feature of his own philosophy, he stands in the Christian tradition which asserts that life is to be found, not as it is anxiously saved, but as it is freely given.

Maurice Merleau-Ponty

Man, the Hero

There are several indications, at least in the world of letters, of a return to peace. Heroes are fading away, and protests, which are cautious today but tomorrow will be bold, are being raised against "heroic" morality. A man of letters who fought in the First World War and who has been silent since the beginning of the Second, writes to a friend, "I was already scandalized to hear Gide in his *Entretiens imaginaires* humming, to a melody by Offenbach: 'We need heroes even if there are none left in the world.' For my part I would much prefer a grain of wisdom, intelligence, and reason. Having myself been a hero in my youth either of necessity or unnecessarily, I distrust heroes just as Mme Cardinal distrusted women."

When he has to judge a novel or play with a heroic ending, a Catholic like Gabriel Marcel implies that there is heroism and heroism; he is perfectly willing that nature be surpassed, but only if this is done according to the rules and by following certain paths. "Artistic" writers claim a separate domain for literature, one which is safe from politics and history.

This kind of debate raises embarrassing questions. How can a hero praise heroism? And how can anyone do so who is not a hero? It would be better to know exactly what there is behind this grand word.

There has always been a cult of the hero. However, insofar as a civilization believes that beyond this world lies another eternal world where good wins out over evil, the great man does not stand by himself

Reprinted from Maurice Merleau-Ponty's *Sense and Non-Sense* (Northwestern University Press, Evanston, 1964), pp. 182–187, by permission of the publisher.

Maurice Merleau-Ponty was one of the most prolific and most revolutionary of the philosophers to emerge in France after World War II. His writings gave rise to the "second school" of phenomenology.

but is the agent of a Providence. The cult of the hero does not take on its tragic cast until the end of transcendent beliefs, or at all events until the emergence of the idea of a world in process. The turning point comes with Hegel. For him, "the individuals of world history" are those who, although born on a certain date, under certain laws, and into certain moral structures just like everyone else, are the first to understand that this system has no future; they forsake happiness and by their deeds and their example create a law and a moral system in which their time will later recognize its truth. At first they stand alone, since they stand against custom; they have a presentiment of the future although, of course, no knowledge of it: they sense it in their tastes, their passions, and their very being rather than see it clearly before them. Their heroism resides in their having worked out and won for others, with nothing certain to go on and in the loneliness of subjectivity, what will afterwards seem the only possible future, the very meaning of history: this is the unexpected junction of reason and unreason.

> They should be called heroes in that they have drawn their goals and their vocation not only from the calmly ordered course of events which the reigning system has consecrated but also from an underground source in the inner spirit whose content is hidden and which has not yet broken through the surface of actual existence but which strikes against the outer world as against a shell and cracks it because such a shell is unsuited to such a kernel. . . . They were people who thought, who knew what was needed, for whom the moment came to know the truth about their time and their world; one might say they were the new race which already existed within the old. . . . That is why the heroes of an era should be recognized as wise men.

If one ceases to believe not only in a benign governor of this world but also in a reasonable course of things, then there no longer is any external support for heroic action; it cannot gather strength from any divine law or even from a visible meaning in history. This heroism which lacks both rules and content is that of the Nietzschean "superman." If the Hegelian hero sacrificed his personal happiness and introduced chaos into his life, it was to save history from chaos; if he questioned the established order, it was to bring another order into the world. The Nietzschean superman is beyond everything that *has been or is to be done;* he is interested only in power itself, and since he refuses to devote it to any particular task, it can only assert itself *against* something or someone. Pure power can only consist in conquering other holders of power and the most powerful opponent of all, death. Hegel had already described this undertaking and this impasse, for all power overcome, just because it is overcome, ceases to have value as power: the death through which the hero has passed was not really death since it could not hold him; the other men whom he has reduced to slavery cannot bear adequate witness to his strength since he was able to conquer them. Therefore, unless he grows old and has himself made an honorary hero, he will always be looking for other risks to run and other men to subdue, knowing in advance that he will never find what he is seeking because he is hoping for the impossible: a life which really integrates death into itself and whose free recognition by others is assured once and for all. For Hegel the true hero is not the master but the slave who has chosen life and who works to transform the world in such a way that in the end there is no more room for the master.

The hero of our contemporaries does not fit either Hegel's or Nietzsche's mold. He is not what Hegel called "the steward of the World Spirit," nor does he believe in any World Spirit which arranges everything for his success and points him clearly on his way. In For Whom the Bell Tolls, Robert Jordan, on the verge of risking his life, asks himself quite frankly whether he is doing so for the materialistic society which is to come. Then part of him says: "Since when did you ever have any such conception? Never. And you never could have. You're not a real Marxist and you know it. You believe in Liberty, Equality, and Fraternity. You believe in Life, Liberty, and the Pursuit of Happiness. Don't ever kid yourself with too much dialectics. They are for some but not for you." It is not that at the moment of risk he is looking for excuses and pretexts. The mission has been accepted and will be accomplished. It is simply a question of his motives, and no matter what he does, Jordan cannot manage to make the society of the future the sole motive for his sacrifice. The society is desirable to him only as the probable guaranty, for himself and for others, of the freedom he is exercising at that very moment.

A Marxist like Kyo in La Condition humaine [by André Malraux] confronts the question at the very core of Marxism. In Marxism, he says, there is both a will and a fatality: when, then, is one to follow the course of events, and when should one force them into a certain channel? If one sticks to the facts, it seems that the Chinese Communists are probably doomed and that the Kuomintang will carry the day. But one can be sure of facts only after giving up the attempt to change them: is it not the moment to bring decisive aid to the Communists, thereby forcing history's hand? No philosophy of history can eliminate this hesitation. "For isn't it true that the essence of life, the basic cause of our anguish, can be defined as freedom of choice? But the Communist gives up a certain degree of free choice and submits to a discipline only because this is necessary for action to be effective. . . ." [Roger Vailland, Drole de jeu]

The hero of Pilote de guerre [by Antoine de Saint-Exupéry] has a different idea of the world but asks himself the same questions. In previous generations the bourgeoisie had its absolute values: one carried out orders; one died for one's country—but perhaps this was because the bourgeoisie had never been face to face with chaos. What sense did it make in June of 1940 to carry out a mission over Arras, at a moment when we could no longer have the slightest effect against the German tanks assembling there, when the announcement could no longer even be broadcast? It is easier to *serve* in a powerful army, at a time when history is clearly heading toward a certain goal. But how can a man help thinking of himself and his own death when the very world goes out of joint and reels before his eyes? How is he to serve if service is useless?

The motto of the contemporary hero is not, however, that of Barrès or Montherlant: he does not serve in order to "blow his own horn" or to prove his mastery in the face of death by means of some "useless service." Saint-Exupéry plunges into his mission because it is an intimate part of himself, the consequence of his thoughts, wishes and decisions, because he would be nothing if he were to back out. He recovers his own being to the extent to which he runs into danger. Over Arras, in the fire of the anti-aircraft guns, when every second of continuing life is as miraculous as a birth, he feels invulnerable because he is *in* things at last; he has left his inner nothingness behind, and death, if it comes, will reach him right in the thick of the world.

But perhaps he will be wounded, perhaps he will have to lie long hours on the ground dying. The same cruel consolation will still be offered him: to be and think like a living person for as long as he does live, to remain poised in the direction of his chosen ends. Wounded behind Fascist lines where he has just blown up a bridge, Robert Jordan has to part from his comrades and even from his beloved Maria.

> Then she started to cry.
> "No, *guapa*, don't," he said. "Listen. We will not go to Madrid now but I go always with thee wherever thou goest. Understand? . . . Thou wilt go now, rabbit. But I go with thee. As long as there is one of us there is both of us. Do you understand? . . . What I do now I do alone. I could not do it well with thee. Do you not see how it is? Whichever one there is, is both."

Later, when he is alone:

> It does no good to think about Maria. Try to believe what you told her. That is the best. And who says it is not true? Not you.

The man who is still alive has only one resource but a sovereign one: he must keep on acting like a living man. We die alone, but we live with other people; we are the image which they have of us; where they are, we are too. Once more and until the very end Jordan submits to that activity which binds him to others and to things and which is beyond judgment because it is the condition of all unhappiness and all happiness. Left alone, he will not commit suicide.

> *And if you wait and hold them up even a little while or just get the officer that may make all the difference. One thing well done can make—*

It is not fascination with death, as in Nietzsche, which allows the hero to sacrifice himself, nor is it the certainty, as in Hegel, that he is carrying out the wishes of history; rather, it is loyalty to the natural movement which flings us toward things and toward others. It is not death that I love, said Saint-Exupéry, but life.

Today's hero is not skeptical, dilettantish, or decadent; he has simply experienced chance, disorder, and failure—in 1936, during the Spanish Civil War, and in June of 1940. He lives at a time when duties and tasks are unclear. He has a sharper sense of human liberty and of the contingency of the future than anyone has ever had before. Taking everything into account, nothing is certain—not victory, which is still so far away, and not other people. Never before have men had such good evidence that the course of events is full of twists and turns, that much is asked of daring and that they are alone in the world and before one another. But sometimes—in love, in action—a harmony is created among them and events respond to their will. Sometimes there is that flash of fire, that streak of lightning, that moment of victory, or, as Hemingway's Maria says, that *gloria* which in its brilliance blots out everything else.

Except in times of faith when man thinks he finds in things the design of a ready-made destiny, *who can avoid these questions and who can give a different answer?* Or rather, is not faith, stripped of its illusions, itself that very movement which unites us with others, our present with our past, and by means of which we make everything have meaning, bringing the world's confused talk to an end with a precise word? This is just what the Christian saints and the heroes of past revolutions have always done—although they tried to believe that their fight had already been won in heaven or in History. This resource is not available to the men of today. The contemporary hero is not Lucifer; he is not even Prometheus; he is man.

Pope Paul VI

The Dignity of the Human Person

. . . What does the Church think of man? What needs to be recommended for the upbuilding of contemporary society? What is the ultimate significance of human activity throughout the world? People are waiting for an answer to these questions. From the answers it will be increasingly clear that the People of God and the human race in whose midst it lives render service to each other. Thus the mission of the Church will show its religious, and by that very fact, its supremely human character.

According to the almost unanimous opinion of believers and unbelievers alike, all things on earth should be related to man as their center and crown.

But what is man? About himself he has expressed, and continues to express, many divergent and even contradictory opinions. In these he often exalts himself as the absolute measure of all things or debases himself to the point of despair. The result is doubt and anxiety. The Church certainly understands these problems. Endowed with light from God, she can offer solutions to them, so that man's true situation can be portrayed and his defects explained, while at the same time his dignity and destiny are justly acknowledged.

For Sacred Scripture teaches that man was created "to the image of God," is capable of knowing and loving his Creator, and was appointed by Him as master of all earthly creatures that he might subdue them and use them to God's glory. "What is man that you should care for him? You have made him little less than the angels, and crowned him with glory and honor. You have given him rule over the works of your hands, putting all things under his feet" (Ps. 8:5–7).

Reprinted by permission of the publisher from *Pastoral Constitution on the Church in the Modern World*, Second Vatican Council, December 7, 1965 (Washington, D.C.: National Catholic Welfare Conference).

But God did not create man to be alone, for from the beginning "male and female he created them" (Gen. 1:27). Their companionship produces the primary form of interpersonal communion. For by his innermost nature man is a social being, and unless he relates himself to others he can neither live nor develop his potential.

Therefore, as we read elsewhere in Holy Scripture, God saw "all that he had made, and it was very good" (Gen. 1:31).

Although he was made by God in a state of holiness, from the very beginning of his history man abused his liberty, at the urging of the Evil One. Man set himself against God and sought to attain his goal apart from God. Although they knew God, they did not glorify Him as God, but their senseless minds were darkened and they served the creature rather than the Creator. What divine revelation makes known to us conforms with experience. Examining his heart, man finds that he has inclinations toward evil too, and is engulfed by manifold ills which cannot come from his good Creator. Often refusing to acknowledge God as his beginning, man has disrupted also his proper relationship to his own ultimate goal as well as his whole relationship toward himself and others and all created things.

Therefore man is split within himself. As a result, all of human life, whether individual or collective, shows itself to be a dramatic struggle between good and evil, between light and darkness. Indeed, man finds that by himself he is incapable of battling the assaults of evil successfully, so that everyone feels as though he is bound by chains. But the Lord Himself came to free and strengthen man, renewing him inwardly and casting out that "prince of this world" (John 12:31) who held him in the bondage of sin. For sin has diminished man, blocking his path to fulfillment.

The call to grandeur and the depths of misery, both of which are a part of human experience, find their ultimate and simultaneous explanation in the light of this revelation.

Though made of body and soul, man is one. Through his bodily composition he gathers to himself the elements of the material world; thus they reach their crown through him, and through him raise their voice in free praise of the Creator. For this reason man is not allowed to despise his bodily life; rather he is obliged to regard his body as good and honorable since God has created it and will raise it up on the last day. Nevertheless wounded by sin, man experiences rebellious stirrings in his body. But the very dignity of man postulates that man glorify God in his body and forbids it to serve the evil inclinations of his heart.

Now, man is not wrong when he regards himself as superior to bodily concerns, and as more than a speck of nature or a nameless constituent of the city of man. For by his interior qualities he outstrips the whole sum of mere things. He plunges into the depths of reality whenever he enters into his own heart; God, Who probes the heart, awaits him there; there he discerns his proper destiny beneath the eyes of God. Thus, when he recognizes in himself a spiritual and immortal soul, he is not being mocked by a fantasy born only of physical or social influences, but is rather laying hold of the proper truth of the matter.

Man judges rightly that by his intellect he surpasses the material universe, for he shares in the light of the divine mind. By relentlessly employing his talents through the ages he has indeed made progress in the practical sciences and in technology and the liberal arts. In our times he has won superlative victories, especially in his probing of the material world and in subjecting it to himself. Still he has always searched for more penetrating truths, and finds them. For his intelligence is not confined to observable data alone, but can with genuine certitude attain to reality itself as knowable, though in consequence of sin that certitude is partly obscured and weakened.

The intellectual nature of the human person is perfected by wisdom and needs to be, for wisdom gently attracts the mind of man to a quest and a love for what is true and good. Steeped in wisdom, man passes through visible realities to those which are unseen.

Our era needs such wisdom more than bygone ages if the discoveries made by man are to be further humanized. For the future of the world stands in peril unless wiser men are forthcoming. It should also be pointed out that many nations, poorer in economic goods, are quite rich in wisdom and can offer noteworthy advantages to others. . . .

In the depths of his conscience, man detects a law which he does not impose upon himself, but which holds him to obedience. Always summoning him to love good and avoid evil, the voice of conscience when necessary speaks to his heart: do this, shun that. For man has in his heart a law written by God; to obey it is the very dignity of man; according to it he will be judged. Conscience is the most secret core and sanctuary of a man. There he is alone with God, Whose voice echoes in his depths. In a wonderful manner conscience reveals that law which is fulfilled by love of God and neighbor. In fidelity to conscience, Christians are joined with the rest of men in the search for truth, and for the genuine solution to the numerous problems which arise in the life of individuals and from social relationships. Hence the more correct conscience holds sway, the more persons and groups turn aside from blind choice and strive to be guided by the objective norms of morality. Conscience frequently errs from invincible ignorance without losing its dignity. The same cannot be said for a man who cares but little for truth and goodness, or for a conscience which by degrees grows practically sightless as a result of habitual sin.

Only in freedom can man direct himself toward goodness. Our contemporaries make much of this freedom and pursue it eagerly; and rightly to be sure. Often, however, they foster it perversely as a license for doing whatever pleases them, even if it is evil. For its part, authentic freedom is an exceptional sign of the divine image within man. For God has willed that man remain "under the control of his own decisions," so that he can seek his Creator spontaneously, and come freely to utter and blissful perfection through loyalty to Him. Hence man's dignity demands that he act according to a knowing and free choice that is personally motivated and prompted from within, not under blind internal impulse nor by mere external pressure. Man achieves such dignity when, emancipating himself from all captivity to passion, he pursues his goal in a spontaneous choice of what is good and procures for himself, through effective and skilful action, aids to that end. Since man's freedom has been damaged by sin, only by the aid of God's grace can he bring such a relationship with God into full flower. Before the judgment seat of God each man must render an account of his own life, whether he has done good or evil.

It is in the face of death that the riddle of human existence grows most acute. Not only is man tormented by pain and by the advancing deterioration of his body, but even more so by a dread of perpetual extinction. He rightly follows the intuition of his heart when he abhors and repudiates the utter ruin and total disappearance of his own person. He rebels against death because he bears in himself an eternal seed which cannot be reduced to sheer matter. All the endeavors of technology, though useful in the extreme, cannot calm his anxiety; for a prolongation of biological life is unable to satisfy that desire for a higher life which is inescapably lodged in his breast.

Although the mystery of death utterly beggars the imagination, the Church has been taught by divine revelation and firmly teaches that man has been created by God for a blissful purpose beyond the reach of earthly misery. In addition, that bodily death from which man would have been immune had he not sinned will be vanquished, according to the Christian faith, when man who was ruined by his own doing is restored to wholeness by an almighty and merciful Saviour. For God has called man and still calls him so that with his entire being he might be joined to Him in an endless sharing of a divine life beyond all corruption. Christ won this victory when He rose to life, for by His death He freed man from death. Hence to every thoughtful man a solidly established faith provides the answer to his anxiety about what the future holds for him. At the same time faith gives him the power to be united in Christ with his loved ones who have already been snatched away by death; faith arouses the hope that they have found true life with God.

The basic source of human dignity lies in man's call to communion with God. From the very circumstance of his origin man is already invited to converse with God. For man would not exist were he not created by God's love and constantly preserved by it; and he cannot live fully according to truth unless he freely acknowledges that love and devotes himself to His Creator. Still, many of our contemporaries have never recognized this intimate and vital link with God, or have explicitly rejected it. Thus atheism must be accounted among the most serious problems of this age, and is deserving of closer examination.

The word atheism is applied to phenomena which are quite distinct from one another. For while God is expressly denied by some, others believe that man can assert absolutely nothing about Him. Still others use such a method to scrutinize the question of God as to make it seem devoid of meaning. Many, unduly transgressing the limits of the positive sciences, contend that everything can be explained by this kind of scientific reasoning alone or, by contrast, they altogether disallow the fact that there is any absolute truth. Some laud man so extravagantly that their faith in God lapses into a kind of anemia, though they seem more inclined to affirm man than to deny God. Again some form for themselves such a fallacious idea of God that when they repudiate this figment they are by no means rejecting the God of the Gospel. Some never get to the point of raising questions about God, since they seem to experience no religious stirrings nor do they see why they should trouble themselves about religion. Moreover, atheism results not rarely from a violent protest against the evil in this world, or from the absolute character with which certain human values are unduly invested, and which thereby already accords them the stature of God. Modern civilization itself often complicates the approach to God not for any essential reason but because it is so heavily engrossed in earthly affairs.

Undeniably, those who willfully shut out God from their hearts and try to dodge religious questions are not following the dictates of their consciences, and hence are not free of blame; yet believers themselves frequently bear some responsibility for this situation. For, taken as a whole, atheism is not a spontaneous development but stems from a variety of causes, including a critical reaction against religious beliefs, and in some places against the Christian religion in particular. Hence believers can have more than a little to do with the birth of atheism. To the extent that they neglect their own training in the faith, or teach erroneous doctrine, or are deficient in their religious, moral or social life, they must be said to conceal rather than reveal the authentic face of God and religion.

Modern atheism often takes on a systematic expression which, in addition to other causes, stretches the desire for human independence to such a point that it poses difficulties against any kind of dependence on God. Those who profess atheism of this sort maintain that it gives man freedom to be an end unto himself, the sole artisan and creator of his own history. They claim that this freedom cannot be reconciled with the affirmation of a Lord Who is author and purpose of all things, or at least that this freedom makes such an affirmation altogether superfluous. The sense of power which modern technical progress generates in man can nourish this belief.

Not to be overlooked among the forms of modern atheism is that which anticipates the liberation of man especially through his economic and social emancipation. This form argues that by its nature religion thwarts this liberation by arousing man's hope for a deceptive future life, thereby diverting him from the contrasting of the earthly city. Consequently when the proponents of this doctrine gain governmental power they vigorously fight against religion, and promote atheism by using, especially in the education of youth, those means of pressure which public power has at its disposal . . .

The Church holds that the recognition of God is in no way hostile to man's dignity, since this dignity is rooted and perfected in God. For man was made an intelligent and free member of society by the God Who created him; but even more important, he is called as a son to commune with God and share in His happiness. She further teaches that a hope related to the end of time does not diminish the importance of intervening duties but rather undergirds the acquittal of them with fresh incentives. By contrast, when a divine substructure and the hope of life eternal are wanting, man's dignity is most grievously lacerated, as current events often attest; the riddles of life and death, of guilt and of grief go unsolved, with the frequent result that men succumb to despair.

Meanwhile every man remains to himself an unsolved puzzle, however obscurely he may perceive it. For on certain occasions no one can entirely escape the kind of self-questioning mentioned earlier, especially when life's major events take place. To this questioning only God fully and most certainly provides an answer as he summons man to higher knowledge and humbler probing.

The remedy which must be applied to atheism, however, is to be sought in a proper presentation of the Church's teaching as well as in the integral life of the Church and her members. For it is the function of the Church, led by the Holy Spirit Who renews and purifies her ceaselessly, to make God the Father and His Incarnate Son present and in a sense visible. This result is achieved chiefly by the witness of a living and mature faith, namely, one trained to see difficulties clearly and to master them. Many martyrs have given luminous witness to this faith and continue to do so. This faith needs to prove its fruitfulness by penetrating the believer's entire life, including its worldly dimensions, and by activating him toward justice and love, especially regarding the needy. What does the most reveal God's presence, however, is the brotherly charity of the faithful who are united in spirit as they work together for the faith of the Gospel and who prove themselves a sign of unity.

While rejecting atheism, root and branch, the Church sincerely professes that all men, believers and unbelievers alike, ought to work for the rightful betterment of this world in which all alike live; such an ideal cannot be realized, however, apart from sincere and prudent dialogue. Hence the Church protests against the distinction which some state authorities make between believers and unbelievers, with prejudice to the fundamental rights of the human person. The Church calls for the active freedom of believers to build up in this world God's temple too. She courteously invites atheists to examine the Gospel of Christ with an open mind. . . .

3
What Is Man's Situation?

In the preceding chapter Reinhold Niebuhr noted that our culture is "credited with the greatest advances in the understanding of nature and with the greatest confusion in the understanding of man." Preoccupied with techniques for the mastery of nature, men noticed too late the confusion and anxiety produced in society by these same techniques. This chapter examines the religious dimensions of man's situation in an era of extremely rapid change—scientific, technological, social, economic, and demographic.

The first three articles describe attributes of the problem. Harvey Cox explores the close relation between the rise of urban civilization and the collapse of traditional religion—the process of "secularization" by which a religious understanding of the world has been bypassed. Kenneth Boulding points out that traditional religious systems developed in response to the problems of ages in which the issues of the contemporary world were unknown and unforeseen. If these new human problems are to be resolved, new models for human conduct must be found. Michael

Harrington describes the predicament of man in a society which has discarded the old models but has so far failed to develop convincing new ones. The absence of models has precipitated "a crisis of belief and disbelief" which offers a common challenge to religion and nonreligion to respond meaningfully to the problems of the twentieth century.

There is evidence that such a response is developing. Barbara Ward's article represents one confrontation of a religious conscience with the difficulties and dangers of man's situation in the modern world. And the Papal Encyclical of Pope John XXIII exemplifies the efforts of one established church to adapt itself to the contemporary needs of a changed world. These two selections suggest that religion may be prepared to accept the responsibility of applying "principles of justice to concrete affairs," that religion has recognized that the problems produced by change, whether scientific, technological, economic, or demographic, are at bottom moral problems and therefore religious problems.

Harvey Cox

The Epoch of the Secular City

The rise of urban civilization and the collapse of traditional religion are the two main hallmarks of our era and are closely related movements. Urbanization constitutes a massive change in the way men live together, and became possible in its contemporary form only with the scientific and technological advances which sprang from the wreckage of religious world-views. Secularization, an equally epochal movement, marks a change in the way men grasp and understand their life together, and it occurred only when the cosmopolitan confrontations of city living

Reprinted with permission of The Macmillan Company from *The Secular City* by Harvey Cox. Copyright © Harvey Cox, 1965.

Harvey Cox is Associate Professor of Church and Society at Harvard University Divinity School.

exposed the relativity of the myths and traditions men once thought were unquestionable. The ways men live their common life affects mightily the ways they understand the meaning of that life, and vice versa. Villages and cities are laid out to reflect the pattern of the heavenly city, the abode of the gods. But once laid out, the pattern of the polis influences the way in which succeeding generations experience life and visualize the gods. Societies and the symbols by which those societies live influence each other. In our day the secular metropolis stands as both the pattern of our life together and the symbol of our view of the world. If the Greeks perceived the cosmos as an immensely expanded polis, and medieval man saw it as the feudal manor enlarged to infinity, we experience the universe as the city of man. It is a field of human exploration and endeavor from which the gods have fled. The world has become man's task and man's responsibility. Contemporary man has become the cosmopolitan. The world has become his city and his city has reached out to include the world. The name for the process by which this has come about is *secularization.*

What is secularization? The Dutch theologian C. A. van Peursen says it is the deliverance of man "first from religious and then from metaphysical control over his reason and his language." It is the loosing of the world from religious and quasi-religious understandings of itself, the dispelling of all closed world-views, the breaking of all supernatural myths and sacred symbols. It represents what another observer has called the "defatalization of history," the discovery by man that he has been left with the world on his hands, that he can no longer blame fortune or the furies for what he does with it. Secularization is man turning his attention away from worlds beyond and toward this world and this time (*saeculum* = "this present age"). It is what Dietrich Bonhoeffer in 1944 called "man's coming of age."

To some, Bonhoeffer's words still sound shocking, but they really should not. He was merely venturing a tardy theological interpretation of what had already been noticed by poets and novelists, sociologists and philosophers for decades. The era of the secular city is not one of anticlericalism or feverish antireligious fanaticism. The anti-Christian zealot is something of an anachronism today, a fact which explains why Bertrand Russell's books often seem quaint rather than daring and why the antireligious propaganda of the Communists sometimes appears intent on dispelling belief in a "God out there" who has long since been laid to rest.

The forces of secularization have no serious interest in persecuting religion. Secularization simply bypasses and undercuts religion and goes on to other things. It has relativized religious world-views and thus rendered them innocuous. Religion has been privatized. It has been accepted as the peculiar prerogative and point of view of a particular person or group. Secularization has accomplished what fire and chain could not: It has convinced the believer that he *could* be wrong, and persuaded the devotee that there are more important things than dying for the faith. The gods of traditional religions live on as private fetishes or the patrons of congenial groups, but they play no role whatever in the public life of the secular metropolis.

Of course there are events and movements which momentarily raise questions about whether secularization has really succeeded in unseating the gods of traditional religion. The self-immolation of a Buddhist monk, the rise of fanatic sects such as Soka Gakkai in Japan, the appearance of the Black Muslims in America, even the new vigor of Roman Catholicism—all seem to suggest that the published obituaries of religion have been premature. But a more careful look will reveal that these phenomena cannot be understood apart from certain swift-flowing secular currents in the modern world. These currents either express themselves in quasi-religious form or else elicit adjustments in religious systems which alter them so radically that they pose no real threat to the secularization process. Thus the revival of ancient Oriental religions gives voice to the nationalistic political aspirations of peoples who preserve antiquated symbols but use them for utterly novel purposes. Pluralism and tolerance are the children of secularization. They represent a society's unwillingness to enforce any particular world-view on its citizens. Movements within the Roman Catholic Church culminating in the Second Vatican Council indicate its growing readiness to be open to truth from all sides. Pluralism is breaking out where once a closed system stood.

The age of the secular city, the epoch whose ethos is quickly spreading into every corner of the globe, *is* an age of "no religion at all." It no longer looks to religious rules and rituals for its morality or its meanings. For some religion provides a hobby, for others a mark of national or ethnic identification, for still others an esthetic delight. For fewer and fewer does it provide an inclusive and commanding system of personal and cosmic values and explanations. True, there are some people who claim that our modern age has its secular religions, its political saints, and its profane temples. They are right in a manner of speaking; but to call, for example, Nazism or communism "religions" is to obscure a very significant difference between them and traditional religions. It also obscures the fact that Nazism was a throwback to a lost tribalism and that every day communism becomes more "secularized" and hence less and less a "religion."

The effort to force secular and political movements of our time to be "religious" so that we can feel justified in clinging to *our* religion is, in the end, a losing battle. Secularization rolls on, and if we are to understand and communicate with our present age we must learn to love it in its unremitting secularity. We must learn, as Bonhoeffer said, to speak of God in a secular fashion and find a nonreligious interpretation of biblical concepts. It will do no good to cling to our religious and metaphysical versions of Christianity in the hope that one day religion or metaphysics will once again be back. They are disappearing forever and that means we can now let go and immerse ourselves in the new world of the secular city. The first step in such an immersion is learning something about its peculiar characteristics. But before we do we must ask more precisely about the other key term we have used in describing the ethos of our time, *urbanization.*

If secularization designates the content of man's coming of age, urbanization describes the context in which it is occurring. It is the "shape" of the new society which supports its peculiar cultural style. In trying to define the term *urbanization,* however, we are confronted with the fact that social scientists themselves are not entirely agreed about what it means. It is clear, however, that urbanization is not just a quantitative term. It does not refer to population size or density, to geographic extent or to a particular form of government. Admittedly some of the character of modern urban life would not be possible without giant populations concentrated on enormous contiguous land masses. But urbanization is not something that refers only to the city. As Vidich and Bensman have shown in *Small Town in Mass Society,* high mobility, economic concentration, and mass communications have drawn even rural villages into the web of urbanization.

Urbanization means a structure of common life in which diversity and the disintegration of tradition are paramount. It means a type of impersonality in which functional relationships multiply. It means that a degree of tolerance and anonymity replace traditional moral sanctions and long-term acquaintanceships. The urban center is the place of human control, of rational planning, of bureaucratic organization—and the urban center is not just in Washington, London, New York, and Peking. It is everywhere. The technological metropolis provides the indispensable social setting for a world of "no religion at all," for what we have called a secular style.

The age of the secular, technological city, like all preceding ages, does have its own characteristic *style*—its peculiar way of understanding and expressing itself, its distinctive character, coloring all aspects of its life. Just as the poets and architects, the theologians and the lovers of the thirteenth century all partook of a common cultural substance, so in our time we all share a fund of unspoken perspectives. Just as the straight aisles and evenly clipped hedges of the eighteenth-century formal garden exhibited a style found also in deist theology and in neoclassic verse, so our secular urban culture makes itself felt in all our intellectual projects, artistic visions, and technical accomplishments.

The French philosopher Maurice Merleau-Ponty (1908–1961) means the same thing when he speaks of a particular *"manière d'être."* He says:

> If indeed philosophy and the film agree, if reflection and techniques of work participate in a common meaning, it is because the philosopher and the film maker have in common a certain manner of being (*manière d'être*), a certain view of the world which is that of a generation.

. . . We must now describe more fully what we mean by the *secular epoch,* and in order to do so it may be helpful to contrast it with two other cultural epochs which expressed different patterns of human community. For purposes of comparison we shall make use of a somewhat contrived word, *technopolis.* It will be used here to signify the fusion of technological and political components into the base on which a new cultural style has appeared. Although the term is an artificial one, it will call to mind the fact that the contemporary secular metropolis was not possible before modern technology. Modern Rome and modern London are *more than* larger versions of their Augustinian or Chaucerian forebears. There comes a point at which quantitative development releases qualitative change, and that point was reached in urban development only after the modern Western scientific revolution. Manhattan is inconceivable before structural steel and the electric elevator. *Technopolis* represents a new species of human community. The fact that it is a neologism will remind us that it is not yet achieved in reality.

By way of contrast to *technopolis,* let us arbitrarily designate the preceding epochal styles, according to their characteristic social forms, the *tribe* and the *town.*

The styles or periods of the tribe, the town, and the technopolis are in no sense merely successive. Nor are they mutually exclusive. If modern Paris is not simply a larger version of medieval Paris, neither should discontinuity be exaggerated. As Lewis Mumford has shown, the roots of the modern city reach back into the Stone Age. Our modern metropolis became possible only after technical advances had solved some of the problems which had heretofore placed iron limits on the size of cities; but the technical metropolis in a sense simply actualized in steel and glass, in pace and personality, what had already been present embryonically in Athens and Alexandria. Nor is tribalism merely a historical category. Even today we can find people in Africa and the South Pacific who still live a tribal existence, and we find residents of New York City with a tribal mentality. Town culture, representing a kind of transition from tribe to technopolis, still persists within and around the urban centers; it forms a residue on the viewpoint of everyone whose youth was marked by small town and rural values—and whose was not?

We are all tribal, town, and technopolitan to some degree, but technopolitan culture is the wave of the future. With this caution let us look at the characteristics of these three epochal styles.

When man appears in history he is already a social animal living in a collective group. Whatever purposes were served by the various social-contract theories of Rousseau or Locke in advancing personal rights, they can now be seen as sheer fiction, as social myths with little grounding whatever in history. The tribe is the setting where man becomes man. It represents an extension of blood and kinship ties, and tribal man celebrates this familial solidarity by singing songs of the common ancestors of all his people. Thus among African pygmies, Australian bushmen, American Indians, wherever remnants of tribal structure have been preserved, the venerable ancestors who are often semidivine beings are ritually conjured in wine, dance, and ballad.

Tribal societies and primitive peoples have supplied one of the recurrent fascinations of modern man. It began perhaps with curiosity about the beginnings of human societies, especially among the French philosophers, who wanted to develop a rational rather than a theological version of man's origins. The interest was fed by the discovery and investigation of the allegedly less civilized peoples of North America and the South Pacific. The romantic myth of the Noble Savage marks one enthusiastic stage of this fascination. More recently it has flowered into the sciences of cultural anthropology.

By *tribal society* we have in mind a stage in human social development which has been described variously as totemic, preliterate, primitive, and even savage or prelogical. The variousness of the terms illustrates the problem, since they include descriptive and pejorative labels as well as terms designed to illuminate different aspects in the lives of peoples who seem increasingly remote from us in the modern technopolis. No one word, not even *tribal,* describes them accurately. . . .

In addition, it has become increasingly clear since the early studies of Frazer, Taylor, and Durkheim not only that primitive societies vary widely from each other, but that even within these societies one can discover greater disparities among personalities than scholars had originally supposed. Paul Radin has reminded a later generation that in any society, for example, one can find some people who take its religion more seriously than others. As he says, there is always the simple pragmatist who wants his religion to "work," as well as the "priest-thinker" who systematizes and orders beliefs.

But one consensus has clearly emerged from modern anthropological studies. It is that the religion and culture of a society cannot be studied apart from its economic and social context. Religion is embedded in behavior and institutions before it is consciously codified, and the alteration of social and economic patterns always entails religious change. As Paul Radin puts it, "No correlation is more definite or more constant than that between a given economic level of society and the nature of the supernatural beings postulated by the tribe at large or by the religious individual in particular." When man changes his tools and his techniques, his ways of producing and distributing the goods of life, he also changes his gods. Tribal, town, and technopolitan existences represent first of all different forms of social, economic, and political community. As such they symbolize different religions or belief systems.

For this reason, tribal societies, despite their idiosyncrasies, do exhibit certain common features.

Tribal life grows out of kinship ties. It is really an expanded family, a group in which tradition prescribes the proper relationship with any person one is likely to meet during a normal lifetime. Tribal societies are compact and enclosed. Prolonged contact with the outside world is bound to be disruptive, but this is precisely what happens to every tribe sooner or later. There are no hiding places left on our shrunken globe for the Noble Savage. Oil wells dot our Indian reservations and industrialism is on the march in Africa. We may be living during the last generation in which it will be possible to study primitive peoples directly.

So tribal life has to be studied as a process, not as a static category. The tribe represents that stage during which man moves from a belief in ghosts and demons to a belief in gods, from spells and incantations to prayers, from shamans and sorcerers to priests and teachers, from myth and magic to religion and theology. All of this happens only when the economic structure of the society allows for a group of self-conscious religious specialists to emerge. There is no time for codification if everyone's energy is spent in simply keeping alive. There is no need for a definition of the relationships between the mythical heroes and divinities until questions are raised or other tribes with other divinities are encountered. But by now the tribe is moving toward a more settled life. The camp, the village, and the town begin to appear.

The transition from tribe to town represents one of the decisive breakthroughs of human history. It is best epitomized by the emergence of the Greek *polis*. The polis appeared when bellicose clans and rival houses met here and there to form a new type of community, loyalty to whose laws and gods replaced the more elemental kinship ties which had previously held force. The gods of the tribes were demoted and a new religion arose, often centering on a common divine ancestor. As the nineteenth-century French scholar Fustel de Coulanges asserts in his classic study *The Ancient City,* the founding of the polis was a religious act. A new cultus was formed whose gods were higher than those of the constituting clans. To be a citizen of the city was to be a member of the new cultus, often centered around a semidivine founder such as Aeneas.

But the conflict of loyalties between family custom and the law of the town, between blood ties and the more impersonal justice of the polis, deeply disturbed the soul of the ancient Greek. Sophocles' tragedy *Antigone* projects this conflict onto the stage. In *Antigone* we watch a struggle between the needs of the arising polis for order and equality, symbolized by King Creon, and the deeper bonds of blood, represented by Antigone. Antigone feels she must bury her brother, Polyneices, who has fallen in a revolt against the polis. Creon has decreed that as a traitor Polyneices must lie unburied, to be devoured by the dogs and the birds. Caught in the fatal contradiction between family and polis, Antigone and Creon collide, with catastrophic effects for both. Though the play is often interpreted and directed as a portrait of religion and the laws of God (Antigone) versus the tyranny and the laws of men (Creon), the Athenians who first witnessed it knew better. They realized that they were watching a reproduction of the anguished struggle going on within their own breasts, a struggle in which gods and values were ranged on both sides. *Antigone* signals the painful transition of a culture from tribe to town, a metamorphosis whose fearful scope and psyche-threatening uncertainty can be matched only by the present transition from town to technopolis.

The tribe was a family writ large. Its roots reached back to a common mythological past and its members were locked together in lines of consanguinity. It bestowed on all its members an unquestioned place and a secure identity. It answered most of the great questions of human existence—marriage, occupation, life goals—almost before they were raised. Tribal tradition gave the answers. Tradition, whether danced, chanted, or carved into masks or figurines, provided a rich, complex, and utterly complete catalog of images, identities, and values.

Tribal man is hardly a personal "self" in our modern sense of the word. He does not so much live in a tribe; the tribe lives in him. He is the tribe's subjective expression. He grasps himself within a closed system of compact meanings in which there is no room for any transcendent point of view or critical detachment. Man and nature, the animals and the gods, all form one continuous life process whose meaning courses through it just below the surface and can erupt anywhere in a transparent moment of magical or religious power.

The appearance of currency and the development of the alphabet supply two essential ingredients in the shattering step from tribe to town. Both devices tend to free individuals from traditionally prescribed relationships and to expand enormously the possible occasions for human contact. A man with a sheep to barter for bread must find a person who both has bread and wants wool or lamb stew. The range of possibilities is small and will tend to be directed by tradition. Sheep-raising and bread-baking will be passed on from father to son. Economic contacts and familial patterns will not be distinguishable. But the man who can sell a sheep and buy bread with the money is at once a more mobile and a more independent operator. The jingle of coins tolls the end of tribal existence and signals the beginning of a more impersonal, more rationalized way of living together.

In the same way, as writing develops, man's dependence on the person of the shaman or the oracle is undercut. Now he can begin to examine documents himself. Books and parchments can circulate and be perused outside the dim circle of the sacred fire where one had to cling to the storyteller's every syllable and defer to his traditional role in order to find out about the world. Writing depersonalizes man's access to information.

Once again the economic framework is crucial in the appearance of writing. It began as a tool of commerce, but quickly became a way to acquire knowledge and therefore power. Thus writing had political and religious consequences. Contact with the "outside," with ideas and possibilities not accessible within the tribe, provided one key to the development of town culture. It was difficult, but not impossible, for strangers to become a part of the town. As Lewis Mumford has correctly seen, one became part of the tribe solely by accident of birth or blood, whereas the town provided a place where strangers could become fellow citizens.

This transformation of "strangers and outsiders" into "fellow citizens and members one of another" recalls, of course, an expression close to the heart of the New Testament message (see Ephesians 2). It suggests one good reason why the early church, from its outset a detribalizing movement in which there was "no longer Jew nor Greek," spread most quickly in the towns and cities. We shall return to this later on, but here it does raise the interesting question of why even the storied Greek polis never realized in full the ideals of town life. It never became fully open or fully universal. It always remained partly a tribe. Athens and Rome felt it necessary to preserve the fiction that all their citizens had sprung from the loins of a common ancestor. Both failed to see that universal citizenship could not be reconciled with slavery and imperialism. There are in fact two reasons why Athens never became a city or a metropolis in the modern sense of the word, why it never achieved the population size, the complexity, the anonymity, or the uncanny vastness of the modern urban area. The first is that these elements were just not possible until modern scientific technology had set the stage. But the second is that the universality and radical openness of the Gospel was not yet present to dispel the remnants of tribalism. Fustel de Coulanges believes that what was missing from the Greek and Roman "cities" was the universal God of Christianity. The ancients, he says, "never represented God to themselves as a unique being exercising his action upon the universe. . . . Religion was entirely local . . . special to each city." It was the lack of that totally inclusive claim of the Gospel that kept the ancients' towns to some extent tribal. Only after the beginning of the Christian era was the *idea* of an inclusive metropolis conceivable, and even then it took nearly two millennia to realize it. "Christianity," Fustel de Coulanges goes on, ". . . was not the domestic religion of any family, the national religion of any city or of a race. It belonged neither to a caste nor to a corporation. From its first appearance it called to itself the whole human race."

Antigone is the tragic figure who symbolizes the painful transition from tribe to town, from kinship to civic loyalties. In a sense Socrates represents a comparable tragedy in the transition from polis to cosmopolis, from the gods of the city to the universal community of mankind. He did not reject the "gods of the city" as his accusers claimed he did. Rather he simply refused to take them with unqualified seriousness. He saw that they have a place, but only a limited and provisional place. His execution marks Athens' refusal to develop from a provincial polis into a universal metropolis.

Perhaps what we have called the "town" will eventually be recognized as itself merely a transitional stage between the tribe and the technopolis, between two forms of communal-collective existence, between the preliterate man of the cave painting and the postliterate man of the electronic image. Without overdrawing the analogies between tribal and technopolitan life, to which we shall return later, it is worth noting that for Marxist theory, the "bourgeois" period (which actually means "the age of the town-dweller") constitutes nothing more than a long, conflict-ridden transition from primitive communism to socialist communism. But before we dismiss the town as being merely transitional, let us briefly examine it in order to remind ourselves of just what it is we are leaving behind as we move into the epoch of the technical city.

Town culture is familiar to us because it is a part of all of us. The age of the towns gave us printing and books, rational theology, the scientific revolution, investment capitalism, and bureaucracy. It gave us many other things as well, but I have listed those which relate closely to what Max Weber, in characterizing the age, has called "rationalization." Especially in the Calvinist Puritanism which was in many ways the prototypical religion of the period, Weber saw a classical instance of what he termed the "routinization of charisma." I have also listed those aspects which provide the most evident contrast with both tribe and technopolis. The shaman is the symbol of tribal man. He dances and chants his religion. The Puritan or maybe even the Yankee is his town-culture counterpart. Town man reads the word and hears it preached. Tribal man merges with his daemon and his group. Town man is a discreet individual who reads *Robinson Crusoe*. Tribal man's gods whirl with him in the night of sensual ecstasy. Town man's God calls him from an infinite distance to work soberly in the daylight of self-discipline. This comparison may make town man sound spare and astringent, but we should not deal with him too harshly, first because he rarely lived up to the image we have painted of him, and secondly because he was preparing the way for technopolitan civilization. Without him it could never have been accomplished.

Kenneth E. Boulding

The Wisdom of Man and the Wisdom of God

. . . The parsimony of the developed society arises because it has to inhabit a spaceship. We have to visualize the earth as a small, rather crowded spaceship, destination unknown, in which man has to find a slender thread of a way of life in the midst of a continually repeatable cycle of material transformations. In a spaceship, there can be no inputs or outputs. The water must circulate through the kidneys and the algae, the food likewise, the air likewise, and even though there must be inputs of

From *Human Values on the Spaceship Earth*, Council Press for the Commission on Church and Economic Life, National Council of Churches, 475 Riverside Drive, N.Y. 10027. © 1966. Used by permission of The National Council of Churches of Christ in the USA.

Kenneth Boulding is Professor of Economics and Research Director, Center for Research in Conflict Resolution, University of Michigan.

energy, because of the dismal Second Law of Thermodynamics, there can be no inputs or outputs of material, short of the transfer of energy into matter; the ratio of energy to matter is so enormous, however, that this seems implausible. In a spaceship there can be no sewers and no imports.

Up to now the human population has been small enough so that we have not had to regard the earth as a spaceship. We have been able to regard the atmosphere and the oceans and even the soil as an inexhaustible reservoir, from which we can draw at will and which we can pollute at will. There is writing on the wall, however; Los Angeles has run out of pure air; Lake Erie has run out of pure water; we are changing the composition of the atmosphere, and even of the oceans to the point where in a few decades this may become the most overwhelming problem facing mankind. Even now we may be doing irreversible damage to this precious little spaceship, simply out of our ignorance and blindness.The brute fact is, we know very little about the earth, either its atmosphere, its oceans, or even its crust. We do not know, even to an order of magnitude, what population the earth would support if we had to recycle everything and live in it like a spaceship. This, of course, would depend on our level of knowledge; nevertheless, there are obvious limits. If this limit is a hundred million, we are obviously in for a rough time, for the population of the earth is almost certainly going to go to six, perhaps to ten billion, before it is stabilized; and there seems to be no way of reducing the human population short of frightful disaster. If the limit is three billion, we had better act fast; if the limit is ten billion, we have some time.

. . . Man's willingness to tolerate change and to provoke and propagate it may arise partly out of the fact that he has never had to live on a spaceship, that he has up to the present lived in effect on an illimitable (if rough) plane, with infinite reservoirs in the atmosphere, the soil, and the sea. Because of his wide horizons he has always had some place to go, over the hill, and he has been able to devote his active and fertile brain to novelty. Perhaps the most depressing aspect of the spaceship era is that novelty itself may have to be economized. The society will be more like that of men in a life boat than of cowboys on the great plains. Indeed, in many ways the cowboy and all that he symbolizes is the very opposite of the spaceship crew. The cowboy can horse around because he doesn't have a boat to rock. Once the fear of rocking the boat of this fragile planet becomes dominant in the human consciousness, something will have gone out of human experience. It may be, of course, that space exploration will recapture the sense of horizon and adventure. Even space exploration, however, must be done in a spaceship even smaller than planet Earth. Furthermore, the trouble with space is that there is so little there except space. There may be things beyond the mountain, but there is an abyss of nothingness beyond the skies. Even Mars, beloved of the science fictioners, is now revealed as a piece of almost inconceivably undesirable real estate, and when man gets out into space, at least in this solar system, he is going to find himself very, very lonely. In this part of the universe, at any rate, spaceship Earth seems to be unique and frighteningly precious. . . .

Ethics and Religion

One of the most interesting and at the same time most difficult questions regarding the developed society or the spaceship Earth is the nature of the ethical and religious systems which will be compatible with such a very different order of human life and society. Man's existing ethical and religious systems were developed for the most part in what might be called the age of civilization. We might almost call this the Biblical Age, for the Bible is perhaps its greatest and most representative work. Nevertheless, the Bible, though it is a product of the age of civilization, clearly looks beyond it. It is a work of prophecy as well as of history. The prophetic vision, both of the Old and of the New Testaments, looks forward to a Messianic age in which the promise that is implicit in the very nature of man is to be fulfilled. This surely is at least one interpretation of the idea of the Covenant which is so fundamental to the Old Testament, that man had in himself a promise which he is destined one day to redeem. In the New Testament, this takes perhaps a more eschatological form; nevertheless, the hope of a Messianic age in the future is continued in the Christian doctrine of a Second Coming.

Furthermore, the Biblical ethic, especially of the New Testament, is more appropriate to the developed society than to the age of civilization. In the age of civilization in which war is a normal state of man, in which the threat system dominates human relations, and in which whatever order there is is maintained precariously by the legitimizing of violence, the ethic of the Sermon on the Mount has remained a counsel of perfection, to be followed only by the specialized religious orders or the separated sect. In the spaceship Earth, we had better learn to love our enemies, or we will destroy each other. Indeed, we had better learn to love ourselves, and our neighbors as ourselves; otherwise, again, we will destroy ourselves, either through conflict or through sheer boredom and ennui. We will have to learn to be poor, or at least parsimonious, in spirit, even in the midst of material affluence. We will have to learn how to mourn, or we will be gobbled up in egotism and pride. We will have to learn how to be meek, or we won't inherit the earth at all. We will have to learn how to hunger and thirst after righteousness, for there will be no effective sanctions. We will have to learn how to be merciful, for we all have to live at each other's mercy. We will have to learn how to be pure in heart, or the corruption of affluence will engulf us. We will even perhaps have to learn how to be persecuted if we are to maintain creatively the kind of tensions which will be necessary if the world is simply not to go to sleep. Tennyson's vision of the time when "the kindly earth shall slumber, lapped in universal law," represents not so much a utopia as a very real danger; and the problem of how to maintain conflict creatively without allowing it to destroy us may be perhaps the most crucial issue facing mankind a thousand years from now.

One of the acute problems which is already beginning to face us is the removal of sanctions for what in the past age has been regarded as sin. Many of the ethical problems of the present period of transition arise out of this. In the developed society or even in the present transitional state, we can already perceive a situation in which we can indulge in lechery without fear of physiological consequences, either in pregnancy or disease; we can indulge in gluttony without getting fat (no-calorie food must be just around the corner) and in drunkenness without getting any hangovers; in avarice without restricting our consumption; in sloth without getting poor; in anger without getting into trouble. There will be no occasion for envy, when everyone can get all he wants; and the whole system, of course, will be able to indulge in pride without even a fall. The fear of earthly consequences, therefore, largely disappears as a motivation towards what has hitherto been regarded as virtue. In the developed society it is the pure heart or nothing.

Ecumenicity and Ecology

Another of the ethical consequences of the spaceship society will be the development of an ethic of extreme conservation to support the material parsimony which we have already seen will be necessary. The historical bases for this are more likely to be found in Eastern religions than in the Judeo-Christian tradition, and it may be precisely at this point that ecumenicity must lead us beyond the stream of history in which we in the West have grown up, and should lead to a genuine dialogue with the religions of South and East Asia. It may be that India, for instance, had to adjust to a highly conservationist economy before the West had to do it, simply because the West was always more expansionist geographically and hence could preserve the illusion of the illimitable plane for a longer period. There is a paradox here, in that the scientific revolution could probably have taken place only in the West, precisely because of the Western expansionism and aggressiveness and the concept of man as the conqueror of nature. The East has never had any illusions about being able to conquer nature, and has always regarded man as living in a somewhat precarious position, as a guest of doubtful welcome, shall we say, in the great household of the natural world.

In the West, our desire to conquer nature often means simply that we diminish the probability of small inconveniences at the cost of increasing the probability of very large disasters. We see this, for instance, in flood control, where the army engineers with their ideology of "conquering" the river actually build up the probability of major disasters, and we see this also in national defense, where we obtain a temporary security at the cost of inevitable long run disaster. Western man, therefore, must learn to live within nature as a member of a great ecological system, and not as a conqueror. Perhaps we can say in the words of St. Paul that we must become "more than conquerors"; man must learn not to enslave the natural order to his own will and his own whims, but to love the natural order and to find his place in it as one member of a great family. This idea, perhaps, is a little uncomfortable in the Judeo-Christian tradition, where God often is set sharply off against nature. Nevertheless, we now live in an age of inevitable contact and cross-fertilization of religious ideas in the whole world, and if we are to move successfully towards a spaceship society, then the Judeo-Christian tradition must learn from the other great tradition of mankind, of South and East Asia, and must learn to develop an ethic of conservation rather than of conquest.

Politics and Economics in the Spaceship Society

The question of what political and economic institutions and practices are most compatible with the spaceship society is a difficult one, to which probably no answer can be found at present. We should beware, for instance, of jumping to the conclusion that the spaceship earth must have a captain, a hierarchical structure, and a highly disciplined crew. This may be all right for a small spaceship or an ocean vessel; it will by no means necessarily be appropriate for a large one with billions of people aboard. . . .

. . . One thing is certain; we are in an age of social invention, just as real and perhaps even more important than mechanical invention. Just as we cannot predict mechanical invention, so we cannot predict social inventions; but it will be surprising if these are not developed, and the appropriate social organization of the spaceship is almost certainly yet to be discovered. It may be neither centrally planned nor a free market economy. It may be neither a conventional democracy nor a dictatorship, but some form of organization beyond all these, which will perhaps take as its goal the maximum amount of individual freedom and creativity which can be attained within the limitations of a socially controlled spaceship society. Within these limitations there may be a considerable number of social forms of organization and behavior available. We should not overlook the fact that a variety of value systems and overall social objectives may also be possible. What is to be rejected is any attempt to identify any particular form of social organization as the only possible one compatible with the spaceship earth.

Religion in the Spaceship Society

The role of religion as distinct from ethics in the spaceship society is a matter of enormous interest, about which we perhaps cannot say very much with confidence. The Marxists, of course, contend that religion will disappear altogether. In their image of the developed society, they regard religion, in terms of this paper, as a phenomenon characteristic of the age of civilization, which will, however, pass away in the communist society of the future, as man reaches full understanding and enlightenment. My own perception of the future is very different from this, even though I do see religion as undergoing profound changes. The Marxists have a certain point in regarding religion in the age of civilization as frequently forming part of the threat system by which a ruling class is able to legitimize and maintain its supremacy. . . . At times, indeed, it has been something of an opiate of the people, enabling them to bear their hard lot and even to legitimize that exploitation on which a preindustrial and prescientific civilization inevitably rests. As, however, the increase of knowledge and technology gradually liberates man from exploitation, the autonomous, prophetic, and mystical role of religion becomes more important, as also does its sociological role in establishing identity and community.

It is particularly striking that in the United States, economic development almost from the founding of the Republic has gone hand in hand with the rise in the popularity and power of organized religion, which was very weak in the late eighteenth century, and has risen to command the allegiance, or at least the membership, of a substantial majority of the population today. Even in the socialist countries, where religion is officially discouraged, it has tended to rise in its internal intensity as its official protection by the state has been removed. The vigor of the Russian Baptists and Orthodox, the Czech Protestants, the Polish Catholics, or the Egyptian Copts, is something which no one would have foreseen a generation ago. It is true that religion is weak in Scandinavia, seems to have been declining in England, and has been perhaps only a little on the increase in France and Germany; however, it is still very much alive in Holland, and even the Common Market is largely a Catholic affair, so that the situation in Western Europe is obscure. In

Japan the vitality of the new religions and of revived Buddhism is quite extraordinary, and even in Islam there seem to be stirrings of renewal. Even though the overall situation, therefore, is hard to assess, we certainly cannot associate the development of and the transition to the developed society with any necessary decline in religion. In fact, the reverse proposition seems to have a good deal of evidence to support it.

The Marxist idea, therefore, that religion is something deliberately cooked up in order to deceive the proletariat into accepting their sad fate, is a theory which does not stand up to examination. . . . Nobody has yet invented a successful religion in which he did not himself believe. Religion in its historical manifestations, that is, has always arisen out of "sacred histories," sets of events which the participants in them themselves have regarded as remarkable and sacred, and which became the symbolic foundations of cultures which have been based on them. . . . It will be extremely surprising if sacred histories do not occur in the future; and it may indeed be that the final movement towards a developed world will be guided by a sacred history yet to come. This is something, however, that we cannot now predict.

The question of what will happen to the old religions, based on sacred histories of the past, is one that we cannot avoid asking, even though we may not be able to give any answers. What seems certain, however, is that the old religions have been changing profoundly under the impact of the great transition, and it would be surprising if they do not change as much in the future. . . .

Human Identity

Deeply involved with all these ultimate problems is a more immediate, practical problem, which might be described as that of developing the human identity. Man cannot live without answering the question, "What am I?" The answers to this question may indeed be various, for one man can play a great many different roles, especially in a complex society. He may say in answer to this question, I am a husband, or a father, or a blacksmith, or a Baptist, or an American. Each of these identities corresponds to certain aspects of his life. Rarely in the present age will he say, "I am a human being"; for the human identity as yet is only latent in mankind. This is mainly because there is no clearly identifiable mode of thought and behavior which is associated with it. If a man says, "I am a father," this means that he concerns himself with his children in innumerable ways. If he says, "I am an American," this means that he votes, concerns himself with political affairs, and so on. If he says, "I am a human being," there is no clear activity which corresponds to this identity, mainly because there is no organizational structure which can express such activity. Every identity has to be embodied in an organization, that of a father and a husband, a wife and a mother, in the family; that of an occupation in an occupational organization such as a firm or a university; that of a citizen in a government. It is only mankind that remains without any protective shell of organization within which the human identity can function. The United Nations is the beginning of this, and it derives a great deal of legitimacy, in spite of its minute size and relative impotence, because it does symbolize, however imperfectly, the human identity. It is this creation of the human identity, however, which is the major problem of the spaceship earth. The crew of a spaceship must identify with the whole enterprise; otherwise there will be a shipwreck.

One of the great obstacles towards the realization of the human identity is the fear that taking on the human identity will destroy our other identities, especially our national and religious identities. This fear is only valid if the other identities demand unconditional loyalty. If we demand unconditional loyalty to our family, we obviously cannot have a wholly satisfactory identity as a citizen, for the larger identity may occasionally demand sacrifice of the smaller. Similarly, if we are to establish the human identity, we must abandon unconditional loyalty either to the national or to the religious identity. This does not mean, however, that we give up these identities; rather does it mean that we redeem them in the promise of the larger and the truer identity. This act of redemption, both of nationalism and of religion, may not be easy. It is, however, an act of redemption and not of destruction. As Jesus himself says, "I come not to destroy but to fulfill"; and the larger identity does not destroy but fulfills the lesser identity. An unconditional loyalty, either to the family or the church or the nation, will in the long run destroy even that to which we are committed. The Christian Church has always maintained that the only unconditional loyalty, either to the family or the church or the nation, will in the long run destroy even that to which we are committed. The Christian Church has always maintained that the only unconditional loyalty was to God himself. This is a doctrine which must be continually refreshed, reinterpreted, and rediscovered; and it is one of utmost importance for mankind in the critical days which lie ahead.

What this means in practice, both in our identity as citizens of a nation and as members of a Church, is that we are going to have to learn to be particular and to abandon our claims for universality. No nation, no church, and no ideology is going to conquer the earth. Each nation and each church is going to have to learn to live as something particular in the midst of a larger universe. Jesus may indeed "reign where'er the sun doth his successive journeys run," but he will reign only in the hearts of those whom he has called, and they will have neither the right nor the will to impose his reign on others. As imperialism is being abandoned in the national sphere, so that each nation will reign only over its home territory, so we must come to the abandonment of imperialism in the religious sphere too. This does not mean the end of missionary effort, nor the end of proclaiming the gospel. It must be proclaimed, however, in a way that says, "He that hath ears to hear, let him hear." In these days even the Roman Catholic Church has had to come to terms with the fact that it is indeed a sect, however large and powerful; and it is preparing for peaceful coexistence, even with the secular religion of Communism. Many Protestants, oddly enough, are far behind the Roman Church in their recognition, however unpalatable the fact may be, of this necessity of the twentieth century. Americans are still less ready to recognize their particularity and "smallness"; the grandiose illusions of being not only "a" but "the" great power are still luring them on to destruction, and at the moment in regard to Viet-Nam, they seem to be seized by a national madness and paranoid delusions of grandeur. . . .

Michael Harrington

The Crisis of Belief and Disbelief

After God died, Man, who was supposed to replace Him, grew sick of himself. This resulted in a crisis of belief and disbelief which made the twentieth century spiritually empty. . . .

I

It was in the nineteenth century that Western man felt, for the first time, the fear of his own power. Out of this mood there came one of

Reprinted with permission of The Macmillan Company from *The Accidental Century* by Michael Harrington. Copyright © Michael Harrington, 1965.

Michael Harrington is Chairman of the Board of the League for Industrial Democracy and an advisor to the government on problems of poverty and unemployment.

the strangest, yet most persistent, definitions of modern society as a spiritual decline: the idea that bread for all is a decadence.

The world of democracy, science, and technology, it was and is still said, must be thin and shallow. In it, men will lose contact with their own depths. The sense of tragedy will vanish, the highest values will smother under the weight of material satisfaction. Ultimately, all this mindlessness, this ignoring of the irrepressible irrationalities of life, will lead to a disaster. Gradual progress prepares an apocalypse.

This theory has profound roots in Western culture. For thousands of years, the exile from the Garden of Eden was a basic certitude. It was written in the divine order of the theologians and the natural order of the philosophers. It was shocking when, with the development of the industrial revolution, there appeared the possibility of abolishing the sweat of the laborer's brow. The reformers and revolutionists set off in search of the New Eden. But others thundered against the blasphemy of ending economic misery.

The greatest among the latter were Nietzsche and Dostoevsky.

The intellectual convergence of the nihilist and the mystic is curious in itself. They saw the same moral rot and predicted the same disaster for opposite reasons. The one feared that the future would be hostile to antifaith, the other to faith, yet they agreed on what was wrong with the present. Basically, what their contradictions shared was the sociology of Adam and Eve, the conviction that social unhappiness is inherent in man. Dostoevsky found the suffering of the people holy unto their salvation, Nietzsche regarded it as necessary for the freedom of the few.

The wars, revolutions, and totalitarianisms since their death have made Nietzsche and Dostoevsky prophets with honor. The nihilist is quoted approvingly by theologians, the impassioned antisocialist is cited in self-criticism by reformers and revolutionists. The times seem to have confirmed the terrible dialectic each, in his utterly different way, announced: that the quest for bread for all would end either in spiritual banality, political slavery, bloody destruction, or all three.

Yet, if one takes Nietzsche and Dostoevsky seriously, as thinkers rather than as fortune-tellers of history, they were in part prophets by accident—and an accident they tragically helped to create. They were right when they saw a potential of vacuousness and violence in the emerging industrial civilization. They were wrong in deducing this doom from inexorable principles, and, above all, they did not see the actual alternatives to it right in front of their own visionary faces. As a result, they mistook a choice for a fate and helped men make the worst decision by convincing them that it was the only one. . . .

It would be hard to imagine two geniuses who disagreed more

fundamentally than Dostoevsky and Nietzsche. The novelist believed in a messianic vision of a Russian Christ; the philosopher rejected all final causes, proclaiming the struggle of "Dionysius against the Crucified," insisting that reality was its own, and only, justification for being. Dostoevsky was antisocialist because "socialism is above all the question of atheism, its contemporary incarnation; it is the question of the Tower of Babel built without God, not in order to reach the heavens from earth, but to pull the heavens down to earth." Nietzsche was antisocialist because socialism was a disguised form of Christian sentimentality, an incomplete nihilism which did not have the courage to break from religious traditions.

So it was that the nihilist and the mystic predicted the coming of totalitarianism for almost exactly opposite reasons. . . .

For [Dostoevsky], the atheist, utilitarian world sets no limits on human action. It had dismantled morality in the name of freedom, but this emancipation made everything licit, including the destruction of freedom. The individual, defined by Christianity as a unique and irreducible soul, was thus transformed into a means to an end. And, Dostoevsky concluded, the holiness of life could only be guaranteed by recognizing a God who was above it.

For Nietzsche, the tragedy was that man was afraid to live without rules of any kind. Having killed God, he continues to act religiously. "The malignant powers," he wrote, "were brought together in the Middle Ages by the Church and through the brute power which it exercised they were, partially at least, assimilated to one another. As this binding broke, as the religious authority disappeared, the powers revolted against one another: . . . And now, the state in the hands of the militarists seeks . . . to organize all things out of itself . . . that is, it wants men to serve it as God, even as the Church did." The holiness of life, Nietzsche concluded, can be guaranteed only if it is recognized that there is nothing above it, neither God, nor the Prussian state, nor socialism. . . .

Nietzsche despaired because the emerging society would place limits upon man, Dostoevsky because it would not. They were irreconcilably divided over the ultimate meaning of the world, yet they had the same intuition of its present meaninglessness. Why?

There is a clue to the resolution of this paradox in an important fact. Both called their completely different versions of what would be wrong with the future by the same name: socialism. Beneath their theoretical conflict, there was a practical agreement that the movements that sought to solve the problem of bread were contradicting the nature of man. Dostoevsky was against them because they violated the supernatural order of grace, Nietzsche because they flaunted the natural order of inequality. For both, the idea of a democratic abundance was an impiety, in the one case against God, in the other against the superman. This analysis illuminated and it blinded. With their dogmatic pessimism, Dostoevsky and Nietzsche could see through the dogmatic optimism of their opponents. As history turned out, theirs was by far the more profound and creative error to make. And yet, for all their psychological acumen, they ultimately derived their predictions from abstractions about man as much as from the men and women before them. They affirmed human unhappiness a priori, as if nothing had changed since the Gates of Eden. These visionaries looked deeply into the next generation's fate; only they ignored the possibilities of their own age. . . .

The prophet did not see deeply into his own age; he mistook a historical moment for a natural law. Nietzsche completely discounted both the human and technical capacity for emancipation in the society which he criticized. As a result, he simplified the future into its catastrophic component, seeing only the stultifying, destructive possibilities in democracy, technology, and science. Most of the liberating potential that Nietzsche ignored never became reality, and this makes him seem right in his predictions. But one of the reasons it was not energized was Friedrich Nietzsche. He made deep deductions from a half-truth which, as they entered into Western history, helped to make his pessimism come true.

Dostoevsky the novelist; Dostoevsky the psychologist of the underground man; Dostoevsky the existentialist poet who understood that bugs and flies always attend moments of high human drama: the greatness of these Dostoevskys is not in question. But Dostoevsky the mystical sociologist who argued that it is what men believe that shapes their economy and society is something else again.

He said that man without God would build a tragic civilization with false idols of science and social progress. But who, then, was this God whose disappearance would be so disastrous? For Dostoevsky, He was Russian peasant society. In the holy of holies of his theological determinism there was, not divinity, but an idealized agricultural order. And in the final analysis, Dostoevsky, the passionate believer, lacked faith. His God could not survive in a modern city.

Dostoevsky set bread against freedom. Western Christianity, liberalism, and socialism, he said, had fallen into a terrible heresy, that of the third temptation of Christ, the conviction that God reveals Himself in an earthly kingdom. And yet, that is exactly the temptation to which Dostoevsky himself succumbed. The God in whose name he anathematized the earthly kingdom to come was Himself the earthly kingdom of the past. . . .

And finally, taking Dostoevsky and Nietzsche together, a strange paradox is revealed. The believer exacerbated the crisis of faith, for it was a Dostoevskian defeatism and identification of God with the social order of the past which caused the churches (particularly in Europe) to lose so much of their hold upon the people, which made God so uncomfortable in the cities of the twentieth century. And the atheist abetted the crisis of antifaith, for his rejection of democratic humanism led, not to the superman, but to the pseudo-religions of barbarian elites, to the metaphysical cults of totalitarianism.

II

The fear of abundance, the conviction that bread for all is a spiritual decadence, persists to this day. Dostoevsky and Nietzsche had a vast intellectual progeny.

Yet, the mystic and the nihilist were necessarily and inevitably misinterpreted. More often than not, they became the patron saints of their enemies. They had proposed impossibilities—the rule of sensitive dictators, the reign of peasant values in the modern world. Once the crisis they announced burst out of men's minds and into the streets, their reactionary utopias were seen as the irrelevancies they were. What remained was their opposition to democracy and socialism. And this inspired both an armed and passive reading of their words.

The point here is not a scholarly critique of Dostoevsky's and Nietzsche's exegetes. Rather, it is to show how history discriminated among their ideas, choosing the negative, discarding the positive. The Russian's old faith and the German's new atheism rejected the only alternative to the catastrophe they predicted: that man, whether inspired by God or his own values, would order his world. Events took ironic vengeance upon their error. . . .

III

Nietzsche and Dostoevsky had asked if society could survive if it believed in the wrong theory. In the twentieth century, a more fearful issue was put. Could society survive if it believed in nothing?

Religion sought its answer. By far and large it took the death of God as a fact. So it was in France, once called the eldest daughter of the Church, Catholics began to speak of their land as a "mission" country. In Protestantism, there was a social gospel which tried to adapt the traditional faith to the new environment. But, more significant, there were the despairing responses. In some cases, God remained only as a symbol (Tillich said that God "is what you take seriously without any reservation," a description that would have struck most premodern Christians as atheistic). In other cases, there was a neo-orthodoxy with its emphasis on original sin and the limitations of man as a reaction to the failures of liberal religion and politics. In almost every instance, the argument for the deity had become Pascalian: He is because He is not apparent, He is *Deus Absconditus*. As the theologian Dietrich Bonhoeffer wrote, "Man has learned to cope with all questions of importance without recourse to God as a working hypothesis."

But this crisis of religion had been anticipated. What came as a surprise was the emergence of a tragic sociology. It developed from within the tradition that held that man could order his own world and thus dispense with a need for God. Now, rationalists announced that reason was becoming irrational. They did not do so as a deduction from philosophic premises, but from an examination of historic experience.

Max Weber was one of the first to formulate this fear analytically. The modern world, he argued, was characterized by a continuous growth in "functional" rationality. In government, in industry, in every aspect of life, scientific principles of organization were becoming more and more dominant. But, at the same time, "substantive" rationality, life as a meaningful experience for individual human beings, as an explicable totality, was on the decline. Technology would progressively bureaucratize and bureaucratize, and in this context it made little difference whether a socialist order would succeed capitalism. The future, under any guise, would be more oppressive and hostile to freedom than the past.

"The fate of our times," Weber wrote, "is characterized by rationalization and intellectualism and, above all, by the 'disenchantment of the world.' Precisely the most ultimate and sublime values have retreated from public life either into the transcendental realm of mystic life or into the brotherliness of direct and personal human relations . . . Today only within the smallest and most intimate circles, in personal situations, in pianissimo, that something is pulsating that corresponds to the prophetic pneuma, which in former times swept through great communities, welding them together."

Weber was a liberal democrat. Karl Mannheim, whose roots were in the socialist tradition, carried his thought to a further irony. For the first time in history, Mannheim said, man stood in danger of losing his utopian vision, his horizon. And, strangely, this was because utopia had moved so much closer to realization and thus become, not a matter of dreaming, but of practical action and compromise. As Mannheim summarized this development:

"The disappearance of utopia brings about a state of affairs in which man himself becomes no more than a thing. We could then be faced with the greatest paradox imaginable, namely, that man, who has achieved the highest degree of rational mastery of existence, left without any ideals, becomes a mere creature of impulses. Thus, after a long, tortuous, but heroic development, just at the highest stage of awareness when history is ceasing to be a blind fate, and is becoming more and more man's creation, with the relinquishment of utopia, man would lose his will to shape history and therewith his ability to understand it."

These theories are aspects of the crisis of disbelief. They do not come from the conservative or religious tradition that thought it unnatural or blasphemous for man to make himself the highest value. They reflect, rather, the liberal and socialist traditions seen from the vantage point of spirituality. They predict, not simply the political and economic consequences of the failure of the party of the poor, but the attendant moral and ethical desolation as well. In a way, they are modern, and empirical, Greek tragedies in which man's assertion of his freedom is simultaneously the working out of a terrible fate.

There were two main ways in which the first half of the century seemed to confirm these fears. In two world wars, on the one hand, the most sophisticated techniques were put to barbarous uses without ethical restraint; and, on the other, peace and prosperity appeared to many as barren, meaningless accomplishments. . . .

For now, there is the crisis of belief and disbelief. The simultaneous undermining of confidence in the two Western ideals of man was parallel to, and related to, the decline of both the capitalist and socialist ideologies. So there is a massive intersection of uncertainties, a time of interregnum, of indeterminacy.

IV

T.S. Eliot once expressed the unique aspect of the contemporary plight. He wrote:

> But it seems that something is happening that never
>   happened before . . .
> Men have left GOD not for other gods, they say, but
>   for no god; and this has never happened before.

As a Christian, Eliot was speaking of a transition from faith to atheism. But the change was even more basic than he imagined.

"God," Nietzsche had said, "is my word for the ideal." The death of the divinity was not to be simply the passing of an ancient religious hero. It was to mark the end of all metaphysics, final purposes, and higher values. Nietzsche thought that a few stoic aristocrats would rejoice in this new, and unrelieved, imminence of the world. He did not understand that the denial of all ideals demanded an intolerable idealism and that a general loss of conviction would therefore peril his antifaith along with the other faiths. He was, as usual, more adept at anticipating the future than in proposing ways to cope with it. Now, Nietzsche's theoretical error has become a problem of Western daily life. The gods and utopias have, temporarily at least, lost their practical meaning to society (faith and antifaith survive, of course, as professed ideas but less and less as cultural forces). If man's purpose is not to be found either in heaven or on earth, does it exist?

So far, this question has been posed under conditions of relative internal stability in the West. The failure of the central visions did not become apparent until after World War II (the socialist prophecy was battered, but intact and whole, until then). It therefore coincided with a sort of prosperity, evoking personal bewilderment rather than mass desperation. But in the crises to come it is possible that the vacuum of values would drive people toward some fabricated, and fanatic, pseudo-faith. This has already happened, for example, in Germany in the thirties. It could happen again.

To avoid this, one must propose a most curious convergence: the united front of atheism and religion.

Religion has lost the discipline, solidarity, and awe of primitive hunger. Short of nuclear catastrophe, it will probably never again build upon such necessities, and in a technological time it cannot possibly construct itself as a mystery cult. The inexplicable natural events which God once made supernaturally reasonable are now scientifically explicable. Either religion will constitute itself as the expression of a higher anguish or else it will have less and less relevance to the future. This, however, is more easily said than done. For if religion is Dostoevskian, if it sees a spiritual leveling down as the only consequence of abundance and is therefore hostile or indifferent to the social task of mastering technology, it has signed its death warrant. The exaltation of man is not a blasphemy against religion, it is religion's only hope. Rootless city people trapped in a sterile, routine, yet perplexing, world will lack both the motive of hunger and that of freedom. They will thus exist in between any need for God.

Atheistic humanism has much the same problem as religion.

The secular tradition has long understood that it did not simply and vindictively seek the death of God but the birth of man as well. The objection to religion was that it mystified the natural. But if the natural, or more precisely the man-made, turns into a mystery, the line of succession is broken. Man can hardly make himself his highest value when he feels himself problematic. He will vegetate as long as that is permitted; he will turn to new irrationalities in time of crisis.

If Weber's deepest pessimism is right—if there is to be an utterly naturalistic world, engineered by man but inexplicable to him as any kind of a meaningful whole—there will probably be an end to faith and anti-faith, at least as the West has defined them. There could be bureaucratic cults, as under Stalin, but that would still mean the death of the Western tradition in all of its variants. The problem of both religion and atheistic humanism is the same: that a puzzled society without hunger or freedom has no need for higher values of any kind. So, in this crisis of belief and disbelief, the antagonism between faith and antifaith is less important than their common challenge: the construction of a world in which the debate between them will be meaningful, in which man chooses between God or himself—and chooses freely.

Barbara Ward
Am I My Brother's Keeper?

. . . One of the consequences of the kind of industrialism and technological change we have experienced in the last hundred years has been to create what is in very truth a *unified* world economy. The industrial powers around the North Atlantic, the rich white nations of the North Atlantic arena, are so far the only nations to make the full break-through to the modern affluent economy—though Japan is close behind, and Russia is coming up. This group of nations have almost by hazard created a world economy in which the impact of the chocolate milkshake drinkers of Manhattan on the cocoa farmers of Ghana is pretty complete. This inner industrial core of wealthy nations has gone out to look for its

Reprinted from *Christianity Amid Rising Men and Nations* (1965), edited by Creghton Lacy. By permission of the publisher, Association Press.

Barbara Ward is Assistant Editor and Foreign Affairs Editor for the *Economist* (London).

raw materials, to bring them back to be fed into the industrial structure of the Atlantic, and in return has sent back manufactures—largely of consumer goods—to satisfy demand in local markets. This movement has made up a sort of systole and diastole of an economy which moves as one all around the world, sometimes shakily, sometimes poorly, but undoubtedly as a single world system.

Now this world economy suffers from a very considerable degree of imbalance—another factor of which, I think, we are insufficiently aware. The Bible of course reminds us that "to him who hath shall be given," and nowhere is this more true than in the uncontrolled, unregulated market economy. If you are rich to begin with, the chances are that you will have every opportunity to get richer still. This tendency is certainly operating at the world level. If you look at the circulation of trade between the wealthy, developed, industrialized Atlantic nations and the great penumbra of developing states—in Asia, in Africa, in Latin America—you will discover again and again that trade tends to serve the interests of the rich nations and to discriminate against the poor. . . .

Every single Western tariff is so arranged that it discourages the growth of manufacturing and processing in underdeveloped countries. The rule is zero tariffs or low tariffs on raw materials; higher tariffs on semi-manufactured goods; full tariffs on manufactures; and then if some of these poor little manufactures manage to creep in, on goes a quota, to make absolutely certain that they are kept out. Again in the field of raw materials, prices tend to instability. Over the last ten years, for instance, in Latin America the entire import of private investment and of public capital has been offset by the fall in primary prices. In fact, there has been a negative outflow of funds over these ten years. In primary prices in general, there was a thirty per cent movement in the terms of trade against the poor countries between 1951 and 1961. Or let us look at the way in which trade is organized. Most gains made by intermediaries—in shipping, in insurance, in much of the marketing as well—tend to remain in the hands of the developed countries.

These are just a few examples of the way in which the world economy has an unconscious bias against the developing world—and does so in a genuinely unified economy with interdependent functions and with a decision-making process, usually carried on in the main cities of the Western world, that can vitally affect economic trends everywhere else. In short, there is interdependence in the world market, even if it is no more than the interdependence of a brute economic kind which occurs when nations impinge upon each other in pursuit of their own interests. There is therefore a priori a case for asking whether some higher form of interdependence, one with some smell of humanity about it, may not be in order.

In technology, in communication, in transportation, in the world market, unity is a fact. How much more our unity is underlined by the possibility of annihilation. Once a neighbor can lob a bomb over your back fence, he is a neighbor whether you like it or not. This is the position in our world. We have, all of us, the possibility of seeing the annihilation of the entire human species. And I sometimes wish, I must confess, that in our modern world it were possible for more people than the astronauts to go up and see this little planet in proper perspective. Think of those men swinging around and living through seven or eight dawns and dusks within twenty-four hours and seeing our planet as it really is—with its tiny envelope of soul, on which all our nourishment depends, and its tiny envelope of atmosphere, through which alone we breathe. I wonder if they reflect that in all the vastness of interstellar space, this planet is all there is to support human existence. It is unimaginable to me that anyone, having seen it thus, should want to destroy it, to blow to smithereens the only center of sentient life in the entire universe. Vulnerable, tiny, unique, infinitely valuable—this is how we must see our planet; this is the kind of insight we need if we are ever to realize our total mutual interdependence against the possibility of destruction.

These, then, are the inescapable unities that now underlie the community of mankind. The concept of the brotherhood of man under the fatherhood of God has of course been a part of Christian belief since its origins. We inherited the faith from the Jewish belief in a single God of the universe and from the universal reason beloved of the Greeks. But the concept of a single humanity could not be realized until our own time, because the means of communication were largely lacking. The most significant change of our time is that the *physical* unity is now a fact. But the economic, military, and technological energies have advanced far beyond our humane, constitutional, and political energies. We have a community that is real in its risks and not yet real in its obligations. This is a wholly new situation, springing from the technological and scientific changes that have compelled us to be unified. We may have dreamt about unity and talked about brotherhood. Now suddenly we are confronted with their physical preconditions—and very disconcerting we find it. We Christians are apparently no more alive to the fact of brotherhood, no more conscious of the common humanity of this entire terrestrial family, than those who have never heard of Christ. . . .

The second consequence of our scientific revolution is, if anything, even more astonishing than physical unity. This is the liberation of physical resources. Until the day before yesterday, the amount that could be done for your neighbor, whatever his misery, was severely limited because, broadly speaking, the limits were always fixed by the size of the harvest. There was only just so much food to go around. If the pressure of population went beyond that point, then people starved. It did not even help much if your neighbor had a good harvest. As long as your transportation was an oxcart, the ox ate as much as he transported, and there was not much left at the end of his day's march. These were the strict physical limitations on charity. You could do a little for the man at the gate, but very little for the man three towns away. These limiting factors upon the concept of charity were, if you like, very like the limiting factors on the concept of brotherhood. You might accept in theory the brotherhood of man; you might accept in theory your duty to your neighbor. In physical fact, it was difficult to realize the one or practice the other.

Now, in the last few decades, the old implacable limitation has been raised. I would implore you to consider just briefly the abundance that is beginning to pour out of our scientific and technologically sophisticated economies. The facts are so startling that we are only just beginning to grasp their scope. At the core of it all stands, naturally, the American farmer. Every time he cuts down his acreage, he puts on more fertilizer and produces twice as much on half the land. This in turn comes up against the technologically unimprovable Western stomach, which refuses to increase its capacity. The result is the piling up of surpluses. The wheat surplus may be the most notorious, but there are others. . . .

What do we do about all this potential increase in supplies? Oversupply in a market system does not resolve itself. Our Western market system has vital characteristics of flexibility and diversity, of productivity, of attention to detail, of the search for profit as a discipline and as the means of making a genuine margin for reinvestment. All these advantages have helped to give us the vast productivity I have described. But the market system has had from the beginning—as Marx, incidentally, foresaw—the problem of keeping demand in step with supply. The first of Marx's prophetic books was, of course, *The Communist Manifesto*. In it, in burning language, he states that the West's so-called Christian society is based upon the exploitation of man by man. Because of this exploitation, the poor will never earn enough to become a market for the system's colossal new outpourings of industrial goods. On the contrary, they will grow poorer; and the system will break down under the weight of what will be called excessive production, but what will in fact be underconsumption.

Do not let us underestimate Marx. He was the first political economist to see that the coming of the industrial revolution, based on the accumulation of the capital applied to technology, would radically remake the face of the earth. He also saw, with outrage, the first stages of primitive accumulation in Britain, carried on in large measure at the expense of the poor. His mistake was to feel that nothing could be done about it. Given the class and political structure of those early bourgeois economies, he believed the poor would go on getting poorer and the rich richer until the final explosion came. He said there would never be enough demand to absorb the new goods, because the workers would never be paid more than a subsistence wage. Therefore they could never become an adequate or expanding market. Supply would pile up—demand would fail. The system would cease to work.

We know that he was proved wrong. The constitutional traditions of European society opened up the vote and the possibility of political action to the workers. They were no longer helpless pawns. At the same time, Christian conscience simply said that even if this degree of exploitation was, as some maintained, essential to the economic system, it would have to stop. These two forces—Christian conscience and liberal constitutionalism—operating in our Western society did, in fact, little by little raise up the mass of the working people. They could organize trade unions and form political lobbies. Their own pressure was added to the conscience of the rich. They secured better wages and a larger share of effective demand. And distributive justice in the shape of progressive taxation added to their opportunities. The hopeless proletarian of the 1860's became bit by bit the fine, upstanding consumer of today. The Marxian prophecy—that demand would never rise to meet the new vast sources of supply—was defeated *within* domestic society.

But when we turn to our present problems of supply, to the new vast ourpouring of wealth and surpluses, we have to see that in our world economy we have not yet acted in any comparable way to build up demand. The enfranchisement of the mass consumer which we were able to achieve within the domestic economy is still a great unfinished business in the world at large. There, in fact, the Marxist prophecy has reappeared. The poor nations grow poorer, while the rich grow wealthier still. The analogy is quite relevant. The conditions of trade which I have described discriminate against primary producers. They cannot earn enough from the work they do for us, in producing primary products, to develop their own capital and technological apparatus. These disadvantages put them in something of the same category as the workers of the 1840's and 1850's in Western domestic society, who could never earn any surplus by their toil and had to see all the gains of productivity drained off to the owners and managers of the new middle class. The proletarians of that time, like the developing countries today, were not able, owing to the functioning of the market, to get their hands on enough purchasing power to become an effective factor in expanding demand.

I think the analogy can be pressed further. One reason that the masses procured a better share of the products of their work was that their own powers of association and self-defense were acceptable to the constitutional tradition of the Western world. Today do we not see something comparable in the emerging part played by the developing world within the United Nations? We talk about "power blocs" and mutter about irresponsible Afro-Asians in our worried way. But in point of fact may we not be seeing something comparable to the earlier creation of useful, necessary, countervailing power within our domestic Western society? Indeed, may not the conference on Trade and Development at Geneva, where trade is being discussed from the point of view of the developing nations, be a very salutary reminder that two-thirds of the human race do not fully profit by the economic system under which they live, that they are beginning to notice the fact and beginning to concert together the policies they need to reverse the disadvantage? This I regard as entirely healthy for the world economy. It is a trend the rich nations should welcome, encourage, and above all actively follow up.

The second great factor in the nineteenth-century transformation of the proletarian into the consumer was the better organization of the internal market. This I have already mentioned, but I would like to add one of the key figures in the revolution—Henry Ford. He realized that if you paid a worker five dollars a day, he might actually buy the car he was producing. If, in the developing world, we can contrive means by which the developing nations can, in the world exchange of goods, earn a better return, they in turn will provide more effective demand for the goods the West can produce. If the Henry Ford analogy can be somewhat expanded, you can say that if we in the West make efforts to put a floor under raw material prices and, through various measures of countervailing finance organized through the International Monetary Fund, put more consuming power at the poor nations' disposal, we shall have given them wider access to the world market—rather as Henry Ford expanded domestic demand, once he had seen that his workers were also his customers.

The third aspect of the analogy concerns, not the organization of trade, but transfers of wealth from rich to poor. Once again, I think, the analogy holds good. It was a combination of constitutional tradition and Christian conscience that compelled statesmen, toward the end of the nineteenth century, to accept the fact that there *is* a mutual obligation between rich and poor and that progressive taxation is a justifiable and useful way of seeing that some of the surplus of the rich is spent upon increasing the opportunities of the poor. I stress this word *opportunities*. The transfer was not a dole. It was not a handout. The transfer went into education, into trade schools; it went into hospitals and better housing. It went into the improvement of factories and cities, in which, although heaven knows they were not perfect, people could work and live with some self-respect. These new opportunities led to the emergence of a skilled working class and to a ladder of mobility and social opportunity. It was, in short, a creative transfer of wealth, and it began to change the exploitative jungle into some semblance of a humane order.

Again, if this analogy is correct, it provides the rationale for foreign aid. Let us for the moment accept the yardstick of one per cent of national income—in fact, only France is achieving it at this time. If this transfer of wealth is devoted to the creation of opportunity, to the building up of skills, to educational programs, to the transformation of agriculture through extension services, to the beginnings of local processing and manufacturing—in other words, into all the creative possibilities of an expanding economy—then it is possible that it will repeat in our international society the civilizing and humane advance that followed from the adoption of income tax within our domestic economy.

Sometimes, I confess, when I hear people talking about economic assistance and the developing world, I am struck more and more forcibly by the resemblance between the two periods—the earlier, domestic phase and the wider world today. It appears to be one of the unattractive features of the rich that they seem unable not to despise the poor. . . . There is hardly a criticism made now about developing societies which was not used in the nineteenth century against the poor. And part of the reason is this bias, this inability of those who are already rich, competent, skilled, intelligent, not to feel in some way that all this is due to their own superior efforts and that therefore other people have failed in the human scale.

Domestic experience shows that if society gives them the opportunity, the education, and the background to develop all their inherent skills, from being miserable proletarians they quietly turn into fine, upstanding consumers. . . .

A world that is one in physical, but not in moral, fact; a world that combines unheard-of abundance with deepening poverty; a world rushing headlong into an urban way of life which already bears threatening marks of deterioration—this is the world that confronts the Christian conscience today and lays all Christians under an inescapable obligation to act.

But how? The short answer is, of course, to turn the abundance into a working tool for the attack on misery and ignorance and urban blight, and to build up a world-wide order with some of the essential underpinnings of solidarity and justice. But the long answer, of detailed work and sustained dedication, has many obstacles to overcome. The first is perhaps to persuade our wealthy societies to accept the fact of affluence. Take America, for instance. Some of your leading businessmen and retired statesmen and elderly senators all too often argue that you are heading for bankruptcy. This is a very odd assumption. To give you one or two examples: The figure today for the savings of the American people has reached one thousand billion dollars—a trillion! This does not sound much like bankruptcy to me. Take another factor, the celebrated drain on gold. A large part of the drain in the last three years has not followed from foreign aid or even military expenditure. It has followed the determination of American businessmen to invest overseas. Excellent —and what happens as a result of investing overseas? A very large flow of resources will return in due season to the United States. How can a country with something like sixty to seventy billion dollars worth of investment overseas talk of bankruptcy?

It is essential for the citizen to get some sense of the abundance that is available. Resources are physical resources, brought together by human intelligence and transformed into utility by machines and human skills. These are the realities underlying the dollars and cents. Owing to the fabulous productivity of modern technology, resources—except in the shortest run—can, in a country as wealthy as America, pretty well be expanded to meet any desirable end. The short run includes the expansion of capacity and the training of new labor. It is true that, without some restraint on short-run demand, it can run ahead of capacity and of employable men, and thus cause pressure on existing resources and hence inflation. But the resources can be quickly expanded, the new men trained, and then the economy proceeds at new levels of abundance. The crucial point is, as we have said, to keep demand expanding. As U Thant once said: "It is no longer resources that limit imagination; it is imagination that limits resources."

Our current economy underlines these facts. The combination of intelligence, capital, and technology now at work in the Western world makes it possible for the nations to spend *eighty billion dollars* a year on arms and still have the national income go up by three to four per cent a year. In 1963–64, America is adding about thirty billion dollars to its national income. If it devoted one per cent of national income to aid and two per cent to the domestic war on poverty, there would still be some fifteen billion dollars for extra consumption at home. Resources will remain abundant. Materials are backed by the immense powers of substitution in the chemical industry. Water will flow from desalinization. Existing energy leads on to atomic energy, to solar energy, to energy from the tides. Labor abounds in a rising birth rate and in the job-reducing tendencies of automation. No, nothing is scarce except imagination.

We have no right, under these conditions, to talk of bankruptcy. We have no right to disguise to ourselves the fact that we are enormously rich. . . . Today when we confront the naked and homeless, the hungry and the sick, all the old alibis are gone—all the old limitations have vanished. We confront a stark moral issue. The resources to act are available; the need for action is obvious. What shall we do?

The need can be expressed in an infinite variety of ways. The need for education, the possibility of building beautiful and creative cities, the possibility of transforming agriculture and building up industry, the introduction of education that gives humane and scientific skills—there is an enormous, exciting range of potential action. We are not talking of doles or handouts. The issue is the creation of a world of opportunity, of repeating in our unified world the successful transformations of our own society. The process will not be quick. There is a century of work ahead. But it can be done—if we will do it. And so we come back to this greatest of all problems facing the Christian conscience. Where are the energies for the task? Where can we mobilize them? Will Christians be in the forefront of the effort? Or has the salt lost its savor after all? It is not so much a question of looking for the answers. It is a question of mobilizing the means and the will to use them, of providing sustained dedication to the task. . . .

This is not the end. Man's destiny is greater than he knows. In a world without much faith in any ultimate vision, it may be the overwhelming duty of Christians to renew a genuine gospel of good tidings. They must proclaim that man is still near the beginning of his evolution. Nothing we can foresee is as strange as what has already occurred. From-amoeba-to-man staggers our imagination. Why should we suppose the future any less stupendous? Christ, as the second Adam, is the firstborn of a new kind of man—still no doubt as rare as *homo faber* in earlier days, but destined to introduce a new humanity and to recreate the face of the earth. In physical terms, man with his Godlike reason has already created some of the physical means of this renewal. What is needed now are the energy and moral vision to set the resources to work. It would be the grossest possible Christian betrayal to give up our whole millennial, messianic tradition at a time when so many messianic possibilities are at hand. . . .

Where are our voices of anger and compassion, raised in outrage that we can spend on chewing gum and cosmetics what would educate half a continent? If we cannot feel in our bones some of that rage and some of that compassion, then the energies will die from Western society and we shall be left holding a tool which is too heavy for us to lift. We shall have created a technology so vast that it will overwhelm us. We shall have created an abundance so unprecedented that it will swamp and sweep us away. Only if we use the energies of our prophetic tradition to mobilize our vast wealth for the redemption of the world—only then will it not crush us, suffocate us, blind us, and make us dead at heart. . . .

Pope John XXIII

Pacem in Terris

Peace demands order; science and technology reveal the marvelous order in living and inanimate nature, and God's greatness as Creator of all things.

Order among men seems difficult to achieve without force, yet it is a postulate of man's conscience. It is erroneous to hold that order among men can be had by the laws governing the irrational universe. God's laws, written in man's nature, govern human relations, including those of a world community.

I: Order Among Men (8–45)

Well-ordered society rests on recognition of man's dignity as a human being having intelligence and free will, and thus as a person having rights and duties of his own which are universal, inviolable and inalienable; man also has a divinely revealed supernatural dignity.

RIGHTS. Man has a right, first, to life, bodily integrity and the basic necessities for subsistence and economic security; to reputation and to free inquiry and exchange of opinions, and to truth about public affairs; to education and training for his role in society and to advancement on merit.

Man also has a right to worship God publicly and privately according to the dictates of conscience; to choose his own state of life; in

Reprinted with permission from *Pacem in Terris* (The America Press, The National Catholic Weekly Review, 106 W. 56 St., New York, N.Y. 10019.) By permission of the publisher. © 1963 America Press, Inc.

The "Summary" from the Encyclical Letter, *Pacem in Terris*. Numbers in the text refer to passages within the Encyclical.

145

marriage, to be aided in maintaining the family as the essential cell of society; to have prior right in educating his children. Man's economic rights include free initiative and the right to a job; also, decent working conditions, with special consideration for the young and for women. Human dignity also demands a sharing in responsibility and a decent family wage. Private property is a natural right, but one having an inherent social aspect.

Man's social nature founds his right to freedom of assembly and of association in groups freely chosen and organized. A variety of such intermediate groups in a society guarantees human dignity and safeguards freedom.

Man has a right to move and dwell where he will, for just reasons. Politically, he has a right to participate in public affairs, and a right to due process and fair play.

DUTIES. Natural rights are linked with duties in the one person. Thus, the right to life involves the duty to preserve it, etc. Reciprocity of rights and duties also exists in society; one cannot demand respect for rights from others without admitting one's duties to them. Man's social nature demands collaboration based on mutual respect for rights and duties along with contributions to the common good. Thus, another's right to subsist means a duty to insure that he has enough food, and society must be organized to secure abundance for all through co-operative effort.

Human dignity also requires the exercise of initiative and responsibility in a society that is free from coercion and inhuman repressions. A sound political society will rest on truth when reciprocal rights and duties are recognized in it. Its citizens will be guided by justice, motivated by charity and organized in freedom. Human society must concern itself with securing and promoting spiritual values, which will influence all its social and cultural institutions. The social order must be a moral one, having principles which are universal, absolute and unchangeable, with God as its ultimate source.

THE CONTEMPORARY SCENE. Our age has three characteristics. First is the improved role and status of the worker; second is the greater equality of women in public life; third is the trend toward national independence. The emergence of new nations everywhere has altered old patterns of distinction based on socio-economic privilege, sex or political standing.

Now, all men, regarding themselves as naturally equal, admit no justification of racial discrimination, but demand respect and equal rights for all. In a society where relations are expressed in terms of rights and duties, men become aware of spiritual values and tend to base their whole lives on their relations to a personal and transcendent God.

II: Relations Between Individuals and Public Authorities (46–79)

NECESSITY AND DIVINE ORIGIN OF AUTHORITY. Society cannot survive without authority, which derives from God and promotes the common good. Thus authority must have moral power to oblige, a power coming from God and used in accord with right reason. Civil authority's chief means of moving men must be, not punishment or reward, but appeal to individual consciences; human dignity rules out any man's coercing another to perform interior acts.

Human authority's power to oblige in conscience comes only when it is related to God's. Human dignity is thus protected, since men reverence God by their obedience to others—and, in so doing, ennoble themselves. Since authority derives from God and the moral order, no law or command can oblige when it contradicts that order or God's will. Though authority comes from God, it does not therefore follow that men lack freedom to choose their rulers or government in a truly democratic way.

ATTAINMENT OF THE COMMON GOOD. Individuals and groups of citizens must contribute to the common welfare and observe general regulations. Civil authorities, likewise, must always act in conformity with present demands of the common good. This common good allows for ethnic differences in a group and looks to the true nature of the human person. It also requires that all share in it according to their circumstances and without discrimination, though justice and equity may demand special consideration for the less fortunate or the disadvantaged.

Since the common good affects the whole man, civil authorities must respect the hierarchy of values and foster the individual's material and spiritual commonweal. Given man's mortal condition, promotion of the common good ought also to include promoting his eternal salvation. In general, the common good is served when personal rights and duties are acknowledged and promoted by civil authorities. Hence a government not acknowledging or safeguarding the rights of man fails in its duty and lacks authority. Its fundamental duty is to regulate society so as to guarantee men's rights and duties or to restore them.

Civil authorities must intervene in economic, political and cultural affairs to eliminate inequalities and insure individual exercise of rights and fulfillment of duties. This will involve providing services on many levels and seeing that citizens are insured against misfortunes. Authorities must also guarantee rights of workers to employment, to fair wages, to a share in industrial responsibility and to autonomy in organizing. In actively promoting the common good, authorities must avoid favoritism or excessive intervention in the economic or other sectors of society.

STRUCTURE AND OPERATION OF THE PUBLIC AUTHORITY. There is no one "best" type of government; rather, a government must be judged in terms of past and present circumstances. It is proper, however, to provide for the legislative, judicial and executive functions of the state, and to spell out the respective rights and duties of state and citizen.

In meeting new problems, legislators must never forget the norms of morality, constitutional provisions and the objective demands of the common good; executives must use discretion; courts must judge impartially. Rights of citizens and groups must be guaranteed under law. A sound juridical structure greatly helps achievement of the common good, but a changing world calls for prudent adaptation of this structure to meet new needs.

Changing relationships in a society call for high competence and integrity in public officials who must act to meet consequent new needs. Human dignity demands that men participate somehow in their own government. Such participation benefits both individuals and government; limited tenure of office for officials also has clear advantages.

THE CONTEMPORARY SCENE. The modern trend favors written constitutions, including a charter of fundamental rights, distinction and limitation of powers, definition of relations between government and governed—with stress on government's responsibilities to the citizenry. The theory that the state, civil rights and authority derive from mere human will cannot be accepted. But current trends make men conscious of their dignity, their right to share in government, and the constitutional limits on authority.

III: Relations Between States (80–129)

States, too, are the subjects of reciprocal rights and duties; relations between them must be grounded on truth, justice, active solidarity and freedom, under the moral law. Public officials, it is clear, as individuals, must observe this law; indeed, they come to such offices precisely because of their high qualities. Moreover, authority disappears when it is abused; hence, it must conform to morality and exist only to serve the common good, which itself demands acknowledgment of and respect for the moral order.

IN TRUTH. Truth in human relations demands the elimination of racism, recognition of individual independence and the right to self-development and respect. Inequalities of endowment between neighbors do not justify one in lording it over the other; the same applies in relations between nations. All men are equal in natural dignity; and likewise all nations. Truth must also regulate the international use of communications media for propaganda purposes.

IN JUSTICE. Justice, too, governs international relations, and so nations must respect the rights of others to existence, self-development, good name and honor; they may not improve themselves at the expense of others. Disagreements between nations must not be settled by force or deceit, but by negotiation and reconciliation of differences. Recent historical developments have given rise to the phenomenon of ethnic minorities and related problems. It is unjust to limit the strength and numerical increase of minorities, and more seriously unjust to aim at their extinction. Justice calls for promoting the betterment of their language, customs and economic growth. Minorities in turn must avoid excessive self-esteem, and recognize that they can profit from contact and exchange with other groups.

IN ACTIVE SOLIDARITY. Great benefits can come from active solidarity between nations, such as already exists in some spheres. Nations must not only avoid hurting others, but seek to co-operate in common enterprises. Both between nations and between ethnic groups in a nation the universal common good demands communication and co-operation.

Mutual collaboration between the have and the have-not nations should extend to sharing capital, goods and manpower. Wherever possible, when needed, work should be brought to workers, to avoid evils linked to dislocation and uprooting of men.

The problem of political refugees saddens Us because of its size and the suffering involved, the problem indicating that some nations deny essential human freedom to their citizens. Such exiles retain their rights as persons, whatever their loss of citizenship, and thus they have a right, where the common good permits, to enter and dwell in a political community with its help. We approve all sound efforts to aid such migrants, especially those efforts of specialized international agencies.

Regrettably, arms stockpiling continues in wealthier nations, burdening the citizenry and hampering needed collaboration with other countries. All this is allegedly justified as a condition of preserving peace, but it makes people live in fear of war breaking out, not as a deliberate act, but as a result of uncontrollable chance.

There is also possible danger for life on earth from continued testing of nuclear weapons. Justice, right reason and humanity demand an end to arms race, reduction of stockpiles, ban on nuclear weapons, progressive disarmament with effective control. Yet none of these can happen without ending the fear of war, and this requires replacing reliance on arms equality by mutual trust—a change which is not only feasible, but also highly reasonable and desirable. This objective is demanded by reason, which calls for basing international relations on the rule of truth, etc.; it is clearly desirable, for everyone must want an end to the threat of war; it promises many benefits for people everywhere.

Therefore We beseech all men, particularly those in high office, to work for this goal. In top-level gatherings let men seek an adjustment founded on mutual trust, sincerity in negotiations and faithful fulfillment of obligations assumed. Our prayers will follow their efforts.

IN FREEDOM. The principle of freedom in international relations forbids unjust oppression or undue meddling. Men are united in one family by many ties and thus the economically developed nations must help others. Consoling progress has been made in this regard and it should continue, but international co-operation must always involve respect for the liberty of developing nations, as Pius XII wisely proclaimed. In particular, wealthier states must respect the moral heritage and ethnic traits of poorer nations and avoid any semblance of political domination in their relations with them.

THE CONTEMPORARY SCENE. Men grow daily more convinced that international disputes must be settled by negotiation rather than by arms. This conviction now rests chiefly on horror at the prospect of destruction in the event of an atomic war; hence, it is hardly possible to imagine that in the atomic era war could be used as an instrument of justice. Still, fear impels nations to spend heavily for arms to dissuade potential aggressors. There is reason to hope, however, that contact through meetings and negotiation may lead to trust and fruitful collaboration.

IV: Relationship of Men and of Political Communities With the World Community (130–145)

INTERDEPENDENCE BETWEEN POLITICAL COMMUNITIES. Progress in science and technology has brought men together in active contacts at several levels, multiplying social relationships and increasing world-wide economic and social interdependence. National isolation has become impossible.

Mankind's unity derives from human equality and postulates a universal common good for the entire human family. Formerly this good could be promoted effectively by normal diplomatic contacts and pacts. Vast changes in the world, however, create new problems that cannot be handled in traditional ways; the international organization and authority available to serve the universal common good does not meet current needs.

The moral order dictates that the structure and function of public authority suffice to promote the common good in a society. Today's world-wide problems of the universal common good demand a public authority of corresponding proportions. Such an authority must be set up, not by force, but by common consent, in order to guarantee its impartiality and avoid suspicion of domination or offense of justified national sensibilities. This authority, by direct or indirect action, must seek the recognition, respect, safeguarding and promotion of the rights of the human person.

Subsidiarity must govern relations between the world community and lesser political communities; it demands that this world authority tackle problems beyond the scope of individual states, not limiting or replacing these political communities, but supplementing them.

THE CONTEMPORARY SCENE. The United Nations, since 1945, has undertaken tasks in the world economic, social, cultural, educational, health and political fields. Of highest importance was its Universal Declaration of Human Rights, approved in 1948. Despite some justified objections and reservations about it, this Declaration recognizes human dignity and is an important step toward the juridico-political organization of the world community. We pray that the structure and means of the UN will evolve to meet its evolving tasks and that it will soon be able to safeguard the universal, inviolable and inalienable human rights of all men.

V: Pastoral Exhortations (146–173)

Christians have a duty to be active in the public life of the entire human community as well as of their own nation. They must bring more than faith and good intentions to this task; they must be equipped, scientifically, technically and professionally, to serve in the various organizations. The task of elevating society to an order founded on truth, justice, love and freedom requires, however, more than these competences; men must learn so to live and act in the temporal order as to create a synthesis between them and spiritual values.

Today, many institutions of traditionally Christian countries show little evidence of Christian influence; though the men who formed these institutions were Christians in name and background, the necessary unity between their temporal activity and their faith and charity was missing. This resulted in great part from the fact that they lacked a solid Christian education to match their scientific formation, a deficiency which must be corrected in today's youth.

It is always difficult to apply principles of justice to concrete affairs; this problem is especially difficult in our times and not susceptible of final solution. We cannot relax in this endeavor, however, since this dynamic age calls for great adaptations in all our institutions.

Most of the doctrinal principles in this encyclical derive from natural-law teachings and thus offer common ground for co-operation with other Christians and all men of good will, without danger of compromise in faith or morals. Where error exists, one must distinguish between it and the person in error, treating the latter as befits his dignity, allowing for his growth in understanding, and hoping for profit from mutual contacts and agreements.

One must also distinguish between false philosophical teachings and various historical movements, even where the one originally inspired the other, since teachings remain fixed while movements evolve, and the movements may even have incorporated some laudable features.

Consequently, the future may permit or call for contacts formerly considered inopportune or unproductive; decisions in this regard are notably difficult, however, and must be made on the scene by those with the best information, subject to the Church's teaching and authoritative guidance.

Some generous souls grow restive over lingering injustices, but human institutions are best reformed from within and gradually, as Pius XII taught. All men of good will must labor to restore order in every area of the human family and thus bring about true peace. Those working to accomplish this in the right way are few, but their number will and must increase, particularly among fervent believers. Indeed, peace in society can be built only where individuals possess inner peace based on God's order.

What We have written springs from awareness of the universal longing of men of good will for the consolidation of world peace. To further this aspiration is Our duty as Vicar of the Prince of Peace, but real peace will come only in an order founded on truth, built according to justice, vivified and integrated by charity, and put into practice in freedom. The task is so exalted that human resources must be augmented by divine aid. For this reason, We look to the Redeemer, who "is our peace," as we are reminded in the liturgy of these holy days.

We pray that Christ's action may turn all men into brothers and thus bring about lasting peace among mankind. As a pledge of this peace, we bless all the faithful and implore from God health and prosperity for all men of good will.

4
What Is Man's Destiny?

Man's response to his situation in the world is partly determined by what he conceives to be his destiny, and any conception of destiny must come to terms with the sure fact of death. Is it man's destiny only to die? Traditional religion answers in the negative with the idea of life after death. As George Shurr points out, the matter of life after death is not merely an academic, theologial concern. How a man treats that idea has an effect on every issue of his life here and now. Norman Brown believes that the effect on man of the notion of the resurrection of the body after death has been repressive, that it has diminished the quality of life before death. He urges man to recognize his destiny as the fulfillment of the rich potential of life in this world.

If man as individual must come to terms with the fact of death, mankind as a species must come to terms with the possibility of extinction. The theory of evolution has demonstrated that mankind's status in the world may turn out to be provisional, that man may be fated eventually to come under the dominion of a higher species or to pass out of

155

existence altogether. Both Julian Huxley and Walter Stuermann argue, however, that such a possibility need not be cause for despair. Huxley makes the point that man "is not only a product of past evolution but an active agent in its future course." Man will find meaning and purpose in life, Huxley says, when he comes to see that it is his responsibility to work for the perfection of human existence. If that responsibility is accepted, it will be man's destiny, as a species carried to its fullest possible development, to influence decisively the evolution of the universe. Stuermann calls on man to have the faith required to shoulder his responsibilities to the universe, to have faith that, although possibly provisional, his existence serves a purpose, that it bears witness to an "overriding, redemptive plan."

But if this plan is to come to fruition, if man's responsibilities to the universe are to be discharged, men of different cultures must realize that they participate together in a common species whose common destiny depends on its internal harmony. In this chapter's concluding essay, Paul Mus raises the question on which man's fate hinges: Can harmony—world order—be arbitrarily imposed upon mankind by external means? Or, must men seek ways to cultivate its natural growth from within the species?

George M. Schurr

Why Bother about Life beyond Death?

A belief in continued individual existence beyond death has traditionally been considered an essential part of Christian theology. This belief has been variously described as belief in "eternal life," "resurrection of the dead," "resurrection of the flesh" or "immortality" of "man" or of the "soul." Though variously described, personal immortality, at least for the elect, has been a touchstone for orthodoxy. However, during the past 100 years the doctrine has been in trouble. On the one hand, many of our contemporaries consider any hope for continued individual existence beyond death to be nothing more than the "archaeological remains" of a former age, the fossil evidence of a previous meaning. As long ago as 1873 Leslie Stephen could write that "the great bulk of the nation continues to think or fancy it thinks in the old formulae, though conscious that a strange numbness is creeping over its faculties." On the other hand, popular "Christian" treatments of life beyond death contain an intolerable amount of emotional language. If asked what they suppose happens after death the majority of professing Christians, including pastors, would probably reply with the kind of words Raynor Johnson has described as "religious-sounding clichés largely concealing fear or ignorance."

Sometimes the pious make the claim that the very difficulty of conceptualizing the belief in life beyond death points to the mystery of belief, and they glory in that mystery. Analysis and argument are rejected as a matter of principle. Mystery is claimed to have its own

Reprinted from *The Christian Century*, April 6, 1966, by permission of the publisher.

George M. Schurr is Associate Professor of Philosophy and Theology at Park College.

significance. William Ernest Hocking writes of those who hold this position: "The 'veil' is beneficent: what is hidden is hidden for our good. And as they feel it, there is a certain philosophical crudity—perhaps an aesthetic and moral crudity as well—in attempting to see behind the curtain which God and Nature have established" (*The Meaning of Immortality in Human Experience*).

Over against this view it may be observed that Christianity has maintained that faith in the Eternal One says—or at least implies—something about man and the world. Some of these implications have been expressed by terms like "eternal life," "resurrection" and "immortality." In these terms an "idea" is put forward for understanding faith. And, as Hocking says, "*Unless an Idea has or can have an intelligible basis in the constitution of things* it is illegitimate, whether for postulate or for faith: we must be able to say what it is we postulate or believe."

This is not to say that all of the mystery can or should be dispelled, but rather that just as many theologians are finding that God's self-revelation in Christ is an accentuation of his hiddenness in mystery, an intelligible statement of the meaning of life beyond death in Christian theology only serves to define the fullness of the mystery of it. Full mystery is realized only as its meaning is defined.

Why Bother, Humanly Speaking?

Another charge is sometimes brought against any concern for life beyond death: that it is irrelevant to contemporary man. The claim is that a "modern" faith does not depend on a belief in life beyond death; it is not the foundation of "modern" ethics, and its interest for "modern" thought is purely historical.

Though the statement seems trite, evidently it needs to be said in rejoinder that this is no abstract question dealing with the sophistication of an intellectual theology. It is a matter of life and death—literally. As Robert McAfee Brown asserts in his foreward to Roger L. Shinn's *Life, Death and Destiny:* "There may be some questions that are 'academic questions' in the sense that they do not really concern our innermost selves, but none of the questions we ask about 'life, death, and destiny' can ever remain academic."

Hocking aptly observes that survival haunts the dark corners of modern consciousness. It has no place in the day's business, save for the florist. It is not a concern of state building, save for the anxious care of the known and unknown "honored dead." It is irrelevant to the sciences, save for the techniques of embalming. It is absent from much philosophy save in the guise of an inheritance.

Drawn, Yet Repelled

Avoiding the question of death by a frantic involvement in life does not seem to work for us. Existentialist thinkers have found in this dark side of life the crucial question of nothingness. Instead of being removed from the universe of meaning, death has become the most vivid symbol of the threat to all that matters. On the one hand modern man runs from an acknowledgment of death, while on the other he is fascinated and terrified by it. When hope in this world fails and life seems out of our control, that which is of the world in each of us asks again the question of Job, "If a man die, shall he live again?" (Job 14:14). Those who are directed to no intelligible reply join voice with Stanton Coblentz' imaginary everyman who says in *The Answer of the Ages:*

> . . . some fear the end, and some pray for it, some mutter resignedly, and some try not to think of it at all; and many find consolation in ancient creeds, while others weep hopeless tears for kinsmen vanished along the self-same route. Nevertheless, among almost all peoples, there have been some ideas of the unknown port; and those ideas have influenced the lives of most races. But none of them are to be trusted—none—none—.

In a world which is learning to take death seriously again, what Christianity has to say about death and life becomes vitally important. It is irrelevant only when the language the church uses seems not to take death seriously. Surely, though, a Christian response is possible precisely because the historic Christian faith *does* take death seriously. Aside from Christ, "Death" *is* the ultimate word.

What Is Its Role in Today's Theology?

At least as far back as Schleiermacher, theology began to shy away from a "pie in the sky by and by" emphasis on life beyond death as the most important doctrine of the faith. Sensitive to the charges of Comte and Marx, contemporary theologians have tended to relegate discussion of life beyond death to the back shelves of divinity school libraries. Actually, much has been written, but it gives one the feeling that it has been written not because it demanded to be written but because some theologian could not avoid the subject.

At least three factors can be discerned in this proliferation of pages with thinness of thought. First, whether it be a matter of development or decision, in most contemporary Christian thought the emphasis has been on *this* world. Second, there has been—at least among liberal thinkers—little really creative and original reflection on the nature of life beyond death since the massive acceptance of a Kantian type of definition of immortality on "moral" grounds for an unknowable self (apparently affirmed on the basis of an implicit metaphysic). Third, it has been felt in this scientific age that it is not "respectable" to speculate about that which cannot be "known" ("scientifically")—and hence not much could be said. For instance, Rauschenbusch was willing to throw out almost all the historic Christian claims about life beyond death. He considered exercises on the subject of life beyond death to be true Christianity meeting prescientific views of the cosmos. In his opinion "eschatology is usually loved in inverse proportion to the square of the mental diameter of those who do the loving."

The Doctrine of Last Things

When Frederick C. Grant writes in *Can We Still Believe in Immortality?*, "It is a situation unique in Christian history when the Church is required to defend the faith in immortality," it behooves us to ask just what many Christian apologists were doing through the centuries, but it seems likely that the need to defend against criticism within the church is at least unusual. Though, as J. E. Fison says in *The Christian Hope*, "the western non-Roman church has for too long appeared to let its whole eschatological position go by default," the need to re-establish eschatological concepts has come about through our discovery that our hope for the world must be grounded in the hope of the world. On the one hand Christians, in company with humanists, have become disabused with progress and the moral impact of the church on society. On the other hand, partly as a result of Schweitzer's uncovering of the eschatological milieu of the historical Jesus, there has been a gradual realization that the foundation of the Christian faith is inseparable from eschatology: the New Testament witness is eschatological.

If the problem of beginnings was the theological issue of the 19th century and the problem of justification by faith the theological issue of the 16th century, the theological issue before the church today is Revelation and the doctrine of Last Things. An awareness of this situation led the second assembly of the World Council of Churches to take the Christian hope as its theme. However, eschatology has entered contemporary theological discussion largely in the guise of a nonpersonal hope. New Testament studies examine the "end of the age." Reinhold Niebuhr pays almost exclusive attention to history and the "final" meaning of history. As a result the hope of the "particular" man has been subordinated to these "larger" issues. Further, when we are dealing with the generalities of eschatology, a certain vagueness about its particularities can go unnoticed. But Christian theology cannot afford to be vague about these particularities. If the Christian witness is that Christ is the conqueror of Death, we must be prepared to say something about what this means for particular individual death—the only Death we know. If we say that Christ is the hope of the world, we must be able to say what this means for individuals who make up the existence of the human world.

In Christian theology eschatological concepts stand in closest relation to the estimate of the person and work of Christ. For Barth, for instance, what is involved in affirmations concerning the resurrection of the dead "is the *substance*, the *whole* of the Christian revelation." The resurrection of the dead and the resurrection of Christ are of one cloth— we cannot have the one without the other. If Christ is truly Lord and truly man, then he is the Lord of man's death.

Are Philosophers Bothered?

Before the end of the nineteenth century the nontheological thinker, noticing the retreat of the theologians, had begun to examine what could be meant by life beyond death, and on occasion tried to establish an immortality without God. Ducasse, among others, follows the same trail today. Philosophical analysts, after going through a period when they considered life beyond death to be strictly meaningless, a contradiction in terms, are now prepared to discuss life beyond death as logically possible and theoretically verifiable. John Hick (in *Faith and Knowledge*) is prepared to opt for eschatological verification as the crucial empirical verification of Christian claims. He considers immortality to be the theoretical vindication of the "meaningfulness of the theistic assertion." No claim is made for proof of the divine existence by this approach, but rather it is claimed emphatically that Christian assertions "make sense."

Unfortunately this renewed interest in life beyond death neglects much of the proper criticism of the earlier analysts. It is assumed that we can simply wait and see and that it will all be perfectly clear. As James Pratt in his *Adventures in Philosophy and Religion* has Mr. Layman say, "If by any chance we . . . should meet in the next world, gentlemen, the beers will be on you." But are the "facts" (including "beers") that patently objective even in this life? Would we recognize life beyond death if we saw it? Though inquiries concerning life beyond death may well be a means of restoring conversation between "secular" philosophy and theology, our enthusiasm over the renewed acquaintance must not blind us to the need to be perfectly clear about just what is to be verified.

At the very least we cannot look for the facts until we know what facts we are looking for, and we cannot know what facts we are looking for unless the statement of the hypothesis is intelligible. The discovery in contemporary physics that where quanta numbers are low (i.e., individuals are being observed) the instruments of observation affect the results observed suggests the importance of the conceptual instruments brought to any problem of verification.

Is God Bothered About Man?

All of the above is a roundabout way of saying that a discussion about life beyond death is one place where theology meets anthropology. Assertions about life beyond death are still a testing ground for the old problem of the relation between science and religion; they are also test cases for claims about the status of man before God. The understanding of life beyond death involves the theologian's conception of human nature as well as of divine action. As in the case of Christology, we must say both man and God.

When theology is slighted, religion means life beyond death, as William James observed, and "whoever has doubts of immortality is written down as an atheist without further trial." The theologian cannot accept such a reduction of religion to human hope for life beyond death. But if the theologian ignores anthropology he is apt to find Luther saying to him, "If you believe in no future life I would not give a mushroom for your God." The Christian affirms that his hope is *in* God, but it is a hope for man; both must be maintained.

In its dual reference—in God and for man—a consideration of life beyond death forces one to deal with the linkage between at least two "language strata"—to use the terminology of F. Weismann. In discussions about life beyond death both theological and anthropological meaning-reference must be included. Dealing as it does with the whole range of questions of God to man and man to God, an examination of the meaning of life beyond death may well prove a better test case for the epistemological status of theological assertions than the much discussed question of the "existence of God." The way man treats the idea of life beyond death affects—and is affected by—almost every other religious and philosophic issue.

Norman O. Brown

The Resurrection of the Body

The path of sublimation, which mankind has religiously followed at least since the foundation of the first cities, is no way out of the human neurosis, but, on the contrary, leads to its aggravation. Psychoanalytical theory and the bitter facts of contemporary history suggest that mankind is reaching the end of this road. Psychoanalytical theory declares that the end of the road is the dominion of death-in-life. History has brought mankind to that pinnacle on which the total obliteration of mankind is at last a practical possibility. At this moment of history the friends of the life instinct must warn that the victory of death is by no means impossible; the malignant death instinct can unleash those hydrogen bombs. For if we discard our fond illusion that the human race has a privileged or providential status in the life of the universe, it seems plain that the malignant death instinct is a built-in guarantee that the human experiment, if it fails to attain its possible perfection, will cancel itself out, as the dinosaur experiment canceled itself out. But jeremiads are useless unless we can point to a better way. Therefore the question confronting mankind is the abolition of repression—in traditional Christian language, the resurrection of the body.

. . . The life instinct, or sexual instinct, demands activity of a kind that, in contrast to our current mode of activity, can only be called play. The life instinct also demands a union with others and with the world around us based not on anxiety and aggression but on narcissism and erotic exuberance.

But the death instinct also demands satisfaction; as Hegel says in the *Phenomenology,* "The life and knowledge of God may doubtless be

Norman O. Brown is Professor of Classics at Wesleyan University.

described as love playing with itself; but this idea sinks into triviality, if the seriousness, the pain, the patience and the labor of the Negative are omitted." The death instinct is reconciled with the life instinct only in a life which is not repressed, which leaves no "unlived lines" in the human body, the death instinct then being affirmed in a body which is willing to die. And, because the body is satisfied, the death instinct no longer drives it to change itself and make history, and therefore, as Christian theology divined, its activity is in eternity.

At the same time—and here again Christian theology and psychoanalysis agree—the resurrected body is the transfigured body. The abolition of repression would abolish the unnatural concentrations of libido in certain particular bodily organs—concentrations engineered by the negativity of the morbid death instinct, and constituting the bodily base of the neurotic character disorders in the human ego. In the words of Thoreau: "We need pray for no higher heaven than the pure senses can furnish, a purely sensuous life. Our present senses are but rudiments of what they are destined to become." The human body would become polymorphously perverse, delighting in that full life of all the body which it now fears. The consciousness strong enough to endure full life would be no longer Apollonian but Dionysian—consciousness which does not observe the limit, but overflows; consciousness which *does not negate any more.*

If the question facing mankind is the abolition of repression, psychoanalysis is not the only point of view from which the question can and should be raised. We have already indicated that the question is intrinsic to Christian theology. The time has come to ask Christian theologians, especially the neo-orthodox, what they mean by the resurrection of the body and by eternal life. Is this a promise of immortality after death? In other words, is the psychological premise of Christianity the impossibility of reconciling life and death either in "this" world or the "next," so that flight from death—with all its morbid consequences—is our eternal fate in "this world" and in "the next"? For we have seen that the perfect body, promised by Christian theology, enjoying that perfect felicity promised by Christian theology, is a body reconciled with death.

In the last analysis Christian theology must either accept death as part of life or abandon the body. For two thousand years Christianity has kept alive the mystical hope of an ultimate victory of Life over Death, during a phase of human history when Life was at war with Death and hope could only be mystical. But if we are approaching the last days, Christian theology might ask itself whether it is only the religion of fallen humanity, or whether it might be asleep when the bridegroom comes. Certain it is that if Christianity wishes to help mankind toward that erasure of the traces of original sin which Baudelaire said was the true definition of progress, there are priceless insights in its tradition—insights which have to be transformed into a system of practical therapy, something like psychoanalysis, before they are useful or even meaningful. The specialty of Christian eschatology lies precisely in its rejection of the Platonic hostility to the human body and to "matter," its refusal to identify the Platonic path of sublimation with ultimate salvation, and its affirmation that eternal life can only be life in a body. Christian asceticism can carry punishment of the fallen body to heights inconceivable to Plato; but Christian hope is for the redemption of that fallen body. Hence the affirmation of Tertullian: *Resurget igitur caro, et quidem omnis, et quidem ipsa, et quidem integra*—The body will rise again, all of the body, the identical body, the entire body. The medieval Catholic synthesis between Christianity and Greek philosophy, with its notion of an immortal soul, compromised and confused the issue; only Protestantism carries the full burden of the peculiar Christian faith. Luther's break with the doctrine of sublimation (good works) is decisive; but the theologian of the resurrected body is the cobbler of Görlitz, Jacob Boehme. When Tillich and Barth finally get round to the substance of things hoped for, their eschatology, they will have to reckon with Boehme. . . .

Whatever the Christian churches do with him, Boehme's position in the Western tradition of mystic hope of better things is central and assured. Backward he is linked, through Paracelsus and alchemy, to the tradition of Christian agnosticism and Jewish cabalism; forward he is linked, through his influence on the romantics Blake, Novalis, and Hegel, with Freud. We have argued that psychoanalysis has not psychoanalyzed itself until it places itself inside the history of Western thought—inside the general neurosis of mankind. So seen, psychoanalysis is the heir to a mystical tradition which it must affirm.

Mysticism, in the mind of the general public, is identified with that flight from the material world and from life preached by such popularizers as Evelyn Underhill and Aldous Huxley—which, from the psychoanalytical point of view, may be termed Apollonian or sublimation mysticism. But there is in the Western tradition another kind of mysticism, which can be called Dionysian or body mysticism, which stays with life, which is the body, and seeks to transform and perfect it. Western body mysticism—a tradition which urgently needs re-examination—contains three main strands: the Christian (Pauline) notion of the "spiritual" body, the Jewish (cabalistic) notion of Adam's perfect body before the Fall, and the alchemical notion of the subtle body. All of these strands unite in Boehme, and even a little knowledge of the real Boehme . . . makes it plain that Boehme and Freud have too much in common to be able to dispense with each other.

Boehme, like Freud, understands death not as a mere nothing but as a positive force either in dialectical conflict with life (in fallen man), or dialectically unified with life (in God's perfection). Thus, says Benz, "Our life remains a struggle between life and death, and as long as this conflict lasts, anxiety lasts also." In Boehme's concept of life, the concept of play, or love-play, is as central as it is in Freud's; and his concept of the spiritual or paradisical body of Adam before the Fall recognizes the potent demand in our unconscious both for an androgynous mode of being and for a narcissistic mode of self-expression, as well as the corruption in our current use of the oral, anal, and genital functions. It is true that Boehme does not yet accept the brutal death of the individual physical body, and therefore makes his paradisical body ambiguously immaterial, without oral, anal, and genital organs; and yet he clings obstinately to the body and to bodily pleasure, and therefore says that Adam was "magically" able to eat and enjoy the "essence" of things, and "magically" able to reproduce and to have sexual pleasure in the act of reproduction. Boehme is caught in these dilemmas because of his insight into the corruption of the human body, his insight that all life is life in the body, and, on the other hand, his inability to accept a body which dies. No Protestant theologian has gone further; or rather, later Protestantism has preferred to repress the problem and to repress Boehme.

Oriental mysticism also, to judge from Needham's survey of Taoism or Eliade's study of Yoga, has reached the same point. Needham (quoting Maspéro) is right in stressing that the Taoist quest for a more perfect body transcends the Platonic dualism of soul and matter. But Needham's enthusiasm for Taoism as a human and organismic response to life in the world must be qualified by recognizing that the Taoist perfect body is immortal: Taoism does not accept death as part of life. . . .

Psychoanalysis accepts the death of the body; but psychoanalysis has something to learn from body mysticism, occidental and oriental, over and above the wealth of psychoanalytical insights contained in it. For these mystics take seriously, and traditional psychoanalysis does not, the possibility of human perfectibility and the hope of finding a way out of the human neurosis into that simple health that animals enjoy, but not man.

As Protestantism degenerated from Luther and Boehme, it abandoned its religious function of criticizing the existing order and keeping alive the mystical hope of better things; in psychoanalytical terminology, it lost contact with the unconscious and with the immortal repressed desires of the unconscious. The torch passed to the poets and philosophers of the romantic movement. The heirs of Boehme are Blake, Novalis,

Hegel, and, as Professor Gray has recently shown, Goethe. These are the poets whom Freud credited with being the real discoverers of the unconscious.

Not only toward the mystics but also toward the poets psychoanalysis must quit its pretension of supramundane superiority. Instead of exposing the neuroses of the poets, the psychoanalysts might learn from them, and abandon the naïve idea that there is an immense gap, in mental health and intellectual objectivity, between themselves and the rest of the world. In the world's opinion, in the eyes of common sense, Novalis is crazy, and Ferenczi also: the world will find it easier to believe that we are all mad than to believe that the psychoanalysts are not. And further, it does not seem to be the case that the psychoanalytical mode of reaching the unconscious has superannuated the poetic, or artistic, mode of attaining the same objective. Anyone conversant both with modern literature and with psychoanalysis knows that modern literature is full of psychoanalytical insights not yet grasped, or not so clearly grasped, by "scientific" psychoanalysis. And anyone who loves art knows that psychoanalysis has no monopoly on the power to heal. What the times call for is an end to the war between psychoanalysis and art—a war kept alive by the sterile "debunking" approach of psychoanalysis to art—and the beginning of cooperation between the two in the work of therapy and in the task of making the unconscious conscious. A little more Eros and less strife.

Modern poetry, like psychoanalysis and Protestant theology, faces the problem of the resurrection of the body. Art and poetry have always been altering our ways of sensing and feeling—that is to say, altering the human body. And Whitehead rightly discerns as the essence of the "Romantic Reaction" a revulsion against abstraction (in psychoanalytical terms, sublimation) in favor of the concrete sensual organism, the human body. "Energy is the only life, and is from the Body. . . . Energy is Eternal Delight," says Blake.

A young critic, whose first book represents a new mode of criticism—a criticism for which poetry is an experience both mystical and bodily—has traced the persistent quest in modern poetry for the resurrection of the body and the perfection of the body. Wordsworth, in contrast with the sublime (and sublimating) tendency of Milton, "considers that his revelation can be expressed in the forms and symbols of daily life" and "sees Paradise possible in any sweet though bare nook of the earth." Hopkins "is engaged on a theodicy, and has taken for his province the stubborn senses and the neglected physical world"; "no one has gone further than Hopkins in presenting Christ as the direct and omnipresent object of perception, so deeply ingrained in the eyes, the flesh, and the bone (and the personal sense of having eyes, flesh, and bone), that the sense of self and the sense of being in Christ can no longer be distinguished." Rilke's plaint throughout his career is that "we do not know the body any more than we know nature": Rilke believes (in his own words) that "the qualities are to be taken away from God, the no longer utterable, and returned to creation, to love and death"; so that the outcome of his poetry is that "for Rilke, the body becomes a spiritual fact." Valéry's poetry "may be considered as the Odyssey of Consciousness in search of its true body"; and "the intellectual pursuit of Valéry is to this end, that the body may be seen as what it virtually is, a magnificent revelation and instrument of the soul. Could it be viewed as such, the eyes would not be symbol, but reality." . . .

The resurrection of the body is a social project facing mankind as a whole, and it will become a practical political problem when the statesmen of the world are called upon to deliver happiness instead of power, when political economy becomes a science of use-values instead of exchange-values—a science of enjoyment instead of a science of accumulation. In the face of this tremendous human problem, contemporary social theory, both capitalist and socialist, has nothing to say. Contemporary social theory (again we must honor Veblen as an exception) has been completely taken in by the inhuman abstractions of the path of sublimation, and has no contact with concrete human beings, with their concrete bodies, their concrete though repressed desires, and their concrete neuroses.

To find social theorists who are thinking about the real problem of our age, we have to go back to the Marx of 1844, or even to the philosophers influencing Marx in 1844, Fourier and Feuerbach. From Fourier's psychological analysis of the antithesis of work and pleasure Marx obtained the concept of play, and used it, in a halfhearted way to be sure, in some of his early utopian speculations. From Feuerbach Marx learned the necessity of moving from Hegelian abstractions to the concrete senses and the concrete human body. Marx's "philosophic-economic manuscripts" of 1844 contain remarkable formulations calling for the resurrection of human nature, the appropriation of the human body, the transformation of the human senses, and the realization of a state of self-enjoyment. Thus, for example, "Man appropriates himself as an all-sided being in an all-sided way, hence as total man. [This appropriation lies in] every one of his human relationships to the world—seeing, hearing, smell, taste, feeling, thought, perception, experience, wishing, activity, loving, in short, all organs of his individuality." The human physical senses must be emancipated from the sense of possession, and then the humanity of the senses and the human enjoyment of the senses will be achieved for the first time. Here is the point of contact between Marx and

Freud: I do not see how the profundities and obscurities of the "philo-sophic-economic manuscripts" can be elucidated except with the aid of psychoanalysis.

Psychoanalysis, mysticism, poetry, the philosophy of organism, Feuerbach, and Marx—this is a miscellaneous assemblage; but, as Hera-clitus said, the unseen harmony is stronger than the seen. Common to all of them is a mode of consciousness that can be called—although the term causes fresh difficulties—the dialectical imagination. By "dialectical" I mean an activity of consciousness struggling to circumvent the limitations imposed by the formal-logical law of contradiction. Marxism, of course, has no monopoly of "dialectics." Needham has shown the dialectical character of Whitehead's philosophy, and he constantly draws attention to dialectical patterns in mystical thought. The goal of Indian body mysticism, according to Eliade, is the "conjunction of Contrarieties." Scholem, in his survey of Jewish mysticism, says, "Mysticism, intent on formulating the paradoxes of religious experience, uses the instrument of dialectics to express its meaning. The Kabbalists are by no means the only witnesses to this affinity between mystical and dialectical thinking."

As for poetry, are not those basic poetic devices emphasized by recent criticism—paradox, ambiguity, irony, tension—devices whereby the poetic imagination subverts the "reasonableness" of language, the chains it imposes? And from the psychoanalytical point of view, if we . . . accept the substantial identity between poetic logic (with its sym-bolism, condensation of meaning, and displacement of accent) and dream logic, then the connection between poetry and dialectics, as defined, is more substantially grounded. Dreams are certainly an activity of the mind struggling to circumvent the formal-logical law of con-tradiction. . . .

We may therefore entertain the hypothesis that formal logic and the law of contradiction are the rules whereby the mind submits to operate under general conditions of repression. As with the concept of time, Kant's categories of rationality would then turn out to be the cate-gories of repression. And conversely, "dialectical" would be the struggle of the mind to circumvent repression and make the unconscious con-scious. But by the same token, it would be the struggle of the mind to overcome the split and conflict within itself. It could then be identified with that "synthesizing" tendency in the ego of which Freud spoke, and with that attempt to cure, inside the neurosis itself, on which Freud came finally to place his hope for therapy. As an attempt to unify and to cure, the "dialectical" consciousness would be a manifestation of Eros. And, as consciousness trying to throw off the fetters of negation, the "dialectical" consciousness would be a step toward the Dionysian ego which does not negate any more.

What the great world needs, of course, is a little more Eros and less strife; but the intellectual world needs it just as much. A little more Eros would make conscious the unconscious harmony between "dialectical" dreamers of all kinds—psychoanalysts, political idealists, mystics, poets, philosophers—and abate the sterile and ignorant polemics. Since the ignorance seems to be mostly a matter of self-ignorance, a little more psychoanalytical consciousness on all sides (including the psychoanalysts) might help—a little more self-knowledge, humility, humanity, and Eros. We may therefore conclude with the concluding words of Freud's *Civilization and Its Discontents:*

> Men have brought their powers of subduing the forces of nature to such a pitch that by using them they could now very easily exterminate one another to the last man. They know this—hence arises a great part of their current unrest, their dejection, their mood of apprehension. And now it may be expected that the other of the two "heavenly forces," eternal Eros, will put forth his strength so as to maintain himself alongside of his equally immortal adversary.

And perhaps our children will live to live a full life, and so see what Freud could not see—in the old adversary, a friend.

Sir Julian Huxley
The Crisis in Man's Destiny

The most bewildering characteristic of the present moment of history is that things are happening faster and faster. The pace of change in human affairs, originally so slow as to be unnoticed, has steadily accelerated, until today we can no longer measure it in terms of generations: Major changes now take place every few years, and human indi-

Reprinted from *Playboy,* Vol. 14, No. 1, January 1967. Copyright © 1966 by HMH Publishing Company, Inc. By permission of the publishers.

Sir Julian Huxley is a world-renowned English author and biologist.

viduals have to make several drastic adjustments in the course of their working lives. Where are these breathless changes taking us? Is change synonymous with progress, as many technologists and developers would like us to believe? Is there any main direction to be discerned in present-day human life and affairs? The answer at the moment is no. Change today is disruptive; its trends are diverging in various directions. What is more, many of them are self-limiting or even self-destructive—think of the trend to explosive population increase, to overgrown cities, to traffic congestion, to reckless exploitation of resources, to the widening gap between developed and underdeveloped countries, to the destruction of wild life and natural beauty, to cutthroat competition in economic growth, to Galbraith's private affluence and public squalor, to over-specialization and imbalance in science and technology, to monotony, boredom and conformity, and to the proliferation of increasingly expensive armaments.

What is to be done? Before attempting an answer, we must look at the problem in a long perspective—indeed in the longest perspective of all, the perspective of evolution. The process of evolution on this planet has been going on for five billion years or so. First of all, it was only physical and chemical—the formation of the continents and oceans and the production of increasingly complex chemical compounds. Then, nearly three billion years ago, this purely physicochemical phase of evolution was superseded by the biological phase—the evolution of living matter, or "life." The threshold to this was crossed when one of the numerous organic chemical compounds built up by ultraviolet radiation in the world's warm, soupy seas became capable of reproducing itself. This compound is a kind of nucleic acid, called DNA for short; its complex molecule is built in the form of a double helix, like a spirally twisted ladder whose complementary halves are joined by special chemical rungs. In favorable conditions, the two halves sooner or later break apart, and both build themselves into new wholes by incorporating organic compounds from the surrounding medium. DNA also has the capacity to build up special enzymes and many other proteins out of its chemical surroundings, with the final result of producing a primitive cell with DNA as its core.

DNA is thus self-reproducing and self-multiplying matter. It is also self-varying, since now and again it undergoes a small change in part of its structure as a result of radiation or some chemical agency (or sometimes spontaneously), and then reproduces itself in this changed form. In modern terms, it mutates, and the mutation is hereditary. And very soon, the sexual process multiplies the variation manyfold by recombining mutations in every possible way.

As a result of these two properties of self-multiplication and self-variation, there results a "struggle for existence" between the different variants, and this in turn results in what Darwin called *natural selection* —a shorthand phrase for the results of the differential death, survival and reproduction of variants.

Crossing the threshold must have been a relatively slow business, taking perhaps 10,000,000 years or more; but once it was crossed, the whole process of evolution was enormously speeded up, major changes taking place at intervals to be measured in hundred-million-year instead of billion-year units. And, as Darwin pointed out over a century ago, and as has become clearer ever since, major change was inevitably progressive, headed in the direction of improvement—improving the organization of plants and animals in relation to their environment, enabling them to surmount more of its dangers and make better use of its resources.

Each major change in biological evolution involved the step-by-step crossing of a critical threshold, leading to the formation of a new dominant type. This is followed by a rapid flowering of the new type and its further improvement along many divergent lines, usually at the expense of its parent and predecessor type. Sooner or later, the process reveals itself as self-limiting: The type as a whole comes up against a limit, and further progress can only be realized by one or two lines slowly achieving a new and improved pattern of organization, and stepping across the threshold barrier to give rise to quite new dominant types.

Thus the amphibians broke through the barrier from water to land, though they still had to live in water as tadpoles or larvae in the early stages of their development; but after about 100,000,000 years, they were succeeded by a new and fully terrestrial dominant type, with shelled eggs containing private ponds to develop in—the reptiles, which, as everyone knows, produced an astonishing variety of specialized lines— crocodiles and tortoises, marine ichthyosaurs and plesiosaurs, aerial pterosaurs and the splendid array of terrestrial dinosaurs.

But after nearly 150,000,000 years, they too reached their limit. A new type of organization was produced, involving hair, warm blood, milk and prolonged development within the mother, and broke through to dominance in the shape of the placental mammals, while most reptilian lines became extinct. This new type again radiated out, to produce all the familiar mammal groups—carnivores and ungulates, rats and bats, whales and primates. Once more, after 50,000,000 years or so, their evolution seems to have reached its limits and got stuck. Only one line among the primates took all the steps—to erect posture, tool- and weapon-making, increased brain size, and capacity for true speech—that led, a mere 100,000 or so years back, to the emergence of man as the new dominant type, and took life across the threshold from the biological to the psychosocial phase of evolution.

This works by cumulative tradition rather than by genetic variation, and is manifested in cultural and mental rather than in bodily and physical transformation. Yet evolving human life progresses in the same sort of way as animal life—by a succession of improved dominant types of organization. However, these are not organizations of flesh and blood and bodily structure but of ideas and institutions, of mental and social structure—systems of thought and knowledge, feeling and belief, with their social, economic and political accompaniments. We may call them psychosocial systems. With the emergence of each new system, man radically changes his ideas about his place, his role and his job in nature—how to utilize natural resources, how to organize his societies, how to understand and pursue his destiny.

Up to the present there have been five such dominant psychosocial systems, five major progressive stages, involving four crossings of a difficult threshold to a new way of thinking about nature and coping with existence. First the crossing from the stage of food gathering by small groups to that of organized hunting and tribal organization. Then the step, first taken some 10,000 years ago, across to the neolithic stage, based on the idea of growing crops and domesticating animals, associated with fertility rites and priest-kings, and leading to food storage and settled life in villages and small towns. Third, nearly 6000 years ago, the radical step to civilization, with organized cities and trading systems, castes and professions, including a learned priesthood, with writing or other means of nonvocal communication, and leading to large and powerful societies (and eventually to empires), always with a religious basis. And fourth, less than 500 years ago, the even more decisive step, marked by the Renaissance, the Reformation and the beginnings of organized objective inquiry, over the threshold to the stage of exploration—geographical, historical, religious and, above all, scientific: in a word, the stage of science. This was associated with increasingly secular representative government, with the idea of progress based on ever-increasing knowledge and wealth, and led to a profit-based economic system, industrialization and competitive nationalism.

What, you may ask, has all this to do with our present troubles? The answer is that they portend a new threshold to be crossed to a new dominant system and a new stage of human advance. During each previous dominant stage, mankind differentiated into competing groups, with divergent trends of thought and action. These were in the long run self-limiting, self-defeating, disruptive or just hampering. But they contained seeds of self-correction: As their unhelpful nature became obvious, this provoked new thinking and new action to reduce their harmful effects, and eventually to make clear the need to attempt the difficult passage into a new stage based on a radically new system. To take but one case, abuses of ecclesiastical power provoked the Reformation, backward-looking and hairsplitting scholasticism helped on the new birth of the Renaissance and of modern science, and the reaction against the Church's ban on "usury" or charging interest on a loan, coupled with the urgent need for large-scale trade ventures, stimulated the birth of the capitalist system.

The same sort of thing is at work today. The population explosion is stimulating birth control, monolithic overplanning in the U.S.S.R. and its satellites is producing liberalizing reactions, while the doctrinaire freedom of enterprise and expression of the U.S.A. and its acolytes is forcing the acceptance of some degree of discipline and planning; the gap between rich and poor nations is stimulating increased aid and assistance; while racial injustice is stimulating campaigns for integration. The inadequacy of our educational systems has called forth efforts for their expansion and reform; the reckless exploitation and careless destruction of the world's varied resources is leading to a multitude of separate attempts to conserve them; traffic congestion and the other frustrations of city life are leading to transportation planning and schemes of urban renewal; in reaction against the conformity and boredom of modern mechanized existence, a whole crop of new outlets for life is sprouting, in sport and art, in adventure and dedicated projects; while to fill the vacuum caused by the enfeeblement of traditional religious belief and expression, new adventures of spiritual and mental exploration are being undertaken. And the giant wars of this most destructive of centuries have provoked a reaction against war itself and generated a general desire for peace and a crop of projects for preserving and fostering it.

But all this is not enough—all these are negative attempts, actions *against* something, instead of positive efforts *for* something. What is needed is a new over-all pattern of thinking and willing that will give us a new vision and a constructive purpose, providing meaning for our lives and incentives for our actions. Only this can bring together the separate reactions against the divergent threats that beset us, and harness them (and all our reserves of suppressed good will) in a single-minded team.

A new vision has been revealed by post-Darwinian science and learning. It gives us a new and an assured view of ourselves. Man is a highly peculiar organism. He is a single joint body-mind, not a body plus a separate mind or soul, but with mind on top, no longer subordinate to body, as in animals. By virtue of this, he has become the latest dominant type in the solar system, with three billion years of evolution behind him and (if he doesn't destroy himself) a comparably long period of evolution before him. Certainly no other organism could oust him from his position: He would quickly become aware of any challenge, whether from rat, termite or ape, and would be able to nip it in the bud. His role, whether he wants it or not, is to be the leader of the evolutionary process on earth, and his job is to guide and direct it in the general direction of improvement.

To do this, he must redefine his aims. In the past, most human groups and most human individuals have aimed at wealth or pleasure or pride of power, though with a sizable minority seeking salvation in a future life, and a smaller minority seeking spiritual satisfactions or creative outlets in this life. During the long march of prehuman evolution, dominant types have split into a multitude of separate biological organizations termed species. Dominant man has also split, but into separate psychosocial and often competing organizations that Konrad Lorenz calls pseudospecies—tribes and nations, empires and religions (though this tendency toward diversity and disunity has been partially offset by an increasing tendency toward convergence and unity).

Clearly, our first aim must be to demote these pseudospecies and recognize the unity of the real species *Homo sapiens*—in other words, the oneness of mankind. And, *pari passu* with that, to construct more effective organs of his unity, in the shape of really effective international (or preferably supranational) institutions, to think, plan and act on behalf of the human species as a whole. A supporting aim must be to increase man's understanding of this new vision of himself, of his destiny and responsibility, of the limitless possibilities of improvement. And to convert understanding into action, he must improve his instruments for actually getting on with the job—new knowledge and new skills, new technological achievements, new social and political mechanisms.

But his most important instrument is his mind; accordingly, one of his most urgent tasks is to improve his own mental and psychological organization. As anthropologist Loren Eiseley has said, ancestral man entered his own head; ever since, he has been trying to adapt to what he found there. What he found there, of course, was a lot of myths and mumbo jumbo, witchcraft and wish fulfillment, the results of primitive thinking trying to cope with his own profound ignorance, with the civil war of conflicting passions inside and with the constricting forces of nature outside.

Man's primitive or fantasy thinking is always projecting his own ideas, his own guilt and his own secret wishes, onto someone or something else; its unconscious cunning is always inventing justifications for his own passions—supernatural justification like shifting the blame for his actions onto God, moral justifications like ascribing wickedness to his enemies or proclaiming his own group as divinely inspired or chosen.

In the natural sciences, man has learned the technique of "reality thinking"—of accepting the facts and phenomena of external nature and trying to understand them objectively, without bias. But he still has to tackle the more difficult task of abandoning primitive for reality thinking in dealing with the facts of his own nature and his own psychosocial creations, like religions and arts, laws and customs, social organizations and political institutions, and all the myths and rationalizations concerning them. In a word, man must improve his mechanisms for thinking about himself.

An obvious aim is to find out further how best to avoid conflict by transcending or transforming it, both internally, within our heads, and externally, in the physical and social world. Another is to ensure that the new pattern of thought and belief (and therefore of potential action) shall not be self-destructive but capable of constructive growth, not self-limiting but open-ended. And the aim of aims must be to provide truly satisfying goals for human beings everywhere, so as to energize our species, to stimulate it to move and to ensure that it moves in the right direction. This involves planning for greater fulfillment for human individuals and greater achievement by human societies, and for fuller realization of man's varied possibilities, both personal and collective. It means aiming at quality rather than quantity—quality of life and personality instead of quantity of people, wealth and material goods. The time is ripe for a new approach to destiny, a new look at human life through the telescope of comprehensive vision of wholes instead of the microscope of analysis into separate parts.

Now I want to take another brief look at some of the unpleasant and threatening trends I spoke of at the outset, to see how the countermeasures we obviously must take against them may help us in planning the practical steps needed to achieve these new integrated ends.

First, population. The world's population is increasing by over 60,000,000 a year—the equivalent of a good-sized town every day of the year, and of nearly 12 baseball teams (with coach) every minute of the day. Its compound interest rate of increase has also increased, from under ½ percent per annum to over 1¾ percent today, and is still increasing a good deal. This applies just as much to Western countries like Britain or Sweden with a slow increase rate or the U.S.A. with a medium rate as to Asian or Latin-American countries with a high rate.

Whatever we do, the world's population will double by the turn of the century. If we do nothing now, life for our grandchildren and great-grandchildren will be much more unpleasant than it is for us, which is saying a good deal. If we go on doing nothing, man will lose his chance of being the beneficent guide of evolution, and will become the cancer of the planet, ruining it and himself with it.

A prerequisite for further human progress is immediate and universal birth control as an instrument of national and international policy, with the immediate aim of reducing man's rate of increase to manageable proportions, well below one percent a year, and the ultimate aim of reducing the total number of human beings in the world.

This means publicizing the need for birth control, incorporating family planning in national health services, adjusting family allowances and taxation systems to discourage overlarge families, and providing birth-control appliances and trained personnel to fit them, in all programs of aid and technical assistance. This means rethinking the whole problem of population, in terms of higher quality of life instead of increasing quantity of people. It also means rethinking the problem of resources, in terms of long-term conservation based on scientific ecology instead of quick exploitation based on mechanized technology.

Next there is the problem of cities. In the last half century, more and more metropolitan areas have grown to monstrous size, up to 12,000,000, 14,000,000, even 16,000,000 in Tokyo, Greater London or Greater New York. If you take as your yardstick the city proper, the central area without its suburban tentacles, the number of cities with over a million inhabitants has grown from 30 at the end of World War Two to over 80 today, only 21 years later. And meanwhile, the population of automobiles is growing twice as fast as that of people. As a result, cities are suffering from traffic thrombosis and their inhabitants from severe vital frustration. We know from experiment that overcrowding in animals leads to distorted, neurotic and downright pathological behavior. We can be sure that the same is true in principle for people. City life today is definitely leading to mass mental disease, to growing vandalism and possible eruptions of mass violence.

Existence in cities must be made not merely tolerable but life-enhancing, as it has so often been in the past. To do this, we must forcibly restrict any further expansion of overbig cities, while undertaking planned and limited expansion of smaller ones; we must create new towns in strategic locations (as is already being done in Britain) to accommodate the overspill of the nation's population: and we must rigorously prevent the horrible unplanned spread of what is neither city nor suburb nor country town, but "slurb"—a compound of slum, suburbia and urban sprawl, which has already blighted Southern California and much of the Atlantic seaboard.

And we must be ready to devote a great deal of money and a great deal of skilled effort to something much bigger and more constructive than what often passes for urban renewal—the conversion of cities from being victims of their own size, ugly or infinitely dreary monuments of profiteering development and general unplanning, or even parasites of the automobile like Los Angeles, into what they should be by definition:

organs for civilized existence; places in which their inhabitants enjoy living, instead of being turned into neurosis fodder; generators of fulfillment instead of frustration.

Science is exploding even more violently than population. Scientists (including technologists) are multiplying over three times as fast as ordinary people. The 1,000,000 or so scientists now at work constitute over 90 percent of all the scientists who have ever lived, and their numbers may well go up to 20,000,000 or even 30,000,000 by A.D. 1999. The number of scientific journals has increased from one in 1665—*The Philosophical Translations of the Royal Society*—to about 1000 in 1865, to over 50,000 in 1965, in which nearly 5,000,000 separate articles are published each year; and the rate of increase is itself increasing. If nothing is done about it, science itself runs the risk of drowning in this torrent of paper; specialization will make scientists in one field more ignorant of work in other fields; and man's advance will be stifled in the mounting mass of unassimilable knowledge that he himself has accumulated.

The situation is made worse by the gross lack of balance between different fields of research. Billions of dollars are spent every year on outer-space research—much of it merely for the sake of prestige, in an effort to get to the moon or Mars before somebody else—as against a few millions on exploring the "inner space" of the human mind; billions on weapons research as against a few millions on the sociology of peace; hundreds of millions on "death control" through medical science as against four or five millions on birth control and reproduction. Biological research has given us the tools for real eugenic improvement, in the shape of artificial insemination with the deep-frozen sperm of outstanding male donors, even after their death, and the speedy prospect of grafting ova from admired female donors—but nothing (except words) has been spent on any such project.

The situation is also made worse by the lack of balance between scientific progress in different countries and regions. There is a big scientific and technological "brain drain" from Britain and Europe to the U.S.A. and Canada, and this is producing an equally big one to Britain and Europe from underdeveloped countries like those of Southeast Asia, the Middle East and Africa. In consequence, the gap between rich and poor nations is widening scientifically as well as economically.

What is to be done? The torrential flow of scientific printed matter could be reduced if the scientific reputation of a man or a department did not depend so much on the number of scientific papers published. This leads, among other things, to postgraduate students being pushed to undertake researches where publishable results rather than scientific importance are the prime consideration. (This holds with even greater force in the humanities, which too often pretend to be "scientific," flooding the learned market with Ph.D. theses crammed with unimportant literary or historical details.)

But what is mainly necessary is a change in approach. Instead of all the separate sciences, like inorganic chemistry or astronomy or systematic botany, pushing on and on along their own divergent lines, and individual scientists competitively striving for new discoveries (or just for publishable facts), more and more scientific manpower should be mobilized to converge on problems that can only be solved by cooperative teamwork between different branches of natural and human science —problems of land use and city planning, of resource use and conservation, of human behavior and health, of communication and education. Beyond all, we need a science of human possibilities, with professorships in the exploration of the future.

Tentative beginnings on a world basis are being made along these lines, like the very successful I.G.Y., or International Geophysical Year, and now the International Biological Program, or I.B.P.; and I am sure that they will incease and multiply in regional, national and professional affairs as well. At the same time we must do our best to get rid of the present imbalance between different branches of science and integrate them in a framework of common effort. This is a necessary step toward a greater goal—the integration of science with all other branches of learning into a single comprehensive and open-ended system of knowledge, ideas and values relevant to man's destiny. This might even lure professional philosophers out of their linguistic burrows and metaphysical towers to take part in rebuilding a genuine philosophy of existence. But before this can happen, we must repudiate our modern idolatry of science and technology, and dethrone them from the exaggerated pedestals on which we have set them. After all, "science" is only the name for a particular system of knowledge, awareness and understanding acquired by particular methods; it must come to terms with other systems acquired by other methods—aesthetic and historical, intuitive and subconscious, imaginative and visionary. A prerequisite for this is the creation of a real science of psychology in place of the array of conflicting heresies at present occupying the field. I venture to prophesy that this will find its root in ethology, the science dealing with the analysis and evolution of animal mind and behavior.

One of technology's most exciting but also alarming achievements is the computer, which is pushing technologically advanced countries like America into an era of computerized automation. I say *alarming* because computerized automation coupled with population increase must tend to split a country into two nations, to use Disraeli's phrase about mid-Victorian Britain. In late 20th century America, the two nations will not be the rich and the poor but the employed and the nonemployed, the minority with assured jobs and high incomes, the majority with no jobs and only unemployment pay. Even though automation can ensure increased production of all kinds of goods, this would be a socially disastrous and politically intolerable situation. Somehow or other, the technologically advanced countries will have to rethink the whole concept of work and jobs. One kind of work that will certainly expand is teaching; another is learning—teaching and learning how to live.

The problems of adjustment will be formidable, and the methods for achieving it will need not only hard thinking but time to work out. Meanwhile, we may be driven to providing everyone, even if they have no job in the customary sense, with a really adequate income to tide them over the period of adjustment.

In regions of dense population and rapid industrial growth, science and technology are producing an alarming increase in pollution and ecological degradation. The volume of solid matter discharged annually into the world's waters amounts to over 65 cubic miles—equivalent to a mountain with 20,000-foot vertical sides and a flat top of over 16 square miles. This includes so much sewage that bathing in many lakes, including even the Lake of Geneva, and on numerous sea beaches has become either disgusting, dangerous to health, or both. Our vaunted Affluent Society is rapidly turning into an Effluent Society. Meanwhile, rubbish dumps and used automobiles are polluting the land, automobile exhausts, domestic smoke and industrial fumes are polluting the air, and pesticides and herbicides are killing off our birds, our wild flowers and our butterflies. The net result is that nature is being wounded, man's environment desecrated, and the world's resources of enjoyment and interest demolished or destroyed.

Here is an obvious case where quality of life and living must take precedence over quantity of production and profit. Compulsory measures against pollution, whatever they may cost, are as necessary as are compulsory vaccination or compulsory quarantine against disease. Meanwhile, science can be set to find better methods of pest control, and technology put to work to reduce effluents, to render them innocuous (or even beneficial, as are some forms of sewage treatment) and to recover any valuable components for future use. Both science and technology must also be called in to reduce the really shocking gap in standards of living and quality of existence between rich and poor countries. If this goes on widening, it will split the world economically into two hostile halves. It will inevitably stir up "envy, hatred, malice, and all uncharitableness," as The Litany puts it, in the poor countries, all too probably combined with racial animosity and with a threat of violence lurking under the surface.

It is all too clear that our present methods of aid and assistance are pitifully inadequate to reduce the gap to below the danger point, let alone close it. To take a single example: The losses inflicted on the countries of Latin America by the falling prices of their primary export products during the Fifties were greater than all the aid they received in the same period. During the present so-called Development Decade, they may well become less instead of more developed.

We have to rethink the whole system. The very idea of aid and assistance, with its implications of charity, of a man satisfying his conscience by giving a beggar half a dollar, must be dropped; for it we must substitute the idea of cooperation in world development, with rich and poor in active though complementary partnership.

This will involve large changes, both in attitude and in practice. First, we must take into account the raw fact that an underdeveloped country cannot be industrialized if its rate of population increase is too high: Too much of the capital and skills required is used up in feeding, housing, educating and generally taking care of the excess crop of human infants; it goes down the drain—the baby drain. Thus expert inquiry has made it clear that unless the Indian birthrate is halved within a generation, it will be impossible for India to break through to modernized economy. Accordingly, all plans for aid must take account of what may be called the recipient country's demographic credit worthiness; if this is too low, some of the aid must go to help the country control its rate of increase, by providing contraceptives and training personnel in their use, and by sending expert advisors.

Secondly, we must somehow transform our international economic system—trade and barter, loans and grants and technical assistance—from the outdated shackles of "free" enterprise and competitive profitability. It is not for a noneconomist to suggest remedies, beyond obvious ones like making loan terms as easy as possible and stabilizing commodity prices. But clearly the job is urgent, and demands a high degree of economic and political statesmanship, in nations, foundations and international bodies.

Both science and automation link up with education. Dorothy Parker once acidly remarked that education consisted in casting sham pearls before real swine. Omitting all questions of the swinishness of its recipients or victims, we must admit that many of its pearls *are* false, flawed or misshapen and, to change the metaphor, that it often involves the forcible feeding of its pupils on unsuitable, unhealthy or even poisonous diets. Just as education in Hitler's Germany was based on stuffing children's brains with National Socialist dogma and anti-Jewish indoctrination, in many Roman Catholic countries it is based on Catholic dogma and anti-Communist and anti-humanist indoctrination; and in

China, the U.S.S.R. and its satellites, it is based on Communist dogma and anticapitalist and antireligious indoctrination. Meanwhile, educational systems in the Western world, and I regret to say in India and most emergent nations in Africa and Southeast Asia, are suffering from the complaint that has been called *examinotosis*—cramming pupils with facts and ideas that are to be regurgitated at appropriate intervals, in subjects that can be marked or graded by the examination process, with the ultimate idea of awarding certificates, diplomas and degrees that will help the examinees in obtaining jobs.

In addition, the world's poor countries suffer grievously from undereducation at all levels. One result of this is that adult illiteracy is actually increasing. A Unesco survey has shown that between 1952 and 1962, 35,000,000 adults were added to the over one billion of the world's illiterates, and the figure is growing yearly. In many countries, only 25, 15, or even 10 percent of the male population is literate, and the illiteracy of women is considerably higher. Meanwhile, surveys have demonstrated that literacy is an indispensable basis for vigorous national life in the world of today, and that 40 percent literacy is the minimum needed for achieving appreciable economic, technological or cultural success. The Shah of Iran has suggested that all nations should contribute one percent of their annual military budgets to a world campaign against illiteracy, and there are numerous other projects for promoting literacy.

Many efforts are also being made to free the examination-ridden educational systems of developed countries from their restrictive practices and liberate them for their true goals—of transmitting human culture in all its aspects and enabling the new generation to lead fuller and more rewarding lives.

The first thing is to reform the curriculum so that, instead of separate "subjects" to be "taken" piecemeal, growing minds are offered a nutritious core of human knowledge, ideas, techniques and achievements, covering science and history as well as the arts and manual skills. The key subject must be ecology, both biological and human—the science of balanced interaction between organisms and their environment (which of course includes other organisms)—together with its practical applications in the conservation of the world's resources, animal, vegetable and mineral, and human. Education must prepare growing human beings for the future, not only their own future but that of their children, their nation and their planet. For this, it must aim at varied excellence (including the training of professional elites) and at the fullest realization of human possibilities.

This links up with the rethinking of religion—a vital task, but one I can only touch on in summary fashion. It is clear that the era of mutually exclusive and dogmatic religions, each claiming to be the sole repository of absolute and eternal truth, is rapidly ending. If mankind is to evolve as a whole, it must have a single set of beliefs in common; and if it is to progress, these beliefs must not be self-limiting but open-ended, not rigid barriers but flexible guidelines channeling men in the general direction of improvement and perfection. Already an effort is being made to find common ground between the world's various religions and churches, and we can be sure that necessity will drive them further in this direction. But this is not enough. In the light of our new and comprehensive vision, we must redefine religion itself. Religions are not necessarily concerned with the worship of a supernatural God or gods, or even with the supernatural at all; they are not mere superstition nor just self-seeking organizations exploiting the public's superstitions and its belief in the magical powers of priests and witch doctors.

The ultimate task will be to melt down the gods, and magic, and all supernatural entities, into their elements of transcendence and sacred power; and then, with the aid of our new knowledge, build up these raw materials into a new religious system that will help man to achieve the destiny that our new evolutionary vision has revealed. Meanwhile, we must encourage all constructive attempts at reformulating and rebuilding religion. My personal favorite is Evolutionary Humanism, but there are many others tending in the same general direction, like Yoga and Zen, ethical and meditative systems, and the cults of release through psychedelic drugs or bodily rituals.

How does this all add up? It adds up to a meaningful whole, something greater than the sum of its parts. We need no longer be afflicted with a sense of our own insignificance and helplessness, or of the world's nonsignificance and meaninglessness. A purpose has been revealed to us—to steer the evolution of our planet toward improvement; and an encouragement has been given us, in the knowledge that steady evolutionary improvement has actually occurred in the past, and the assurance that it can continue into the future.

It is especially encouraging to know that biological improvement has been born of struggle, and that conflict has often been disinfected of open violence and sometimes even converted into cooperative bonding; and it is especially significant that the most vital of all improvements has been the improvement of mind—awareness, knowledge and understanding—coupled with ability to learn and profit from experience. What is more, improvements in the human lot, in man's ways of coping with the problems of existence, have always depended on improvements in his awareness, knowledge and understanding; and today the explosive increase of knowledge has given us a wholly new understanding of our role in the universe and wholly new hopes of human improvement. We are still imprisoned in a mental cage, whose walls are made of the forces of nature as we have experienced them, whose bars are the constructions of our own primitive thinking—about destiny and salvation, enjoyment and ethics, guilt and propitiation, peace and war.

Today the individual man or woman need not feel himself a meaningless insect in the vast spaces of the cosmos, nor an insignificant cog in a huge, impersonal social machine. For one thing, the individual human is the highest and most wonderful organization we know of. In developing his own personality, he is making his own unique contribution to the evolution of the universe.

Secondly, he is a unit of mankind; and mankind is the highest type in the solar system, the only organism we know of in whom mind has broken through to dominate existence. Mankind is not only a product of past evolution but an active agent in its future course: The human individual can help mankind shoulder this responsibility.

Our first objective is to clarify the new vision of our evolution. The next is to define the tasks required to carry out our responsibilities. Our over-all aim is improvement. Our immediate tasks are to achieve the peaceful unity and cooperative development of mankind, to encourage varied excellence and greater achievement, to think in terms of ecology and to practice conservation, and to build a fulfillment society underpinned by some new system of beliefs. The final aim will be the eugenic transformation of man's genetic nature, coupled with the cultural transformation of his social environment. Meanwhile, all can help in understanding and spreading the new revelation of human destiny.

Walter E. Stuermann

The Human Prospect When God Is Dead

The twentieth century was directed to its place in one of the rear pews in the sanctuary of history by an usher, who, to the communicant's embarrassment, did not so much whisper but shout, "God is dead! Today we shall have an anti-Christian service—and I am its herald!" Later, when the young church-goer learned that this enigmatic usher died while insane, he judged that this was quite understandable and proceeded promptly to forget him. And now it is only when he is faced with a catastrophe of stellar magnitude and calls to his aid the witches of Endor, that this caustic apparition appears for a moment to speak again the same terrifying words. Nietzsche was a fusion of the spirits of Amos and Socrates. The result was comparable to a nebular explosion. This Elijah of a new anti-Christian era is one of the most important and fascinating philosophers in the West.

Friedrich Nietzsche (1844–1900) is notorious for many things, including his violent attack on Christian morality, his doctrine of the superman, and the idea that the strong and creative man stands above and beyond good and evil. This misplaced Socrates has also been suspect because he has been falsely regarded as an anti-Semite and an early proponent of the high nationalism and military ambitions of the German Reich. This misunderstanding of Nietzsche can be traced mainly to the activity of his sister, Elizabeth Foerster-Nietzsche, wife of a leader of the German anti-Semitic movement, Bernard Foerster. Walter Kaufmann's *Nietzsche: Philosopher, Psychologist, Antichrist* (1950) analyzes the Nietzsche myth and provides us with a scholarly and engaging picture of the real Nietzsche and his thought. The philosopher is often discovered

Reprinted from *McCormick Quarterly*, XIV, 2, 1961, by permission of the publisher.

Walter E. Stuermann, formerly Professor of Philosophy at the University of Tulsa, is Associate Editor of *ETC.: Review of General Semantics.*

185

giving a distinctly prophetic and Christian criticism of the complacency and self-righteousness of the men of his day. Admittedly he was frequently too caustic and vociferous. And when his illness began to move in and take toll of him, his inhibitions were lowered. But there is scarcely any doubt that Nietzsche was one of the great philosophers of all times, in spite of the fact that he did not follow the beaten paths of philosophical thought and formulated no system. As a matter of fact, his greatness lies precisely in his originality and his rejection of all block-views of the universe. Indeed, Nietzsche was one of the very few men who maintained to the end the critical spirit of a Socrates. Most philosophers start with Socratic skepticism but eventually fall prey to certainty, dogmatism, and the passion for a system. "Here the ways of men part: if you wish to strive for peace of soul and pleasure, then believe; if you wish to be a devotee of truth, then inquire," says the self-styled Antichrist.

One of the curious but profound Nietzschean themes suggests a delusion which has developed in modern man's thinking about himself and his world. "God is dead, and woe is us!" This prophetic exclamation sounds like an inspired utterance of a Jeremiah who lacks the faith of Jeremiah. Nietzsche proclaims that God is dead and that he is the herald of an anti-Christian era which is dawning in human history. The philosopher feels like a solitary prophet on a tortuous mission; he must be the first to declare the message, and, being the first, he must suffer the hatred of men. No man has an easy lot who must preach disaster in the midst of complacency. God is dead—this curious news must reach the ears of men. We cannot deal with the many ramifications of this intuition. We shall indicate one part of its meaning and try to develop this single insight in order to lay bare a delusion to which Western culture has been subject.

When Nietzsche proclaimed that God is dead and that we men have killed him, he was not preaching atheism. He was an agnostic in the interests of intellectual integrity he refused to let his mind come to rest finally in any position. For atheism is as much a firm metaphysical conceit as is dogmatic theism. The uncompromising believer and the firm denier have both given up inquiring; that is, they both have died intellectually. As one Danish thinker expressed it, holding a firm opinion presupposes too much intellectual complacency—it is like being married. To philosophize is to inquire continuously, to experiment everlastingly, to be ever ready to call your presuppositions into question. In this sense Nietzsche was a rare spirit, an authentic heir of Socrates. Men who arrive at firm opinions and formulate systems—Aristotle, Aquinas, Spinoza, or Hegel— are of a different, less noble company.

The formula, God is dead, was Nietzsche's way of saying that the modern world has so far advanced in the sciences as to outrun and render antiquated the received Christian interpretation of God. The classical idea of God is no longer commensurate with the world as it is now understood, though that conception may have been appropriate for a pre-Copernican world.

Before the fifteenth century men's interpretation of the world in which they lived was quite simple. This view is associated with the name of Ptolemy of Alexandria (ca. A.D. 127–151). In brief, it held that the earth was the fixed center of the world. About the earth, the sun, moon, and other celestial bodies revolved in epicycles. In the minds of most men, God and his spiritual hosts resided in heaven above the strata of earth, water, and air. The lair of Satan was below the earth's surface. Here was a simple, comfortable three-story world, with man squatting on his real estate at the center. Neither heaven nor hell was far removed. Man must therefore walk with caution; for invaders from heaven or from hell quite frequently put in their appearance, and they were to be treated with appropriate attitudes of reverence and fear. While man lived in this world with caution, he nevertheless felt "at home." He sat at the center of the scheme of things. The beloved of the race who had fallen asleep in the Lord were not far removed. The saints, angels, and the Lord of creation were all within calling distance and a long arm's reach. There was a certain comfort and security for a man who lived in this Ptolemaic world. He lived in familiar surroundings, both physical and spiritual. It counted heavily with him that all things seemed to revolve about him and were directed largely to minister to his body and soul. He was at home in the world.

This sense of feeling at home, based upon the current scientific explanation of the world, was also fortified mightily by another factor. Man had learned well the ancient lesson that the welfare of his soul was a chief concern of God the Creator and Redeemer of life. God had sent his only begotten Son into the world that he might suffer and die for the purpose of saving human souls. The whole drama of Christian redemption was focused upon man. The Lord had created man by a special act, setting him apart from other creatures over which he was to have dominion. The privileges of Eden were originally bestowed upon him. The whole epic of scriptural history was a recitation of God's attempts, now by punishment and now by invitation to blessedness, to win back the wayward creature. Finally, to climax the drama, God himself came in human form to restore by sacrificial love the descendants of Adam. Man could look forward to a great day of the Lord when triumph would be spelled out in terms of men of faith being raised up into the celestial company of God's own chosen. The Christian drama of redemption was centered upon man. The history and destiny of the race was the center of divine attention. Religiously as well as scientifically, the world revolved about man. The cosmos was not only geocentric but also anthropocentric.

The work of men like Copernicus, Galileo, Brahe, and Kepler shattered the geocentric theory of the world's structure. Copernicus and his scientific heirs produced a world-view where the sun stood at the center of the system and the earth was shoved off toward the margins of the world-structure. That it required several centuries for such thinking to be generally accepted is testimony to the reluctance of man to be dispossessed of his central position. But man was dispossessed—and God was evicted from heaven, his third-story apartment. Man had a residence only in the marginal areas of this new world, and God seemed to have been forced into the life of a celestial hobo. The Ptolemaic world-view had ministered to the conceit of man that surely he must have the seat of honor in the astronomical festivities. It was a sharp and hard blow to his vanity and his dreams of eminence to be thrust aside. His sense of being at home began to wither away. Now he was a stranger in space. The terrifying distances and machine-like movements of the planets, even of his own celestial vehicle, caused him to tremble. His friendly, familiar environment had disappeared as a dream, and he stood alone and unarmed against a world which seemed to be little concerned for his hopes and aspirations. We note Pascal's poignant expression of the thought that the infinite reaches of space terrified him. The old God was dead in such a world as this. The news of it did not, however, get around quickly.

The Copernican revolution shattered the geocentricity of the world which had been built in the image of man's dreams and of his grandeur. But the delusion still persisted in another form. The prejudice that man was at the center of things religious, social, and historical did not die—and it has not yet died. Man shook off the dust of his feet against Copernicus. The picture he holds of the new, widened world is still anthropocentric. To be sure (he says), the earth is an infinitesimal blob of mass in a huge solar system, which is but one small part of a nebula among innumerable other nebulae. To be sure—but man is still set apart from other creatures by a special act. Man is still the focus of divine attention, and the whole drama of redemption simply says that God is moved to minister particularly to the human soul. The Protagorean spirit is still dominant: man is yet the measure of all things. Thus we confront a curious situation. Man is not at the center of things—yet he is at the center. Man is not significant—yet he is most significant. We have here a kind of spiritual schizophrenia. Our sense of our insignificance, in terms of our scientific understanding of the universe, wars within us against our sense of importance, in so far as religious prejudices go. The old God is dead; but still he is not dead.

Human conceit was to suffer another serious setback. The dawning of the scientific hypothesis of evolution in the mid-nineteenth century leveled another blow at man's unusually high opinion of himself. This hypothesis had been anticipated by a few early Greek and later philosophers. It did not gain a controlling position in human thinking until after the work of Charles Darwin (1809–1882). The publication of the hypothesis in *The Origin of Species* (1859), and *The Descent of Man* (1871) provoked much controversy and distress in religious circles, for it was looked upon as a dire threat to the Christian persuasion that man is a creation of God. In part it was a vision of the distressing effect upon man of the hypothesis of evolution that prompted Nietzsche to declare without qualification, "God is dead."

The chagrin men first felt upon learning that their species was naturally selected in an intricate line of development of life in a whole complex evolution of the physical world, of plant and animal life, was soon conquered. To be sure, man emerged, sometimes gradually and sometimes by mutation, over many millions of years from lower forms of life. Certainly, other species of animals underwent a similar development, and some poorly equipped creatures were rolled under by the selective impetus of nature. But, so the transfigured prejudice runs, man is the culmination of this whole intricate process. The human creature is the most complex and sensitive of beings, and it is equipped with a tool no other creature has in like measure: reason. Man's peculiar facilities for behavior and communication have purchased for him an everlasting lease on the cosmos. The anthropocentric conceit of man is most acutely expressed in his opinion that he is the culmination of the process of evolution. The whole of nature subserves his interests. The conceit also involves the idea that the human species simply cannot suffer the fate of those classes of beings now called extinct. Onward and upward the process goes and any further development in man must be an improvement of man as man. "Organic life, we are told, had developed gradually from the protozoon to the philosopher; and this development, we are assured, is indubitably an advance. Unfortunately, it is the philosopher, not the protozoon, who gives us this assurance." Of course, this sort of thinking about man's exceptional position in the process of evolution proceeds on the assumption that the process is undergirded by a Power or Spirit at work to produce a moral and rational being as its end-product. What idolatry is to be found, even among pious Christians, when it is assumed by them that the end of God's purposes is to be identified with a happy end of human life on this planet! Such an assumption not only testifies to human conceit but also to a niggardly conception of God. Deity is trussed up in the bonds of human pride. This is the principal idolatry of man. And the Christian doctrine of redemption is idolatrous to the extent to which it expresses this conceit that the end of God's purposes is to be identified with the preservation and beatification of man in the universe.

It has not been Christian theology alone which has tried to legislate for the universe on the basis of man's intense desire to be an everlasting tenant in the cosmos. In modern times there has arisen a whole family of optimistic philosophies of evolution which, while trying to be modern by making the category of evolution central to their position, have nevertheless been antiquated by reason of interpreting the evolutionary process either as progressive or as anthropocentric. A very clear example is the work of Lecomte du Nouy in his *Human Destiny*. This family includes such different children as Spencer, Hegel, Bergson, and Marx. Despite the mutual fratricide which exists within the family, all the members raise their voices as one to assure us that "the future, though we cannot foresee it, will be better than the past or the present." The reader of these philosophies is like "the child which expects a sweet because it has been told to open its mouth and shut its eyes." The philosophies of evolution, as well as Christian theology, speak of man's conceit concerning his cosmic importance and express his persuasion that, come what may, he cannot be set aside either by nature or by God.

Now, if one were to make a probable judgment about man's place and prospects in the volutional history of the world on the basis of the evidence available, the best guess would be that man as a species will pass away in the midst of the fortunes and misfortunes of history. Man will fade into the shades of the eons with Tyrannosaurus and Stegosaurus. If dinosaurs could have reflected upon their status and spoken about it, we may be sure that they would have complimented themselves on being the eminent end-product of evolution and would have confused dominion with superiority and the immortality of the species. In this connection we cannot fail to call attention to Loren C. Eiseley's suggestive articles, "The Fire Apes" and "The Snout" (*Harper's Magazine*, Sept. 1950, and Sept. 1949). To put the question in theological terms, may not the glory of the Creator and Sovereign of life require that the human species pass away and be supplanted by another reigning family? May not the purposes of God go beyond the happiness and survival of this one group of his creatures? God may one day discover that the human experiment was a failure! Is faith in God strong enough to survive the shock which comes upon learning that his purposes outrun the survival and felicity of man? Unfortunately, in most religious circles it is not. The issue is laid bare, then, as to which is more important to man: his own happiness or the glory of God. The terror with which men flee before the prospects of annihilation or the ridicule they shower upon the idea simply testifies to the fact that they cannot have a grand conception of God as

Creator and one which does not identify God's purposes with their own good fortune. The aged Deity they worship shortly died, and the prospect for them is an ignominious death. Of course, there is no other prospect than death—but it need not be ignominious!

The first conceit concerning man's place in the world, geocentricity, was shattered by the Copernican revolution. The second, anthropocentricity, remains yet to be thoroughly destroyed. As there has been no return to Ptolemy, there will (probably) be no return to the anthropocentric view of the universe, once it has been buried alongside the other conceit. The old God is dead. Christian theology becomes a subdivision of geriatrics, if not of necromancy. It is imperative for the spiritual welfare of men that they raise their sights religiously and conceive God in grander, more subtle terms. The hypothesis of God must be formulated in terms that are commensurate with the rejection of geocentric and anthropocentric theories of the world and of history.

The Christian drama of redemption, which is focused upon man and his salvation, was a great factor in establishing and crystallizing the anthropocentric view of the world. If the conceit is abandoned, then some thorough reconstruction of the doctrine of salvation will be required. Now the Christian tradition is not completely devoid of insights upon which to build a broader, less anthropocentric doctrine of salvation. The idea of God as Creator and Sovereign of all life furnishes an ample foundation upon which to build an understanding of God's dealings with his creatures in such a way as not to set man apart as a specially treated species. It is just possible that God is equally concerned for the life and destiny of all living forms. Salvation may be conceived as a creative restoration of the healthy integrity of all of creation. Besides the doctrine of God as Creator, another element in the tradition useful for the suggested reconstruction is that of the glory of God. This thought, mostly to the fore in the Calvinistic tradition, insists that God's activities are designed to serve finally, not human interests, but the Deity's own honor and good pleasure. Let God be God! If a concept of God is worth having, it ought not be limited in such a way as to serve human prejudices.

One must look sharply these days to discover a man with a faith which confesses that God may employ the death of all human kind for a higher purpose. But perhaps this should not be the case at all. The doctrine of resurrection from death has perhaps been improperly restricted to men as individuals. The dismal prospect of the death of mankind may be the foreshadow of the cross which the species must bear in the interests of God's overriding, redemptive plan. It may not be that God will have to declare the human experiment a failure, as we said above, but that he will find that the race has, in its allotted time, completely served his purposes. The atonement of Christ does not release men as individuals from the penalty of death. We ought not expect it to purchase a pardon for the race. Possibly the death of the race effects a generic atonement on behalf of the whole of creation. The crucifixion of Christ is a sign, not merely of the death of each man, but of the death of mankind. And the symbol of the resurrection is a sign that the realization of God's purposes requires the crucifixion of the race. It is quite possible that the chief end of man is simply to glorify God, without enjoying him forever. Man's prospect is death. Our faith must be deep enough and wide enough to comprehend this. We should not be too much concerned with the human prospect when the old God is dead. We should be intensely concerned with the divine prospect when man is dead.

Paul Mus

Buddhism and World Order

. . . The quotation from an ancient Chinese author, Mo-ti, selected by Professor F. S. C. Northrop as an epigraph for his book, *The Meeting of East and West* (1946), still retains its relevance: "Where standards differ, there will be opposition. But how can the standards in the world be unified?" . . .

The lesson is that a plan for world order, no matter how well-devised and realistic, may not even constitute a step toward world order if it provokes a sufficient amount of opposition—even unfounded opposition.

Religions, especially in Asia, represent, even today, more than "folkloristic residues" . . . Moreover, no great Asian religion, whether

Reprinted from *Daedalus* (Summer 1966), Journal of the American Academy of Arts and Sciences, pp. 813–827, by permission of the publisher, The American Academy of Arts and Sciences, Cambridge, Mass.

Paul Mus is Professor of Civilizations of the Far East at the College de France in Paris and Professor of Civilizations of Southeast Asia at Yale University.

Hinduism, Buddhism, or the popular Chinese mixture of Confucianism, Taoism, and Buddism, may be categorized among "single factors." For these traditions, world order is not, as it is for us, a matter to which they may sometimes turn their attention. It is not, according to Professor Northrop's penetrating analysis, a *postulation*, a prospective and provisional scheme which we formulate, check against experience, and more or less successfully try to improve upon. It asserts itself as an autonomous, continual, and all-embracing process in which we find and may more effectively insert ourselves. The total, not the individual, comes first—a mode of thinking coinciding with Durkheim's much discussed but fundamentally sound description of society as an organic whole rather than as a mechanical addition of parts and circumstances.

Many centuries before the Stoics elaborated the idea of world order along lines still largely accepted by the Western world—though in a quite different spirit because of the penetration of Christian values—world order was generally conceived, throughout a wide cultural area extending from Egypt to China, not as a more or less direct religious preoccupation. On the contrary, it was religion itself, in its highest and impersonal expression, reflected on earth and personalized in a Pharaoh, a King of Kings, a Son of Heaven, or a King of the Wheel.

This can be seen, for instance, in Joseph Needham's suggestive *aperçu* of the Chinese version of the Pattern of Patterns:

> The highest spiritual being known and worshipped was never a Creator in the sense of the Hebrews and the Greeks. . . . The Chinese world-view depended upon a totally different line of thought. The harmonious cooperation of all beings arose not from the orders of a superior authority external to themselves, but from the fact that they were all parts in a hierarchy of wholes forming a cosmic pattern and what they obeyed were the internal dictates of their own nature.

Under various formulations, this high level of temporal and religious organization seems to retain, though with obvious differences, something of a previous, more primitive period, when divine powers may have been less directly conceived as personal figures. The outcome is often called Asian pantheism—a term which should be accepted only with the reservation that, as in the previous stage, the site was more divine than the genius, often theriomorphic and especially ophidian, that haunted it. In the same spirit, now, the total image of the world and of world order remains more divine than the pantheism it accommodates. . . .

We have not fully realized the implications of the fact that the major Asian civilizations view world history as essentially cyclical. In contrast with our own Western conception of an open, indefinite progression, they recognize progress and regress—that is, an alternation, at the cosmic level, of general improvement and deterioration of world order, bringing us periodically back where we began, thus to start all over again.

As a result, each of these different traditions considers that the Golden Age existed when their own patterns of thought and collective as well as private behavior were naturally followed all over the world. The notion that things could have been otherwise does not even arise. Degenerescence—whatever be its final reason—began when an increasing number of people went astray. This is a view which Westerners often do not understand, but which it is essential for us to know. How can the Asian civilizations fail to hold us and our activities responsible for the ever deeper obscurity of this Iron Age, where the leading powers in the world appear to have lost their bearings so that we not only openly expect—and dread—Armageddon, but prepare for it with all our might? . . .

Buddhist Concern in This World: Historical Background

Since the Geneva Agreement of 1954, which marked the end of the Colonial period in what was once called French Indochina, many new political factors have come to the fore in the whole of Southeast Asia. None has taken our experts more by surprise than the role played in many tense circumstances by the various schools of Buddhism in Mahāyānist Viet-Nam, as well as in the countries of Theravāda obedience, Cambodia, Laos, Thailand, and Burma, all of which claimed Ceylon as their religious metropolis. Although Buddhism there was recognized as having deep roots, governing peoples' lives and behavior, it was reputed to be non-political.

I have attempted to explain elsewhere that this erroneous assessment of the political influence of the Doctrine of the Elders (Theravāda) derives from data, texts, translations, and exegesis mainly established through the sustained activity of the Pali Text Society, first in Ceylon and later in Burma. The British Raj had put an end to the local Buddhist dynasties in these two countries in 1802 and 1885 respectively. In both cases, this left a kind of rump Buddhist society deprived of the vitally important support of the faith which the temporal authority is canonically in charge of. This temporal Buddhism was based on the commemoration and cult of the Master, with the Church, for its part, entrusted with the perpetuation of his teachings.

No critical account seems to have been taken of this grave mutilation. Our vision is of a Southern Buddhist monasticism that has turned its back to the world in quest of an egoistic, personal salvation, to be fulfilled in a monastic career extending over several lives, in accordance with the basic belief in transmigration.

When viewed in this manner, Buddhism becomes a complete enigma. How was it possible for a religion so lamely equipped doctrinally to conquer half the world? In his well known book on *The Religion of India,* Max Weber, noting that the Buddha's teaching gave birth to "one of the great missionary religions on earth," inserts this mystified comment:

> This must seem baffling. Viewed rationally, there is no motive to be discovered which should have destined Buddhism for this. What could cause a monk who was seeking only his own salvation and therefore was utterly self-dependent to trouble himself with saving the souls of others?

According to Hermann Oldenberg, our most authoritative expert, "princes and nobles, Brahmans and merchants, we find among those who 'took their refuge in Buddha, the Law and the Order,' i.e., who made their profession as lay believers; the wealthy and the aristocrat, it seems . . . exceeded the poor." Were such people attracted by "the giddiness of annihilation" and by the final negation of self and soul, fading away in the unfathomable vacuity of Nirvana?

Oldenberg asserts that the belief in transmigration had put the last touch to the dreadful picture of the condition that the thought of India, exposed to the woes of a tropical climate, was convulsing itself into. Elaborating on the vedic hymns, most of which concerned, according to him, the legacy of happier times, Oldenberg says that the ritualists

> on all sides . . . descried gloomy formless powers, either openly displayed or veiled in mysterious symbols, contending with each other and like harassing enemies, preparing *contretemps* for human destiny. The tyranny of death also is enhanced in the estimation of the dismal mystic of this age; the power of death over men is not spent with the one blow which he inflicts. It soon comes to be averred that this power over him, who is not wise enough to save himself by the use of the right words and the right offerings, extends even into the world beyond and death cuts short his life yonder again and again; we soon meet the conception of a multiplicity of death-powers of whom some pursue men in the worlds on this side and others in the worlds beyond.

Thus, even death, the supreme recourse of the unfortunate in case of extreme misery, failed the degenerate and endarkened scions of the "tall, blond, dolichocephalic" race that so valiantly had entered the country a few centuries earlier.

In fact, and quite apart from such mistaken ideas of ours, the philosophy and *Weltanschauung* of the Vedas, reflecting the·impact of the Indo-European tribes in India, had very strong positive characteristics. To the variegated and at first disconcerting appearance of the Indian world and its denizens, they opposed, as a deliberate counterweight, the massive unity of an ideal world. This world was bolstered by endless sacrifices, the soul and repository of which were to be found in the vedic texts. The epitome of Indo-European traditions and values thus became the cultural program of the invaders. In the course of the centuries, it had to cope with indigenous and mixed traditions and products, such as the belief in local spirits and gods and, above all, transmigration. The outcome was Hinduism, in which the positive values, previously built on sacrifice (*yajña*), were transferred to a more personal devotion (*bhakti*) to a personalized cosmic power,. Ishvara "The Lord." Ishvara was seen as the Lord of the Universe and, pantheistically, as that universe itself. The self (*ātman*) of the devotee, once built on his sacrificial achievements (*karma*), was now more and more authenticated by, and at the same time finally reabsorbed in, the omnipresence and omnipotence of these Ishvaras (Shiva and Vishnu). The world, in such a perspective, tended to become, a mere picture, an illusion (*māyā*), supreme religious values being everywhere. For the initiate, it was a refuge from the real world and its problems.

This is precisely what the Buddhist revelation sweeps out: the whole mental construction is shattered and with it the prestige and profits which the Brahmans derived from it. At the same time, it becomes less surprising that the new doctrine should have rejected the notion of the person (*ātman*), and yet presented itself, to all objective assessment, as the most rigorous "personalism." It builds each individual entirely on himself and his own actions, without ritual alibis or escapes by atonement. Thus, the conventional self of the Hinduistic rites and devotion was definitively eliminated, leaving everyone to face his own responsibilities: "none but the door of the deed will reap the fruit of the deed." It was a reformation of a kind. The days of the indulgences were past.

The real innovation was to reject final identification with the obscure and unpredictable notion of the cosmic total and to assert that the truth of the transient substantive "states" (*beings*) lay in their very transience, determined by their moral—instead of their ritual—actions (*karma*). Hence the interest shown by early, basic Buddhism in the temporal world. For these early Buddhists, there was (in contrast with the Brahmanical views) no other world on which to rely in order to reach liberation from this one. It is the way in which we handle this world of ours, reducing its beings and finally our being into ways and means of action (*karma*), that leads, thanks to the Buddha's illuminating disclosures, to the "way out" (*nirvana*).

Cosmic Law and World Order: The Burmese Experiment

But was this sufficient to justify a temporal Buddhism, which was overseen by faithful kings and tended to maintain and develop not only order, but prosperity and even abundance in this world—a remarkable anticipation of our "continuing dynamics of development" as the basis for world order? How can such an anticipation of our concept of the Welfare State, with which the historical Maurya king, Ashoka (3rd century B.C.), has been especially credited, be reconciled with the strict doctrine of personal action and retribution, clear of all indulgences, recourses to "others," and alibis?

What is a king, but a figurehead in the inexorable, though not fatal, process of transmigration, in which everyone may count on his own actions, and on nothing else whatsoever, to improve his future conditions?

Professor Emanuel Sarkisyanz, in his remarkable exposition of *The Buddhist Backgrounds of the Burmese Revolution,* has found solid reasons for denouncing local attempts at re-enacting the great Maurya king's *saga* as tragically inconsistent with the ethics and teachings of the Master. Under the pretext of emulating Ashoka, whose glory is to have replaced the drum and weapons of war by the weapons and drum of the Law—the sound of which was the signal of his moral conquests—Burmese historical sovereigns ended in a bath of blood their unfruitful attempts to extend their power over their neighbors. One of them went so far as to boast of having built pyramids of heads. If the Buddhist Cosmic Law is, as canonically described, a peaceful, all-embracing ordering of the world, what has it to do with such cruel and unfortunately too authentic stories?

The notion of cosmic law can be derived from several sources in which the proportion of observation and positive verification, in contrast to pure theorizing, varies greatly. The Brahmanical sacrificial approach of pre-Buddhistic times, centering essentially on the typical Aryan family and its head (*pati*), was related to the ultimate abstract power of the sacrificial formula (brahman), in harmony with the seasons of the year. However, the Buddhist mode of salvation took into consideration a finally impersonal sequence of actions and retributions (*karmaphala*), which was mistaken by "unawakened" (lit. "childish") minds for a "self" or "soul" (*ātman*).

In early Vedic times, the ritualistic approach, with its extensive and strict pattern of sacrificial procedures (*karma*) which covered and authenticated all actions and circumstances of human life, could harmoniously organize that society to meet the short-range interests and elements of routine existence. They developed a hand-to-mouth, autarkic economy. There were, of course, occasional wars against the aborigines, the results of which, as the outcome demonstrates, were usually favorable.

But as soon as we transpose the problem from the simple, comparatively uneventful schedule of a *grihapati's* life, ancient-style, to what befalls a kingdom, its population, and its cities, especially during the uncertain and agitated centuries that followed the advent of Buddhism, an oversimplified and ritualistic conception of cosmic law and world order can no longer work satisfactorily.

Max Weber, following Oldenberg, appears to strike the right note when he stresses the fact that "rural surroundings, cattle and pasture were characteristic of the ancient Brahmanical teachers and schools, at least in the early times of the Upanishads, whereas the city and the urban palace with its elephant-riding kings were characteristic of Buddha's time." This applies, of course, to Hinduized India as well us to Buddha's time.

Wars, invasions, and political and religious revolutions obscured what had been, for a while, a clear and somewhat monotonous conception of world order as the frame of a prosperous "Aryan" life. The final effect was that all Indian religions from then on had to accommodate themselves to a more intricate, more rhythmic, and broader vision of the world—the theory of the recurrent ages—which might well have originated in the Middle East in connection with early astrology and astronomy. It told of a vanished Golden Age. The turn taken by contemporary history, especially in Northern India, thus announced the cataclysmic approach of an end of the world. Early Buddhism associated these ideas with belief in a gradual recession of the Buddha's teaching, leading to the disappearance of the Doctrine of the Church. It found comfort, however, in the expectation of a new Golden Age, to be brought back to earth by the coming of a new Buddha, Maitreya. Though evidently unfounded scientifically, this way of thinking comes remarkably close to what we would call the graph of a periodic phenomenon—in this case, the phenomenon of phenomena, that is, the phenomenon of the world or worlds as a whole.

If such a graph were known with perfect accuracy, we would be able to predict effectively the turn that our lives and the world's affairs would be expected to take. However, no Indian system has ever claimed this degree of accuracy, least of all Buddhism. It was essential to its doctrine not to submit to any fatalistic predestination: the act (*karma*) was to build the world in accordance with the full responsibility of the actors.

Thus, the Buddhists, in the pangs of the present Iron Age, were bound to attach ever greater importance, just to be able to see ahead of themselves, to the exact position of our world as shown on its graph. This made sense of the royal power, of its social activities, its attempts at a peaceful conquest of the earth, establishing a Welfare State that would take charge of the entire world, an ideal nearly attained by Ashoka. Such a reign was a check and, in the case of success, a signal: It meant that the Buddha to come was not indefinitely deferring his coming. There might still be many centuries to wait, but a turning point must have already been reached as things seemed to be improving instead of growing worse. The psychological value of such speculations is not to be slighted. We have recently had ample occasion to appreciate the deep impression made on the Buddhist world by the conviction that we have reached, with the 2500th anniversary of the Buddha's birth, the precise point when we could consider ourselves halfway between his "revelation" and his expected successor, Maitreya.

The West cannot remain indifferent to the fact that so many millions of our contemporary "fellow men" look in that direction in their expectation of an oncoming world order.

The massacres perpetrated by the Buddhist kings who tried to emulate the Maurya Emperor thus make more sense—if a dire and forbidding one. They should be understood as a kind of test or ordeal. Such wars were initiated as a check of the point reached by world affairs on the graph of the ages of the world. The history and, even more clearly, the legend of Ashoka's reign established the pattern of such an experiment. Whatever his final relation to the oncoming Buddha, a point which, in the present state of our documentation, cannot be clearly assessed, after a bloody beginning, a moment had come when—because of his past merits and the accumulated merits of all men and of his contemporaries —the latter spontaneously turned to him and submitted to his sway without further resistance. Such is evidently the signal that the Burmese conquerors sought—and that finally did not come.

There would be great profit in reading Professor Sarkisyanz's remarkable book in the light of such preconceptions, still alive among the masses. This would make it easier to understand why U Nu, commonly taken in 1960 to be the impersonation of the King of the Wheel (cakravartin) that forebodes the coming of the Buddha, or even as the "incarnation" of the Buddha himself, should have been quasi-unanimously borne to power, and nevertheless failed in the eyes of his fellow countrymen and found little support among them against General Ne Win, when the latter deposed him in 1962. U Nu had remained short of the expected "signal": bringing around the Communists to his charisma. This political or, more accurately, cosmic test had, to all appearances, failed.

Conclusion

Relying largely on Professor Sarkisyanz's admirable analysis of the Buddhistic backgrounds of the Burmese crisis, I have tried to show how difficult it is for Westerners to comprehend a vision of the world and world order which is neither *normative* nor purely *objective*, but, shall we say, *prospective*. Still deeply affected by their traditionally half-Buddhistic, half-folkloristic approach to such problems, the masses bet heavily on what they imagine will or might happen—their stakes being themselves. The closest analogy with our modern methodology would be Claude Bernard's famous *Expérience pour voir*. U Nu has been given precisely that chance and has not lived up to it—his achievements as well as his failure offers a remarkable illustration of both sides of the question.

Thus, far from considering "lay" Buddhism, Ashokan style, as a mere pragmatic accretion to the Theravāda faith, a closer study of its intimate connection with the doctrine will help to reconstruct a more human and convincing picture of both the social and political expansion of the Southern School and the eventual grounds for its reconciliation on such matters with the much more open and active leanings of the Mahāyānist or Northern School which prevails in Central and Eastern Asia, Viet-Nam included.

If, before the arrival and interference of the Westerners, a kind of political, quasi-national Buddhism was established on authentic Theravāda and Mahāyāna values, it would seem possible to build, at least between the various Indochinese denominations, a new covenant on that strong and lasting foundation: the Buddha's message.

5
Is God Necessary for Modern Man?

Traditional religion, dazed by the rise of secularization and the collapse of definitive religious patterns, has been forced to ask itself if God is necessary for modern man. It is becoming increasingly clear that the language of traditional religion is no longer understood. Its vocabulary has become outmoded. With one exception, the essays in this chapter reflect the determination of contemporary religion to develop a new language with which to speak to contemporary man.

According to Richard Shaull, this new language will have to use the vocabulary of "becoming" rather than "being." Modern man is in the midst of a revolution in his perception of reality and his understanding of himself. If religion is to speak to him of the direction and dimensions of this ongoing change, it must employ the vocabulary of change.

But to understand fully what idioms it must now adopt, religion must examine closely the idioms it has used in the past. An example of this kind of examination is the essay by Charles Rieck, who contends that study of the genesis of "God-talk" will lead to a better understanding of its meaning and logic. Perhaps such a revived understanding will, as Thomas Parker suggests, enable religion to continue to employ at least part of its traditional vocabulary, yet communicate effectively with contemporary man.

One of the earliest and most persuasive of contemporary advocates for the reappraisal of the vocabulary of religion, and, indeed, of the entire perspective out of which that vocabulary arises, was Dietrich Bonhoeffer, whose *Letters and Papers from Prison* sent scholars and pastors in quest of a "theology of the secular." Bonhoeffer's example is in large part responsible for the predominately progressive mood of contemporary religion. But there remains a minority mood which cannot be ignored and for which Billy Graham is one spokesman. Graham is no less disturbed by religion's failure to communicate with contemporary man, but his recommendation is not that religion move into new contexts but that it return to old ones with a new fervor. Graham's message is an example of conservative reaction to the trend of current theology.

Richard Shaull.

The Presence of God and the Human Revolution

There was a time, not long ago, when theology spoke with a great deal of confidence about where God was at work and what he was up to in the world. For those Christians, however, who are involved on the front lines of revolution today, this is not often the case. The reason, I believe, is to be found in the fact that the same forces that have produced

Reprinted from *McCormick Quarterly*, January 1967, (McCormick Theological Seminary, Chicago) by permission of the publisher.

Richard Shaull is Professor of Ecumenics at Princeton Theological Seminary.

the revolution—many of them having their roots in Christianity—now create a new context for Christian faith, in which our traditional theological categories are called into question.

We use the term human revolution here to refer to the fundamental changes in man's understanding of reality and in his self-understanding, which have occurred in recent times. The breakdown of the older metaphysical world view has opened the way to concern for the fullness of historical existence as that which is real and important for man. The de-sacralizing of all creaturely reality—nature, social and political institutions, the family, human experience and emotions—has cut away the foundations of traditional structures of authority and of religious immediacy as well. With the growth of scepticism about man's ability to know the essence of things has come the discovery of the utility of functional thinking together with a functional approach to all social institutions. As a result of all this, modern man finds himself thrust into full historical existence, with no solid ground under his feet and no authoritarian order around or above him, but with an amazing new freedom to choose and create his own future. If he feels insecure and threatened in this new situation, he is also aware that any return to the former structures of authority and security can only be, at this stage, a dehumanizing regression.

The social revolution taking shape around us is one of the most natural and authentic expressions of this wider revolution in human self-understanding. Modern technology, a product of this changed attitude toward life and world, is now the most powerful instrument for its diffusion. As it undercuts old authorities, makes use of a functional approach in all spheres, and gets results in the domination and use of the world, technology awakens new hopes and contributes to intensified awareness on the part of great numbers of people of all social classes in many parts of the world.

At the same time, the changes required in our social institutions by the dynamics of technology and by its functional approach have not yet come about to any significant degree. By and large, economic growth and technical rationality have not satisfied the hopes they have awakened in many people for greater economic well-being, participation in determining their own future, or liberation from those forces by which they have been enslaved. In fact, as Herbert Marcuse has indicated, technology and the *ethos* accompanying it in the West—and in Communist society—have tended toward a total system of domination in which those who have awakened to new possibilities of existence find themselves more and more frustrated. It is not surprising, therefore, that in many parts of the world those most sensitive to what is happening around them choose revolution as the only way ahead. This revolutionary involvement, in turn, leads to new discoveries of the wider dimensions of the revolution in self-understanding now going on.

At this point, a strange paradox emerges. Theologians rightly see God at work in all this. Yet in that case, what he is doing would seem to make it more difficult, if not impossible, for us now to perceive or speak of God's presence in the midst of revolution. The de-sacralization of the world has removed the possibility of experiencing the immediacy of God's presence, and man's coming of age makes God unnecessary. Most of the categories for describing God's action in the world are so identified with the "religious" or metaphysical understanding of transcendence that they do little to point to the "beyond in the midst of life." And the whole religious framework in which our talk about God is set identifies him with the order which must be repudiated if man come of age is to move toward meaning and fulfillment in contemporary terms.

Our contention here is that in this situation it no longer makes any sense for us to work out, in theological isolation, a systematic interpretation of *Heilsgeschichte* and from that try to deduce what God is now doing in our world. The alternative open to us is to be fully involved, as theologians, in this historical moment, and from within it work out the terms for a fruitful dialogue with the heritage of faith. Whatever these terms turn out to be, they should represent a description, in secular language, of the possibilities open for the renewal of man and for the transformation of society that can be perceived as we look at our world through the eyes of faith. If God is at work in this revolutionary situation, this type of dialogue should not only provide us with some clues to his actions but also lead us eventually to a new language, new imagery, and new concepts for speaking authentically about him.

Some brief remarks may be in order regarding this approach and its implications:

1. Our understanding of the Triune God and of his relationship to the world and to the ongoing history of man, frees us to approach the problem in this way. All spheres of the created order have lost their sacral character; at the same time, they are set in the context of God's redemptive purpose and action. For Bonhoeffer, this means that all earthly and human reality lies "embedded in . . . the reality of God"; the "reality of Christ . . . has already encompassed, seized, and possessed" it. Thus, "the whole reality of the world is already drawn in into Christ and bound together in him, and the movement of history consists solely in divergence and convergence in relation to this center" (*Ethics,* p. 64). The Apostle Paul in Colossians speaks of Jesus Christ as the center of all worldly reality. In him all things were created; it is he who holds all

things together, and in and through him, God is at work reconciling all things unto himself (vs. 15–19). The world as history is the sphere of the Lordship of Christ; it is there that the Holy Spirit is at work.

All this does not provide a basis for a new natural theology; it does suggest, however, that what we have in biblical revelation is not some esoteric truth but the disclosure of what is ultimately real in man's historical existence. God's redemptive activity does not occur in a corner, but in the center of the world. It creates a new reality at the disposal of all men. Theology is concerned about the resources which revelation provides for reflection upon man and his future in the world. But these resources can only take meaningful conceptual form in the midst of the concreteness of historical existence, as the terms for authentic dialogue are worked out again and again.

2. A theological approach to reality, in order to be faithful to its biblical sources, can be neither metaphysical nor empirical, as these terms are usually understood. Because of the centrality of the eschatological in biblical thought, Becoming takes priority over Being, and the concrete reality of the present must be understood in the light of the future. If this is the case, theological reflection about man will not produce an anthropology, but rather a description of what is involved in the renewal of man, as we move from the First to the Second Adam. And Christian social thought will not offer either a justification for the present order or a pattern for a new one, but will help us to comprehend what is involved in the transformation of our present social structures in the direction of the Kingdom of God.

In this perspective, the way may be open for a more fruitful confrontation between theology and the various secular disciplines. As long as the theologian, the social scientist, or the philosopher looks upon the reality with which he deals as that which *is* in either an ontological or empirical sense, we can have little hope of moving beyond the present impasse. When, however, the stabilities of each discipline are upset by the pressures of the future and by the concern for humanization, these inter-disciplinary relationships may well undergo a significant change. Moreover, when theology is true to its vocation in these terms, it can once again become a force of transgression and transcendence in its impact upon other disciplines.

In relation to the development of theology itself, the issue here raised is that of the theologian's choice of a partner for dialogue. Contemporary conceptualizations of faith will hardly emerge except as they come out of such dialogue. If the theologian must always be careful not to give normative value to any philosophy or ideology, he should also recognize that not just any secular partner for dialogue will do. If our thesis here is correct, those who are most intensely concerned about understanding their spheres of reality in relation to the future of man should merit our special attention. To speak more specifically, perhaps the time has come when we will find it helpful theologically to turn from Martin Heidegger to Ernst Bloch.

3. We have suggested that to speak of the presence of God in the world today means to point to concrete possibilities for the renewal of human life and the transformation of society on the road to the future. But this in itself is not of much help to us, even if we have a satisfactory Christian description of the shape of the human. Christian existence is historical existence, and the interaction between God and man in history implies that, at certain specific moments, the task and possibilities of humanization are defined in quite specific ways. And yet, when the theologian attempts to "discern the signs of the times," he is on very uncertain ground. Any hypothesis he offers for such discernment must be highly tentative, and open to constant correction and revision.

Nevertheless, the attempt must be made, and recent studies by Bonhoeffer, Van Leeuwen and others may give us a basis for it. If the work of Christ in the world has cut away the foundations of ontocratic patterns of life and forced man to come of age, then God may be pushing us to the point where we can discover our humanity as we accept the collapse of old structures and find the resources we need to live without stability or security. In other words, human renewal may be a question of appropriating the freedom to which we are now called in order to explore new possibilities of *vita experimentalis* within a framework of growing responsibility. The presence of God will then be perceived along this road to maturity, as a new style of life emerges.

In the social sphere, the breakdown of the ontocratic order creates a situation in which the integration of community or nation must come as people are united in a common effort to create the type of future they want. But given the present structures of social institutions and the system of social domination now being established by technology, this process leads increasingly toward social revolution. The presence of God may therefore be discerned most clearly at those points where the powers of the old order are being confronted by new messianic movements for human liberation, i.e., in the midst of the breakdown of old institutions, the eruption of conflict and violence, and the search for *new* solutions for our most pressing social problems.

4. The contribution of theology to reflection upon the renewal of man and society cannot be made any longer in the framework of a total, metaphysical system. In addition to its being abstract and non-historical, such thought will always have a certain heteronomous character for modern man. What we do have at our disposal, however, is a wealth of biblical and theological images and symbols, of myths, parables, and

stories, which can give new insight into human and social reality, call attention to dimensions of that reality that are often overlooked, provide us with clues as to what is most important, and make possible a clearer vision of the whole.

Professor Paul Ricoeur, in a number of recent writings, especially his two-volume study of *Finitude et Culpabilité*, has given a great deal of attention to this approach. For him, symbol and myth are primarily means by which "man understands himself in his world." By relating reminiscence and expectation to the present moment, and by pushing beyond that which is immediately perceived to new and hidden dimensions of reality, the symbol has the power to illumine the situation in which man finds himself. By its very nature, it aims at unifying the rich variety of human experiences and thus offering a vision of totality. The symbol expresses what is sacred in the world and for the self, at the same time that it relates the sacred to the realm of immediate experience. Thus myth and symbol can become the basis for a new *logos*.

The task before us then, is that of rediscovering the meaning and wealth of our Christian imagery, especially of those clusters of myths and symbols which help us to discern the nature and direction of God's humanizing activity in the world: among them

—those describing man's pilgrim existence, on the road from Exodus to Promised Land, from Exile to the new Jerusalem;

—those describing life as a gift, as response to the surprises of grace;

—the great symbols of crucifixion and resurrection and their implications for man's historical existence;

—those which give us a basis for iconoclasm, for an attitude of radical transgression and transcendence in relation to every established order;

—those which describe the dialectical relationship between conflict and reconciliation, stability and change;

—the images that point to signs of hope in the midst of the social struggle in which we are now involved.

5. The new *logos* that may emerge from the confrontation of the biblical images with contemporary reality will not necessarily be a *Christian logos*. In fact, the primary concern of the theologian should be to contribute as much as possible to the broadening, deepening, and revitalization of *secular* thought.

There will always be a place, within the discipline of theology, for historical studies and for efforts to formulate an integrated under-standing of what the Christian faith is all about. But beyond this, the theologian who works creatively on the basic images and symbols of faith will discover that almost everything he has to say will be related to questions that are being dealt with in other disciplines. The fact that theology has its own starting point—in revelation—does not mean that the theologian can fence off any area which he can then claim exclusively as his own. Within the present framework of academic disciplines in the university, his position will always be very insecure; and whenever he speaks, he will probably be considered an intruder by the social scientist, the philosopher, and others.

We may not enjoy being forever in such a position, but there is no reason why we should be too unhappy about it. The material with which we work makes this inevitable, and we will hardly be prepared to interpret the meaning of death and resurrection for modern man unless we discover what it means for us as theologians to run the risk of dying daily in order to live creatively. Moreover, the theologian who follows this path may be free to discover that our rigid structure of disciplines is fast becoming obsolete. In an electronic age in which insight depends upon the discovery of pattern and configuration, rather than upon the mastery of information, new instruments are needed for a more adequate interpretation of reality. When theology focuses its attention on image and symbol, and struggles to find new categories of thought in this context, it may be in the process of responding creatively to the presence of God in the revolution of our time, and thus be on the road toward new forms of witness in a secular world.

Charles J. Rieck

Is God Dead?—A Positivist's Dialectic

It is an interesting thing about theology that the most burning questions and perennial issues have always been "metaphysical" in character. The point under discussion may run through a whole gamut of topics; the theologian may be discussing the mode of Christ's divinity, predestination and grace, Christ's presence in the Eucharist, the divine nature, or the life of the Trinity.

Any approach to these questions that claims respectability and durability will be framed in a complicated network of concepts and intuitions that most people would term scientific or "metaphysical." The revival of positive theology and studies in the source of Revelation in recent years has, however, often obscured this fact. In Protestant circles, the influence of Barth and Bultmann and their emphasis upon Scripture have inspired a kind of anti-intellectualism. Among Catholics, too, the liturgical, patristic, and biblical revivals have at times clouded the basic questions.

God Is Dead

Nevertheless, in our own day—one might say in our own hour—these recent tendencies have come to an abrupt halt. It is in England and America that this event is most tangible. Never swept away by the European pessimism which afflicted post–World War I thinkers and post–World War II students, Anglo-American thinkers have kept in close touch with the fundamental optimism of the culture around them.

Reprinted from *Listening—Current Studies in Dialog,* Spring 1966, Vol. I, No. 2, by permission of the publisher. © 1966.

Charles J. Rieck is Associate Editor of *Listening; Current Studies in Dialog,* Dubuque, Iowa.

This culture—and this holds true for the whole of the West—is coming to a new stage of self-confidence. At this moment in history, these nations are coming to a vivid consciousness of the power and vitality of the human intellect. The Kennedy myth, the Great Society, the Common Market, de Gaullism and the East-West *détente* are both causes and symptoms of the growing awareness that we in the West are entering upon a second Enlightenment in which technology, the social and nature science—reason in all its forms—are about to create a new world.

As theology tries to remain loyal to the present modes of human vitality and enter into dynamic interplay with them, it swerves from a preoccupation with its roots in the past and comes face to face with the world about it. In its own way this event recalls the thirteenth century when the students of the *Sentences*—that great historical sketchbook— fell under the sway of Aristotle and awoke to nature's depths, the sweep of reason and science, and the mind's power to mold the world to its own purposes. Paralleling the efforts of St. Thomas and St. Albert with their *Summae*, theologians today are coming to grips with the issue of secu- larity—an earnest attempt to take the world seriously, to realize that *this* is the stage on which the believing Christian re-enacts the drama of grace.

It is inevitable, as a result, that theologians should question the meaning of their endeavor vis-à-vis the world around them. And since the world around them is more and more a vibrant, positive experience, evoking the total loyalty of the masses, theologians will attempt to interpret the structures of belief in terms of reason, nature, and science.

Of course, one cannot escape the fact that God, in some sense of that term, is the leitmotif of theology, the subject of theological inquiry. Hence, the first sector the theologians will reassess will inevitably be the notion of God and, more generally, the nature of that which claims to be above nature. For this is what the theologian feels the buoyant self-confi- dence of the new Enlightenment threatens—as indeed it does. Is God dead?—the world asks the theologian.

Bishop Robinson first brought public attention to this problem in his *Honest to God*. Though he has borrowed heavily from both Bultmann and Tillich, Robinson uses the latter as his chief inspiration for the God- question. But Tillich's ideas have long been current among the existen- tialist theologians. What brings life to Robinson's book is not Tillich's abstractions but the way Robinson applies them to the vital question of God-talk in a scientific culture. What is provocative, however, is not always adequate. Robinson is not a metaphysician; in fact, his treatment of these metaphysical questions is so muddled and confused that almost every critic has wrung his hands.

Robinson's chief defect is his failure to bring philosophical precision to bear upon the problem of God. Others, chiefly the British analysts, have not been so ill-prepared for this task, however; this paper will explore the implications of some of this work.

The Problem

The task is really two-fold. First, how can we possibly talk about "God" if we do not experience him. In what way can we set out to find the applicability or non-applicability of our language if we have no tangible object that will gauge its validity.

Clearly, God is not something experienced, at least not by many people. In the language of the analysts, "there's nothing to see." But if God is not experienced, we can not even begin to describe him. This is a simple question of logic. To attribute some predicate to God, to say, for instance, that "God is love" or "God is the first cause" there must be an *"an sit"* of the subject of such a proposition, i.e., God. The proposition, for instance, "Socrates *is* a white man" is neither true nor false and thus in a real sense is meaningless because Socrates no longer exists. A fortiori, if an object never has been nor ever will be experienced, the existence of the object remains an open question and propositions about it will, in analytical terminology, be totally meaningless. Thus, an answer to the question *"an sit"* implies some point of contact, some cognitive exchange between God and the mind; we can only speak of what we know or are at least aware of in some way. What cannot be spoken must remain unuttered. But where would be the opening for such a contact if our experience is so firmly rooted in sense data and its intelligible structure?

There is a further question: If, as theists claim, God is completely transcendent, in what sense do the predicates attached to his name have any meaning? Study of works attempting to describe this transcendent entity show that the language employed is derived from the ordinary experiences of structured sense-data: wisdom, cause, love, and so on. But if God transcends sense experience, in what way do these descriptions have any content left?

Of course, these are the classical objections which were most concisely articulated by Kant's *Prolegomena* and *Critique of Pure Reason*. Yet these are also the pivotal issues of empirically minded theologians. Over and above treating these questions separately, what this article hopes to contribute is a clear explanation of the precise mode in which these two questions reduce to a single question. Perhaps it is only with the advent of linguistic analysis as a clearly defined thought form that this question has been broached in the contemporary period.

By way of summary and preview, this article will prove the "logical" status of god-talk, such statements, that is, as "God is," "God is infinitely wise," and so on. In the course of this inquiry, examination will be made of a) the point of contact with the reality of God (what the medievals termed "proofs for the existence of God") and b) the logical characteristics of the terms used by the statements which describe this "experience" (the so-called "attributes" of God). It will be seen, finally, how closely related these two considerations are.

"Experience" and Beyond

Before these questions can be studied, some preliminary groundwork must be laid. First, it is true that man's cognitive life is centered upon what is termed "experience" in a Kantian framework. Knowledge, that is, is man's immersion in the stream of structured sense-data. This is the cardinal tenet of the Aristotelians; it was elaborated by Hume, given its classic expression by Kant and rediscovered by modern-day empiricists. The first group often emphasized the disparate character of the basic constituents, categorizing them as sensible and intelligible. Hume, in the polish of perfect English, began the long trek towards integrating what often seemed to be split asunder, focusing his attention upon the most palpable factor, the sensible. Kant did justice to the ineffable interplay between sense and intellect, but blurred his perspective by falling victim to the idealist tendencies inherited from Descartes and Leibniz.

The initial field of cognitive experience is a panorama of sense data, loosely organized in the phenomenon of perception. The mind, taking this term for the combined interplay of sense and intellect, becomes aware of the similarities of things, both in reference to themselves across the span of time and in reference to other things across the sweep of space and time; it sees, that is, the generic and permanent features of these perceptually organized sense-data. The mind views these objects, thus, in a state of abstraction, where what it savors and exploits in the objects are the common, permanent factors, passing over the particular, individuating features. The faculty of sense is that which brings the mind into contact with the sense-data, while the faculty of intellect is posited as the source of the mind's ability to focus its attention upon only select sense data, ignoring the individuating limitations of space, time, precise dimension, and so on. This moment of intellect yields the subject-matter of natural science; the intellect guides sense so that the mind contacts stable, universal objects upon which science can be erected.

The mind, however, does not stop here, and this is where the real problem begins. There are a variety of phenomena which pose troublesome questions. The problem of motion or event is one of these. Every physical motion or event is observed to have a predecessor-event, an efficient cause. By a process of argument, however, it can be shown, the medievals claimed, that an event here and now cannot really be explained by efficient causes.

If one event, that is, occurs after, or because of, another event (the causal bond), the next event must take place because of some other, and so on. The inquiry leads to an interminable list of events, each trying to explain the one next to it. Hence, the mind never reaches a single object that presents a decisive explanation, i.e., an explanation itself free of further explanation. This is a violation of the whole scientific program; the mind is incapable of decisive explaining with the objects of knowledge at its actual or possible disposal. Yet the mind is driven to seek a final explanation. Always the question of the mind is "Why?" For the mind which takes this dilemma seriously, a distracting tension pursues it. On the one hand, the mind says, there must be a physical explanation; yet the mind can establish that there is none, but only an interminable series of cascading answers.

Towards Non-Explanation

But is this dilemma the full tale? There is, in fact, a domain of reality with which the mind has *some* contact and which at the same time escapes some of the exigencies of physical, material, sensible existence—the intellect. True, the mind does not know itself, as intellect, as an object; it knows only the material directly. On the other hand, in terms of a peculiar reflective process, it does have a limited ability to take in its ken, in some sense, its own presence—as the "I think" (Kant) or "arena" (Hume) which accompanies and unifies all cognitive experience of material objects. Yet the mind also knows that this "I think," this "arena" rises above the exigencies of space-time existence, transcending to some extent the objects which it directly knows, i.e., the purely material and physical. True, the intellect does not "exist," in the sense of providing an object of direct knowledge that can be empirically, sensibly verified through experience. Yet the word intellect has some "meaning," some kind of entity, therefore, for man has an over-the-shoulders awareness of it and "*esse*, in the wide sense, *est percipi*, in the wide sense."

Perhaps, one says, there is something, some entity like the intellect, in some vague sense "responsible" for, somehow "explanatory" of, this interminable series of intermediate causes. If the mind is driven to seek a cause and finds none among the ordinary objects of direct experience, perhaps the mind is being oriented to a new realm of entity of a status similar to the freedom from materiality which characterizes the intellect (I hesitate to use "existence" and use instead "entity" since from an empiricist point of view, "existence" means "knowable as a material object," i.e., *esse est percipi* as an object of sense). This reality does not in any as yet *recognizable* sense "cause," i.e., serve as an explanation, because all explanations to this point have been material events and objects. Yet if the mind does not attain a "cause" of the series, it does see the glimmer of an entity that "lurks behind" this series; at least the mind becomes aware of the fact that because of this series it is oriented beyond the series *in the sense that* its scientific quest is vain and frustrated if it remains within the series.

This seems to be what has been described as the moment of *"separation."* It is a negative judgment often phrased as *"non est omne ens huiusmodi,"* i.e., not every being is material. Though "being" (*ens*) or "existence" must be equated with the sensible and material, i.e., the directly sensibly knowable, yet there is an "entity," i.e., something which in some way, indirect as it may be, confronts the mind, a quasi-*ens*, and yet is not directly knowable, i.e., is not an *ens*, or the sensible and physical. This judgment is framed negatively because the entity is not directly experienced; hence a statement as "there is a being which is immaterial" (*est ens immateriale*), would be misleading because it seems to imply direct cognitive exchange. The negative form, however, emphasizes the *in*adequacy of the *ens* (*materiale*) which is directly perceived. All we can say, in substance, is that the series points beyond itself, i.e., is inexplicable on its own terms, and then apply to it, project upon it, the peculiar awareness we have of our own freedom from restraint to matter.

In no sense does the dialectic through efficient causes, as examined above, yield an "explanation" in the strict sense. In fact, the whole point is that there *is none* and *cannot* be any decisive explanation strictly so-called for this series, however hard this may be for the mind to accept. It is this lack of explanation which the mind, as it were, hypostatizes, projecting its indirect self-experience outwards in an attempt to attribute some reality to that which the mind instinctively tries to find.

"God" as Verifiable

This whole inquiry leading to such an hypostatized non-explanation can be approached from a different tack. It is part and parcel of the whole analytic movement that those statements are meaningful which can in some way be verified, under conditions laid down by the verification principle. That is, before a statement can be judged true or false it must be empirically meaningful. This meaning, according to the verification principle, is framed in terms of a "test." If there is some sense-data test whose truth or falsity will decide for or against the proposition, then it is meaningful. The proposition "God exists" is meaningful in this way, provided extreme care is taken in search for the empirical test which can either verify or falsify this statement.

The test in this case is the dilemma to which consistent application of the principle of causality leads. If the causality principle were false, our dialectic would never even begin and there would be no reason to postulate the existence of some unseen entity. But in fact the causality principle is true, at least in the macro-domain, and it leads to an interminable series of superimposed non-decisive explanations and a resulting mental stalemate. Thus "God exists" is a meaningful statement.

The proof for the existence of God from order in the universe also yields novel insights when interpreted as a "*separatio*." Garrigou-La-grange seems to have presented the most plausible form of this proof in its classical form. There are (at least some) things in nature which behave, i.e., encounter other objects dynamically, in regular patterns. For example, an electron always attracts a neutron with precisely the same force. Two atoms of hydrogen and one of oxygen always produce water when they interact under suitable conditions. But such regularity of behavior under different environments proves that the source of this determinate behavior is from the "within" of the object.

Thus within an object we have a positive orientation towards another object and towards specific behavior with it; the objects are in some fashion united. Yet the two objects are substantially independent, autonomous. It is clear, that is, that in nature there is no such object which embraces the two autonomous entities. Thus the two are one and yet they are not one. Hence, a puzzle, a tension.

Yet, as with the dialectic of causality, there may be some kind of resolution, a mitigation of this polarity. After all, the mind knows through reflection "over its shoulder" that it unifies objects which are substantially different in the framework of a single concept: the concept of interaction in the case of the electron and proton, for instance. Perhaps there *is* some "entity"—not an "existent," since by definition this is what is directly known in terms of sense data and we experience no such unifying thing— which unites these two objects in some way paralleling the intellect's unification.

It is interesting to note that this proof leads to a theism that does not immediately avoid pantheism. Perhaps after all the objects really are one, i.e., are not totally independent, but are really integral parts of one quasi-substance, the cosmos, which in some mysterious way unites and embraces the two seemingly independent things. Only further analysis of the possible simplicity of this "principle" could remove the possibility of pantheism which dogs the tracks of any argument from order and design.

Here again we can characterize this dialectic as a "*separatio*."

(Material) being does not satisfy the intellect's instinct for explanation; *non est omne "ens" huiusmodi*—not all explanations are material.

There is, then, justification for maintaining that a domain of inquiry exists which passes beyond the physical sciences. Such a study—metaphysics, and, in particular, natural theology—does not, as the less alert of the positivists maintained, belong to a stage of knowledge that historically precedes the physical sciences. Far from being a kind of animism, or poetry or a characteristic of the historical era termed metaphysical (Comte), it is an outgrowth, an epiphenomenon of scientific pursuits. This is not to say, of course, that it participates in the instability which characterizes many of the sophisticated domains of science that have only a provisional character. Rather, it is an area of interest that is opened up soon after the first halting but stable and certain steps of scientific knowledge are made.

God-Talk: Models and Qualifiers

What can be said about the nature of the methodology and language that will be employed by this "science"? In particular, what of God-talk? How does it stand, as Heidegger might say, with regard to the logics which control these strange usages of language? Here again the achievements of the analysts become especially valuable. The work of Ian Ramsey in this direction has taken great strides.

In the first place, what is the status of the language used to describe the first moment of contact with this new domain of being, the moment of "*separatio*"? There are, for example, terms such as "first cause," "first intellect," etc. An analysis of "first cause" will illustrate the gains made by linguistic analysis.

In an expression of this kind, there are two elements, exemplified in this case by "first" and "cause" taken separately. "Cause" serves as the "model," and "first" as the "qualifier," in Ramsey's terminology. A "model" "is a situation with which we are all familiar, and which can be used for reaching another situation with which we are not so familiar; one which, without the model, we should not recognize so easily." In the argument from causality the "model" starts us, for example, with this tree, or this human being, and puts them in a causal setting. We can go in either direction. We can think of this tree in relation to the acorn from which it came; or of this tree, over a long period of time and under certain pressures, becoming coal. With the "model," then, we are given straightforward sense-data pictures.

The "qualifier" has two separate functions. First, it prescribes a special way of developing the "model" situations. In the case of "cause," "first" prescribes that we move backwards to the ancestors, and not forwards to the progeny. If we are dealing with a tree, for example, we move backwards to the acorn, or, in the case of human generation, from the son to the father, or in Thomas' metaphors of per se subordination, from the son to the sun. But more than that, the word "first" in its initial function, presses us to *keep* moving backwards, in search of a decisive explanation; what results is an interminable series of causal bonds.

"Disclosures"

Somewhere during the midst of this dialectical retreat, a "disclosure" takes place—one such as we described above. The mind sees it can never reach a decisive explanation, a "first" cause in the ordinary sense of "first."

After this disclosure, the word "first" takes on a second function. In reality, it now seems to mean "not-first," i.e., there is *no* first cause. In a sense, "first" means "there is no first"; there is no object of scientific inquiry that serves as a decisive, a "first" explanation.

And yet, according to ordinary language, God *is* the *first* cause, he is not a not-first cause. He is posited as *the* decisive explanation—where "explanation" is taken in the broad sense sketched above as being applicable to some non-material, non-physical reality. Obviously we must commit this second usage of "first" to deeper scrutiny.

In Ramsey's terms, God's explanatory function is logically *prior* to the intermediate causal explanations; he is "first" in that he is in some sense the *first* word among the words of explanation used to explain, for instance, the presence of this tree here and now.

The word "God" is placed "first" at the head of all causal stories, presiding over and uniting all the material causal explanations. Otherwise expressed, the word "God" "completes," and is logically prior to, all causal stories

in the series. God, then, stands outside the series of subordinated causes, sustaining the whole series with its intermediate links—sustaining in the sense of giving some kind of explanation, albeit a non-scientific one.

St. Thomas' treatment of the dialectic of motion or causality in his commentary on the *Physics* dovetails with this analysis, and illuminates this second function of "first." The object whose motion we are trying to explain is the tip, the last piece of a stick. (Consider the here and now conjoined movers as parts of a long stick.) The tip is moved by the part next to it, that part by the one next to it, and so on—perhaps *ad infinitum*. Note that the stick itself is in motion; each part moves the next only because it itself is in motion. Now, what of the stick as a whole with its motion as a whole? Clearly, no material object is moving it, since by our definition of the stick, every physical mover in the series is part of the stick. Yet the motion of the whole seems to beg for some explanation: whatever occurs, occurs because of something else. Again, our familiar tension, the mental dilemma. If the stick has a mover, this ultimate, "first" mover is completely separate from the stick since it is immaterial. Thus, this "first" mover is not "first" in the sense of being the other end of the stick; it is not part of the stick. It is "first" in the sense that it "presides over" the whole motion—not in the sense that it is the last term of a series.

A Misconception

Thus the objections to this kind of a dialectic which are based upon a misconception of the logical role of "first" can be met. If "first" means the end of the series, one might legitimately ask, "does not the word 'cause' always imply a causal predecessor?" Does not every material object or event have a preceding cause? If one were to reply facilely that this cause is not material, the charge would be made that this is nonsense talk—that this is not a (physical) explanation. But if the "first" cause does have a (physical) predecessor, how can it be "first"?

On the basis of what has been said, the proper response is that, despite grammatical similarity, "first cause" is not at all logically parallel to either "proximate cause" or "remote cause" or "first item in a series"; rather, the "first cause" has the complex logical structure indicated. "First cause" does not explain some successor, the way remote or proximate cause does. Such a "first cause" would have to be material, and thereby a contradiction in terms. Rather, it is logically first, i.e., outside the series, "explaining" the series as a whole, and not the motion of its successor link rather than another intermediate link further down the line.

Ramsey gives another example of how the metaphysical character of theological words must be carefully scrutinized. In working through the dialectic of design and noting the order of certain segments of the universe, finally coming to recognition of a first designer or "eternal purpose," we must be extremely careful in assessing the results. "Purpose" usually means "adjusting means to some end." It is a way of overcoming difficulties, i.e., of reaching some non-obtained end by proper and judicious choice of intermediate steps. Hence, if we predicate "eternal purpose" of God in this sense of "purpose," we destroy his omnipotence, rendering him subject to some autonomous external end which he is striving to attain, and confining him to a limited range of means. But this annoying result stems from failure to see how our logics have been altered. As in the discussion of causal situations, so in the dialectic of order we begin with purposeful situations, where causality and purpose are used in their ordinary, experiential senses. But as in the first proof "first" takes the term "cause" of "first cause" out of the original model situation, so too "external," the qualifier, lifts "purpose" out of the original model situation "purpose(ful behavior)." The divine intellect posits the ends *and* the means, giving the means their outward thrust to the end. Creatures, on the other hand, opt for an end and are then bound to choose those—and only those—means which have pre-established orientations to the end.

Attributes

The type of analysis Ramsey conducts to establish the existence of God has broad implications when we pass on to consider the attributes of God, the *"quomodo (non) sit."* One word which dominates analysis of each of the attributes is "infinite." For the purposes of this paper, we shall restrict our attention to this rubric. Moreover, we shall confine our interests to the epithet "infinitely wise."

Classically, this phrase means the unadulterated, potentiality-free condition of pure act, what has as its correlative *"ipsum intelligere subsistens."* The procedures of linguistic analysis, however, provide deeper insight into the meaning of this term by isolating the peculiar logical function which such a phrase serves.

Such a notion is often derived from a dialectic that bears resemblance to the Platonic (fourth) proof of Aquinas. Focusing first upon the model "wise" we consider various examples of intelligence: the bee, the university professor, the grammar school student. But the qualifier "infinitely" in its first logical function puts a direction to this rumination. We consider first an amoeba, *then* the bee, *then* the grammar school student, *then* a high school student, *then* a university professor, *then* some world-renowned scientist or philosopher, and so on. What we are presented with is a series which we would classify as an ascending chain, each member of which is wiser than its predecessor.

Somewhere during this dialectic, a "disclosure" occurs. "Wisdom" is experienced in these examples as a perfection that admits of more or less. Hence it is somehow independent of its varying degrees of manifestation. There is an "infinite wisdom." At this point, "infinite" exerts its second logical role. It might be objected, for instance, that if the word "wise" is to have any verifiable meaning, every "wise" thing can be excelled by some further increase of wisdom. Thus, the concept of "infinite wisdom" is a self-contradiction; it is the highest, purportedly, and yet, not the highest.

The Logic of "Infinite"

But this statement betrays a misconception of the logical force of "infinite." The qualifier "infinite," in its second logical role, removes the "wisdom" which it modifies from the series of ascending wisdoms. It is not at one end of the series, higher than its successors—and thus within the series. Rather, it presides over the series as a whole, from without. Simply speaking, therefore, it is not what people ordinarily mean by "wisdom" at all; if it were, it could be exceeded, with the proper genetic care at least. "Infinite wisdom," rather, expresses the consternation which the intellect is gripped by when it detects the newly found quasi-autonomy of wisdom vis-à-vis the individual expressions to which it seemed so firmly rooted. It is not directly experienced; it is the fringe of an experience that the mind cannot reach, and the outer limit of the experience that the mind has attained.

An analogy can be drawn with the number "2." According to the Whitehead-Russell scheme of mathematical analysis, "2" in one sense is a peculiar kind of number. Consider, for example, the series of finite sums: $1, 1 + \frac{1}{2}, 1 + \frac{1}{2} + \frac{1}{4}, 1 + \frac{1}{2} + \frac{1}{4} + \frac{1}{8}, 1 + \frac{1}{2} + \frac{1}{4} + \frac{1}{8} + \frac{1}{16}$, etc. Clearly, this series of increasing sums represents the first logical function of "infinite" in "infinite sum." That is, after the "model" presents us with each of the sums, the qualifier "infinite" directs us to consider them as they increase in magnitude, approaching "2." After a while, we notice that while the sums are always exceeded by "2," at the same time they become increasingly close to "2." That is, "2" represents an "infinite sum"—but not in the sense that the other members are sums; for we cannot write out an infinitely long expression. "2" is a "sum" in the sense that it presides over the series of sums from without—the second logical function of "infinite." In short, "infinite" in " '2' is an infinite sum" has two logical functions. First, it points out that in following the ascending terms, we come increasingly nearer to "2"; second, "infinite" removes "2" from the series by pointing out that none of the sums is ever exactly equal to "2," but is somewhat less.

Conclusion

At this point, we can reflect back upon the proposal made earlier that linguistic analysis could point out the close relationship between the genesis and meaning—the *an sit* and *quomodo sit*—of God-talk.

In fact, much more than a close relationship is disclosed. The logical status of the words used in describing the attributes of God can be understood only in terms of the empirical context from which the proofs of God's existence are drawn. Expressions like "infinite," when used of the attributes, immediately conjure up the model embedded in natural experience and impose upon it the two logical functions of direction and withdrawal which govern man's response to this model. But careful scrutiny of certain examples has shown that this model, and this treatment of it, is in structure and content very similar to the type of dialectic which generates the *an sit* of non-subjective, immaterial being, as shown in the first section of this paper. In fact, it appears to be identical with the so-called Platonic proof of Aquinas.

Thomas D. Parker

How Can We Think of God? Another Look at Transcendence

. . . Transcendence, reality, and encounter are three concepts that appear to be required if we are to speak of "God" as a *name* for an "other" whom we meet as that which supports and limits our existence as Christians and as human beings, and to which we respond in faith and love. If these three concepts are meaningless in a secular-technological world, then all talk of "God" which names a reality beyond ourselves is ruled out along with all traditional theology. This stricture applies equally to Brunner's cosmic "Thou" and to Tillich's "God beyond the god of theism." It might even eliminate so this-sided a definition of God as "the whence" of my being placed under ethical obligation and supported by my neighbor. Even the god-substitutes of Radical Theology cannot stand if these categories are no longer meaningful. Altizer's radical

Reprinted from *McCormick Quarterly,* January 1967 (McCormick Theological Seminary, Chicago), by permission of the publisher.

Thomas D. Parker is Instructor in Systematic Theology at McCormick Seminary, Chicago, Ill.

immanence, Hamilton's unconditional significance of Jesus, and van Buren's strange conception of freedom all fall before such a limitation.

Perhaps the key question of this essay could be put in two related but distinct parts:

a) Is the exclusion of transcendence (and its corollaries "reality" and "encounter") as a category of thought a necessary implication of secularity?

b) Is the exclusion of human capacity to respond to that which transcends the human sphere a necessary implication of secularity?

Putting the questions this way points to the assumption that our real problem is not rapid social change *per se*, but the kind of rapid social change taking place in our day and its secular pre-suppositions regarding the nature of man and the human enterprise. It seems clear that this is in fact the case. It is also clear that we cannot maintain the fiction of being able to articulate our faith in categories which no longer relate to our real commitments in the real world. If we try to do this, our language of faith simply becomes a rhetoric which holds a decaying institution together, and has no more of a truth claim than the monetary slogan "In God We Trust." Does our situation, then, make it impossible to use these fundamental categories of thought to articulate and to interpret faithfully our lives in the world as Christians? Can we think "theologically" at all in our day? About anything?

"Secularity" is a difficult reality to conceptualize because it is so broadly characteristic of our contemporary world and more nearly represents a mood or a posture than a particular set of positions. The understanding of secularization has changed from the time it was first used to indicate the "worldly" political and economic sphere as opposed to the spiritual or religious sphere in a system which made room for both spheres. When the synthesis which made the system viable gave way to antitheses of discordant elements in the seventeenth and eighteenth centuries, first one realm then another was removed from the control and interpretation of the ecclesiastical authorities. Nationalism challenged the Church's baptized concept of *imperium*, capitalism challenged the Church's moral laws, and the new science questioned the Church's dogmatic pretensions. In the nineteenth century explicit use of the term to describe a this-worldly stance self-consciously set against any religious, supernatural interpretation of reality came to the fore, and modern secularism was born. Here secularism is a specific philosophy, humanist and pragmatist in orientation. The process of secularization was now interpreted in such a way that it appeared as a reaction against and competitor of Christian faith.

The point has been often made, however, that the development of secularized autonomy need not entail an anti-religious posture. What we have is a historical process and an interpretation, both of which use the term *secular*. Our concern with secularity is with the historical reality, for this is the reality of our world which any theological reflection must refer to. Taken in this way, secularity is not so much a point of view to be refuted as it is simply an assumption of our lives. C. West has defined the process of secularization as "the withdrawal of areas of thought and life from religious—and finally also from metaphysical—control, and the attempt to understand and live in these areas in the terms which they alone offer." Here secularization may have its theoretical aspects—simply foregoing ultimate questions in favor of proximate ones, turning from contemplation of mystery to cooperation in problem-solving, etc. But it is important as a style of life which supports such a theoretical perspective. It is the way in which contemporary men make it possible to live in the world in worldy terms and upon worldly presuppositions. It was contended at the beginning of this essay that this basic style had conditioned the processes of rapid social change in our day, and that the question of transcendence and its implicates was raised in relation to secularity more than to rapid social change as such. This is because the revolutionary social, political, and economic changes of our day are profoundly secular in their orientation.

Does this secular style exclude either transcendence as a category or the affirmation that human beings may respond to that which transcends human being? *Analytically, neither transcendence nor its implicates are ruled out as useful concepts by the secular style of life.* Even a thoroughly humanistic, this-worldly view of life has room for the transcendence of the human spirit over the conditions of this-worldly reality. It also recognizes that human life is set in a context (the universe) which transcends it and is really "other." And, except for occasional solipsists (who are non-secular), the concept of encounter is a meaningful category of thought as well. *Secularity in no way rules out the possibility of a human response to that which goes beyond the human sphere.* Men may be conceived as responsive beings in a broader and more significant way in a secular world than was the case when human-ness was restricted to rational man in a Ptolemaic world.

We must, however, be very careful to stay within the limits of the question and the interpretation of the answer. It is easy to err at this point and assume that we have laid the ground for another kind of theistic argument. But even if our analysis shows that secular men also presume a transcendent reality to which they respond, it does *not* thereby validate an experience of the transcendent *God*. Of course secular men presume a transcendent—in fact they assume many of them! There are all kinds of things which lead secular men beyond themselves and their culture into new areas of discovery and invention. There are all kinds of realities to which men reach and by virtue of which they exist in an exciting world even if they may not grasp all they reach for. In fact, there is so much that transcends man and his world today that men have given up the attempt to be encyclopedists. We live in an increasingly open universe which precludes any formulation of all knowledge in any kind of universal synthesis. Rapid social change itself has brought its own awareness of transcendent realities into the picture. In our time accepted structures and systems are being broken, and new ones are appearing which genuinely "go beyond" the previous possibilities. Yet the reality of transcendence is not enough to ground a new religious interpretation of culture which entails a faith in God. That would destroy secularity in principle. It would also involve us in the same logical leap that is made at some point in all theistic proofs: the assertion that "this all men call God."

Nevertheless, a negative answer to the two parts of our question is an important gain. If it cannot establish faith in a transcendent God, it can at least accomplish two other things which are essential to the formulation of a theological perspective on the realities of our life. It may prepare the way to speak intelligently about God, and at the same time relativize the very secular processes of social change.

a) As a preparation for speaking about God, we are offered a new and potent way of understanding transcendence, reality, and encounter which puts meaning into these old terms. These terms have a secular meaning in their own right, a more dynamic meaning than they were given in some of the models by which they were conceived in times past. The Christian may use new understandings of transcendence and its corollaries to articulate the genuine otherness and relatedness of that One whom the Christian community has addressed as "God" in its confession and its prayer. Thus, not only may we use the concepts without destroying our secularity, but we may use them in ways more appropriate to the biblical confession of faith in God than could ever be the case with transcendence conceived as supranatural. They may be used to express the otherness and relatedness of the "God" whom Christians meet as the ultimate source of their life through Jesus the Christ. They may be used when the community reflects on its confession of faith and seeks to communicate it to other men. In such uses, "ultimate source" is not a dead reality that the community arrives at by peeling the onion of existence down to the (non-existent) core of essence; it is a genuine other who supports and limits their existence as Christians and as human beings.

"God" is transcendent in his relationship to human beings, and not otherwise.

b) The negative answer to the question of the exclusion of these categories of thought in a secular world also provides us with a way of going beyond secularism. According to a common view, secularism is a self-stultifying view of secular reality. It cannot provide the dynamic to motivate the pursuit of genuine good. It offers no ground for the search for a better secularity, for it lacks the religious motive which impels men to seek that good. Put in a less traditional way, the point is that human autonomy and secular relativism are incompatible; secularism relativizes man himself, and thus destroys his spontaneity and autonomy. Human beings become "man," an entity which is manipulable for selected secular ends. At the end of the road, the question "Who am I?" and "What are we?" appears in a form which cannot be answered by the road itself. In such a situation, the affirmation of God as a transcendent reality which we encounter in the midst of life, and from which we live by grace, is at the same time an affirmation of the centrality of human existence.

Secularity refuses to mystify history and to picture to itself any Absolute. It is pragmatic in orientation. It attempts to understand every area of life in terms implicit to its concrete reality. It forfeits the luxury of system-building. Yet this very effort has the effect of neutralizing critical relations to other areas of life and of producing a myopia which finally lacks any standpoint of judgment over what is positive and "historical." Instead of a kingdom of a universal system, we have a collection of fiefdoms, each responsible only to itself. And a new historicism develops in which practically any goal or strategy may be justified. It is not only theologians who are concerned to find a critical point of judgment over history. Albert Camus asked what reality could transcend the merely secularist (historical) reality in order to save mankind. His answer was anthropological: there is a human structure which persists in the midst of all historical change and gives the ground for rebellion when men are being destroyed for the sake of man, progress, or utopia. In form, this is not far different from the work of theologians such as Tillich and Niebuhr, or even Barth, although the content of the transcendent reality varies. All would agree that men must not be objectivized and relativized by any historical process, no matter how "secular." The assumption is that men are related to a reality which transcends the merely secular and offers a point of judgment upon it. And only if there is such a reality can life be kept genuinely secular.

One of the chief problems implicit in thinking theologically about rapid social change in our day is to reflect on the meaning of the *theos* implied in the adverb "theologically." There can be no theological frame of reference, adequate for interpreting and giving direction to human existence, apart from a sustained and critical examination of this key term. In an effort to "place" the term, the following considerations have been offered:

a) The term "God" is a *name* by which Christian men speak of a reality beyond themselves, disclosed in the historical life of Israel and the Church as expressed in Jesus the Christ. The primary form in which this name is uttered is confession and prayer, for this form of speech corresponds to a faith-relation to "God."

b) It is impossible to conceive the One named by Christian men apart from some kind of category of transcendence. This is so because transcendence implies a reality beyond ourselves which meets us in our existence, and to which we respond in faith.

c) Yet the secular milieu hardly appears to allow for the category of transcendence. Immanence is more appropiate. A second glance at transcendence shows us that it is not a contradictory but a correlate of immanence. It is *not* necessarily excluded by the style of secular life.

d) This keeps open the possibility of naming "God" in faith. There are two uses of "transcendence" in a theological perspective which keep it theological. 1) It allows us a way to speak of God in relation to our existence in the world. 2) It provides us with a way of affirming the centrality of man and of preventing the relative secularity of the world from being absolutized.

It is difficult to see how a theological perspective could be formulated that did not name God in its confession as a transcendent reality which meets us in our (secular) existence. And, if such a view could be formulated, it is even more difficult to see what relevance if any it would have for the interpretation and guidance of human life in our time. Of course, the problem of "God" is not solved by these conclusions. It remains to be shown that that which the Christian community names "God" is more than a communally inspired illusion. In addition, it remains to be shown how that which the Christian community names "God" differs from other realities which transcend us, and to which we give other names: being, the universe, the Unconditioned, etc. But these further problems could not even be dealt with if it were no longer possible to speak of God as a transcendent reality.

Dietrich Bonhoeffer

Two Letters from Prison

8th July 1944

A little while ago I wrote you a letter with some very theoretical philosophy about heat. In the last few days I have been trying it on my own body. I feel as if I were in an oven, and I am wearing only a shirt that I once brought you from Sweden, and a pair of shorts . . . and the only reason why I don't complain about it is that I can imagine how badly you must be suffering from the heat, and how frivolous my former letter must have seemed to you. So I will try to squeeze a few thoughts out of my sweating brain, and let you have them. Who knows—it may be that it will not have to be too often now, and that we shall see each other sooner than we expect. The other day I read a fine and striking remark in Euripides, in a scene of reunion after a long separation: "So, then, to meet again is a good."

Now for a few more thoughts on our theme. Marshalling the biblical evidence needs more lucidity and concentration than I can command at present. Wait a few more days, till it gets cooler! I have not forgotten, either, that I owe you something about the non-religious interpretation of biblical concepts. But for today, here are a few preliminary remarks:

The displacement of God from the world, and from the public part of human life, led to the attempt to keep his place secure at least in the sphere of the "personal," the "inner," and the "private." And as every

Dietrich Bonhoeffer was a pastor-theologian who took part in the German resistance and was imprisoned by the Nazis for two years before his execution in 1945.

man still has a private sphere somewhere, that is where he was thought to be the most vulnerable. The secrets known to a man's valet—that is, to put it crudely, the range of his intimate life, from prayer to his sexual life—have become the hunting-ground of modern pastoral workers. In that way they resemble (though with quite different intentions) the dirtiest gutter journalists—do you remember the *Wahrheit* and the *Glocke,* which made public the most intimate details about prominent people? In the one case it is social, financial, or political blackmail, and in the other, religious blackmail. Forgive me, but I cannot put it more mildly.

From the sociological point of view this is a revolution from below, a revolt of inferiority. Just as the vulgar mind is not satisfied till it has seen some highly placed personage "in his bath," or in other embarrassing situations, so it is here. There is a kind of evil satisfaction in knowing that everyone has his failings and weak spots. In my contacts with the "outcasts" of society, its "pariahs," I have noticed repeatedly that mistrust is the dominant motive in their judgment of other people. Every action, even the most unselfish, of a person of high repute is suspected from the outset. These "outcasts" are to be found in all grades of society. In a flower garden they grub around only for the dung on which the flowers grow. The more isolated a man's life, the more easily he falls a victim to this attitude.

There is also a parallel isolation among the clergy, in what one might call the "clerical" sniffing-around-after-people's-sins in order to catch them out. It is as if you could not know a fine house till you had found a cobweb in the furthest cellar, or as if you could not adequately appreciate a good play till you had seen how the actors behave offstage. It is the same kind of thing that you find in the novels of the last fifty years, which do not think they have depicted their characters properly till they have described them in their marriage bed, or in films where undressing scenes are thought necessary. Anything unclothed, veiled, pure, and chaste is presumed to be deceitful, disguised, and impure; people here simply show their own impurity. A basic antisocial attitude of mistrust and suspicion is the revolt of inferiority.

Regarded theologically, the error is twofold. First, it is thought that a man can be addressed as a sinner only after his weaknesses and meannesses have been spied out. Secondly, it is thought that a man's essential nature consists of his inmost and most intimate background; that is defined as his "inner life," and it is precisely in those secret human places that God is to have his domain!

On the first point it is to be said that man is certainly a sinner, but is far from being mean or common on that account. To put it rather tritely, were Goethe and Napoleon sinners because they were not always faithful husbands? It is not the sins of weakness, but the sins of strength, which matter here. It is not in the least necessary to spy out things; the Bible never does so. (Sins of strength: in the genius, *hubris;* in the peasant, the breaking of the order of life—is the decalogue a peasant ethic?; in the bourgeois, fear of free responsibility. Is this correct?)

On the second point: the Bible does not recognize our distinction between the outward and the inward. Why should it? It is always concerned with *anthropos teleios,* the *whole* man, even where, as in the Sermon on the Mount, the decalogue is pressed home to refer to "inward disposition." That a good "disposition" can take the place of the total goodness is quite unbiblical. The discovery of the so-called inner life dates from the Renaissance, probably from Petrarch. The "heart" in the biblical sense is not the inner life, but the whole man in relation to God. But as a man lives just as much from "outwards" to "inwards" as from "inwards" to "outwards," the view that his essential nature can be understood only from his intimate spiritual background is wholly erroneous.

I therefore want to start from the premise that God should not be smuggled into some last secret place, but that we should frankly recognize that the world, and people, have come of age, that we should not run man down in his worldliness, but confront him with God at his strongest point, that we should give up all our clerical tricks, and not regard psychotherapy and existentialist philosophy as God's pioneers. The importunity of all these people is far too unaristocratic for the Word of God to ally itself with them. The Word of God is far removed from this revolt of mistrust, this revolt from below. On the contrary, it reigns.

Well, it's time to say something concrete about the secular interpretation of biblical concepts; but it's too hot! . . .

16th July 1944

. . . Now for a few more thoughts on our theme. I am only gradually working my way to the nonreligious interpretation of biblical concepts; the job is too big for me to finish just yet.

On the historical side: There is one great development that leads to the world's autonomy. In theology one sees it first in Lord Herbert of Cherbury, who maintains that reason is sufficient for religious knowledge. In ethics it appears in Montaigne and Bodin with their substitution of rules of life for the commandments. In politics Machiavelli detaches politics from morality in general and founds the doctrine of "reasons of State." Later, and very differently from Machiavelli, but tending like him towards the autonomy of human society, comes Grotius, setting up his natural law as international law, which is valid *etsi deus non daretur*, "even if there were no God." The philosophers provide the finishing touches: on the one hand we have the deism of Descartes, who holds that the world is a mechanism, running by itself with no interference from God; and on the other hand the pantheism of Spinoza, who says that God is nature. In the last resort, Kant is a deist, and Fichte and Hegel are pantheists. Everywhere the thinking is directed towards the autonomy of man and the world.

(It seems that in the natural sciences the process begins with Nicolas of Cusa and Giordano Bruno and their "heretical" doctrine of the infinity of the universe. The classical *cosmos* was finite, like the created world of the Middle Ages. An infinite universe, however it may be conceived, is self-subsisting, *etsi deus non daretur*. It is true that modern physics is not as sure as it was about the infinity of the universe, but it has not gone back to the earlier conceptions of its finitude.)

God as a working hypothesis in morals, politics, or science, has been surmounted and abolished; and the same thing has happened in philosophy and religion (Feuerbach!). For the sake of intellectual honesty, that working hypothesis should be dropped, or as far as possible eliminated. A scientist or physician who sets out to edify is a hybrid.

Anxious souls will ask what room there is left for God now; and as they know of no answer to the question, they condemn the whole development that has brought them to such straits. I wrote to you before about the various emergency exits that have been contrived; and we ought to add to them the *salto mortale* (death-leap) back into the Middle Ages. But the principle of the Middle Ages is heteronomy in the form of clericalism; a return to that can only be a counsel of despair, and it would be at the cost of intellectual honesty. It is a dream that reminds one of the song *O wüsst ich doch den Weg zurück, den weiten Weg ins Kinderland* ("Oh if only I knew the way back, the long way back to the land of childhood."). There is no such way—at any rate not if it means deliberately abandoning our mental integrity; the only way is that of Matt. 18:3, i.e. through repentance, through *ultimate* honesty.

And we cannot be honest unless we recognize that we have to live in the world *etsi deus non daretur*. And this is just what we do recognize—before God! God himself compels us to recognize it. So our coming of age leads us to a true recognition of our situation before God. God would have us know that we must live as men who manage our lives without him. The God who is with us is the God who forsakes us (Mark 15:34). The God who lets us live in the world without the working hypothesis of God is the God before whom we stand continually. Before God and with God we live without God. God lets himself be pushed out of the world on to the cross. He is weak and powerless in the world, and that is precisely the way, the only way, in which he is with us and helps us. Matt. 8:17 makes it quite clear that Christ helps us, not by virtue of his omnipotence, but by virtue of his weakness and suffering.

Here is the decisive difference between Christianity and all the religions. Man's religiosity makes him look in his distress to the power of God in the world: God is the *deus ex machina*. The Bible directs man to God's powerlessness and suffering; only the suffering God can help. To that extent we may say that the development towards the world's coming of age outlined above, which has done away with a false conception of God, opens up a way of seeing the God of the Bible, who wins power and space in the world by his weakness. This will probably be the starting-point for our "secular interpretation."

Billy Graham

A New Theology

The message that I shall give tonight is one I do not want to give, but God the Holy Spirit has laid it upon my heart so definitely that I cannot escape it. I want to speak not only to the masses of people who are here from the Miami area, but to the delegates, to the pastors, to all of you as you get ready to go back home to minister and to evangelize.

I want you to turn to the book of Jeremiah which I read nearly every day. I think this book describes our conditions today probably more accurately than any other book in the Bible. I want to read the prophet's words from Jeremiah 6:

From a message given by Billy Graham, June 27, 1965, at the Baptist World Alliance in the Orange Bowl at Miami Beach, Fla., and printed in *NEW*, Volume I, No. 2. Reprinted with permission of the author.

Billy Graham is a well-known evangelist.

For from the least of them even unto the greatest of them every one is given to covetousness; and from the prophet even unto the priest every one dealeth falsely.

They have healed also the hurt *of the daughter* of my people slightly, saying, Peace, peace; when *there is* no peace.

Were they ashamed when they had committed abomination? nay, they were not at all ashamed, neither could they blush: therefore they shall fall among them that fall: at the time *that* I visit them they shall be cast down, saith the Lord.

Thus saith the Lord, Stand ye in the ways, and see, and ask for the old paths, where *is* the good way, and walk therein, and ye shall find rest for your souls. But they said, We will not walk *therein.*

. . . Here, O earth: behold, I will bring evil upon this people . . . your burnt offerings *are* not acceptable, nor your sacrifices sweet unto me.

Jeremiah was speaking to the church of his day. He said to Israel: "You have departed from the faith of your fathers. Israel, return, return, return to the old ways and the old paths!"

The nineteenth century was the age of the exclamation mark. The twentieth century has become the age of the question mark. Everything we once believed in is being questioned today. Youth is saying: "If what you believe is right: why is the world in such a mess today?" Some have even said that Christianity has failed. They say: "Look at the suffering, the agony, the disease, the poverty, the hate, the racial injustice, the war, the blood being spilled all over the world. If God is a God of love, why doesn't He stop it? Christianity has failed." I agree with G. K. Chesterton who said that Christianity "has not been tried and found wanting. It has been found difficult and left untried."

There are those today who say that we should disregard the old things of our fathers, that we need something new. Even church leaders are beginning to say that in certain areas. And so new ideas have emerged, claimed by their exponents to be superior to the old. Some of these new ideas are invading the church with deadly effect.

Now, let me focus on what is called "a new theology."

One of the most popular words today is "new" or "neo." We have neo-orthodoxy, neo-liberalism, neo-evangelicalism, neo-fundamentalism. We seem to think that everyone must be put in one category or another. He's a fundamentalist; he's a liberal; he's this; he's that. I am not sure I claim any of them; I am just a plain Christian. Solomon said: "There is nothing new under the sun."

Today some of the old creeds are being revised, and often they are scaled down to match a dwindling faith. One of our great denominations is taking giant steps toward a new confession of faith. One clergyman suggested that we have a moratorium on God for a year, and another said it should be for twenty years—don't mention the name of God for twenty years!

Recently a Baptist preacher said in print: "There is no such thing as a devil." When I read that I felt like the prize fighter whose opponent was beating him almost to death. As the boxer leaned on the ropes about to fall, his manager said: "Get up! He's not even hitting you." The fighter replied: "Well, watch that referee; somebody's hitting me." If there is no devil, then who is hitting us?

As I study some of these new books and read some of the many articles, I have to admit that they raise questions that must be answered. As I study some of these new things, I find that they revolve around three points: (1) They question the authority of the Scriptures; (2) they deny the existence of judgment and of hell; (3) they accept and teach a form of humanism. Seeing this, I have thought to myself: "Well, that's not new at all. That is all found in the very beginning of the Bible."

Turn to the third chapter of Genesis and read the devil's words to Eve: "Now the serpent was more subtle than any beast of the field which the Lord God had made. And he said unto the woman, Yea, hath God said, Ye shall not eat of every tree of the garden? And the woman said unto the serpent, We may eat of the fruit of the trees of the garden: But of the fruit of the tree which is in the midst of the garden, God hath said, Ye shall not eat of it, neither shall ye touch it, lest ye die. And the serpent said unto the woman, Ye shall not surely die. For God doth know that in the day ye eat thereof, then your eyes shall be opened, and ye shall be as gods."

Three times the devil said: "Yea, hath God said?" Baptists have always believed in the authority of the Word of God, the Bible. We may disagree as to the details of how it was inspired, but we believe in its authority. Two thousand times in the Old Testament the prophets claimed that God spoke.. In the Pentateuch we find such expressions as these:

> The Lord said unto Noah
> God spoke unto Israel
> God said
> The Lord commanded

In the books of the prophets we read these statements:

> Hear the word of the Lord
> Thus saith the Lord
> I put My words in your mouth

Now, either God did speak to these men as they wrote by inspiration, or they were the most consistent liars the world has ever known. That they should tell and record more than 2,000 lies seems incredible. And did Jesus deliberately deceive us? For, you see, Jesus quoted from the Old Testament constantly; and not once did He say: "Watch out! You can't trust that. You can't trust the other." He quoted Noah, Moses, Jonah, three of the men in the Old Testament whose writings some persons today find it hardest to accept. He used many quotations from the Old Testament, and the apostles constantly quoted from the Scriptures.

When I began to preach a few years ago, I had many questions and some doubts about this book. Intellectually, I could not figure it all out. Do you know what I did? One day in 1949 I opened up my Bible, and I said: "Oh, God, I do not understand everything in this book. There are problems I cannot figure out. But, oh, God, from this day on, I am going to accept this book by faith as the authority for my life and ministry." I tell you, my ministry changed overnight. I found that I carried a sword in my hand. Tonight I attest with Job: "I have esteemed the words of his mouth more than my necessary *food*" (Job 23:12b).

This Bible is not a book of science. Do not come to it expecting it to be like the science textbook you have in the university. It is a book of redemption. It is a book about God. It is a book about man. It is a book about salvation. It is authoritative, and it was inspired by God the Holy Spirit.

The devil's second statement to Eve was: "Ye shall not surely die." A. C. Dixon once said: "If we had more hell in the pulpit, we might have less hell in the community."

In one village where Jesus had cured a man, the people said to Him: "Leave us alone." And people today say the same thing because they do not want to hear about death and judgment and hell. Too often we picture God as a kindly old man with a long white beard, sitting on a cloud, saying sentimentally to everybody: "Love, love, love." God *does* love; God *is* love; but this same Bible tells us that God is a God of judgment. Let me make this very clear. There is coming a Day of Judgment when every man, lost, without Christ, will be judged. There is coming a day of accounting when every believer in Christ must answer for every deed, every thought, every intent of his life. You and I will face a holy, righteous God. Acts 17:31 says: "Because he hath appointed a day, in which he will judge the world in righteousness by *that* man whom he hath ordained."

The third thing the serpent said to Eve was: "Ye shall be as gods." That is humanism, and today humanism has pervaded the university campuses from one end of the world to the other. The object of humanism is to replace religion with a national, man-centered philosophy of natural progress and improvement. Humanism is simply the worship of man. "Glory to man in the highest," sings the humanist, for man is the master of all things. This has become the idolatry of our age—the worship of man. It is all the more dangerous for being so sophisticated and civilized in its expressions. And it is even invading the church.

As Baptists we have always believed in the sinfulness of man and in his lost condition. Baptists believe in the dignity of man. No denomination in all the world believes more strongly in the dignity of man and the freedom of the human will. But we also believe that man has sinned and rebelled against God, that this sin has affected his life, his will, his conscience, his whole human personality. Whoever you are, before God you are a sinner.

It is interesting to note that the devil has not changed his tactics. He still knows that we can be fooled and deceived. Our minds are clouded by sin, and he does not have to change his approach at all. He uses today the same three lies that he used in the Garden of Eden.

Now I sympathize with those people who want a new method of communicating the gospel in the twentieth century. I am not saying, for instance, that we must imprison the gospel message in the Old English language of the King James Version of the Bible. But neither must we disregard the truth because it is old.

No mathematician would look at the multiplication table and say: "Why, that's old stuff," would he? "Two plus two is four. That's old. I learned that when I was in school. Don't you have something new?" When I was in school I learned that at sea level water will boil at 212° and freeze at 32° Fahrenheit. I learned that twenty-five years ago in school. Should I disregard it because it is old? Water still boils at 212° Water still freezes at 32°. It will always be so.

In the spiritual realm, as in the mathematic, there are certain truths that are constant, fixed, firm. *God is constant.* The Scripture says: "For I *am* the Lord, I change not" (Malachi 3:6). *The Word of God is constant.* Jesus said: "Heaven and earth shall pass away, but my words shall not pass away" (Matt. 24:35). *Our Lord Jesus Christ is constant.* "Jesus Christ the same yesterday, and today, and for ever" (Hebrews 13:8). *The way of salvation is constant.* "Neither is there salvation in any other: for there is none other name under heaven given among men, whereby we must be saved" (Acts 4:12). These truths are fixed and firm. They cannot be changed. They cannot be altered.

Speaking of my message in our Los Angeles crusade two years ago, a local pastor told the press that I had set the church back fifty years. I replied to the newspaper reporter, "I am disappointed. I had hoped to set it back 2,000 years."

Faithful Baptists have influenced the whole world. Let us stand with John Bunyan and Roger Williams and Charles Spurgeon and William Carey and Lee Scarborough and George Truett and all the great heroes of the past. Let us believe as they believed.

I believe in God the Father Almighty, Maker of heaven and earth; and in Jesus Christ His only Son our Lord: who was conceived by the Holy Ghost, born of the Virgin Mary, suffered under Pontius Pilate, was crucified, dead, and buried; the third day He rose again from the dead; He ascended into heaven, and sitteth on the right hand of God the Father Almighty; from thence He shall come to judge the quick and the dead. I believe in the Holy Ghost; the holy universal church; the communion of saints; the forgiveness of sins; the resurrection of the body; and the life everlasting. Amen.

That is our faith. Let us stand on it and believe it and carry it around the world. Let us reaffirm our faith in those constants of our fathers and of the early apostles.

part two
Social
Issues

6
Social Morality

It may be that, in its aims, the social revolution we are living through today is no different from the social revolutions of previous generations; but it is more intense and more open. And, as more and more issues of moral and immoral conduct are reviewed, religion is being transformed.

Charles Ketcham demonstrates that the social revolution of today is not confined to college campuses. Not only students but many other men as well, theologians prominently among them, are "involved in the search for a new morality," for a new humanism which begins by asking the twin questions of identity and authenticity, "Who am I?" and "How can I be myself?" These are the underlying questions to which the essays in this chapter are directed.

Joseph Fletcher argues for the acceptance by society of a "situational" code of ethics. Situationism follows a course between the poles of legalism and antinomianism. It rejects rigid, prefabricated regulations but does not discard regulations altogether. Rather, it brings to any

239

ethical situation a set of flexible ethical priorities to be used as "illuminators" rather than final determinants.

The essays by Robert Fitch, Winfred Overholser, and Howard
Moody all apply the test of humanism to social problems. Fitch surveys
contemporary attitudes toward sex, finds that they tend to separate sex
from love, and calls for a new sex code that emphasizes personal sexual
roles and responsibilities. Examining the laws on homosexuality and the
social attitudes reflected in those laws, Winfred Overholser attacks both
the laws and the attitudes as irrational and asks that society recognize
that homosexuality is a problem not of some subspecies of life but of
human beings. And Moody, scrutinizing fundamental and subtle moral
biases, dramatizes the irony of the self-righteousness of a society in which
sexuality is considered more obscene than the desecration of human life.
How pale is the evil of pornography, says Moody, compared to the
obscenity of Dachau or Hiroshima.

Charles B. Ketcham
The Search for the New Morality

We are "Beyond Berkeley"—or so we are being told. The free
speech movement has lost its charismatic charter; Mario Savio, the not-so-
charismatic leader, has been left knocking at a door he could once have
opened by himself; and the Berkeley Radicals have ostensibly gone back
to the primary task of getting an education.

Last November [1965], at the Washington, D.C., protest march
against American policy in Vietnam, the New Radicals found themselves
delivered by the experienced old hands of Dr. Benjamin Spock into the

Reprinted from *The Christian Century* (October 12, 1966), pp. 1236–1239,
by permission of the publisher.

Dr. Ketcham is James M. Thoburn Professor of Religion at Allegheny
College, Meadville, Pennsylvania.

everlasting arms of Norman Thomas under the maternal eye of Mrs. Martin Luther King. To some critical observers, this must seem like poetic justice for a movement which not long before had stated: "We trust no one over 30," and then, under pressure of justification, stated even more categorically: "Now we don't trust anyone at all."

I

What has happened to the great revolt? Does the decline of demonstrations, their loss of power and lack of leadership—Staughton Lynd, Paul Potter, Joan Baez, Bob Dylan notwithstanding—mean that Berkeley was merely the symbol of student frustration at the impersonality of the multiversity? Such a conclusion would seem to support the contention that the problem of revolt and estrangement has been overstated; that the problem is technical rather than moral or spiritual; that it can be, and in part has been, solved by establishing self-contained colleges within the university, by introducing new curriculums or by improving the university's "internal" public relations and counseling services. But such technical, methodological analysis of the problem is all too simple.

Perhaps a key to understanding the revolt of the New Radicals is to be found in its lack of form and focus, its lack of leadership and organization, and its persistent lack of articulation. Most of us expect a revolution to be going somewhere, to have a goal or gospel; yet here we apparently have those who think of themselves as "rebels without a cause." It is, as Jack Newfield terms it, a "Revolt without Dogma."

What meaning can we find in this seemingly meaningless college? I think it becomes clear that the New Radicals, the so-called activists, are not out to overthrow democracy but to achieve it; they are not out to change civil rights but to implement them—to make them consistent with human rights; they are not out to change higher education but to become truly educated. What they desire, they state, is not their own way but a way of their own.

For these Radicals, the villain in every case is the Structure, the System, the Regulation, the Establishment, which prevent one from experiencing the full life, an authentic life. It is the Establishment, which includes the Multiversity, Big Business, Big Labor, Big Government, the Military, and even Big Church, that prevents any genuine, human self-realization and any meaningful commitment. Most of the New Radicals believe that to become part of such a System is to become a participant in its crimes. To act meaningfully is to act personally in such a way as to draw maximum attention to the injustice of impersonal society. The System is the agent of depersonalization, the landlord for Harrington's

"Other America." In short, the New Radicals believe that the Establishment has failed to translate educational, political and social ideals into realities.

II

This may be enough justification for the point I should like to make: that the protest—the revolution, if you will—taking place on campuses across the nation is not an isolated, academic affair. It spills over into our cultural, political and spiritual life. What has been examined thus far is simply the academic syndrome of a protest of much wider scope. That academe has received such attention is due in part to the improvident handling and consequent publicity of the Berkeley demonstration.

As the students are involved, so are many men involved in the search for a new morality. Our lack of authenticity, our loss of true humanism and spiritual identity, mark all aspects of our culture. The Establishment, if not the source of evil, is at least the partial occasion of its expression; and it is well for us to see this and see it clearly lest, concentrating on the student's rebellion, we find the apple and miss the snake.

Now that our affluence has put us on the verge of Eden, some of us fear that what we are about to achieve is not paradise but purgatory—that the Great Society now envisioned is more threat than treasure, that mass society means mass-man subject to mass taste made available by mass production. Such total exposure to mediocrity and total availability of common goods can prove stifling to any imaginative or creative life. Mass-man is trained to structure his life within a mass economy which militates not only against values but against any form or idea of individuality. The resulting depersonalization convinces one that he is in fact expendable. Mass culture mutilates meaning. It produces, as Herbert Marcuse suggests, a one-dimensional man. It produces a nonvalue society, marked, as Jack Newfield suggests (in *motive* for October 1965), by "hypocrisy called Brotherhood Week; assembly lines called colleges; conformity called status; bad taste called Camp; and quiet desperation called success." The frightening fact which begins to emerge is the continuous growth and seeming inevitability of such Structure. As more and more people crowd the earth the necessity of conformity mounts, so that even a protest against conformity necessarily employs the very System and Structure it seeks to destroy—as the civil rights movement has learned in trying to cope with "black power," and as the free speech movement reluctantly had to admit as it turned to computers for organizational help. Thus the protest carries with it—in Berkeley as elsewhere —the seed of its own destruction.

This dilemma does not imply that the rebels are committed to some irrational or irresponsible thanatology. Philosophically eclectic, the protest movement incorporates insights from diverse sources. From Martin Buber, for intance, comes support for the fundamental assertion that the necessary world *It* (Structure) can never fulfill the function of the intimate world of *Thou* (personal relation), which is self-informing and self-affirming. "Without *It* man cannot live," writes Buber. "But he who lives with *It* alone is not a man." The world of *It* becomes evil only when it presumes to have being and seeks total mastery over life. From Martin Heidegger comes the radical's inheritance of the existential revolt. Heidegger cautions man about the imposed "ersatz" or imitation world and equally cautions man to "let truth be." Uninhibited self-expression is the ground of truth.

III

To be sure, such insights are not confined to students, but that is *just* the point. The protest movement is not confined to campus. So let us look briefly at the broader aspects of this revolt against suffocation by System and see if any hints of an emerging morality are there, which coincide with what one observes on the college campus. Historically one of the oldest but most enduring protests is represented in the movement called Dadaism in art. The search for freedom, for integrity, began with the recognition that Formalism, Stylization and System severely limit if they do not preclude much of what an artist has to express of himself and his perception of the world. Marcel Duchamp, who painted the famous "Nude Descending a Staircase," stated: "Dada was a metaphysical atti-tude—a sort of nihilism . . . a way to get out of a state of mind—to avoid being influenced by one's immediate environment, or by the past; to get away from clichés—to get free." Dadaism emphasizes the irrational in an attempt to avoid the stultifying superficiality induced by formal patterns. In such artists as Duchamp and Picasso one can detect a protest movement not simply against mediocrity of expression but also against decadent morality.

The same revolt against Form is evident in the music of such contemporary composers as Boulez, Lukas Foss and Vincent Persichetti. In "Shimah B'Koli" (Psalm 130), Persichetti composes atonally and ametrically, without key-signature and without bar lines. It would seem that Persichetti, by freeing himself from any conventional system of composition, hopes to free the listener from his passive or analytical role for an active involvement with the music and the text; the power of the Psalmist's words ("Out of the depths . . .") must not be permitted to fail because they are framed by an artful fugue.

Further evidence for this search is to be found in writers and directors. Negatively speaking, the rejection of System and Formalism can be seen in the emergence of the antinovel with its obscurantism, absence of plot, amorality, and endless variation on a situation. This rejection, however, is more universally represented in the antihero; e.g., Updike's "Rabbit" Angstrom in *Rabbit Run* or Beckett's Vladimir and Estragon in *Waiting for Godot*. A radical response to form also occurs in the irrationality of the Theater of the Absurd, or in Total Theater, with its shock of uninhibited "happenings." Rejection is evident in such television spoof-productions as "Batman" and "Get Smart." But the revolt against form is not all negative—as even some of the above would indicate. The search for genuine expression, for freedom, for authenticity, for identity, is much in evidence in the antispectacular, intensely personal, often introspective movies of such directors as Antonioni, Bergman and Fellini. However, one of the finest and most informative expressions of the revolt in its positive sense appears in the first of *six nonlectures* by e. e. cummings. "Let me cordially warn you," cummings admonished his Harvard audience, "at the opening of these so-called lectures, that I haven't the remotest intention of posing as a lecturer. . . . For while a genuine lecturer must obey the rules of mental decency, and clothe his personal idiosyncrasies in collectively acceptable generalities, an authentic ignoramus remains quite indecently free to speak as he feels. This prospect cheers me, because I value freedom; and have never expected freedom to be anything less than indecent. . . . Since I can't tell you what I know (or rather what I don't know) there's nothing to prevent me from trying to tell you who I am—which I'd deeply enjoy doing."

Finally, one can trace the same revolt against the ultimacy of Structure and Form in contemporary existentialist theology, particularly in the "death of God" movement. These contemporary theologians are desperately trying to avoid the oppressive conformity of an outmoded orthodox cosmology which, they maintain, restricts man's creativity, ignores his responsibility and destroys his freedom to be. To subject man in the name of religion to categories of thought which no longer have the power to point beyond themselves or to involve man religiously is, for God's sake, idolatry. Whether destructive or constructive, what these theologians are attempting to do is to shock us out of our nonreligion into the act or commitment of faith which must be free, personal, total, authentic and holy. Theirs is the search for a new humanism which would recognize that man is not created in the image of God but is created to image God who freely confronts him.

IV

All these protests seem to give some support for claiming that the campus revolt is really a scholastic synecdoche for the longings of men caught in an age of crisis. It is an age when the world population explosion, an incomprehensible science, political and military hostilities and racial tensions combine to produce a total experience exposure in which man, seeking self-expression, is overwhelmed by the necessity of massive response in terms of massive power—both of which seem to rob him of his individuality, his humanity, his life.

The solution suggested by each of our witnesses—students, artists, musicians, writers, theologians, et al.—involves a major change in our thinking. The search for meaning, for the new morality, does not begin by first asking, "Where are we going?"—though direction is important; nor by determining by what laws mankind must go at all—though order is necessary to avoid chaos. The search on the campus and in the culture really begins by asking the twin questions of identity and authenticity, "Who am I?" and "How can I be myself?" For all the New Humanists (if I may arbitrarily choose a term for our protesters), the point of contact with reality is the point of immediate personal context. What we truly want to do, as e. e. cummings suggests, is to tell people who we are, not what information we have; for we have begun to perceive that information cannot end our estrangement and alienation, but love can.

For the agnostics among us life, with its possibilities of love, joy, courage and creativity, witnesses to itself. If, as Heidegger suggests, we have been "thrown into existence," we have picked ourselves up, looked about and decided that, whatever our source, things could be worse. Our positive expression, our affirmation of life-here-and-now is self-authenticating. For such a position, however, the problem of personal evil becomes increasingly difficult to explain or avoid.

For the religiously informed radical, the movement seems to be toward a contextual ethic which maintains that the love, joy, courage and creativity are all part of man's responsive Yes to the world and thereby to the One who created him a little lower than the angels. Personal evil is seen to exist (or to be experienced) when one fails to live or wills not to live responsibly, i.e., in response to that Ultimate Reality which has called one into existence and continues to sustain that existence. In this contextual ethic, in which one is created free to image God, self-expression becomes movement toward identity, and freedom is the ground of its expression. System and Structure can thus never be primary but only secondary; they can exist only in so far as they prompt and permit man to express authentically his reality in the context of forces in which he finds himself. Thus freedom, for such an ethic, is not described primarily as freedom *from* or freedom *to;* this is to beg the question of Structure. Freedom is the spontaneous, uninhibited expression of the self as it interacts responsibly with the rest of the created world. To act so responsibly is, obviously, to invite rules, but rules primarily as supportive and instructional rather than as restrictive and judgmental. Life is more precious than law.

V

Life is also more precarious than law, for to live authentically, creatively, freely is to live in the presence of personal doubt and to risk the reaction of public guilt. The authenticity of another is always catalytic for me, for it forces me to live authentically myself, or to reject the other as a threat, or to surrender my individuality to another. Many men fear to live authentically, to be truly alive. The authority for their lives is simply turned over to another. For some of these, religion with its creeds, dogmas and ritualistic rubrics pointing toward a tidy Kingdom fulfills this idolatrous function. For others, the state with its laws of economics, social organization and status pointing toward a Great Society fulfills this idolatrous function.

Neither of these patterns for pseudo-living is acceptable to our group of New Humanists who will accept nothing less than authenticity, whatever the cost. Creeds? Yes, as guides to authentic expression, not as ends in themselves. A Great Society? Yes, as that society which is open to and encouraging of man's spontaneous, creative self. Otherwise, life has become a matter of style or technique, which is what the New Humanist revolt is all about.

The search for the new morality comes at a critical and late date. Mass-man with his mass culture and his pseudo-personality has almost destroyed the possibility of effective individual expression. It takes the power of a mass movement, or of mass communications, to deal effectively with the power of this authoritative Establishment—as civil rights action has shown us. But mass movements of protest in any sustained sense are antithetical to the creative, free spirit which initiates them. Consequently, it is encouraging to see the primary protests coming in the church, in the arts and in the universities. Here is our hope—the point of immediate entree to the society and maybe, in a world already sated with mediocrity, the only possibility of power we shall have for an authentic expression of life.

Joseph Fletcher

Three Approaches

There are at bottom only three alternative routes or approaches to follow in making moral decisions. They are: (1) the legalistic; (2) the antinomian, the opposite extreme—i.e., a lawless or unprincipled approach; and (3) the situational. All three have played their part in the history of Western morals, legalism being by far the most common and persistent. Just as legalism triumphed among the Jews after the exile, so, in spite of Jesus' and Paul's revolt against it, it has managed to dominate Christianity constantly from very early days. . . .

There is an old joke which serves our purposes. A rich man asked a lovely young woman if she would sleep the night with him. She said, "No." He then asked if she would do it for $100,000? She said, "Yes!" He then asked, "$10,000?" She replied, "Well, yes, I would." His next question was, "How about $500?" Her indignant "What do you think I am?" was met by the answer, "We have already established *that*. Now we are haggling over the price." Does any girl who has "relations" (what a funny way to use the word) outside marriage automatically become a prostitute? Is it always, regardless of what she accomplishes for herself or others—is it *always* wrong? Is extramarital sex inherently evil, or can it be a good thing in some situations? Does everybody have his price, and if so, does that mean we are immoral and ethically weak? Let's see if we can find some help in answering these questions.

1. Legalism

With this approach one enters into every decision-making situation encumbered with a whole apparatus of prefabricated rules and

From *Situation Ethics*, by Joseph Fletcher. The Westminster Press. Copyright © 1966 by W. L. Jenkins. Used by permission.

Joseph Fletcher is Professor of Social Ethics at Episcopal Theological School, Cambridge, Mass.

regulations. Not just the spirit but the letter of the law reigns. Its principles, codified in rules, are not merely guidelines or maxims to illuminate the situation; they are *directives* to be followed. Solutions are preset, and you can "look them up" in a book—a Bible or a confessor's manual.

Judaism, Catholicism, Protestantism—all major Western religious traditions have been legalistic. In morals as in doctrine they have kept to a spelled-out, "systematic" orthodoxy. The ancient Jews, especially under the post-exilic Maccabean and Pharisaic leadership, lived by the law or Torah, and its oral tradition (halakah). It was a code of 613 (or 621) precepts, amplified by an increasingly complicated mass of Mishnaic interpretations and applications.

Statutory and code law inevitably piles up, ruling upon ruling, because the complications of life and the claims of mercy and compassion combine—even with code legalists—to accumulate an elaborate system of exceptions and compromise, in the form of rules for breaking the rules! It leads to that tricky and tortuous now-you-see-it, now-you-don't business of interpretation that the rabbis called pilpul—a hairsplitting and logic-chopping study of the letter of the law, pyramiding from codes (e.g., the Covenant and Holiness) to Pentateuch to Midrash and Mishna to Talmud. It was a tragic death to the prophets' "pathos" (sharing God's loving concern) and "ethos" (living by love as *norm*, not program). With the prophets it had been a question of sensitively seeking "an understanding of *the situation.*"

Any web thus woven sooner or later chokes its weavers. Reformed and even Conservative Jews have been driven to disentangle themselves from it. Only Orthodoxy is still in its coils. Something of the same pilpul and formalistic complication may be seen in Christian history. With Catholics it has taken the form of a fairly ingenious moral theology that, as its twists and involutions have increased, resorts more and more to a casuistry that appears (as, to its credit, it does) to evade the very "laws" of right and wrong laid down in its textbooks and manuals. Love, even with the most stiff-necked of system builders, continues to plead mercy's cause and to win at least partial release from law's cold abstractions. Casuistry is the homage paid by legalism to the love of persons, and to realism about life's relativities.

Protestantism has rarely constructed such intricate codes and systems of law, but what it has gained by its simplicity it has lost through its rigidity, its puritanical insistence on moral rules. In fact, the very lack of a casuistry and its complexity, once people are committed to *even the bare principle* of legalistic morality or law ethics, is itself evidence of their blindness to the factors of doubt and perplexity. They have lost touch with the headaches and heartbreaks of life.

What can be worse, no casuistry at all may reveal a punishing and sadistic use of law to hurt people instead of helping them. How else explain burning at the stake in the Middle Ages for homosexuals (death, in the Old Testament)? Even today imprisonment up to sixty years is the penalty in one state for those who were actually consenting adults, without seduction or public disorder! This is really unavoidable whenever law instead of love is put first. The "puritan" type is a well-known example of it. But even if the legalist is truly *sorry* that the law requires unloving or disastrous decisions, he still cries, "*Fiat justitia, ruat caelum!*" (Do the "right" even if the sky falls down). He is the man Mark Twain called "a good man in the worst sense of the word."

The Christian situation ethicist agrees with Bertrand Russell and his implied judgment, "To this day Christians think an adulterer more wicked than a politician who takes bribes, although the latter probably does a thousand times as much harm." And he thoroughly rejects Cardinal Newman's view: "The Church holds that it were better for sun and moon to drop from heaven, for the earth to fail, and for all the many millions who are upon it to die of starvation in extremest agony . . . than that one soul, I will not say should be lost, but should commit one single venial sin."

A Mrs. X was convicted (later cleared in appellate court) of impairing the morals of her minor daughter. She had tried to teach the child chastity but at thirteen the girl bore the first of three unwanted, neglected babies. Her mother then had said, "If you persist in acting this way, at least be sure the boy wears something!" On this evidence she was convicted and sentenced. The combined forces of "secular" law and legalistic puritanism had tried to prevent loving help to the girl, her bastard victims, and the social agencies trying to help her. Situation ethics would have praised that woman; it would not have pilloried her.

In the language of classical ethics and jurisprudence, the more statutory the law, the greater the need of equity. For, as statutes are applied to actual situations, something has to give; some latitude is necessary for doubtful or perplexed consciences. Inexorably questions arise as to whether in a particular case the law truly applies (doubt), or as to which of several more or less conflicting laws is to be followed (perplexity). The effort to deal with these questions helpfully, even though hamstrung and corseted by rules and "sacred" principles, is what casuistry is. When a law ethic listens to love at all, it tries to rise above its legalism; paradoxically enough, the development of Catholic casuistry is powerful evidence of less legalism in the Catholic fold than the Protestant.

Legalism in the Christian tradition has taken two forms. In the Catholic line it has been a matter of legalistic *reason*, based on nature or natural law. These moralists have tended to adumbrate their ethical rules by applying human reason to the facts of nature, both human and subhuman, and to the lessons of historical experience. By this procedure they claim to have adduced universally agreed and therefore valid "natural" moral laws. Protestant moralists have followed the same adductive and deductive tactics. They have taken Scripture and done with it what the Catholics do with nature. Their Scriptural moral law is, they argue, based on the words and sayings of the Law and the Prophets, the evangelists and apostles of the Bible. It is a matter of legalistic *revelation*. One is rationalistic, the other Biblicistic; one natural, the other Scriptural. But both are legalistic.

Even though Catholic moralists deal also with "revealed law" (e.g., "the divine positive law of the Ten Commandments") and Protestants have tried to use reason in interpreting the sayings of the Bible (hermeneutics), still both by and large have been committed to the doctrines of law ethics.

2. Antinomianism

Over against legalism, as a sort of polar opposite, we can put antinomianism. This is the approach with which one enters into the decision-making situation armed with no principles or maxims whatsoever, to say nothing of *rules*. In every "existential moment" or "unique" situation, it declares, one must rely upon the situation of itself, *there and then*, to provide its ethical solution.

The term "antinomianism" (literally, "against law") was used first by Luther to describe Johannes Agricola's views. The ethical concept has cropped up here and there, as among some Anabaptists, some sects of English Puritanism, and some of Wesley's followers. The concept is certainly at issue in I Corinthians (e.g., ch. 6:12–20). Paul had to struggle with two primitive forms of it among the Hellenistic Jew-Christians whom he visited. They took his attacks on law morality too naïvely and too literally.

One form was libertinism—the belief that by grace, by the new life in Christ and salvation by faith, law or rules no longer applied to Christians. Their ultimate happy fate was now assured, and it mattered no more *what* they did. (Whoring, incest, drunkenness, and the like are what they did, therefore! This explains the warning in I Peter 2:16, "Live as free men, yet without using your freedom as a pretext for evil; but live as servants of God." This license led by inevitable reaction to an increase of legalism, especially in sex ethics, under which Christians still suffer today.) The other form, less pretentious and more enduring, was a Gnostic claim to special knowledge, so that neither principles nor rules were needed any longer even as guidelines and direction pointers. They would just *know* what was right when they needed to know. They had, they claimed, a superconscience. It is this second "gnostic" form of the approach which is under examination here.

While legalists are preoccupied with law and its stipulations, the Gnostics are so flatly opposed to law—even in principle—that their moral decisions are random, unpredictable, erratic, quite anomalous. Making moral decisions is a matter of spontaneity; it is literally unprincipled, purely *ad hoc* and casual. They follow no forecastable course from one situation to another. They are, exactly, anarchic—i.e., without a rule. They are not only "unbound by the chains of law" but actually sheer extemporizers, impromptu and intellectually irresponsible. They not only cast the old Torah aside; they even cease to think seriously and *care-fully* about the demands of love as it has been shown in Christ, the love norm itself. The baby goes out with the bath water!

This was the issue Paul fought over with the antinomians at Corinth and Ephesus. They were repudiating all law, as such, and all principles, relying in all moral action choices solely upon guidance in the situation. Some were what he called *pneumatikoi*, spirit-possessed. They claimed that *their* guidance came from outside themselves, by the Holy Spirit. Of what use are principles and laws when you can depend on the Holy Spirit? It was a kind of special-providence idea; a version of the inspiration theory of conscience. Other antinomians claimed, and still do, that their guidance comes from within themselves, as a sort of built-in radarlike "faculty," a translegal or clairvoyant conscience as promised in Jer. 31:31–34, written "upon their hearts." This second and more common form of Gnostic antinomianism, found among both Christians and non-Christians, is close to the intuition theory or faculty theory of conscience.

Perhaps a good example of the guidance idea in today's scene is Moral Re-Armament. It has a doctrine of special providence and daily guidance by "spiritual power" to right and wrong actions and causes. Its basic doctrines were first worked out under the leadership of Frank Buchman in the twenties, when it was called "The First Century Christian Fellowship." It has won to itself, not so surprisingly, even the French Catholic existentialist philosopher, Gabriel Marcel.

In its present form, with its wealthy clientele, it is a "sawdust trail in a dinner jacket." Part of its ideology, understandably, is the perfectionist notion that "members of the fellowship" can achieve and should live by *absolute* purity (sexual!), *absolute* truth, *absolute* unselfishness, and *absolute* love. Its separation of love from unselfishness is as puzzling as its call for "absolute" virtue and perfectionism and is as pretentious. But after all, if we have the power of the Spirit to tell us daily in a special way *what* the good is, surely we can expect to *do* it "absolutely"! Curiously, the Moral Re-Armament ethic is of the kind one would logically expect to find in the Holiness and Pentecostal movements, and yet, in spite of their self-styled pneumatic character, they are for the most part quite legalistic morally—not antinomian about their ethics at all.

Another version of antinomianism, on the whole much subtler philosophically and perhaps more admirable, is the ethics of existentialism. Sartre speaks of "nausea," which is our anxious experience of the *incoherence* of reality. For him any belief in coherence (such as the Christian doctrine of the unity of God's creation and his Lordship over history) is "bad faith." In every moment of moral choice or decision "we have no excuses behind us and no justification before us." Sartre refuses to admit to any *generally* valid principles at all, nothing even ordinarily valid, to say nothing of universal *laws*. Simone de Beauvoir in *The Ethics of Ambiguity* cannot quite bring herself to accept either "the contingent absurdity of the discontinuous" or "the rationalistic necessity of the continuous," proving herself to be less sturdily existentialist than Sartre, but she admits that the real world is after all "bare and incoherent." She shrinks from a candid antinomianism. But the plain fact is that her ontology—her idea of basic reality—is, like Sartre's, one of radical discontinuity, so that there can be no connective tissue between one situation or moment of experience and another. There is no fabric or web of life, hence no basis for generalizing moral principles *or* laws. Every situation has only its particularity!

On this view, of course, the existentialists rightly reject even all principles, all "generally valid" ethical norms or axioms, as well as all rules or laws or precepts that legalistically absolutize (idolize) such general principles. Radical discontinuity in one's theory of being forces the "absolute particularity" of *tout comprendre, tout pardonner*. Sartre is at least honest and tough-minded. In the absence of any faith in love as the norm and in any God as the norm-giver, he says resolutely: "Ontology itself cannot formulate ethical precepts. It is concerned solely with what is, and we cannot possibly derive imperatives from ontology's indicatives." He is, on this score at least, entirely correct!

3. Situationism

A third approach, in between legalism and antinomian unprincipledness, is situation ethics. (To jump from one polarity to the other would be only to go from the frying pan to the fire.) The situationist enters into every decision-making situation fully armed with the ethical maxims of his community and its heritage, and he treats them with respect as illuminators of his problems. Just the same he is prepared in any situation to compromise them or set them aside *in the situation* if love seems better served by doing so.

Situation ethics goes part of the way with natural law, by accepting reason as the instrument of moral judgment, while rejecting the notion that the good is "given" in the nature of things, objectively. It goes part of the way with Scriptural law by accepting revelation as the source of the norm while rejecting all "revealed" norms or laws but the one command—to love God in the neighbor. The situationist follows a moral law or violates it according to love's need. For example, "Almsgiving is a good thing *if* . . ." The situationist never says, "Almsgiving is a good thing. Period!" His decisions are hypothetical, not categorical. Only the commandment to love is categorically good. "Owe no one anything, except to love one another" (Rom. 13:8). If help to an indigent only pauperizes and degrades him, the situationist refuses a handout and finds some other way. He makes no law out of Jesus' "Give to every one who begs from you." It is only one step from that kind of Biblicist literalism to the kind that causes women in certain sects to refuse blood transfusions even if death results—even if they are carrying a quickened fetus that will be lost too. The legalist says that even if he tells a man escaped from an asylum where his intended victim is, if he finds and murders him, at least only one sin has been committed (murder), not two (lying as well)!

. . . We might say, from the situationist's perspective, that it is possible to derive general "principles" from whatever is the one and only universal law (*agapē* for Christians, something else for others), but not laws or rules. We cannot milk universals from a universal!

. . . Our obligation is relative *to* the situation, but obligation *in* the situation is absolute. We are only "obliged" to tell the truth, for example, if the situation calls for it; if a murderer asks us his victim's whereabouts, our duty might be to lie. There is in situation ethics an absolute element and an element of calculation . . . But it would be better to say it has an absolute *norm* and a calculating method. There is weight in the old saying that what is needed is "faith, hope, and clarity." We have to find out what is "fitting" to be truly ethical, to use H. R. Niebuhr's word for it in his *The Responsible Self*. Situation ethics aims at a contextual appropriateness—not the "good" or the "right" but the *fitting*.

A cartoon in a fundamentalist magazine once showed Moses scowling, holding his stone tablet with its graven laws, all ten, and an eager stonecutter saying to him, "Aaron said perhaps you'd let us reduce them to 'Act responsibly in love.'" This was meant as a dig at the situationists and the new morality, but the legalist humor in it merely states exactly what situation ethics calls for! With Dietrich Bonhoeffer we say, "Principles are only tools in God's hands, soon to be thrown away as unserviceable."

One competent situationist [E. LaB. Cherbonnier at Trinity College, December 14, 1964], speaking to students, explained the position this way. Rules are "like 'Punt on fourth down,' or 'Take a pitch when the count is three balls.' These rules are part of the wise player's know-how, and distinguish him from the novice. But they are not unbreakable. The best players are those who know when to ignore them. In the game of bridge, for example, there is a useful rule which says 'Second hand low.' But have you ever played with anyone who followed the rule slavishly? You say to him (in exasperation), 'Partner, why didn't you play your ace? We could have set the hand.' And he replies, unperturbed, 'Second hand low!' What is wrong? The same thing that was wrong when Kant gave information to the murderer. He forgot the purpose of the game. . . . He no longer thought of winning the hand, but of being able to justify himself by invoking the rule."

This practical temper of the activist or *verb*-minded decision maker, versus contemplative *noun*-mindedness, is a major Biblical rather than Hellenistic trait. . . . A "leap of faith" is an action decision rather than a leap of thought, for a man's faith is a hypothesis that he takes seriously enough to act on and live by.

There are various names for this approach: situationism, contextualism, occasionalism, circumstantialism, even actualism. These labels indicate, of course, that the core of the ethic they describe is a healthy and primary awareness that "circumstances alter cases"—i.e., that in actual problems of conscience the situational variables are to be weighed as heavily as the normative or "general" constants.

The situational factors are so primary that we may even say "circumstances alter rules and principles." It is said that when Gertrude Stein lay dying she declared, "It is better to ask questions than to give answers, even good answers." This is the temper of situation ethics. It is empirical, fact-minded, data conscious, inquiring. It is antimoralistic as well as antilegalistic, for it is sensitive to variety and complexity. It is neither simplistic nor perfectionist. It is "casuistry" (case-based) in a constructive and nonpejorative sense of the word. We should perhaps call it "neocasuistry." Like classical casuistry, it is case-focused and concrete, concerned to bring Christian imperatives into practical operation. But unlike classical casuistry, this neocasuistry repudiates any attempt to anticipate or prescribe real-life decisions in their existential particularity. It works with two guidelines from Paul: "The written code kills, but the Spirit gives life" (II Cor. 3:6), and "For the whole law is fulfilled in one word, 'You shall love your neighbor as yourself' " (Gal. 5:14).

. . . *Christian* situation ethics has only one norm or principle or law (call it what you will) that is binding and unexceptionable, always good and right regardless of the circumstances. That is "love"—the *agapē* of the summary commandment to love God and the neighbor. Everything else without exception, all laws and rules and principles and ideals and norms, are only *contingent,* only valid *if they happen* to serve love in any situation. Christian situation ethics is not a system or program of living according to a code, but an effort to relate love to a world of relativities through a casuistry obedient to love. It is the strategy of love. This strategy denies that there are, as Sophocles thought, any unwritten immutable laws of heaven, agreeing with Bultmann that all such notions are idolatrous and a demonic pretension.

In non-Christian situation ethics some other highest good or *summum bonum* will, of course, take love's place as the one and only standard—such as self-realization in the ethics of Aristotle. But the *Christian* is neighbor-centered first and last. Love is for people, not for principles; i.e., it is personal—and therefore when the impersonal universal conflicts with the personal particular, the latter prevails in situation ethics. Because of its mediating position, prepared to act on moral laws or in spite of them, the antinomians will call situationists soft legalists, and legalists will call them cryptoantinomians. . . .

Robert E. Fitch

A Common Sense Sex Code

A common sense code of sexual morality is all that is left for young people today. Indeed, it is all that is left for Christian young people when their elders answer their most pressing questions only with loose discourse about the "liberating power of the gospel" and how "in Jesus Christ we are freed from myth and from law." In all such discourse it is apparent that we are to be freed from old myths in order to be credulous about current myths, liberated from an ancient law to become

Reprinted from *The Christian Century* (October 7, 1964), by permission of the publisher.

Dr. Fitch is Dean of the Pacific School of Religion, Berkeley, California.

slaves to the law of our present folkways, emancipated from the authority of the past only to be brought into more secure bondage to the tyranny of contemporary prejudice.

Certainly common sense affirms the primacy of love. But it does not envisage love as a dangling emotion without organic connection to the larger realm of thought, feeling and action which makes us whole as human beings. Common sense will always prefer the flat Yes or No to the ambiguous "Who knows?" The flat answer at least offers alternatives to action and occasions for significant inquiry. Because we are all sinners and fall short of the ideal, the practices of charity and of humility continue to be in order. But it is not charity to teach that you can be a person without having principles; and irresponsibility is a hypocritical substitute for humility.

Herewith, therefore, a code—and let us not be afraid to call it that!—for sexual morality today:

(1) *Either you control sex, or sex controls you.* Needed right now are bigger and better inhibitions. Let no one be afraid to speak to young people today in this manner. It is a message they have not heard in a quarter of a century, and it will come to them with all the charm of novelty. Currently they have a respectful awareness that they must curb their appetites for food, drink and tobacco. This message comes to them with all the authority of science, of the federal government and of the beauty parlor. Surely there is something ludicrous in the notion that while liquor, cigarettes and ice cream must be put under the most strict and rational controls, sex, on the contrary, is something to which you may help yourself when, as and if you please.

At the same time there is needed a recovery of the sense of personal responsibility. This means giving up the perpetual alibi of the environment. We are told, for instance, that it is hypocritical to tell young people to practice self-control when they are surrounded by solicitations to license by all kinds of commercialized sex. But they are equally surrounded by solicitations to license in eating, drinking, smoking and in buying automobiles, clothes and cosmetics. Besides, I remember vividly my first parish, years ago, on a barren midwestern prairie, with no magazines, no movies, no radio, no TV, no advertising, no commercialized sex—with nothing but dust storms, traveling evangelists, circuses, gumbo mud and wild oats instead of wheat for a crop. Here there was an even greater temptation to license in sexual activity, simply because there was nothing else to do. One way or the other you can always use the environment as an alibi—if you don't ever want to grow up to be a man.

Nor has personal responsibility disappeared because now you can depend on the pill. There may be an infallible pill, but, as every doctor knows, there is no such thing as an infallible patient. The proportion of persons with enough disciplined regularity of habit to take a prescribed pill at the specified time, without fail from day to day, is scarcely as much as one in 25. When impulse and passion are mingled with the business, then the proportion must be even lower. And in this sort of thing, a miss is as good as a mile.

So either you control sex, or sex controls you. It may control you by forcing you into parenthood or marriage or a job before you really want any of these things. Or it may control you more subtly by clouding your judgment of members of the opposite sex, so that you do not turn to the kind of companionship you most deeply desire. Or it may trap you into an illusory romance where a temporary ecstasy of the senses is only a cover for a hunger of the mind and of the spirit. It's up to you!

(2) *Sex is for human beings.* To be sure, it is also for vegetables and for animals. Aristotle knew that. Today we are almost constrained to admit that it must be for machines, too. Not that any machines have yet been invented which can copulate in a biologically creditable manner. But there are some people who attempt to mechanize sex, and to dispose of it as an impersonally automated product. Sex is also for uncomplicated, primitive peoples—the idyllic South Sea islander of the poet and the cultural anthropologist. There is no question in my mind that such islanders are fully human beings. But when someone out of a complex culture—with high-strung nerves, an educated intellect and sophisticated senses and emotions—tries to put himself back into the simpler pattern, there will be nothing idyllic about him: he will become less than human.

Let each creature, then, take sex according to his own order and degree. We must take sex according to the order and degree of our own humanity. And what is it that makes human beings human? The Greek answer is intelligence; the Christian answer is love. Sex for us as human beings has to be blended with intelligence and with love. But intelligence as disciplined inquiry into truth, as Socrates knew it, and love as the highest spiritual excellence, as St. Paul spoke of it, are something more than a mere impulse of curiosity or a sudden leap of lust.

The tragedy of contemporary civilization is the way it has exalted sex and debased love. It has not known how to hold them together because it has not known which should be in command nor even what is the true character of the commanding principle. For this reason contemporary literature—on stage or in the novel—is marked by the absence of true passion, which I define as a deep and powerful emotion attached to a worthy and ennobling object. Instead, we have hysteria, violence and tantrums or grunts, snorts, groans and shrieks. Perhaps this would please a Kinsey, who had a scarcely concealed resentment against religion (love) and higher education (intelligence) because he wanted us all to get back to the simpler animal condition. In any case, when we take our sex we must decide whether we take it as pigs or as people.

(3) *Sexual compatibility is not the essential in a happy marriage.* This statement will scandalize the sentimentalists of sex. But let us look at the facts. Theoretically there are four possible combinations: happiness, with sexual compatibility, or without it; unhappiness, with sexual compatibility, or without it. Only two of these cases supply critical evidence.

Can people be sexually compatible and still develop an unhappy marriage? Obviously Yes. The fact is that the ordinary normal person is capable of having physically satisfied sexual relations with millions of members of the opposite sex. The difficulty arises when he discovers that that is the only satisfactory relationship he has. When that discovery is made, the sex relationship itself degenerates.

Can people be sexually incompatible and still have a happy marriage? The answer must vary with the kind and degree of incompatibility. The important thing is whether the other factors in a happy marriage are present or absent. But any marriage counselor knows that there are happily married couples whose experience of the usual consummation of sexual intercourse is limited or infrequent. In such circumstances it may still be possible to have children, to create a home, to develop a significant fellowship one with the other.

And here we are at one point where premarital experiments in sexual intercourse are radically misleading. Whether consciously or not, the participants tend to make an absolute out of the sexual relationship. But happiness in marriage depends still more on other factors. It depends on a love and a loyalty which can stand the long-range test for better for worse, for richer for poorer, in sickness and in health. It depends on the standards of craftsmanship (housekeeping, earning a living) and of morality (fair play, generosity, fidelity) that go into the mixture. And it depends on the degree to which the intimate communion of the lovers is enriched and corrected by higher and wider forms of fellowship. No premarital relationship can test these things, nor can any short-term trial marriage.

(4) *Sex is social.* In our society sexual relations may have their origin in the free choice and consent of individuals. But the outcome is always social. That is why there is no society whatsoever, from the most primitive to the most complex, that does not regulate sexual conduct by its folkways. This is true even with what may look to us like patterns of promiscuity—which, however, are socially defined and circumscribed in the most careful manner. Sex has a social outcome that is biological—in

the form of babies. But it also has social outcomes that are vocational, economic, civil, political, aesthetic and religious.

The big deception that lies at the basis of premarital experiments is the illusion of the isolated individual. I still recall the ironic contradiction between the experience and the creed of a young social worker in the case of an unwanted baby. Said the social worker in defense of her client, "But of course it's nobody's business but hers!" Nobody else's business—when a clergyman, a social worker, a legal officer, an adoption agency, foster parents and, in this instance, a good piece of the machinery of the United States government were involved in cleaning up the mess! But, says someone, let us leave out the baby. Very well, then, leave it out (when you can). The social consequences of the sexual intimacies of two persons are still enormous in extent.

Moreover, not only the *outcome* but also the *test* of satisfactory sexual relations is social. Love is not just a matter of the feeling of emotional sincerity or of the experience of a beautiful relationship consummated furtively at a one-night stand in a motel. Love may be initiated by two private individuals, but it is *in effect* a public transaction which must meet social standards. Nor does love even know itself as love until it has entered into community with groceries, the rent, a salary, taxes, civic responsibilities and religious forms of association. Moreover, what makes love a truly individual affair is precisely this social experience. As Thielicke observes, "Not uniqueness establishes marriage, but marriage establishes uniqueness."

(5) *Sex is for persons.* It is an ultimate evil to depersonalize sex. Being a person implies the full social context and also involves the genuine emotion of love. Yet people will still argue that sex can be cut off from its organic relationship to the affections and to the social order, and taken in isolation by itself. Of course it can. So can you cut off a hand or an arm or a head and take it by itself. But what happens to the separated organ, what happens to the dismembered person? If someone practicing such a dismemberment of sex argues "What I'm doing can't harm anyone else," then the answer ought to be clear. The dismemberment will not, at once, harm any but you—by gradually converting you into a selfish sensualist incapable of loyalty and affection for another.

In Rostand's *Last Night of Don Juan* the devil, in the guise of a puppeteer, comes at last to bring the great lover to his reward. Don Juan pleads for more time, argues that he was always in love with his women, asks that his mistresses be brought back to testify for him. As they parade past him each holds a mask to her face. He steps up eagerly to identify one and then the other—"Henriette! Louise! Jeanne!" But in each instance there is the tinkling laughter of mockery as the mask is withdrawn to show the mistake in identity, while the woman bows ironically and goes her way. Don Juan, with all his famous affairs, had never known a woman as a person. He had long ago ceased to be a person himself. And he had never really been in love with anyone—but himself and his own narcissistic sensations. So the devil takes Don Juan to his reward, with the decree that one who has made himself a puppet in this life must be forever hereafter a puppet in hell.

And that surely is the heart of the matter. Sex must be a part of the self as a person. Like any other healthy appetite, it requires regulation and control. Nor shall we get the most out of it, or out of ourselves, unless we mingle it with those elements that are moral and spiritual and social, that call forth the highest in our humanity.

Winfred Overholser

Homosexuality: Sin or Disease?

There is nothing new about homosexuality. Just as the sexual drive has existed since the dawn of mankind, so have deviations from the accepted modes of expression of that drive been manifested. The account of the destruction of Sodom and Gomorrah (Genesis 19:1–28) makes it clear that among the early Jews homosexuality was held in the greatest abhorrence. The men of Sodom, we are told, demanded Lot's male visitors for sexual purposes, spurning his offer to turn over his unmarried daughters to the crowd's demands. Indeed, the name of Sodom has come down to the present, sodomy (or buggery) being the term applied to

Reprinted from *The Christian Century* (September 11, 1963), pp. 1099–1101, by permission of the publisher.

Winfred Overholser is Professor of Psychiatry, Emeritus, at George Washington University, Washington, D.C.

anal coitus, a principal form of male homosexual relations, the other common form being mouth-genital contact, known as fellatio.

Among the great Western civilizations, the Greek has been almost alone in tolerating homosexuality. The names of Socrates and of Sappho, the great poetess of Lesbos, have been applied, respectively, to male and female homosexual activities. In the Anglo-Saxon world the legal penalties have been severe—life imprisonment in some instances—and the church has vigorously denounced such activities as against the laws of God and man. It is of some interest, as illustrating the tremendous emotional hold attaching to discussions of this type of sexual activity (and indeed of matters sexual in general), that as far back as the time of Henry VIII it was referred to as "the abominable and detestable crime against nature." Some of our own statutes have followed that wording— at the same time refraining from the use of such emotionally charged epithets in regard to murder, robbery and rape!

Homosexuality has been defined as a sexual propensity for persons of one's own sex. Since the male is much more aggressive in expressing the sexual drive, the homosexual is usually thought of as a man. But female homosexuality is far from unknown; although we have only very undependable statistics, there is reason to suspect that the incidence among women may be almost as high as among men, especially in prisons. Legal prosecutions of women are, however, extremely rare; indeed, they are virtually unknown.

Homosexuality is not an "all or none" phenomenon. It exists in many degrees, and in many persons a latent tendency may never become overt. Some individuals are the active partners in overt relations, while others prefer the passive role. The aggressiveness with which the homosexual impulse is expressed varies markedly. There are the homosexual "wolves" who seek out victims, using bribes, blandishments or even force to overcome resistance. On the other hand, there are those who become involved only on occasion, or while under the influence of alcohol, physical or mental disease, or senile deterioration. Both types are found on all levels of society and of intelligence. The homosexual is certainly not a special order of creation! Nor is homosexual activity incompatible with a heterosexual adjustment, at least of a sort. Though some homosexuals apparently use marriage as a "front," cases are far from unknown in which married men live as good husbands and fathers yet at the same time engage in homosexual activities.

The late Alfred Kinsey, a long-time student of human sexual behavior, constructed what may be termed a 7-point scale of sexuality, with a rating of 6 for sexual arousal with other males only, 3 for arousals and acts equally with either sex, and 0 for exclusive heterosexuality. There is thus seen to be a continuum, not a sharp demarcation.

Shrouded in Uncertainty

The question is often asked: How prevalent is homosexual behavior? Nobody knows. We may be sure of one thing, however: it is considerably more prevalent than is generally believed. As to whether it is increasing, again one cannot give a dogmatic reply. I would guess that it is not—but that is only a guess. Any increase in arrests can well be due to increased police activity rather than to an increase in homosexual acts. It is a fact that matters sexual are being much more freely discussed than was the case even a decade or two ago—and one must admit that on this as on other important aspects of life the spread of knowledge is preferable to ignorance. It is also a fact that there seems to be a slackening of the force of prohibitions and moral sanctions in the sexual realm; presumably such slackening prevails equally in the hetero- and homosexual fields.

Dr. Kinsey estimated that about 4 per cent of the male population were exclusively homosexual and that 37 per cent had had homosexual experience at some time during their lives—usually sodomy or mouth-genital contacts or mutual masturbation. Whatever one may think of the validity of Dr. Kinsey's figures or his selection of subjects, the fact remains that he made an intensive study of the sexual activity of more persons than have been studied by any other investigator. Obviously, any determination of number or proportion is rendered almost impossible by the fact that sexual activities are carried out in private and that queries on these topics seldom elicit the truth.

Why do some adults develop into homosexuals? In one group are those persons who exhibit an imbalance of the ductless glands, so that they have a higher output of the estrogens of the opposite sex than is normal. Such men have a feminine configuration and hair distribution (little or no beard, for instance) and tend to have the mincing gait and high-pitched voice which the popular mind associates with the homosexual. There are similar reversals in some women: lack of secondary sex characteristics, deep voice, perhaps a beard, and so on. However, it is probable that such physically conditioned types constitute a relatively small proportion of homosexuals. Not infrequently a typical "he-man" turns out to be latently or even overtly homosexual. Endocrine imbalance probably does not account for the aberrations of more than a small fraction of the whole group.

Since the time of Freud and his associate Ferenczi, psychiatrists have studied the problem of homosexuality and have attempted to explain its existence. Freud's formulation of psychosexual development may be briefly stated as follows: The young child is first interested in himself and his mother, and may become so attached to her that he vies with his father for her attention (the Oedipus situation). Somewhat later, but still in the pre-adolescent period, the child goes through a period when he scorns the opposite sex; he hero-worships leaders of his own sex, develops "crushes" on playmates and may engage in sexual experiments with them. This is referred to as the homosexual stage of psychosexual development. There is often, however, no overt homosexual activity.

Normally, with the onset of puberty the heterosexual or adult stage is entered, with developing interest in the opposite sex. For various reasons, largely environmental, an undetermined proportion of adults never fully reach this stage; they become fixated partially or wholly at an earlier level. Incidentally, there is no certain evidence that homosexual seduction at an early age is a substantial factor accounting for later homosexual behavior.

It follows from what has been said that homosexual trends are present to some degree in many persons, though rigidly repressed. Indeed, it may be fear of these repressed impulses that accounts for much of the extreme abhorrence and suspicion and fear of the homosexual expressed in our laws and mores.

Aspects of Treatment

Homosexuality is treatable, provided the patient recognizes that his way of life is rejected and indeed despised by society, and that for that reason if no other modification is urgent. The most important factor in successful therapy is cooperation on the part of the subject, and a readiness to undergo therapy which may take a long time. Except for the few organically conditioned cases, the approach is basically psychoanalytic. This involves a long series of sessions in which the patient (analysand) brings out through "free association" material from the unconscious which may have been long repressed or "forgotten"—especially occurrences, sometimes painful, of early childhood.

As the roots of the problem are uncovered and examined, there is at least a moderate likelihood that the patient will achieve understanding and an ability to face reality in a truly adult way. This process is one which should be undertaken only by a trained psychiatrist. It is rare that mere cautionings or threats—for example, by a clergyman or a representative of the law—will have any lasting effect on the patient's conduct, except perhaps to make him somewhat more cautious and determined to try a bit harder not to be caught. It is, I hope, unnecessary to add that anyone—physician, clergyman or friend—to whom the homosexual appeals should continually bear in mind that he is dealing with a person who needs treatment and who therefore is entitled to sympathetic consideration.

Though one of the tragic consequences of illicit sexual activity, namely illegitimacy, need not exercise the community with regard to homosexuals, homosexuals would do well to remember that they run the danger of contracting venereal disease. Too often they must come to terms with the fact that "the wages of sin" can well be syphilis.

In the Eyes of the Law

There are undoubtedly psychological reasons why the law is so savage in assessing penalties for this sort of behavior, and why the public so strongly disapproves of the homosexual. He is looked on as a pariah. The government in both its civil and military branches will not employ him, even though the only blot on his record may have to do with an isolated act committed years earlier. And if he is already in government employ when accusations are made, he is likely to be summarily dismissed with hardly more than suspicion as evidence. The furor which stemmed from the accusations made by the late Senator Joseph R. McCarthy still leaves its mark on bureaucratic thinking and acting. Yet many of the men accused are competent and intelligent, a fact which makes their plight all the more tragic. Tragic too is the fact that the prevalent public attitude opens the door wide to blackmail and police entrapment.

Fortunately, our courts are coming to recognize more fully the psychological aspects of homosexuality. Not infrequently a court places an offender on probation, conditioned perhaps on his accepting psychiatric treatment. The enactment of the so-called "sexual psychopath" laws in some 20 states is in itself recognition of the fact that some sexual offenders (not only homosexuals) are not amenable to ordinary penal treatment but are subjects for psychiatric attention. A reasonable proportion of homosexuals may be treated by psychotherapy and a few by glandular therapy, provided they are willing to cooperate. Some there are, however, who prefer not to attempt any change, professing to look at themselves and their kind as superior beings.

Although in this country the legislatures have mostly contented themselves with verbal abuse and with increased penalties in dealing with the problem, the British lawmaking bodies have viewed it more objectively. In 1954 a parliamentary committee under the chairmanship of Sir John Wolfenden was established. Its report, filed three years later after many hearings, is recommended reading. Acting on the principle that "unless a deliberate attempt is to be made by society . . . to equate the sphere of crime with that of sin, there must remain a realm of private morality and immorality which is, in brief and crude terms, not the law's business," the report recommended "that homosexual behavior between consenting adults in private no longer be a criminal offense." The committee made it clear, however, that there should be no relaxation of the law when persons under 21 are involved, or when force is used.

The Wolfenden program, which expressed basically the continental attitude, has not been adopted in England and probably will not be adopted in the near future. Given the present state of American emotions on the subject, however, I would venture the opinion that Britain will probably anticipate this country in moving on to saner ground in this regard. The fact that a parliamentary committee could make such recommendations indicates at the very least that reason is being applied to a very troublesome problem. It would seem to point the way to a more rational dealing with the homosexual in this country as well. When such rationality is achieved, we may expect that, in the case of the consenting adult, understanding—and, where indicated, treatment —may take the place of vilification and indiscriminate punishment.

Howard Moody

Toward a New Definition of Obscenity

It was no accident that one of the issues in the Presidential campaign [of 1964] was the "breakdown" of morality and the "deterioration of decency." We are obviously in the midst of what is simultaneously a moral and an artistic revolution, and it is usually difficult to tell where one leaves off and the other begins. All the way from the police department "put-down" of "dirty poetry" in coffeehouses in the early Fifties to

Reprinted from *Christianity and Crisis*, Vol. XXIV, No. 24 (January 25, 1965), by permission of the publisher.

Howard Moody is minister of Judson Memorial Church in Greenwich Village and lectures at the New School for Social Research.

the recent persecution of that most tragic of all shamans, Lenny Bruce, we have felt the reverberations of a battle that is as old as the country itself.

In the last few years slick-paper sex magazines like Ralph Ginzburg's *Eros*, as well as classics like *Fanny Hill*, have been banned and unbanned with disarming regularity. More recently the new wave of offbeat film makers experimenting with weird and strange themes have been arrested and their films banned from public places. Everything from topless bathing suits for women to bottomless bathing suits for men (in a Greenwich Village sportswear shop) are subjects for legal action.

To some people the foregoing is merely evidence of the decadence and coming destruction of American civilization, while to others it is the dawn of a new day of freedom of expression and the demise of shackling censorship. Whatever one's point of view as to the significance of the present revolution, it will be impossible to understand the present situation without knowing something of the history of the problem. How continuously, and sometimes obsessively, we as a people have been bent upon what Morris Ernst and Alan Schwartz have called "the search for the obscene." (*Censorship: The Search for the Obscene* is their valuable study of this question from which I have drawn much of the legal-historical material in this article.)

Though the Puritans have often been blamed for "blue laws" and censorship, they actually were a great deal freer than they are often given credit for. In his revealing volume *The Not-Quite Puritans* Henry Lawrence refers to no fewer than sixty-six confessions to fornication in one small town between 1761–65 (that was only those who confessed).

As a matter of fact, our first anti-obscenity law did not come into existence until the nineteenth century. Our forefathers, the Revolutionists and fashioners of the Constitution, did not seem so concerned with obscenity or pornography (and don't think there wasn't plenty around, cf. *The Fyfteen Plagues of a Maidenhead* and Ben Franklin's *Advice to a Young Man on Choosing a Mistress*, a ribald essay not published but freely circulated). Their concern is contained in the words of the First Amendment about Congress making no law abridging freedom of speech, religion and the press.

The real beginning of censorship—the establishment of prudery by legal sanctions—was the work not of Puritans and Pilgrims but of nineteenth century Protestants. This will come as a surprise to those who label Roman Catholics as the book banning "bad boys" of censorship and the first antagonists of pornography. After all it was Anthony Comstock, a fanatical 24-year-old grocery clerk, who with the decisive help of the YMCA badgered the country and the Congress into passing a law that still governs obscenity in the mails. State after state followed the Congress and enacted "Comstock Laws." The major support for Comstock came, ironically enough, from the Babylon of sin and iniquity, New York City. The crusaders were not Irish Catholics; their top leadership was from the Protestant social hierarchy of New York, and J. P. Morgan's name led all the rest.

Using the Law

The leaders of censorship crusades used several means to gain their end, beginning with the law. From the late 1880's on, the crusaders have been confounded in attempts to get a definitive ruling on the meaning of obscenity in the courts of the land. The definition in the Comstock Law was terribly unclear, and since that time the courts have played the "synonyms game" (obscene is "dirty," "lewd," "lascivious," "scurrilous").

The protesters seemed to be disturbed by several matters as they pressed by law for the banning of books, and later films. They were deeply offended by "dirty words." One of the most important court cases was the Woolsey case, named after Judge John M. Woolsey, which dealt with the question of whether James Joyce's *Ulysses* might be distributed in this country. The basic objection to this book was the use of "four-letter words." The counsel, Morris Ernst, gave a historic exposition. The following is his dialogue with the judge.

> Counsel: Judge, as to the word "fuck" one etymological dictionary gives its derivation as from "facere"—to make—the farmer fucked the seed into the soil. This, Your Honor, has more integrity than a euphemism used every day in every modern novel to describe precisely the same event.
> Judge Woolsey: For example . . .
> Counsel: "They slept together." It means the same thing.
> Judge Woolsey: (smiling) But, Counselor, that isn't even usually the truth!

The final opinion of Judge Woolsey was that *Ulysses*, in spite of its vulgar language, did not excite sexual impulses or lustful thoughts and that its net effect was only that of a somewhat tragic and very powerful commentary on the inner lives of men and women.

This was the beginning of a whole series of significant legal cases on "obscenity" and attempts to control pornography.

One of the most important cases on obscenity was the Roth case, which involved an outright challenge to an obscenity law and its constitutionality under the First Amendment. Justice Harlan's decision in this case ought to be read by every fair-minded person interested in the problem of freedom and censorship.

Roth had been convicted by a lower court for selling books that "tend to stir sexual impulses and lead to sexually impure thoughts." This would, of course, condemn much of the world's great literature, and moreover, Justice Harlan asserts: ". . . in no event do I think that limited federal interest in this area can extend to mere 'thoughts.' The federal power has no business, whether under the postal or commerce laws, to bar the sale of books because they might lead to any kind of 'thoughts.'"

And in sections of the decision Justice Brennan's understanding of human nature is comparable to his judicial wisdom. He says:

> However, sex and obscenity are not synonymous; obscene material is material dealing with sex in a manner appealing to prurient interest. The portrayal of sex, e.g., literature, art and scientific works, is not itself sufficient reason to deny material the constitutional protection of freedom of speech and press. Sex, as a great and mysterious moving force in human life, has indisputably been a subject of absorbing interest to mankind through the ages; it is one of the vital problems of human interest and public concern.

The culmination of the long court battle was the Supreme Court's decision [of January 25, 1965] declaring *Tropic of Cancer* and the film "The Lovers" not to be obscene.

Sanction, Accusation, Intimidation

The peddlers of prudery also used another technique for the enforcement of their morality on the community as a whole: social and religious sanction. This was an effective weapon as long as a people dominated by a common Protestant ethos or Christian moral understanding controlled both legally and socially the normally accepted standards of behavior for the society.

However, with the "passing of Christendom," and the accompanying breakdown of religious authority, control has become much more difficult.

The censors in more recent years have used more desperate techniques such as that of quasi-legal and police action. Since the higher courts keep refusing to make irrevocably clear what is obscene, censors are driven to vigilante tactics that are extra-legal, highly undemocratic and probably unconstitutional. Self-appointed citizens' clean-books councils are springing up all over the country. Their tactics are intimidation and their appeals are sloganeering. Operating under the very appealing objective of "keeping filth and smut from our children," they move on to cleaning from libraries such books as *Brave New World, Black Boy, Catcher in the Rye* and others.

One of the more renowned private citizens' groups in this country is an interfaith organization in New York City called Operation Yorkville, which has garnered financial support and the backing of religious and political leaders for its task of guarding the morals of the city's youth. Most recently its chief targets of "malignancy" are the American Civil Liberties Union, the Supreme Court of the United States and every Court of Appeals judge who refuses to accept their "book-burning" standards. In order to punish the "pushers of pornography," methods are used, including accusations, that violate the rights of others.

One would not for a moment deny the right of these individuals acting in concert to make their point of view felt by means of persuasion. But when they use intimidating threats and slanderous name-calling as in the recent attack on the Supreme Court Justices for their June 22 [1964] ruling as "nurturing degeneracy," then these groups have gone beyond the boundary of what constitutes responsible citizens' action.

Class Prudery or Blasphemy

The question that comes to the Church and to individual Christians at this point is what should be our posture in the midst of these revolutions going on about us? I think Christians should look carefully at the confusion regarding the meaning of obscenity and then make a major contribution by raising our own standard for judging obscenity. The Supreme Court, in its most recent case prior to last June's decision, defined it as follows: Obscene material is material which deals with sex in a manner appealing to prurient interest, and the test of obscenity is whether to the average person, applying contemporary community standards, the dominant theme of the material appeals to prurient interest (Justice Brennan: Roth v. U.S., 1957).

The dictionary defines "prurient" as "having an uneasy or morbid desire or curiosity: given to the indulgence of lewd ideas; impure minded." It is almost too obvious to say that even the wisest gods, let alone mortal men, would have an exceedingly difficult time deciding under this definition what is obscene, who is an average person, whose community standard, and what constitutes dominant theme. More basic than such highly ambiguous matters is the larger question of the legitimacy of using sex (even in a prurient way) as the sole basis for determining what is obscene. Here we are up against the most important aspect of the definition of obscenity: at least two of the important grounds for censorship are "dirty words" and "sexual subjects."

Relative to the matter of vulgar language, what righteous indignation can we Christians muster about our Anglo-Saxon forebears? Can we really pretend that the use of "coarse" and "vulgar" words is somehow tantamount to an affront to God Almighty? (Do we have to be so ashamed of the "bawdy" talk of Martin Luther?) Vulgar speech and four-letter words are not blasphemous or immoral, and our shame and prudery over them are basically class matters. (Even the derivation of the word "lewd" is interestingly traced to a "lewd-frere," a lay brother; unlearned, unlettered, rude, artless, belonging to lower orders.) Vulgar and bawdy language may well be objected to on the bases of aesthetics and social manners, but it is hardly justifiable to make a moral or theological case against raw language as the Church has tended to do.

I remember my father telling me as a youth that uttering the profanity "Goddamn" was the unforgivable sin of blasphemy as well as the breaking of the Third Commandment. It is the Christian's devious manner of avoiding the hard truth that "taking God's name in vain" is a far more profound sin than profanity. It is not the vulgar utterance from our lips but our deeds that truly profane human life. Christ always warned that you can't judge a man by his speech. Not everyone who says words like "Lord, Lord," even spoken with great reverence and piety, "does the truth" of those words; conversely many people who speak roughly in the raw language of vulgarity live in awe of and respect for the mystery of humanity.

The true profanity against God is to refuse to take him seriously; the truly "dirty" word is the one used to deny and to denigrate the humanness of another person. Language is symbolic, not literal; when a person speaks in raw language he may be trying to say something that nice and prosaic words will not communicate.

My point here is that, from a theological or ethical perspective, "dirty words" are a terribly inadequate base from which to write a definition of obscenity.

In the same way, we do not do justice to the Christian perspective upon human evil and immorality if we see sex as the dominant and determinative factor in the judgment of what is obscene. Sex, by our understanding of creation, is vital and a potent force in human behavior, though shot through with human sin and distortion. To make sex the sole determinative factor in defining "obscenity" or "pornography" or "filth" is to relegate it to the shadowy regions of immorality (depending on who says it in what community and how much). This completely fails to explain what all Christian faith and tradition teaches us is really obscene in this world.

For Christians the truly obscene ought not to be slick-paper nudity, nor the vulgarities of dirty old or young literati, nor even "weirdo" films showing transvestite orgies or male genitalia. What is obscene is that material, whether sexual or not, that has as its basic motivation and purpose the degradation, debasement and dehumanizing of persons. The dirtiest word in the English language is not "fuck" or "shit" in the mouth of a tragic shaman, but the word "nigger" from the sneering lips of a Bull Connor. Obscenity ought to be much closer to the biblical definition of blasphemy against God and man.

The censors tell us that the "filth" must be stopped because it is leading our children into acts of violence, rape, narcotic addiction and prostitution. They say that young minds are being poisoned and perverted by "pornographic books."

Are we really worried about the pornographic pictures peddled by shady characters on street corners? I remember all those "dirty" comic books in high school, i.e., "Popeye," "Maggie and Jiggs"—they made me feel I was "illicit" and they made me laugh, but I wasn't moved to ravish my teacher as a result.

I do not conceive that a picture is "dirty" because sex is its dominant theme. (The tragic disservice of slick-paper sex magazines is not that they display nudes in suggestive poses but that they become anti-sexual by pushing sex to the point of satiety, thus making it a deadly bore.) A picture is not dirty that shows a man and woman in one of the 57 recommended positions for intercourse (unaesthetic perhaps, possibly bad taste, but hardly obscene!). The dirty or obscene [picture] is the one that shows the police dogs being unleashed on the Negro demonstrators in Birmingham. The "lewdest" pictures of all—more obscene than all the tawdry products of the "smut industry"—are the pictures of Dachau, the ovens, and the grotesque pile of human corpses.

Let us as Christians write a new definition of obscenity based on the dehumanizing aspects of our contemporary culture. Can we not see the hypocrisy of our prudery when we spend time, words and money trying to prevent the magazine *Eros* from going through the mails and never raise an eyebrow about the tons of material that vilify human beings and consign whole ethnic groups to the lowest kind of animality? Do we not have to admit the duplicity that allows our police to guard George Lincoln Rockwell as he mouths blasphemous obscenities of the most inhuman order on public streets, while the same police are used to harass Lenny Bruce in the confines of a night club while he vulgarly satirizes our human hypocrisies?

Should we not as Christians raise a new standard of "obscenity" not obsessed with sex and vulgar language, but defined rather as that material which has as its dominant theme and purpose the debasement and depreciation of human beings—their worth and their dignity? Such a definition might include some material dealing with sex but this would be a minor aspect of pornography. The "words" that would offend us and from which we want our young protected would not be "Anglo-Saxon" but English, French, German, which carried within their etymology and meaning outrages against human individuals and groups.

The pornographic pictures would be those that showed humans being violated, destroyed, physically beaten. (The prize obscene film might be a three-minute documentary of a fully clothed man, twitching and writhing as the shock of electricity applied by our officials burns through his body.)

All the resources of our Christian teaching and tradition, all the theological armament in the Church could be called up in the warfare against "the new obscenity." The significant concomitant of this is that it would lessen the distortion and perversion of sex in our society that the present definition of obscenity has created. A further advantage to this new understanding would be that the Church and many literary critics would be saved the embarrassment of having to defend every mediocre form of literature and art against the wild attacks of the book-banners.

We would be saved the somewhat ludicrous spectacle of "far-out ministers" and "hip theologians" eloquently testifying in court for what may be lousy literature or atrocious art. (There was a laughable scene in the recent court case against Lenny Bruce when a minister was forced into justifying why he didn't use four-letter words in his homiletical exercises on Sunday. I can already see some enterprising seminary developing a new course in "The Use of Pornography in Preaching.")

Norman Podhoretz has stated the matter succinctly: ". . . it is the extent to which law has forced criticism into hypocrisy that, in order to defend freedom of expression, one must always be exaggerating the literary merits of any piece of erotica that happens to get published."

If it is asserted that this position skirts dangerously close to "license" and the accompanying breakdown of moral order, I can only reply that it is one of the hard truths of Christian tradition that we have been released to a freedom whose burden is a terrible risk. This freedom of the Christian man has already sent Christians in our time against the law, to prison and even to death. With this new definition of obscenity we will run a risk by allowing our children and ourselves to see "obscene pictures" of the instant destruction of 200,000 persons at Hiroshima with one bomb—the risk that we may come to accept this as a natural and realistic way of solving conflicts between men and nations. This is a real danger, but the alternative is mental slavery, a restricted thought process, a closed society. Consequently in the battles of censorship in a pluralistic society Christians may find themselves coming down regularly against the inroads of censorship at the risk of being called licentious and immoral.

It may be, as some politicians claimed in the past campaign, that this nation is in a state of moral decadence. If so, I am convinced that the evidence of this is not to be found in salacious literature, erotic art or obscene films but in the "soul-rot" that comes from the moral hypocrisy of straining at the gnat of sexuality and swallowing the camel of human deterioration and destruction.

Protestant Christian liberals in this country have been very adept at accommodating Christian faith and ethics to the social and economic revolutions of the past thirty to forty years. However, we display every evidence of being ill at ease and unprophetic in relating our Christian insights and teachings to the moral and sexual revolutions in American life. There are a few clues that the wind is changing, but much more study and reflection in honesty is needed.

7
Politics

Should religion participate in secular politics? What connection is there, or ought there to be, between the broad and timeless ethical ideals of religion and the particular social system of any one time and place? Should religion dedicate itself to the individual sphere—the training of the soul—or to the social sphere—the transformation of society? Or is it possible to fight on both fronts at once? These are the kinds of questions shaping the internal debate of contemporary religion.

G. P. Fedotov helps to place today's debate in historical perspective. Tracing religion's part in the historical ebb and flow of social justice, Fedotov notes the irony of the fact that the emergence of socialism from Christian utopianism came about because of Protestantism's increasing preoccupation with individualism and mysticism. Fedotov's essay demonstrates that, one way or another, the attitude of religion toward society will affect the politics of society.

What might be called a "conservative" statement of the role of religion in politics is made by the Editor of *Christianity Today,* who

275

argues that the duty of ecclesiastics is to strive for the transformation not of any particular manifestation of social ethics but of man, who brings about such manifestations. The conservatives fear that, in the dust raised by ecclesiastical participation in any particular political conflict, the fundamental religious principles that should inform all political and social behavior will be obscured and eventually, perhaps, forgotten.

Ecclesiastical liberals, on the other hand, contend that immediate crises must be met immediately, that political issues are often moral issues, and that ecclesiastical participation in political activities, far from obscuring fundamental religious principles, dramatizes those principles by bringing them to life. Two examples of a religious approach to critical mid-century issues are included in this chapter. Both Martin Luther King's now classic statement on civil rights and the position paper by the Committee of Clergy and Laymen Concerned about Vietnam reflect the conviction of religious liberals that religion has a responsibility for the affairs of the world and that failure to exercise that responsibility would betray some of religion's most fundamental principles.

G. P. Fedotov
The Church and Social Justice

The two answers given to the question as to the social ideal of Christianity are in direct contradiction to each other. On the one hand, Christianity is said to be a religion of personal salvation, having nothing to do with the problem of social organization. This is the view of most Protestants and of many modern Eastern monks. On the other hand it is

Reprinted from *Cross Currents* (Fall 1964), pp. 417–432, by permission. Previously published in St. Vladimir's Seminary Quarterly. Translated by N. Duddington.

G. P. Fedotov was one of the leading Orthodox thinkers of the past one hundred years.

maintained that Christianity has a social ideal of its own, and the only possible one. But attempts to define that ideal greatly differ. For some people it is the patriarchal autocratic monarchy, for others—democracy, or socialism, or communism. Both points of view are wrong, however convincing they may appear on the surface.

Christianity as an absolute religion cannot depend in its ethics upon any social system. Its ideal is so high, indeed unattainable—"be ye perfect even as your Father which is in Heaven is perfect" (Matt. 5:48)—that no social system can satisfy it. From this unquestionble truth an erroneous conclusion is drawn that social life is a matter of indifference to a Christian and that he must not aim at saving other people but seek his own salvation. St. John Chrysostom, the famous bishop and preacher who lived at the end of the fourth century, admirably shows how untenable such religious egoism is: "Do not let us be content with seeking our own salvation: that would merely mean losing it. At war and in the ranks a soldier whose sole concern is to save himself by escaping, ruins both himself and his comrades. A brave soldier who fights for others, together with others, saves both himself and others." (*Ninth Homily on Matthew*, 5).

It would be difficult to express more forcibly the principle of solidarity, comradeship and brotherhood in the Christian ideal of life. Since a social system does affect people's moral and spiritual welfare and can either demoralize or train them in the right principles, it obviously cannot be a matter of indifference to a Christian. What social system must he, then, strive for? For one which best embodies justice and the principles of brotherhood, which makes struggle against evil more easy and provides more favourable conditions for the spiritual development of personality. . . .

The Christian Church was born in Jerusalem, in the small community of disciples united by faith in the risen Christ and expecting Him to return in glory to judge the world. What were the social relations established among the first Christians? We read in the Acts of the Apostles: "And the multitude of them that believed were of one heart and of one soul: neither said any of them that aught of the things which he possessed was his own; but they had all things common" (Acts 4:32–33). It would not be contrary to truth to call this kind of brotherly life, where "*they had all things, common,*" communism. From the story of Ananias and Sapphira (Acts 5), it is evident that this communism was neither complete nor compulsory. Everyone could preserve for himself a part of his possessions. This free communism might be described as a communism of love (Troeltsch). It exists between lovers, between husband and wife, in every closely-knit family and sometimes between intimate friends. Love "seeketh not her own" (1 Cor. 13:5), but seeks communion in all things, earthly and heavenly, small and great. Communistic features are present in every union born of love.

Another peculiarity of the Jerusalem communism was, apparently, its uneconomical character, its lack of connection with labour and production. The apostles and their disciples did not intend to settle securely and permanently upon the earth. Their thoughts were directed towards the Lord Who was to come. It is not surprising that in the enthusiasm of prayer and expectation the material side of life was neglected.

Two dangers always threaten attempts to realize communism, whether religious or purely economical in the life of society. In the first place, every diminution of love (and still more, its complete absence) leads to tyranny, for communism without love means doing violence to the natural (not merely egoistic) needs of the individual. Secondly, communism that is practicable with regard to the distribution of goods generally breaks down on the problem of production; disinterested service of society cannot alone replace the motives of self-interest and of self-preservation. The modern communism of Russia has brought both these dangers to light—both tyranny and inefficiency. Apostolic communism in Jerusalem, strong in love, was economically weak and could not serve as a pattern for imitation.

Does this mean that it was a mistake? No, any more than the expectation of the Second Coming in the apostolic age was a mistake or a delusion. It was a heroic expression of the Christian social ideal—social maximalism which in spite of its "failure" preserves its decisive significance. The perfect ideal of brotherly Christian life is a communism of love. Later on, the monastery will provide another instance of it, but this time on the basis of external discipline and economic foresight.

In addition to its unrealized social ideal, the Jerusalem community bequeathed to the Church of the future a social institution which retained for centuries its vital and efficient character. That was the institution of deacons whose immediate task was social service (Acts 6:1-5). "Serving tables" were set apart from "ministry of the word" as a special socially religious function. The social service of the deacons to the community was of earlier date than their service of the cult. The deacons retained that function, together with their liturgical duties, throughout Christian antiquity, and in the West during the Middle Ages as well. We have a right to say that social service in the Church is essentially the deacons'.

We do not find communism in any other Christian churches known to us from the New Testament. Not one of the Apostles attacked the political or social foundations of the world of antiquity. Slavery and inequality remained, but they were tempered by love. Common meals—

the so-called love-feasts (*agape*)—brought the faithful together, reminding them that the sharing of goods was the highest ideal of life. Those meals were combined with the Eucharist, i.e., with partaking of Christ's Body. Communion with Christ went together with human intercommunion—in love and bread.

The love-feasts were not merely a symbolic act. In the ancient Church the communities actually took upon themselves the responsibility for social evil. As a matter of principle and of fact the poor were supported by the Church. That was why church property managed by the bishop was regarded as belonging to the poor. But the broadest possible charity could not satisfy the ideal of love which retained all its binding force: "Thou must not refuse the needy but share everything with thy brethren. Say not that this is thy property, for if you enjoy together the eternal blessings, it should be the more so with temporal ones." This is said in the *Didache,* one of the earliest (second-century) records of Christian literature.

When persecutions ceased, two ways were open to the Christian Church: either to remain a small community of the pure, expecting Christ to return and judge the world and meanwhile leaving the world to inevitable perdition, or to go into the world in order to teach and save it, to engraft in it as far as possible some features of the unattainable Christian ideal, inevitably lowering that ideal to the world's level. The Church followed the second path—the path of "condescension."

Having set before itself the task of christianizing the Graeco-Roman world, the Church had to accept its established social and political structure. To change it was beyond its power. Life developed in the direction of universal enslavement, and increasing social burdens laid on the lower classes. All that the Church could do was to lighten that burden by appealing to individuals, by restraining them from abusing wealth and power and instilling into them mercy for the weak.

The Church whose possessions had greatly increased went on supporting the poor. But the glaring inequalities within the world which had now become Christian persisted and even received justification. Theories were framed to the effect that wealth and poverty have been created by God in order to supplement and serve each other. The rich man was saved by giving alms, the poor man by patiently enduring his lot. . . .

The thousand years that passed between the fall of the Western Roman Empire and the fall of its Eastern half, Byzantium—the so-called Middle Ages—was a time when Christianity as the state religion held undisputed sway. One might think that the social structure of that period corresponded most fully to the principles of Christian ethics. But as against all attempts to idealize the past, it must be admitted that the christianization of life has never been deep or comprehensive. Throughout its history the Church has never been the victor on earth. Its relation to the world was one of struggle, compromise and training. Hence the thorough duality of the Christian civilization. Saints and villains are to be found both outside and within the Church, and indeed within its select "spiritual" circles.

Social and political life proved to be far harder and less yielding to Christian influences than the sphere of personal morality. And so the Church chiefly reserved for itself the individual sphere—the training of the soul. And yet the influence of Christianity made itself felt even in the "hard" social sphere, gradually transforming and humanizing it.

In Byzantium the Church inherited from antiquity a society based upon slavery and a state based upon despotism. Having given up paganism in religion, the state remained pagan in all its forms of life. The demoralizing influence of the East outweighed the ennobling influence of the Church. Renouncing the task of reforming the cruel structure of public life, the Church kept reminding the people about mercy. Within its holy precincts it continued the philanthropic works bequeathed to it by the Christian past. In the big cities of the Empire thousands of the poor were kept at Church expense. Patriarchates and bishoprics founded hospitals, hostelries, and practiced other forms of social service. The biggest monasteries did the same. As far as "social welfare" institutions were concerned, Byzantium apparently was ahead of Western Europe. But the social influence of the Greek Church can only be fully appreciated by considering the lives of its saints. We shall find that the saints most remote from social work like Antony the Great or Simeon the Stylite intervened in public life, sending letters, petitions and warnings to the rich, strong and powerful in the interests of the poor, weak and oppressed. Justifying in theory the social structure of the Empire, the Church strove to humanize it for the sake of those groups of the population that suffered most from it. . . .

Mediæval culture broke down, making room for the culture of the Renaissance and the Reformation, characterized by the triumph of individualism both in the secular and the spiritual sphere. The new epoch breaks away from the traditions of social Christianity. Exclusive preoccupation with personality and with its religious, purely mystical path leaves hardly any room for a religious reconstruction of society. The influence of religion in the cultural sphere weakens; religion has to give over to secular forces in one domain after another—the state, economic relations, science—and reserve for itself only the deep and intimate life of the heart, inaccessible to society.

This is why the new economic force, capitalism, met with hardly any moral obstacles or restrictions from the Christian Church. Indeed, in

Calvanistic countries it was religiously justified. Economic individualism was connected with religious individualism. The struggle for existence was predominant in the material sphere, and the struggle for personal salvation in the spiritual. The destruction of the masses in this struggle was a sad but inevitable law. The moral force of the few was triumphant —a sign of divine grace. Puritanism regarded wealth as a visible Divine blessing, and poverty as the consequence of idleness, vice, or Divine punishment. Denunciations of the rich were heard no longer, and preaching concerned with social questions consisted chiefly in urging the poor to submit to their lot. Almsgiving was reduced to the level of an insignificant correction to the divinely appointed social system. During the later centuries Christianity in the West becomes aristocratic, and the upper class (the nobles and the bourgeoisie) entrust to it the defense of their rights and privileges.

It is only fair to recognize that in modern times, too, Christian churches did social work. It is sufficient to point out the activities of the parish in Protestant countries where it carries on a considerable amount of public philanthropic duties, and certain Catholic bodies that do social work, especially those connected with the name of Vincent de Paul, such as "the daughters of mercy" who have served as a pattern for the secular Red Cross, and so on. But all this work seems quite insignificant by comparison with the social activities of the mediæval church or with the crying evils of the new capitalist society.

It is noteworthy that in the sixteenth century the social work of the Church declined in Orthodox Russia also. From that time onward the monasteries acquire more and more the character of the ecclesiastical economic communities. The stern political and military tasks which faced Russia made life in Muscovy very hard for the masses, and the Church could no longer temper it by its intercessions. But it was the reform of Peter the Great that finally put an end to the social service of the Russian church. A series of harsh and violent measures deprived the Church of property, independence, and of all care for the people. All that was left to it was the narrow sphere of personal piety. Through theological and cultural influences of the West the Protestant and neo-Catholic ethics of religious individualism penetrated into the Russian church. Religious consciousness withdrawn into its own depths found food for thought in the individually-ascetic tradition of the ancient East. Thus the two types of individualism, the Protestant and the monastic, determined the social or, rather, the antisocial attitudes predominant in the Russian church up to the present.

This new style of Christianity was a betrayal both of its ancient and mediæval traditions. Retribution was swift to follow. The downfall first of the aristocratic and then of the capitalist system, filling with the din of revolutions the last hundred and fifty years of European history found the Church in the camp of the privileged classes waging a losing battle in self-defense. Hence the hatred of the masses—especially of factory workers—for the Church and Christianity in a number of countries. Up to the end of the seventeenth century all social movements of the lower classes were under the banner of Christianity—orthodox or sectarian—and had a religious character. In the French revolution the social ideal, whether it be called freedom, equality or socialism—acquired an anti-Christian and finally an atheistic bias. The most powerful movement of our time, socialism, in its main forms and especially in Russia is hostile to Christianity and indeed to all religion. This is the fruit of the deplorable history of the last centuries and of forgetting the social foundations of Christianity.

The modern forms of socialism and particularly of communism certainly contain much that is incompatible with Christianity: materialism, the ethics of hatred and class egoism, the faith in the power of brute force, the emergence of personality in the collective unity of class and party. If, however, one reflects upon the actual basis of the social ideas of our age, it is not hard to discover their Christian origin. The social problem in our sense of the term never had, and never could have arisen in any but a Christian civilization. It is a practical conclusion from the postulate of Christian brotherhood.

In studying the early history of socialism we see that it took shape over a hundred years ago, in the thirties and forties of the last century in France among the ardently religious and revolutionary-minded intellectuals. Most of the so-called "utopian" socialists, Saint-Simon, Fourier, Pierre Leroux, Georges Sand, were people of romantically Christian, though not orthodox, views. Catholics like Lamennais and Lacordaire joined forces with them, and it was in this high-minded, dreamy, and religious *milieu* that socialism was born. Marx translated it into the language of materialism, but he took over the socialistic ideal and its moral foundations ready-made. It had been fashioned in Christian, though secular, circles. Apart from this (essentially Christian) datum, no socialistic ideal could possibly be deduced from economic materialism.

Marx's interpretation of socialism was a terrible distortion of it. But the revolutionary socialism of the nineteenth century has in any case the merit of formulating the social problem. Its significant and menacing nature could not fail in the end to awake from their long slumber the representatives of Christian churches. From the middle of the nineteenth century down to the present day, the Christian social movement in many different forms has been growing steadily.

In England and America socialism and the preaching of social justice in general are closely connected with Christianity; but this is not the case in continental Europe. Apart from socialism in the narrow sense, almost all humanitarian social reforms of the nineteenth century in Anglo-Saxon countries were directly prompted by the Christian conscience: abolition of slavery, labor laws, mitigation of war and struggle for an international organization of peace. In the rest of modern Europe the influence of the Christian conscience showed itself indirectly and unconsciously, often in direct hostility to historical Christianity (the French Revolution, socialism); in England and America, however, the connection between Christianity and social justice has not been severed to this day.

In Orthodox Russia there have never been any important organizations or movements of social Christianity. But in the realm of religious thought highly significant developments took place. The philosophy of the Slavophils, the first original Russian Orthodox thinkers, had a social coloring. They had an utopian idea of finding in the Russian village commune and autocracy the means of realizing social justice. At the end of the nineteenth century a profound and extremely original Orthodox thinker N. Fyodorov, put the practical solution of the social question at the center of his philosophical speculation. In the nineteenth century there arose a whole school of Orthodox philosophers, to some extent originally connected with marxism. Many of them, like S. N. Bulgakov and N. A. Berdyaev, strove to take away from Marx and give back to Christ the social domain of which the Church had been wrongfully deprived.

At present in communist Russia as everywhere else, the social Gospel of Christ is struggling with Marx's black theology. The destinies of the world depend upon the issue of the struggle. For in spite of the apparent helplessness of Christianity in the stream of events, it alone contains the spiritual forces that are constructive and not destructive and can create not a prison but a free communion of persons. Without Christianity there is class war, war between nations, and—if civilization is not wiped out altogether—the prospect of an unheard of tyranny of the "social" state. The outlines of a Christian system which is to replace the degenerating and chaotic capitalism are not yet clear. It is of no importance whether it will be socialistic in name. What matters is that while safeguarding human freedom it should be a step towards the ideal of brotherhood which, though never fully realizable on earth, has been the undying dream of Christianity ever since the early days of the first Church of Jerusalem.

The Editor, Christianity Today

Evangelicals in the Social Struggle

Evangelical Christianity today confronts a "new theology," a "new evangelism," and a "new morality," each notably lacking in biblical content. A "new social ethics" has also emerged, and some ecumenical leaders mainly interested in politico-economic issues speak hopefully of a "new breed of evangelical" in this realm of activity. The red carpet rolls out when even a few evangelicals march at Selma, when they unite in organized picket protests and public demonstrations, when they join ecclesiastical pressure blocs on Capitol Hill or at the White House, or when they engineer resolutions on legislative matters through annual church meetings.

Since most evangelical churchmen traditionally have not mobilized their social concern in this way, non-evangelical sociologists are delighted over any and every such sign of apparent enlightenment. Moreover, they propagandize such church techniques as authentically Christian, and misrepresent evangelical nonparticipation as proof of social indifference in conservative Christian circles and as a lack of compassion. This favorite device of propagandists is effective among some evangelicals who desire to protect their genuine devotion to social concern from public misinterpretation. The claim that evangelicals as a whole are socially impotent, moreover, diverts attention from the long-range goals of social extremists by concentrating attention on existential involvement on an emergency basis.

That Christians are citizens of two worlds, that a divine mandate enjoins both their preaching of the Gospel and their promotion of social

Reprinted from *Christianity Today* (October 8, 1965), pp. 3–11, by permission of the publisher.

justice, that the lordship of Christ over all of life involves socio-cultural obligations, that Christians bear a political responsibility, are historic evangelical emphases. Evangelicals regard government and jurisprudence as strategic realms of vocational service to humanity. They stress that government exists for the sake of all citizens, not simply for certain favored groups, and that a just or good society preserves for all citizens equal rights before the law. This emphasis has equally critical implications for a society that seeks special privilege for one race above another and for any church that seeks partisan and sectarian benefits from government.

The heritage of evangelical Christianity includes both Jesus' sermon on the mount and his delineation of the Good Samaritan, and Paul's account of civil government as an agent of justice. Evangelical Christians recognized the moral claim of these scriptural elements long before Protestant liberalism distorted them into a rationalistic politico-economic perspective. The Evangelical Revival in eighteenth- and nineteenth-century Britain attested the devotion of believers, not only to the observance of public statutes, but also to the vigorous promotion of just laws. The seventh Earl of Shaftesbury headed the movement in Parliament that led in 1807 to the abolition of slavery in the British Empire. As a result of his own conversion Wilberforce led great reform programs, including child-labor laws. The Evangelical Revival placed evangelicals in the forefront of humanitarian concerns, not only for an end to the slave trade, but also for child labor laws, prison reforms, improved factory labor conditions, and much else in the sphere of social justice. It was evangelical social concern, in fact, that preserved the shape of Anglo-Saxon society from tragic revolutionary onslaught. An eminent church historian writes:

"No branch indeed of the Western Church can be refused the honor of having assisted in the progress of humane ideas, and non-Christians have participated largely in the work of diffusing the modern spirit of kindness; but the credit of the inception of the movement belongs without doubt to that form of Protestantism which is distinguished by the importance it attaches to the doctrine of the Atonement. . . . History shows that the thought of Christ on the Cross has been more potent than anything else in arousing a compassion for suffering and indignation at injustice. . . . The later Evangelicalism, which saw in the death of Christ the means of free salvation for fallen humanity, caused its adherents to take the front rank as champions of the weak. . . . Prison reform, the prohibition of the slave trade, the abolition of slavery, the Factory Acts, the protection of children, the crusade against cruelty to animals, are all the outcome of the great Evangelical revival of the eighteenth century. The humanitarian tendencies of the nineteenth century, which, it is but just to admit, all

Christian communities have fostered, and which non-Christian philan-
thropists have vied with them in encouraging, are among the greatest
triumphs of the power and influence of Christ."[1]

Liberal Impact and Evangelical Reaction

For two generations liberal social ethics has been markedly influential in American public life in the areas of education, government, and
labor. Liberal ecclesiastical reformers have only themselves to blame for
the present lack of fixed governing principles in public policy, and for the
declining spiritual influence of their churches in the private sector of
national life. One theologian addicted to a radically secular version of
Christianity—Professor William Hamilton of Colgate-Rochester Divinity
School—tells us candidly that "we are well into the opening phase of the
breakdown of organized religion in American life, well beyond the time
when ecumenical dialogue or denominational mergers can be expected to
arrest the breakdown" (*The Christian Scholar*, Spring, 1965). Professor
Hamilton fails to recognize, however, that the modernist dilution of
historic Christian theology was largely responsible for compromising the
message and power of institutional Christianity. In no century of recent
history have public structures been so directly influenced by American
churchmen as they are in our time through the pressures of liberal social
thought. Churchmen have increasingly manipulated the machinery of
ecumenical Christianity in support of socio-economic objectives, including specific legislative proposals. Not even the breakdown of the League
of Nations or the deformation of the United Nations, each endorsed as
the world's best hope for peace, has encouraged "second thoughts" about
the efficacy or legitimacy of the nature of their social activity.

This does not mean that evangelical Christians have reason to
boast about social alertness on the explosive frontiers of public life. They
were undeniably concerned with personal behavior in public social life,
and with responsible community involvement in keeping with the standards and vocations of believers. To their further credit they realized that
not an ethic of grace but rather an ethic of justice should govern social
structures (including international relations, national government, and
legal institutions generally). But evangelical Christians elaborated no
Bible-based ethic impinging on the basis, method, and function of social
structures and groups such as the state, labor movements and business
corporations, minorities, and so on.

If excuses for neglect are in order, this may be the right place to
note them. Evangelicals could plead, of course, that the "social gos-

---

[1] F. J. Foakes-Jackson, "Christ in the Church: The Testimony of History,"
in H. B. Swete, *Cambridge Theological Essays* (New York, 1905), pp. 512–514.

peler's" neglect of God's good news of salvation for sinners imposed upon conservative Christianity the burden of biblical evangelism and missions throughout a perishing world—a staggering task indeed. Evangelical capability was decimated by liberal control of denominations, schools, and other ecclesiastical resources. But evangelical withdrawal from the arena of public life came mainly in reaction to the Protestant liberal attempts to achieve the Kingdom of God on earth through political and economic changes. The modernists so excluded supernatural redemptive facets of the Christian faith and so modified the proper content of the Christian ethic that, as evangelicals saw it, they had altered the very nature and mission of the Church. Evangelical Christianity reacted against the liberal Protestant concentration of effort in this area of concern by non-involvement, and this withdrawal yielded the field to the speculative theories of liberal churchmen and largely deprived evangelicals of an ethical witness in the mainstream of public life.

Fallacies of Liberal Ethics

Precisely what is objectionable in liberal social ethics from the evangelical viewpoint? This is no small matter, for criticism extends to presuppositions, methods, and goals.

The theological presuppositions of liberal social ethics are hostile to biblical theology. A generation ago the "social gospel" theologians deleted the wrath of God and dissolved his righteousness into benevolence or love; today the revolt has been extended. Dialectical and existential moralists surrender the objective being of God, while secular theologians disown his transcendence and, for that matter, his relevance as well. What passes for Christian social ethics in such circles dispenses with the supernatural essence of the Christian religion as foreign to problems of social justice and public righteousness. Evangelicals who insist on obedience to divinely revealed precepts, and who hold that redeemed men alone can truly fulfill the will of God and that only men of good will can enlarge the boundaries of God's Kingdom, are caricatured as "rationalists," despite the fact that Scripture specifically associates Jesus' mission with an era of good will on earth. Yet while existentialists reject the absolutes of a transcendent morality for an absolute of their own decision, thereby making each person his own church, and reject an ethics based on principles because they consider it impossible to achieve moral obedience by decree, they nonetheless agitate for laws to compel others to act in a predictable, principled way.

It may seem pedantic, if not picayune, in a secular society so perilously near doom, to surround the moral demand for *agape* with a complex of theological distinctions. After all, is not *agape* itself the central Christian moral motif? But the reply is simple: *"agape"* stripped of supernatural elements is no longer biblical *agape*. For biblical *agape* is first and foremost the love of God. Biblical *agape* is nowhere simply a matter of humanistic charity toward one's neighbors. "You shall love the Lord your God with all your heart, and with all your soul, and with all your mind, and your neighbor as yourself"—love them, as a well-phrased prayer reiterates, "with a pure heart, fervently." Although just laws are desirable and imperative, law has the power only of outward restraint; it lacks power to ensure outward obedience and inner conformity to its command. In the absence of moral men—of men willing to do the good— no body of law, however just, can ensure a good society. Authentic Christian ethics concerns what is done through a desire to do God's will, in obedience to his command; this is made possible only by spiritual regeneration. No other motivation can counter the selfish drives that haunt the noblest of unredeemed men and correct the faulty vision of an unredeemed society. The current existential appeal for everyman's "identification with others" naïvely presupposes that the "identifiers" are morally equipped with motivations unthwarted by selfishness. But universal love, even in diluted forms, is a requirement that far exceeds the capacity of unregenerate men; for a Jew to have loved Hitler must have posed a problem not unlike that involved in a Selma marcher's love for the governor of Alabama, or a Birmingham demonstrator's affection for the local sheriff. The modern devotion to mankind *in place of* God, on the premise of "the infinite worth of the individual," indicates the inability of some Western intellectuals to assimilate the basic lessons of recent history. They blandly overlook the power of evil in human nature and man's limitations in coping with it—witness not only the patent egoism of individuals and social collectivities and the barbarism of the dictators, but also the tragic fact of two world wars at the pinnacle of Western scientific development and the unresolved threat of imminent universal destruction. As George F. Thomas says, "man is neither infinite nor perfect, and his ideal ends are worthy of devotion only insofar as they are subordinated to the purpose of One who is both."[2]

The evangelical Christian mobilizes for social action in the spiritual context of transcendent justice, supernatural law, revealed principles, concern for God's will in human affairs, and love of God and man. Against ecclesiastical "young Turks" who propagandize the notion that social concerns cannot be expressed within the inherited theology, the evangelical contends that insofar as social concerns are authentically biblical, they can be adequately expressed and fulfilled only within scriptural theology. What the evangelical does in the social order, as in

[2] *Religious Philosophies of the West* (New York: Charles Scribner's Sons, 1965), p. 351.

every other realm of life, he does as a matter of principled spiritual obedience to the Lord of life.

Differences in Goals

It is, moreover, a gross underestimation of differences in social action between evangelicals and non-evangelicals to imply that, beyond motivation, they agree wholly on goals and differ only in method. The liberal Protestant identification of Christian love with pacifism, then with socialism, even with Communism by some modernists in the recent past, is too fresh a memory to allow one to blunder into the notion that the Bible sanctions whatever social goals the liberal moralists endorse. Even the Communist hostility toward supernatural religion as an unscientific myth has moderated into tactical tolerance of religion as useful for promoting a social consciousness agreeable to the Soviet politico-economic ideology. Repudiation of private property, of the profit motive, and of inequality of wealth, and other Marxist ideals have been arbitrarily promoted by liberal social reformers in supposed devotion to the biblical vision of the Kingdom of God. Even their emphasis on equal rights has cheaply surrendered property rights as a fundamental human right, and also man's right to work apart from compulsory union membership.

Whenever the Church advances a political ideology or promotes partisan legislation, its ecclesiastical leaders are soon forced into the position of impugning the integrity of influential Christians who sincerely dissent from the official views. It should surprise nobody, therefore, that as the National Council of Churches comes under increasing fire, its spokesmen tend to demean critics of its political commitments as reactionary advocates of arrogant nationalism and of social, economic, and racial privilege.

Not a few goals approved by modern social theorists are wholly desirable, and evangelical differences in such cases concern the means of achieving these ends. Elimination of poverty, opportunity for employment, racial equality, and many other goals that stand at the heart of contemporary social agitation are not only acceptable but highly desirable. Evangelicals are not indifferent to the desirability of such objectives even if liberal social ethics mistakenly conceives the Kingdom of God as basically a politico-economic phenomenon and tends to dilute redemptive spiritual forces into sociological ingredients. In fact, as evangelicals see it, such features of social life are essential to a just and good society.

Evangelicals no less than liberals recognize social justice as an authentic Christian concern, despite serious differences over definition and content. If evangelicals came to stress evangelism above social concern, it was because of liberalism's skepticism over supernatural redemptive dynamisms and its pursuit of the Kingdom of God by sociological techniques only. Hence a sharp and costly disjunction arose, whereby many evangelicals made the mistake of relying on evangelism alone to preserve world order and many liberals made the mistake of relying wholly on socio-political action to solve world problems.

Conflict over Method

It would be naïve to argue from this, however, that liberals and evangelicals need each other for complementary emphases. Over and above differences of motivation and of goals stand the differences between evangelical and liberal ethics in respect to methodology. Most evangelicals reject outright the liberal methodology of social reform, in which more and more liberals call for a "new evangelism" that substitutes sociological for spiritual concerns. Just as in his theological view of God the liberal dissolves righteousness into love, so in the political order he dilutes social justice into compassion. This kind of merger not only destroys the biblical view of God on the one hand but also produces the welfare state on the other. This confounding of justice and love confuses what God expects of government with what he expects of the Church, and makes the state an instrument for legislating partisan and sectarian ideals upon society. Ideally the purpose of the state is to preserve justice, not to implement benevolence; ideally, the purpose of the Church is to preach the Gospel and to manifest unmerited, compassionate love.

Many sociologists and political scientists dislike this way of stating the case. But it is noteworthy that these particular disciplines are especially barren of evangelical perspectives; they tend to be theologically illiterate in respect both to eschatology and to a basic theology of justice. Current proposals to detach the Gospel from "right-wing" social reaction and current pleas for "political compassion" are rooted in leftist political ideology more often than in an authentic spiritual view of the role of government.

But in the present explosive era of history the problem of acting on an acceptable methodology is an urgent one for evangelicals. It is one thing to deplore ministerial marches and picket lines and well-publicized public pressures; but if evangelical conscience is to be a remedial and transforming social force, then evangelical convictions require articulate mobilization on their own account.

Evangelicals and Social Concern

Despite the present confusion caused by ecclesiastical intervention in political affairs, evangelicals have something socially relevant to say to both the secular man and the church man. The Christian has social duties not simply as a Christian but as a man, and his sanctification therein does not come about automatically without pulpit instruction in sound scriptural principles. Evangelicals as a people consider themselves bound to the Word of God; for this reason they consider themselves a spiritual people with a divine message for themselves and for others in regard to social action. Evangelicals acknowledge a divine call to identify themselves with others—not with social customs or social vices or social discontents, but rather with persons in their survival needs: physical and moral and spiritual. These survival needs include material help in destitution, social justice, and the redemption that is in Christ Jesus.

Surely evangelical Christianity has more to offer mankind than its unique message of salvation, even if that is its highest and holiest mission. While it rightly chides the liberal for regarding the world as a unity (rather than divided into unregenerate and regenerate), it also has a message for all men as members of one society. The Christian is not, by his church identification, isolated from humanity, or from involvement in the political and economic orders. Not only is he called to identify himself with society: he *is* identified, by the very fact of his humanity, and as a Christian he bears a double responsibility in relation to the social needs and goals of mankind. Social justice is a need of the individual, whose dignity as a person is at stake, and of society and culture, which would soon collapse without it. The evangelical knows that spiritual regeneration restores men to moral earnestness; but he also knows the moral presuppositions of a virile society, and he is obligated to proclaim the "whole counsel" of God. He may have no message for society that insures unrepentant mankind against final doom—nor even against catastrophic destruction in our own time, while its leaders insist upon arbitrary human authority at the expense of the lordship of Jesus Christ. But he can and ought to use every platform of social involvement to promulgate the revealed moral principles that sustain a healthy society and that indict an unhealthy one. More than this, the evangelical Christian should be represented, in his personal convictions, on the frontiers of government and in the corporate processes of society. Convinced that the cooperation of godly men in the social and collective order can be decisively influential, he should be concerned about relations between nations and about minority rights. There is no reason at all why evangelical Christians should not engage energetically in projecting social structures that promote the interests of justice in every public realm; in fact, they have every legitimate sanction for social involvement.

Of course the Church is to be ruled distinctively by an ethic of grace. But the Church is also in a world that is to be ruled by justice, an ethic of justice that does not *per se* require regenerate social structures.

In this context, a positive ethic and corrective principles enunciated on the broad world scene by regenerate believers who are engaged in the social struggle can have decisive influence. Such an ethic will include (1) the Church's faithful exposition of divinely revealed standards of human justice as the only basis for a stable society and as the criteria by which the world will be finally judged; and (2) the Christian's energetic promotion and support of just laws as the formal hallmark of a good society. When Christian believers become thus involved in the struggle for justice, the world may recognize in a new way the presence of regenerate realities; noting the community of twice-born men that sees the restoration of sinners to fellowship with God and to holiness as the aim of the Gospel, the world may even recognize the validity of regenerate structures through their moral impact.

Any Christian engaged in the pursuit of social justice is painfully aware that, in a tragic world of fallen men, government decisions often involve a choice between greater and lesser evils rather than between absolutes of good and evil, and that only the Church of Christ can witness to a manifestation of absolute good in history. He will, however, avoid both the liberal error of "absolutizing relatives," as if these were identical with the will of God, and also the fundamentalist temptation to consider any gain short of the absolute ideal in history as worthless or unworthy.

Law and Gospel

But evangelicals must not perpetuate the liberal Protestant failure to distinguish between the social concerns of *Law* and the social concerns of *Gospel*. In law and justice—that is, the province of government—all men are obliged to support man's God-given rights as universally due to human beings whatever their race, color, or creed. The evangelical knows that no improvement can be made on a government that assures every man his rights, and that limits the freedom of citizens where and when it intrudes upon the rights of others. Evangelicals do not view government as an instrument of benevolence or compassion, since love is preferential and shows favor or partiality. Constantly pressing the question, "Don't you care?," liberals enlist support for legislating programs of benevolence. Such an appeal to "compassion" in support of legislative programs commits a twofold error, however: it diverts government from an ideal preservation of equal human rights before the law, and it shifts to the state a responsibility for compassion or benevolence that belongs properly to the Church. By concentrating on government to achieve the goals of both state and Church in a "benevolent partnership," liberalism reflects a reliance on political techniques in society to the neglect of the redemptive dynamisms inherent in Christianity. This reliance on political techniques to achieve ecclesiastical objectives means the loss of a genuine supernatural grounding of ethical concerns, the loss of the Church as Church in society, the loss of the redemptive evangel in deference to secular solvents of social malformity, and the loss of evangelical loyalties in the congregation.

What distinguishes evangelical Christianity is its refusal to impose sectarian obligations upon government, upon government which then employs compulsion to enforce a program of benevolence that individual citizens might or might not approve. Even if they did approve, they might consider the provision of such benevolences moral only if performed voluntarily; or they might consider it immoral to use taxation to compel others to do what they do not think to be right. While liberals justify their breaking of laws that appear unjust on the grounds of sensitivity to conscience, they nonetheless promote other laws that some persons regard as preferential and unjust.

To the evangelical Christian, the best alternative to the "welfare" state is the just state, and the best alternative to political demonstrations is civil obedience. The evangelical champions and strives for just legislation, and for obedience to law and respect for judicial process rather than for directly coerced action. The evangelical sponsors a principled ethic whose course is determined by divinely revealed moral principles. Much of contemporary liberal social action is not a matter of obeying laws; rather, it is a case of everyone's being on his existential own. Dialectical-existential ethics cannot indicate in advance what the moral agent ought to do, and looks upon any structured objective ethics as mere rationalism.

The evangelical holds that all persons are divinely obligated by the Scriptures to love their neighbors. While progress has been slow in the area of race tensions, nonetheless there has been progress. Yet even evangelical believers fall short of their highest moral aspirations, and laws are necessary to hold just social standards before Christians and non-Christians alike. All citizens should strive to replace discriminatory laws by non-discriminatory laws. The evangelical recognizes, however, that without public enthusiasm only moral earnestness vouchsafed by spiritual conviction and renewal assures the necessary devotion to right that guarantees social fulfillment. While the glory of ancient Rome was its genius for universal law, through its lack of heart for righteousness the Roman Empire sank into oblivion. The problem of racial discrimination can be permanently met only by Christian behavior that faces up to the ugliness of bias, the evils of immorality and delinquency, and the whole complex of problems that surrounds race feeling. The predilection for public issues over personal holiness in liberal social ethics is all the more disconcerting in view of this fact. Although liberal churchmen will throw their energies behind a public health program, they tend to remain silent about many of the personal vices; such concerns are left to the "purity nuts."

The history of Christian mission in the world makes it clear that evangelicals were interested in education, hospitals, care for the aged, and many current social concerns long before modern secular theory was ever born. Evangelicals were active in social work not only in the slums of America but also on distant mission fields a full century before the rise of modern welfare programs. To this day, rescue missions all across the land reflect a long-standing inner-city missionary concern for people in material and spiritual poverty. Evangelicals have not been as active as they need to be in the social arena; on the other hand, they have been far more active than they are sometimes said to have been.

The weakness of public demonstrations as the approved means of Christian social action is its limitation and externalization of Christian concern. It is arbitrary to imply that only those who demonstrate at a given point manifest authentic social concern. Moreover, since local demonstrations gain national significance through radio and television, the implications of massive civil disobedience are the more distressing. Ecclesiastical demonstrators who never persuade observers to become disciples of Jesus Christ ought to ask how effectively Christian is such amorphous "witness by demonstration." The motivations for demonstrating are internal, and apart from verbal interpretation might equally well be sub-Christian, non-Christian, or anti-Christian. As a matter of fact, Jews and humanists resent a Christian interpretation of their demonstrating. If authentic social concern demanded the ecumenical chartering of planes to officially designated out-of-town points, it would require a large expense account to enable everybody to travel to somebody else's home town "to identify." If every supporter of an item of disputed legislation had to march to Capitol Hill, if every Christian citizen had to put in a personal appearance to let legislators know what laws he thought God specially wanted, what would tourist-jammed Washington be like then? If the representative role of congressmen were superseded by the group pressures of ministers, the whole machinery of American government would soon collapse. The question remains, moreover, Whose conscience answers for whom? These clergy are received by congressmen, not on the premise that they speak only for themselves, but as voices for their churches. No one disputes a clergyman's right as an individual to picket or demonstrate anywhere he wishes (the right of conscience is a Protestant principle). It is unlikely, however, that pastors can wholly detach themselves from responsibilities to their congregations. When prominent churchmen parade as Reverend Church, moreover, they are simply encouraging future counter-demonstrations at 475 Riverside Drive or the Witherspoon Building [New York and Philadelphia offices of the United Presbyterian Church].

What many socially sensitive ministers especially deplore is the implication left by the well-publicized minority of marchers that non-marchers are lacking or inferior in social concern. "I don't mind another minister's marching if he must relieve his conscience that way," said one Washington minister, "but I don't see why my social concern—never before questioned—should now be in doubt because I didn't engage in this form of exhibitionism." In Copenhagen, when Evangelist Billy Graham opened his crusade, a heckler interrupted him with the cry: "Why didn't you march in Selma?" But Graham had been integrating meetings in the South long before some of the marchers had become existentialized and, moreover, had done so in the context of biblical Christianity. It is a neat propaganda device to imply that evangelical social concern is immobile because it does not conform to liberal methods —it merely proves that political propagandism is a technique in which liberal ecclesiastical leaders have become adept. In some ecclesiastical circles, the defense of this one controversial method of action has apparently justified the repudiation of all theological grounds of social concern.

Evangelical Distinctives

When evangelicals manifest social concern, they do so first by proclaiming the supernatural revelation of God and the historical resurrection of Jesus Christ. Thus they emphasize the transcendent basis of justice and the divine basis of the Gospel. They declare both the standards by which Almighty God will judge the human race and the redemption from sin unto holiness that is to be found in Jesus Christ. They affirm God's institution of civil government to preserve justice and order, and the Church as a spiritual fellowship of redeemed men who esteem their neighbors in holy love and dedicate themselves to social righteousness.

The evangelical Christian's social concern is first directed towards the family as the basic unit of society. He finds a hollow ring in the social passion for "one world" that simultaneously lacks indignation over divorce, infidelity, and vagrancy in the home. Because liberalism fails to see society as a macrocosm of the family, it is bankrupt to build a new society. Liberalism changes ideological loyalties and social perspectives every generation; evangelical Christianity treasures the family bound to the changeless will of God and to the apostolic faith. Hence evangelical Christianity regards the Sunday school, the prayer meeting, and the family in the church as a cohesive social unit that reflects in miniature the ideal social order. No new era of brotherliness and peace is likely to emerge in the absence of a new race of men. Evangelicals consider alliances of nations uncommitted to transcendent justice to be as futile a foundation for future mutuality as premarital promiscuity. As evangelical Christians see it, the vision of One World, or of United Nations, that is built on geographical representation rather than on principial agreement is as socially unpromising as is a lawless home that neglects the commandments of God. Walter Lippmann has somewhere said: "We ourselves were so sure that at long last a generation had arisen, keen and eager to put this disorderly earth to right . . . and fit to do it. . . . We meant so well, we tried so hard, and look what we have made of it. We can only muddle into muddle. What is required is a new kind of man."

Evangelical Christianity finds the most natural avenue for social witness beyond the family circle in the world of work when it is viewed as a divine calling. How sadly liberal Christianity, during its past-generation domination of ecclesiastical life, has failed in the organized church's social witness is nowhere more apparent than here. Almost all political leaders of the race-torn states are church members; Alabama's Governor Wallace belongs to the Methodist Church, which is in the forefront of liberal social action programs. Almost all congressmen are church members. Either the religious social activists have failed miserably in inspiring churchmen in political life to view their vocations as avenues for the advancement of social justice, or an elite ecclesiastical cadre is pressuring leaders to conform their political judgments to the partisan preferences of a special bloc of churchmen—or perhaps both are true. Since everyone lives in a world of labor and economics, evangelical Christianity emphasizes that man's work is a divinely appointed realm in which man is to glorify God and invest his talents for the good of his fellows; it is not only a means of livelihood but also an avenue of service.

This concept of divine vocation, of work as a calling, has all but vanished from the work-a-day world at the very time in modern history when liberal social action commissions have conspired with the labor unions in their skyrocketing material benefits. Meanwhile evangelical Protestants have organized a Christian Medical Society, Christian Business Men's Committee, Christian Professional Women's Club, Christian Law Society, Christian Teachers Association, Officers Christian Union in the Armed Forces—even a Christian Labor Union—in order to emphasize the spiritual responsibilities of vocation. It must be conceded that many of these Christian organizations serve mainly an evangelistic role, or one of vocational fellowship; only a beginning has been made in the equally urgent task of shaping an ethic for the social structures in which these groups operate. Beyond fulfilling person-to-person Christian opportunities, such agencies have an opportunity to supply guidance to both

Christian and non-Christian on what is implied in a specified social order in the way of justice.

Evangelical Christians consider this recognition of the priestly nature of daily work to be more basic to social renewal than is a reshuffle of economic features that locates the fundamental flaws of society in man's environment rather than in man himself and his works. The importance of just laws is not in dispute, since civil government is divinely designed as a coercive force to restrain evil, preserve order, and promote justice in a fallen and sinful society. Because there is no assurance that all men will repent and seek the will of God, and because even Christian believers must contend with the remnants of sin, just laws are indispensable in human history, and God's common grace in the lives of men everywhere matches conscience with law in the interest of social preservation. But evangelical Christianity is not so infatuated with the external power of coercion as to exaggerate its potentialities, nor so skeptical of the spiritual powers of regeneration as to minimize its possibilities. Precisely because law does not contain the power to compel obedience, evangelical Christianity recognizes that a good society turns upon the presence of good men—of regenerated sinners whose minds and hearts are effectively bound to the revealed will of God—and upon their ability under God to influence humanity to aspire to enduring values.

Although society at large has seldom been overwhelmed by the Church's proclaiming the Gospel from the pulpit, the obedient fulfillment of the Great Commission has called new disciples one by one into the circle of regenerate humanity. The voice of the Church in society has been conspicuously weaker whenever the pulpit of proclamation has been forsaken for mass pressures upon the public through the adoption of resolutions, the promotion of legislation, and the organization of demonstrations. Whenever the institutional church seeks public influence by mounting a socio-political platform, she raises more fundamental doubts about the authenticity and uniqueness of the Church than about the social aberrations against which she protests.

To evangelical Christianity, history at its best is the lengthened shadow of influential men, not the compulsive grip of impersonal environmental forces. A change of environmental forces will not transform bad men into good men—let alone into a good society. But transformed men will rise above a bad environment and will not long be lacking in a determination to alter it.

At the present time, involvement in the race problem is the crucial test of devotion to social justice. Of the evangelical Christian's love for men of all races the long-standing missionary effort leaves no doubt; from Adoniram Judson and David Livingstone to Hudson Taylor and Paul Carlson, the story is one of evangelical sacrifice of creature comforts, even of life itself, that men of every land and color might share the blessings of redemption. In mid-twentieth-century America, humanism and liberalism and evangelicalism alike were slow to protest political discrimination against the Negro, although evangelical missionaries have deplored the incongruities of segregation. Regrettably, the Negro's plight became for some liberal reformers an opportunity for promoting social revolution, and for some conservative reactionaries an occasion for perpetuating segregation and discrimination. Evangelical Christianity has a burden for social renewal but no penchant for revolution or reaction. Because it champions the redemptive realities inherent in the Christian religion, evangelical Christianity will in the long run vindicate the judgment that the Negro is not only politically an equal but also spiritually a brother.

Some Governing Principles

A new breed of evangelical? Yes, indeed! But not because evangelicals are switching from proclamation of the good tidings to pronouncements, picketing, and politicking as sacred means of legislating Christian sentiment on earth. Rather, evangelicals are a new breed because redemptive religion seeks first and foremost a new race of men, new creatures in Christ. Whenever Christians lose that motivation, they surrender more than their New Testament distinctiveness; they forfeit the New Testament evangel as well.

In summary, evangelicals face the social predicament today with four controlling convictions:

1. The Christian Church's distinctive dynamic for social transformation is personal regeneration by the Holy Spirit, and the proclamation of this divine offer of redemption is the Church's prime task.

In the twentieth century the ecumenical movement has failed most conspicuously in its mission to the world by relying on political and sociological forces, and by neglecting spiritual dynamisms.

2. While the corporate or institutional church has no divine mandate, jurisdiction, or special competence for approving legislative proposals or political parties and persons, the pulpit is responsible for proclaiming divinely revealed principles of social justice as a part of the whole counsel of God.

3. The most natural transition from private to social action occurs in the world of daily work, in view of the Christian's need to consecrate his labor to the glory of God and to the service of mankind.

4. As citizens of two worlds, individual church members have the

sacred duty to extend God's purpose of redemption through the Church, and also to extend God's purpose of justice and order through civil government. Christians are to distinguish themselves by civil obedience except where this conflicts with the commandments of God, and are to use every political opportunity to support and promote just laws, to protest social injustice, and to serve their fellow men.

Martin Luther King, Jr.

Letter from Jail

The Clergymen's Statement

April 12, 1963

"We the undersigned clergymen are among those who, in January, issued "An Appeal for Law and Order and Common Sense," in dealing with racial problems in Alabama. We expressed understanding that honest convictions in racial matters could properly be pursued in the courts, but urged that decisions of those courts should in the meantime be peacefully obeyed.

Since that time there had been some evidence of increased forbearance and a willingness to face facts. Responsible citizens have undertaken to work on various problems which cause racial friction and unrest. In Birmingham, recent public events have given indication that we all have opportunity for a new constructive and realistic approach to racial problems.

However, we are now confronted by a series of demonstrations by some of our Negro citizens, directed and led in part by outsiders. We

Reprinted from *Liberation* (June 1963), by permission of Martin Luther King, Jr.

recognize the natural impatience of people who feel that their hopes are slow in being realized. But we are convinced that these demonstrations are unwise and untimely.

We agree rather with certain local Negro leadership which has called for honest and open negotiation of racial issues in our area. And we believe this kind of facing of issues can best be accomplished by citizens of our own metropolitan area, white and Negro, meeting with their knowledge and experience of the local situation. All of us need to face that responsibility and find proper channels for its accomplishment.

Just as we formerly pointed out that "hatred and violence have no sanction in our religious and political traditions," we also point out that such actions as incite to hatred and violence, however technically peaceful those actions may be, have not contributed to the resolution of our local problems. We do not believe that these days of new hope are days when extreme measures are justified in Birmingham.

We commend the community as a whole, and the local news media and law enforcement officials in particular, on the calm manner in which these demonstrations have been handled. We urge the public to continue to show restraint should the demonstrations continue, and the law enforcement officials to remain calm and continue to protect our city from violence.

We further strongly urge our own Negro community to withdraw support from these demonstrations, and to unite locally in working peacefully for a better Birmingham. When rights are consistently denied, a cause should be pressed in the courts and in negotiations among local leaders, and not in the streets. We appeal to both our white and Negro citizenry to observe the principles of law and order and common sense.

Bishop C. C. J. Carpenter, Bishop Joseph A. Durick, Rabbi Milton L. Grafman, Bishop Paul Hardin, Bishop Nolan B. Harmon, Rev. George M. Murray, Rev. Edward V. Ramage, Rev. Earl Stallings.

Dr. King's Reply

My dear Fellow Clergymen,

While confined here in the Birmingham City Jail I came across your recent statement calling our present activities "unwise and untimely." Seldom, if ever, do I pause to answer criticism of my work and ideas. If I sought to answer all of the criticisms that cross my desk, my secretaries would be engaged in little else in the course of the day, and I would have no time for constructive work. But since I feel that you are men of genuine goodwill and your criticisms are sincerely set forth, I would like to answer your statement in what I hope will be patient and reasonable terms.

I think I should give the reason for my being in Birmingham, since you have been influenced by the argument of "outsiders coming in." I have the honor of serving as president of the Southern Christian Leadership Conference, an organization operating in every Southern state, with headquarters in Atlanta, Georgia. We have some eighty-five affiliate organizations all across the South—one being the Alabama Christian Movement for Human Rights. Whenever necessary and possible we share staff, educational and financial resources with our affiliates. Several months ago our local affiliate here in Birmingham invited us to be on call to engage in a nonviolent direct action program if such were deemed necessary. We readily consented and when the hour came we lived up to our promises. So I am here, along with several members of my staff, because we were invited here. I am here because I have basic organizational ties here.

Beyond this, I am in Birmingham because injustice is here. Just as the eighth century prophets left their little villages and carried their "thus saith the Lord" far beyond the boundaries of their home towns; and just as the Apostle Paul left his little village of Tarsus and carried the gospel of Jesus Christ to practically every hamlet and city of the Graeco-Roman world, I too am compelled to carry the gospel of freedom beyond my particular home town. Like Paul, I must constantly respond to the Macedonian call for aid.

Moreover, I am cognizant of the interrelatedness of all communities and states. I cannot sit idly by in Atlanta and not be concerned about what happens in Birmingham. Injustice anywhere is a threat to justice everywhere. We are caught in an inescapable network of mutuality, tied in a single garment of destiny. Whatever affects one directly affects all indirectly. Never again can we afford to live with the narrow, provincial "outside agitator" idea. Anyone who lives inside the United States can never be considered an outsider anywhere in this country.

You deplore the demonstrations that are presently taking place in Birmingham. But I am sorry that your statement did not express a similar concern for the conditions that brought the demonstrations into being. I am sure that each of you would want to go beyond the superficial social analyst who looks merely at effects, and does not grapple with underlying causes. I would not hesitate to say that it is unfortunate that so-called demonstrations are taking place in Birmingham at this time, but I would say in more emphatic terms that it is even more unfortunate that the white power structure of this city left the Negro community with no other alternative.

In any nonviolent campaign there are four basic steps: 1) Collection of the facts to determine whether injustices are alive. 2) Negotiation. 3) Self-purification and 4) Direct Action. We have gone through all of these steps in Birmingham. There can be no gainsaying of the fact that racial injustice engulfs this community.

Birmingham is probably the most thoroughly segregated city in the United States. Its ugly record of police brutality is known in every section of this country. Its unjust treatment of Negroes in the courts is a notorious reality. There have been more unsolved bombings of Negro homes and churches in Birmingham than any city in this nation. These are the hard, brutal and unbelievable facts. On the basis of these conditions Negro leaders sought to negotiate with the city fathers. But the political leaders consistently refused to engage in good faith negotiation.

Then came the opportunity last September to talk with some of the leaders of the economic community. In these negotiating sessions certain promises were made by the merchants—such as the promise to remove the humiliating racial signs from the stores. On the basis of these promises Rev. Shuttlesworth and the leaders of the Alabama Christian Movement for Human Rights agreed to call a moratorium on any type of demonstrations. As the weeks and months unfolded we realized that we were the victims of a broken promise. The signs remained. Like so many experiences of the past we were confronted with blasted hopes, and the dark shadow of a deep disappointment settled upon us. So we had no alternative except that of preparing for direct action, whereby we would present our very bodies as a means of laying our case before the conscience of the local and national community. We were not unmindful of the difficulties involved. So we decided to go through a process of self-purification. We started having workshops on nonviolence and repeatedly asked ourselves the questions, "Are you able to accept blows without retaliating?" "Are you able to endure the ordeals of jail?" We decided to set our direct action program around the Easter season, realizing that with the exception of Christmas, this was the largest shopping period of the year. Knowing that a strong economic withdrawal program would be the by-product of direct action, we felt that this was the best time to bring pressure on the merchants for the needed changes. Then it occurred to us that the March election was ahead and so we speedily decided to postpone action until after election. When we discovered that Mr. Connor was in the run-off, we decided again to postpone action so that the demonstrations could not be used to cloud the issues. At this time we agreed to begin our nonviolent witness the day after the run-off.

This reveals that we did not move irresponsibly into direct action. We too wanted to see Mr. Connor defeated; so we went through postponement after postponement to aid in this community need. After this we felt that direct action could be delayed no longer.

You may well ask, "Why direct action? Why sit-ins, marches, etc.? Isn't negotiation a better path?" You are exactly right in your call for negotiation. Indeed, this is the purpose of direct action. Nonviolent direct action seeks to create such a crisis and establish such creative tension that a community that has constantly refused to negotiate is forced to confront the issue. It seeks so to dramatize the issue that it can no longer be ignored. I just referred to the creation of tension as a part of the work of the nonviolent resister. This may sound rather shocking. But I must confess that I am not afraid of the word tension. I have earnestly worked and preached against violent tension, but there is a type of constructive nonviolent tension that is necessary for growth. Just as Socrates felt that it was necessary to create a tension in the mind so that individuals could rise from the bondage of myths and half-truths to the unfettered realm of creative analysis and objective appraisal, we must see the need of having nonviolent gadflies to create the kind of tension in society that will help men to rise from the dark depths of prejudice and racism to the majestic heights of understanding and brotherhood. So the purpose of the direct action is to create a situation so crisis-packed that it will inevitably open the door to negotiation. We, therefore, concur with you in your call for negotiation. Too long has our beloved Southland been bogged down in the tragic attempt to live in monologue rather than dialogue.

One of the basic points in your statement is that our acts are untimely. Some have asked, "Why didn't you give the new administration time to act?" The only answer that I can give to this inquiry is that the new administration must be prodded about as much as the outgoing one before it acts. We will be sadly mistaken if we feel that the election of Mr. Boutwell will bring the millennium to Birmingham. While Mr. Boutwell is much more articulate and gentle than Mr. Connor, they are both segregationists, dedicated to the task of maintaining the status quo. The hope I see in Mr. Boutwell is that he will be reasonable enough to see the futility of massive resistance to desegregation. But he will not see this without pressure from the devotees of civil rights. My friends, I must say to you that we have not made a single gain in civil rights without determined legal and nonviolent pressure. History is the long and tragic story of the fact that privileged groups seldom give up their privileges voluntarily. Individuals may see the moral light and voluntarily give up their unjust posture; but as Reinhold Niebuhr has reminded us, groups are more immoral than individuals.

We know through painful experience that freedom is never voluntarily given by the oppressor; it must be demanded by the oppressed. Frankly, I have never yet engaged in a direct action movement that was "well timed," according to the timetable of those who have not suffered unduly from the disease of segregation. For years now I have heard the words "Wait!" It rings in the ear of every Negro with a piercing familiarity. This "Wait" has almost always meant "Never." It has been a tranquilizing thalidomide, relieving the emotional stress for a moment, only to give birth to an ill-formed infant of frustration. We must come to see with the distinguished jurist of yesterday that "justice too long delayed is justice denied." We have waited for more than three hundred and forty years for our constitutional and God-given rights. The nations of Asia and Africa are moving with jet-like speed toward the goal of political independence, and we still creep at horse and buggy pace toward the gaining of a cup of coffee at a lunch counter. I guess it is easy for those who have never felt the stinging darts of segregation to say, "Wait." But when you have seen vicious mobs lynch your mothers and fathers at will and drown your sisters and brothers at whim; when you have seen hate filled policemen curse, kick, brutalize and even kill your black brothers and sisters with impunity; when you see the vast majority of your twenty million Negro brothers smothering in an air-tight cage of poverty in the midst of an affluent society; when you suddenly find your tongue twisted and your speech stammering as you seek to explain to your six-year-old daughter why she can't go to the public amusement park that has just been advertised on television, and see tears welling up in her little eyes when she is told that Funtown is closed to colored children, and see the depressing clouds of inferiority begin to form in her little mental sky, and see her begin to distort her little personality by unconsciously developing a bitterness toward white people; when you have to concoct an answer for a five-year-old son asking in agonizing pathos; "Daddy, why do white people treat colored people so mean?"; when you take a cross country drive and find it necessary to sleep night after night in the uncomfortable corners of your automobile because no motel will accept you; when you are humiliated day in and day out by nagging signs reading "white" and "colored"; when your first name becomes "nigger" and your middle name becomes "boy" (however old you are) and your last name becomes "John," and when your wife and mother are never given the respected title "Mrs."; when you are harried by day and haunted at night by the fact that you are a Negro, living constantly at tip-toe stance never quite knowing what to expect next, and plagued with inner fears and outer resentments; when you are forever fighting a degenerating sense of "nobodiness"; then you will understand why we find it difficult to wait. There comes a time when the cup of endurance runs over, and men are no longer willing to be plunged into an abyss of injustice where they experience the blackness of corroding despair. I hope, sirs, you can understand our legitimate and unavoidable impatience.

You express a great deal of anxiety over our willingness to break laws. This is certainly a legitimate concern. Since we so diligently urge people to obey the Supreme Court's decision of 1954 outlawing segregation in the public schools, it is rather strange and paradoxical to find us consciously breaking laws. One may well ask, "how can you advocate breaking some laws and obeying others?" The answer is found in the fact that there are two types of laws: There are *just* and there are *unjust* laws. I would agree with Saint Augustine that "An unjust law is no law at all."

Now what is the difference between the two? How does one determine when a law is just or unjust? A just law is a man-made code that squares with the moral law or the law of God. An unjust law is a code that is out of harmony with the moral law. To put it in the terms of Saint Thomas Aquinas, an unjust law is a human law that is not rooted in eternal and natural law. Any law that uplifts human personality is just. Any law that degrades human personality is unjust. All segregation statutes are unjust because segregation distorts the soul and damages the personality. It gives the segregator a false sense of superiority, and the segregated a false sense of inferiority. To use the words of Martin Buber, the great Jewish philosopher, segregation substitutes an "I-it" relationship for the "I-thou" relationship, and ends up relegating persons to the status of things. So segregation is not only politically, economically and sociologically unsound, but it is morally wrong and sinful. Paul Tillich has said that sin is separation. Isn't segregation an existential expression of man's tragic separation, an expression of his awful estrangement, his terrible sinfulness? So I can urge men to disobey segregation ordinances because they are morally wrong.

Let us turn to a more concrete example of just and unjust laws. An unjust law is a code that a majority inflicts on a minority that is not binding on itself. This is difference made legal. On the other hand a just law is a code that a majority compels a minority to follow that it is willing to follow itself. This is sameness made legal.

Let me give another explanation. An unjust law is a code inflicted upon a minority which that minority had no part in enacting or creating because they did not have the unhampered right to vote. Who can say that the legislature of Alabama which set up the segregation laws was democratically elected? Throughout the state of Alabama all types of conniving methods are used to prevent Negroes from becoming registered voters and there are some counties without a single Negro registered to vote despite the fact that the Negro constitutes a majority of the population. Can any law set up in such a state be considered democratically structured?

These are just a few examples of unjust and just laws. There are some instances when a law is just on its face and unjust in its application.

For instance, I was arrested Friday on a charge of parading without a permit. Now there is nothing wrong with an ordinance which requires a permit for a parade, but when the ordinance is used to preserve segregation and to deny citizens the First Amendment privilege of peaceful assembly and peaceful protest, then it becomes unjust.

I hope you can see the distinction I am trying to point out. In no sense do I advocate evading or defying the law as the rabid segregationist would do. This would lead to anarchy. One who breaks an unjust law must do it *openly, lovingly* (not hatefully as the white mothers did in New Orleans when they were seen on a television screaming "nigger, nigger, nigger"), and with a willingness to accept the penalty. I submit that an individual who breaks a law that conscience tells him is unjust, and willingly accepts the penalty by staying in jail to arouse the conscience of the community over its injustice, is in reality expressing the very highest respect for law.

Of course, there is nothing new about this kind of civil disobedience. It was seen sublimely in the refusal of Shadrach, Meshach and Abednego to obey the laws of Nebuchadnezzar because a higher moral law was involved. It was practiced superbly by the early Christians who were willing to face hungry lions and the excruciating pain of chopping blocks, before submitting to certain unjust laws of the Roman empire. To a degree academic freedom is a reality today because Socrates practiced civil disobedience.

We can never forget that everything Hitler did in Germany was "legal" and everything the Hungarian freedom fighters did in Hungary was "illegal." It was "illegal" to aid and comfort a Jew in Hitler's Germany. But I am sure that if I had lived in Germany during that time I would have aided and comforted my Jewish brothers even though it was illegal. If I lived in a Communist country today where certain principles dear to the Christian faith are suppressed, I believe I would openly advocate disobeying these anti-religious laws. I must make two honest confessions to you, my Christian and Jewish brothers. First, I must confess that over the last few years I have been gravely disappointed with the white moderate. I have almost reached the regrettable conclusion that the Negro's great stumbling block in the stride toward freedom is not the White Citizen's Council-er or the Ku Klux Klanner, but the white moderate who is more devoted to "order" than to justice; who prefers a negative peace which is the absence of tension to a positive peace which is the presence of justice; who constantly says "I agree with you in the goal you seek, but I can't agree with your methods of direct action"; who paternalistically feels that he can set the timetable for another man's freedom; who lives by the myth of time and who constantly advises the Negro to wait until a "more convenient season." Shallow understanding from people of goodwill is more frustrating than absolute misunderstanding from people of ill-will. Lukewarm acceptance is much more bewildering than outright rejection.

I had hoped that the white moderate would understand that law and order exist for the purpose of establishing justice, and that when they fail to do this they become dangerously structured dams that block the flow of social progress. I had hoped that the white moderate would understand that the present tension in the South is merely a necessary phase of the transition from an obnoxious negative peace, where the Negro passively accepted his unjust plight, to a substance-filled positive peace, where all men will respect the dignity and worth of human personality. Actually, we who engage in nonviolent direct action are not the creators of tension. We merely bring to the surface the hidden tension that is already alive. We bring it out in the open where it can be seen and dealt with. Like a boil that can never be cured as long as it is covered up but must be opened with all its pus-flowing ugliness to the natural medicines of air and light, injustice must likewise be exposed, with all of the tension its exposing creates, to the light of human conscience and the air of national opinion before it can be cured.

In your statement you asserted that our actions, even though peaceful, must be condemned because they precipitate violence. But can this assertion be logically made? Isn't this like condemning the robbed man because his possession of money precipitated the evil act of robbery? Isn't this like condemning Socrates because his unswerving commitment to truth and his philosophical delvings precipitated the misguided popular mind to make him drink the hemlock? Isn't this like condemning Jesus because His unique God-Consciousness and never-ceasing devotion to His will precipitated the evil act of crucifixion? We must come to see, as federal courts have consistently affirmed, that it is immoral to urge an individual to withdraw his efforts to gain his basic constitutional rights because the quest precipitates violence. Society must protect the robbed and punish the robber.

I had also hoped that the white moderate would reject the myth of time. I received a letter this morning from a white brother in Texas which said: "All Christians know that the colored people will receive equal rights eventually, but it is possible that you are in too great of a religious hurry. It has taken Christianity almost two thousand years to accomplish what it has. The teachings of Christ take time to come to earth." All that is said here grows out of a tragic misconception of time. It is the strangely irrational notion that there is something in the very flow of time that will inevitably cure all ills. Actually time is neutral. It can be used either destructively or constructively. I am coming to feel that the people of ill-will have used time much more effectively than the people of goodwill. We will have to repent in this generation not merely for the vitriolic words and actions of the bad people, but for the appalling silence of the good people. We must come to see that human progress never rolls in on wheels of inevitability. It comes through the tireless efforts and persistent work of men willing to be co-workers with God, and without this hard work time itself becomes an ally of the forces of social stagnation. We must use time creatively, and forever realize that the time is always ripe to do right. Now is the time to make real the promise of democracy, and transform our pending national elegy into a creative psalm of brotherhood. Now is the time to lift our national policy from the quicksand of racial injustice to the solid rock of human dignity.

You spoke of our activity in Birmingham as extreme. At first I was rather disappointed that fellow clergymen would see my nonviolent efforts as those of the extremist. I started thinking about the fact that I stand in the middle of two opposing forces in the Negro community. One is a force of complacency made up of Negroes who, as a result of long years of oppression, have been so completely drained of self-respect and a sense of "somebodiness" that they have adjusted to segregation, and, of a few Negroes in the middle class who, because of a degree of academic and economic security, and because at points they profit by segregation, have unconsciously become insensitive to the problems of the masses. The other force is one of bitterness and hatred and comes perilously close to advocating violence. It is expressed in the various black nationalist groups that are springing up over the nation, the largest and best known being Elijah Muhammad's Muslim movement. This movement is nourished by the contemporary frustration over the continued existence of racial discrimination. It is made up of people who have lost faith in America, who have absolutely repudiated Christianity, and who have concluded that the white man is an incurable "devil." I have tried to stand between these two forces saying that we need not follow the "do-nothingism" of the complacent or the hatred and despair of the black nationalist. There is the more excellent way of love and nonviolent protest. I'm grateful to God that, through the Negro church, the dimension of nonviolence entered our struggle. If this philosophy had not emerged, I am convinced that by now many streets of the South would be flowing with floods of blood. And I am further convinced that if our white brothers dismiss as "rabble rousers" and "outside agitators" those of us who are working through the channels of nonviolent direct action and refuse to support our nonviolent efforts, millions of Negroes, out of frustration and despair, will seek solace and security in black nationalist ideologies, a development that will lead inevitably to a frightening racial nightmare.

Oppressed people cannot remain oppressed forever. The urge for freedom will eventually come. This is what happened to the American Negro. Something within has reminded him of his birthright of freedom; something without has reminded him that he can gain it. Consciously and unconsciously, he has been swept in by what the Germans call the *Zeitgeist*, and with his black brothers of Africa, and his brown and yellow brothers of Asia, South America and the Caribbean, he is moving with a sense of cosmic urgency toward the promised land of racial justice. Recognizing this vital urge that has engulfed the Negro community, one should readily understand public demonstrations. The Negro has many pent up resentments and latent frustrations. He has to get them out. So let him march sometime; let him have his prayer pilgrimages to the city hall; understand why he must have sit-ins and freedom rides. If his repressed emotions do not come out in these nonviolent ways, they will come out in ominous expressions of violence. This is not a threat; it is a fact of history. So I have not said to my people "get rid of your discontent." But I have tried to say that this normal and healthy discontent can be channelized through the creative outlet of nonviolent direct action. Now this approach is being dismissed as extremist. I must admit that I was initially disappointed in being so categorized.

But as I continued to think about the matter I gradually gained a bit of satisfaction from being considered an extremist. Was not Jesus an extremist in love—"Love your enemies, bless them that curse you, pray for them that despitefully use you." Was not Amos an extremist for justice—"Let justice roll down like waters and righteousness like a mighty stream." Was not Paul an extremist for the gospel of Jesus Christ —"I bear in my body the marks of the Lord Jesus." Was not Martin Luther an extremist—"Here I stand; I can do none other so help me God." Was not John Bunyan an extremist—"I will stay in jail to the end of my days before I make a butchery of my conscience." Was not Abraham Lincoln an extremist—"This nation cannot survive half slave and half free." Was not Thomas Jefferson an extremist—"We hold these truths to be self-evident, that all men are created equal." So the question is not whether we will be extremist but what kind of extremist will we be. Will we be extremists for hate or will we be extremists for love? Will we be extremists for the preservation of injustice—or will we be extremists for the cause of justice? In that dramatic scene on Calvary's hill, three men were crucified. We must not forget that all three were crucified for the same crime—the crime of extremism. Two were extremists for immorality, and thusly fell below their environment. The other, Jesus Christ, was an extremist for love, truth, and goodness, and thereby rose above his environment. So, after all, maybe the South, the nation and the world are in dire need of creative extremists.

I had hoped that the white moderate would see this. Maybe I was too optimistic. Maybe I expected too much. I guess I should have realized that few members of a race that has oppressed another race can understand or appreciate the deep groans and passionate yearnings of those that have been oppressed and still fewer have the vision to see that injustice must be rooted out by strong, persistent and determined action. I am thankful, however, that some of our white brothers have grasped the meaning of this social revolution and committed themselves to it. They are still all too small in quantity, but they are big in quality. Some like Ralph McGill, Lillian Smith, Harry Golden and James Dabbs have written about our struggle in eloquent, prophetic and understanding terms. Others have marched with us down nameless streets of the South. They have languished in filthy roach-infested jails, suffering the abuse and brutality of angry policemen who see them as "dirty nigger lovers." They, unlike so many of their moderate brothers and sisters, have recognized the urgency of the moment and sensed the need for powerful "action" antidotes to combat the disease of segregation.

Let me rush on to mention my other disappointment. I have been so greatly disappointed with the white church and its leadership. Of course, there are some notable exceptions. I am not unmindful of the fact that each of you has taken some significant stands on this issue. I commend you, Rev. Stallings, for your Christian stand on this past Sunday, in welcoming Negroes to your worship service on a non-segregated basis. I commend the Catholic leaders of this state for integrating Springhill College several years ago.

But despite these notable exceptions I must honestly reiterate that I have been disappointed with the church. I do not say that as one of the negative critics who can always find something wrong with the church. I say it as a minister of the gospel, who loves the church; who was nurtured in its bosom; who has been sustained by its spiritual blessings and who will remain true to it as long as the cord of life shall lengthen.

I had the strange feeling when I was suddenly catapulted into the leadership of the bus protest in Montgomery several years ago that we would have the support of the white church. I felt that the white ministers, priests and rabbis of the South would be some of our strongest allies. Instead, some have been outright opponents, refusing to understand the freedom movement and misrepresenting its leaders; all too many others have been more cautious than courageous and have remained silent behind the anesthetizing security of the stained-glass windows.

In spite of my shattered dreams of the past, I came to Birmingham with the hope that the white religious leadership of this community would see the justice of our cause, and with deep moral concern, serve as the channel through which our just grievances would get to the power structure. I had hoped that each of you would understand. But again I have been disappointed. I have heard numerous religious leaders of the South call upon their worshippers to comply with a desegregation decision because it is the *law*, but I have longed to hear white ministers say, "follow this decree because integration is morally *right* and the Negro is your brother." In the midst of blatant injustices inflicted upon the Negro, I have watched white churches stand on the sideline and merely mouth pious irrelevancies and sanctimonious trivialities. In the midst of a mighty struggle to rid our nation of racial and economic injustice, I have heard so many ministers say, "Those are social issues with which the gospel has no real concern," and I have watched so many churches commit themselves to a completely other-worldly religion which made a strange distinction between body and soul, the sacred and the secular.

So here we are moving toward the exit of the twentieth century with a religious community largely adjusted to the status quo, standing as a tail-light behind other community agencies rather than a headlight leading men to higher levels of justice.

I have travelled the length and breadth of Alabama, Mississippi and all the other southern states. On sweltering summer days and crisp autumn mornings I have looked at her beautiful churches with their lofty spires pointing heavenward. I have beheld the impressive outlay of her massive religious education buildings. Over and over again I have found myself asking: "What kind of people worship here? Who is their God? Where were their voices when the lips of Governor Barnett dripped with words of interposition and nullification? Where were they when Governor Wallace gave the clarion call for defiance and hatred? Where were their voices of support when tired, bruised and weary Negro men and women decided to rise from the dark dungeons of complacency to the bright hills of creative protest?"

Yes, these questions are still in my mind. In deep disappointment, I have wept over the laxity of the church. But be assured that my tears have been tears of love. There can be no deep disappointment where there is not deep love. Yes, I love the church; I love her sacred walls. How could I do otherwise? I am in the rather unique position of being the son, the grandson and the great-grandson of preachers. Yes, I see the church as the body of Christ. But, oh! How we have blemished and scarred that body through social neglect and fear of being noncon-formists.

There was a time when the church was very powerful. It was during that period when the early Christians rejoiced when they were deemed worthy to suffer for what they believed. In those days the church was not merely a thermometer that recorded the ideas and principles of popular opinion; it was a thermostat that transformed the mores of society. Wherever the early Christians entered a town the power structure got disturbed and immediately sought to convict them for being "disturbers of the peace" and "outside agitators." But they went on with the conviction that they were "a colony of heaven," and had to obey God rather than man. They were small in number but big in commitment. They were too God-intoxicated to be "astronomically intimidated." They brought an end to such ancient evils as infanticide and gladiatorial contest.

Things are different now. The contemporary church is often a weak, ineffectual voice with an uncertain sound. It is so often the arch supporter of the status quo. Far from being disturbed by the presence of the church, the power structure of the average community is consoled by the church's silent and often vocal sanction of things as they are.

But the judgment of God is upon the church as never before. If the church of today does not recapture the sacrificial spirit of the early church, it will lose its authentic ring, forfeit the loyalty of millions, and be dismissed as an irrelevant social club with no meaning for the twentieth century. I am meeting young people every day whose disappointment with the church has risen to outright disgust.

Maybe again, I have been too optimistic. Is organized religion too inextricably bound to status quo to save our nation and the world? Maybe I must turn my faith to the inner spiritual church, the church within the church, as the true *ecclesia* and the hope of the world. But again I am thankful to God that some noble souls from the ranks of organized religion have broken loose from the paralyzing chains of conformity and joined us as active partners in the struggle for freedom. They have left their secure congregations and walked the streets of Albany, Georgia, with us. They have gone through the highways of the South on tortuous rides for freedom. Yes, they have gone to jail with us. Some have been kicked out of their churches, and lost support of their bishops and fellow ministers. But they have gone with the faith that right defeated is stronger than evil triumphant. These men have been the leaven in the lump of the race. Their witness has been the spiritual salt that has preserved the true meaning of the Gospel in these troubled times. They have carved a tunnel of hope through the dark mountain of disappointment.

I hope the church as a whole will meet the challenge of this decisive hour. But even if the church does not come to the aid of justice, I have no despair about the future. I have no fear about the outcome of our struggle in Birmingham, even if our motives are presently misunderstood. We will reach the goal of freedom in Birmingham and all over the nation, because the goal of America is freedom. Abused and scorned though we may be, our destiny is tied up with the destiny of America. Before the pilgrims landed at Plymouth we were here. Before the pen of Jefferson etched across the pages of history the majestic words of the Declaration of Independence, we were here. For more than two centuries our fore-parents labored in this country without wages; they made cotton king; and they built the homes of their masters in the midst of brutal injustice and shameful humiliation—and yet out of a bottomless vitality they continued to thrive and develop. If the inexpressible cruelties of slavery could not stop us, the opposition we now face will surely fail. We will win our freedom because the sacred heritage of our nation and the eternal will of God are embodied in our echoing demands.

I must close now. But before closing I am impelled to mention one other point in your statement that troubled me profoundly. You warmly commended the Birmingham police force for keeping "order" and "preventing violence." I don't believe you would have so warmly commended the police force if you had seen its angry violent dogs literally biting six unarmed, nonviolent Negroes. I don't believe you would so quickly commend the policemen if you would observe their ugly and inhuman treatment of Negroes here in the city jail; if you would watch them push and curse old Negro women and young Negro girls; if you would see them slap and kick old Negro men and young boys; if you will observe them, as they did on two occasions, refuse to give us food because we wanted to sing our grace together. I'm sorry that I can't join you in your praise for the police department.

It is true that they have been rather disciplined in their public handling of the demonstrators. In this sense they have been rather publicly "nonviolent." But for what purpose? To preserve the evil system of segregation. Over the last few years I have consistently preached that nonviolence demands that the means we use must be as pure as the ends we seek. So I have tried to make it clear that it is wrong to use immoral means to attain moral ends. But now I must affirm that it is just as wrong, or even more so, to use moral means to preserve immoral ends. Maybe Mr. Connor and his policemen have been rather publicly nonviolent, as Chief Pritchett was in Albany, Georgia, but they have used the moral means of nonviolence to maintain the immoral end of flagrant racial injustice. T. S. Eliot has said that there is no greater treason than to do the right deed for the wrong reason.

I wish you had commended the Negro sit-inners and demonstrators of Birmingham for their sublime courage, their willingness to suffer and their amazing discipline in the midst of the most inhuman provocation. One day the South will recognize its real heroes. They will be the James Merediths, courageously and with a majestic sense of purpose, facing jeering and hostile mobs and the agonizing loneliness that characterizes the life of the pioneer. They will be old oppressed, battered Negro women, symbolized in a seventy-two-year-old woman of Montgomery, Alabama, who rose up with a sense of dignity and with her people decided not to ride the segregated buses, and responded to one who inquired about her tiredness with ungrammatical profundity: "my feet is tired, but my soul is rested." They will be the young high school and college students, young ministers of the gospel and a host of their elders courageously and nonviolently sitting-in at lunch counters and willingly going to jail for conscience's sake. One day the South will know that when these disinherited children of God sat down at lunch counters they were in reality standing up for the best in the American dream and the most sacred values in our Judeo-Christian heritage, and thusly, carrying our whole nation back to those great wells of democracy which were dug deep by the founding fathers in the formulation of the Constitution and the Declaration of Independence.

Never before have I written a letter this long (or should I say a book?). I'm afraid that it is much too long to take your precious time. I can assure you that it would have been much shorter if I had been writing from a comfortable desk, but what else is there to do when you are alone for days in the dull monotony of a narrow jail cell other than write long letters, think strange thoughts, and pray long prayers?

If I have said anything in this letter that is an overstatement of the truth and is indicative of an unreasonable impatience, I beg you to forgive me. If I have said anything in this letter that is an understatement of the truth and is indicative of my having a patience that makes me patient with anything less than brotherhood, I beg God to forgive me.

I hope this letter finds you strong in the faith. I also hope that circumstances will soon make it possible for me to meet each of you, not as an integrationist or a civil rights leader, but as a fellow clergyman and a Christian brother. Let us all hope that the dark clouds of racial prejudice will soon pass away and the deep fog of misunderstanding will be lifted from our fear-drenched communities and in some not too distant tomorrow the radiant stars of love and brotherhood will shine over our great nation with all of their scintillating beauty.

Yours for the cause of Peace and Brotherhood,

Martin Luther King, Jr.

The Executive Committee of Clergy and Laymen Concerned
about Vietnam

Vietnam—The Christian's Dilemma

The Need to Speak

*A time comes when silence is betrayal. That time has come for us
in relation to Vietnam. As members of American churches and syna-
gogues, we voice not only our own convictions, but seek also to
articulate the unexpressed fears and longings of millions of Americans.
The Old Testament forbids us to prophesy "smooth things," and in
the face of any evil, the mandate of Albert Camus is laid upon all
men, whether religious or not, that they "should speak out, loud
and clear, and that they should voice their condemnation in such a
way that never a doubt, never the slightest doubt, could rise in the
heart of the simplest man. That they should get away from abstraction and confront the blood-stained face history has taken on today."*

Our share of responsibility for that blood-stained face haunts us
today and prompts our outcry. We confess that we should have spoken
sooner and with clearer voice, but we do speak now, hoping it is not too
late, adding our voice to the voice of Pope Paul, the World Council of
Churches, the Synagogue Council of America, the National Council of
Churches, the National Conference of Catholic Bishops, and other religious bodies, in urging a reappraisal of our policy in Vietnam.

Our allegiance to our nation is held under a higher allegiance to
the God who is sovereign over *all* the nations. When there is a conflict
between those allegiances, the priorities are clear: "You shall have no
other gods before me." "We must obey God rather than men." Each day
we find allegiance to our nation's policy more difficult to reconcile with
allegiance to our God.

A position paper prepared by the Executive Committee of Clergy and
Laymen Concerned about Vietnam for distribution at the Washington Mobilization,
January 31–February 1, 1967.

Both the exercise of faith and the expression of the Democratic privilege oblige us to make our voices heard. For while we speak as members of religious communities, we also speak as American citizens. Responsible expression of disagreement and dissent is the lifeblood of Democracy, and we speak out of a loyalty that refuses to condone in silence a national policy that is leading our world toward disaster.

We speak in full awareness that no easy answers are available. But we believe that issues must be pressed and questions forced, if new answers are to be forthcoming. For the old answers no longer satisfy us.

The Ongoing Anguish

No one planned the type of war in which we are involved. It has slowly escalated from one small move to the next small move, each presumed to be the last that would be necessary, so that now we find our nation able to offer only military answers to political and human questions. We sympathize with the dilemmas that face our President and congressmen in dealing with a situation all decent men abhor. But a recognition of past mistakes does not entitle us to repeat and compound those mistakes by continuing them on an ever-widening scale.

We are unable to support our nation's policy of military escalation, and we find those to whom we minister caught as we are in confusion and anguish because of it.

1. This anguish is based first of all on *the immorality of the warfare in Vietnam. We* add our voice to those who protest a war in which civilian casualties are greater than military; in which whole populations are deported against their will; in which the widespread use of napalm and other explosives is killing and maiming women, children, and the aged; in which the combatants are systematically destroying the crops and production capacity of a country they profess to liberate; in which the torturing of prisoners by both sides has been a commonplace.

All who believe that man is made in God's image must be horrified by such crimes committed against God and man. There is guilt on all sides in such a war as this, but the guilt is ours far more than we have courage to admit. We can only tremble at the thought that God is just.

2. Even those of us who recognize that sometimes evil must be done lest greater evil prevail, feel a sense of anguish in *the inconsistency between our stated aims and the consequences they produce.*

Our ongoing escalation, far from bringing the war closer to an end, serves rather to increase its duration and intensity.

Our bombing of the North, far from bringing our enemies to their knees, serves rather to strengthen their will to resist us.

Our military presence in Vietnam, far from stemming the tide of

Communism, serves rather to unite more firmly those Communist societies which might otherwise develop separate destinies.

Our widening military involvement, far from demonstrating to the world our firmness and resolve, serves rather to make the world suspicious of us and fearful of our use of power.

Our unilateral action in Vietnam, far from strengthening our influence among other nations, serves rather to jeopardize new alliances we might be creating.

At home, we find the war threatening the very goals we claim to be defending in Vietnam. Programs to help members of minority groups realize their own human dignity are jeopardized if not destroyed. A spurious type of patriotism is challenging the right of dissent and the open debate of public issues. Financial and psychological preoccupation with the war is destroying creative plans to alleviate poverty, overcome disease, extend education, replace city slums and exalt human dignity. We grieve over lost opportunities that may never be reclaimed.

Many of us are called upon to counsel young men of draft age who in conscience question our presence in Vietnam. The moral dilemma they face is part and parcel of our own. Their anguish is frequently motivated by a high patriotism that forces them to challenge, often at great personal cost, policies they believe will stain their nation's honor. How can we counsel them to participate in such a war as this? When they decide that they cannot condone the war by their personal involvement, we must support them in that decision.

3. Our anguish is deepened by *the discrepancy between what we are told by our government and what we discover is actually taking place.*

We are told that the other side gives no indication of desire to negotiate, and we then discover that such indications have been given, but that we have responded either with rebuff or military escalation.

We are told that our nation is prepared to negotiate with all concerned, and we then discover that certain of the combatants will not be welcome at the conference table.

We are told that certain cities have not been bombed, and we then discover that they have been.

We are told that civilian targets have been avoided, and then we discover that they have not been.

Such actions not only play into the hands of those who distrust us, since they can consistently discount our word, but the continuous discovery of discrepancies between our nation's word and deed has already shaken the confidence of our own people in the word of their government. We fear the immediate and long range consequences for our nation of this increasing deterioration of trust.

This, then, is our ongoing anguish: A crisis of conscience concerning what we *do* know, and a crisis of confusion concerning what we do *not* know.

The Need for Clarification

The public debate is forcing us to choose between wrong alternatives in Vietnam. Consequently, agreeing with the American Roman Catholic Bishops that it is "our duty to magnify the moral voice of our nation," we ask for clarification of the real alternatives.

The choices usually presented to the American people are three: (1) We could escalate rapidly and "win the war" in the foreseeable future; or (2) we could withdraw our troops and accept defeat; but (3) since to most Americans these alternatives are unsatisfactory, we must continue our present course, i.e., gradually escalate the war until the other side capitulates to our increasing pressure.

We believe the realistic alternatives are closer to the following: (1) We can continue to fight a hard, bloody, increasingly bitter and frustrating war for many years, a war we can conceivably "win," but at the price of destroying the land and people we presume to liberate, of sacrificing more and more of our own young men to death, of widening the probability that other nations will enter the conflict, of engendering increasing hostility against ourselves throughout the rest of the world, and of emerging at the end with no "victory" worth what it has cost; or (2) we can commit ourselves unequivocally to seek now rather than later for a negotiated peace, realizing that history does not present us with easy choices and that the road to such a peace would be long and torturous. Just as there has been frustration and heartache in our gradual escalation, so too there would be frustration and heartache in the development of new initiatives leading to a negotiated peace. Just as the risks of extending the war are great, so too the risks of seeking new initiatives for negotiated peace are great.

But confronted by such a choice, we believe the American people will choose the path of initiatives for negotiation, and that the risks involved in such a choice are well worth taking.

And so we put these questions to our government:

1. Will you help our nation confront the choice between the expansion of a war no one can "win" without destruction so terrible as to negate its stated aim, and the immediate pursuit of a negotiated peace no one can "win" in the conventional sense?

2. Will you make clear to all that we are not trying to win through negotiation what we have been unable to win through military

might, and that we seek a peace without victory—a peace that can come only on terms agreeable to all at the conference table?

3. Will you make more credible use than has yet been made of international agencies that could help us find ways to initiate negotiations?

The Preconditions of Negotiation

The possibility of negotiation will depend in large part on how such questions are answered. Many in our nation already feel that all efforts toward a negotiated peace have been made by us, and that any further initiatives must come from the other side. But certain preconditions that seem indispensable to negotiations are not yet present in our policy, and without them other nations can hardly be expected to take seriously our intent.

1. The first precondition is implied in our questions and involves an assurance from our government that we are genuinely ready to negotiate, and that we are not merely trying to win diplomatically what we have not won militarily. There will be no reason for response from the other side unless we indicate a willingness to seek peace without prior assurance that all details of the peace will follow our desires.

2. There must be some action by our government to lend credibility to our willingness to negotiate. It is increasingly clear that one indispensable prerequisite is our willingness unconditionally to cease the bombing of North Vietnam.

We are at an impasse. We have said we will not cease the bombing until there is a sign from the other side of willingness to negotiate, and yet when such signs have come we have ignored them. They have said they will give no further sign of willingness to negotiate until we cease the bombing, and yet when we have briefly ceased the bombing, no sign has come.

There is no way beyond this impasse until someone takes a fresh initiative. We, as the stronger nation, have both the obligation and the opportunity to take that initiative.

The initiative must be unconditional. Having ceased the bombing, we must be prepared to wait until the other side responds. We have no reason to expect that a response will come soon, for it will take time to gain credibility for our intent. In the interval, while diplomatic channels are explored, we will call upon religious leaders in other countries to intercede and urge that positive response be made.

3. If we truly do not intend to dictate the terms of peace in advance, then we cannot exclude from the conference table any who are involved in the present struggle. Our nation must accept the National

Liberation Front as a partner in the peace talks in its own right. The previous assurances of our leaders have failed to state this clearly.

4. Other conditions are desirable, such as a de-escalation of the ground war to a degree commensurate with the protection necessary for those already there. But since the destiny of all nations is involved in a negotiated peace, we must not seek it unilaterally, but must ask the full cooperation of all agencies designed to deal with international tensions. These must include an increasing role for the United Nations, and a recognition of the potential role of the International Control Commission in reducing ground hostility by providing an international presence under cover of which foreign troops might ultimately be withdrawn from Vietnam.

Although we address these appeals particularly to our own nation, we are fully aware that negotiations involve more than one participant, and we lay the seriousness of our concern upon all men everywhere to offer further help in transforming possibilities into realities.

Recommendations for Further Action

There are further steps that Americans can take to indicate our desire to play a creative rather than destructive role in the future of Vietnam.

1. Our congressmen will shortly begin debate on an appropriations bill. Their response to that bill will say much about our true intentions in Vietnam. We urge that additional time be allocated for a careful estimate of the costs of the war by a number of congressional committees, such as the Joint Economic Committee, the Ways and Means Committee, the Education and Labor Committee, the Judiciary Committee and the Foreign Affairs Committee, in addition to the Appropriations Committee and the Armed Services Committee, to determine what costs are necessary (1) to maintain the current level of military operations, (2) to finance new stages of build-up and escalation, and (3) to provide the type of military and civilian security that would be needed during a period of prolonged negotiation. In this way, members of the Congress can choose the type and degree of military operation they wish to support.

2. We ask the Congress to reexamine the international agreements to which the United States is pledged. To an unprecedented degree, today's world order and human life itself depend upon the exercise of constraint in the conduct of foreign affairs. The origin and conduct of the war in Vietnam must be examined in this light. Particular attention must be focused on the destruction of civilian life and property, the use of gas and other chemicals, and the treatment of prisoners of war.

Our country must pledge itself anew to conform policy and practice in Vietnam to international law, as embodied in the several agreements of Geneva and The Hague, the Nuremberg judgments, the Charter of the United Nations, and other such documents. The abandonment of constraint leads our country and the world down the path of brutalization and destruction.

3. Our religious bodies must assume a particular responsibility for prisoners of war in both the North and South. We call upon international religious agencies to take the initiative in developing effective programs for speedy repatriation and humane treatment of prisoners, with special attention to nutritional and medical needs. Under no circumstances can our nation condone brutal treatment of prisoners on the ground that the other side does so.

We must immediately support efforts to insure that victims of bombing and terrorism, particularly those who have been burned by napalm, are given proper hospitalization wherever adequate facilities are available, including the United States. We welcome the formation of the Committee of Responsibility that is working to this end, and urge governmental support for its efforts.

We urge all religious organizations to follow the example of the World Council of Churches in arranging special offerings for the relief of all victims of warfare in Vietnam, whether in the North or South, to be administered through the International Red Cross or similar agencies.

5. At such time as negotiations have begun, further creative opportunities should be opened up for both the public and the private sectors of our nation. There will be need for the development of a genuinely representative government in the South. Members of our Congress and our legal profession can offer their services, under the auspices of Asian members of such bodies as the International Parliamentary Union, for whatever counsel the Vietnamese desire in the development of a Constitutional Assembly.

Those with special skills in such fields as education, land reform, housing, nutrition, medicine and job training can be prepared to help in Vietnam during the long and involved period of negotiations. The resources of various Catholic, Protestant and Jewish relief agencies can be coordinated for these and other ventures, and we urge foundations to support extended opportunities for service in these areas.

We are eager that many of our citizens pledge themselves to acts of mercy and rebuilding and reconciliation. These are a particular American responsibility because of the deep measure of American involvement in acts of injury and destruction. But such acts will have enduring meaning only when our nation has pledged itself to seek negotiated peace in more courageous terms than have yet been under-

taken. Otherwise we will appear to be using small gestures of creativity
to excuse massive acts of ongoing destruction. . . .

In all such ventures, however, there is a danger to which Americans must be particularly sensitive. We must not seek to export the
American way of life, or impose an alien culture on the Vietnamese. By
insisting that our help be channeled through international agencies, we
can clarify our desire to serve only as others choose to use us, and not as
we dictate. We must convey by word and even more by deed, our desire
to let the Vietnamese be the arbiters of their own destiny, and insist only
on such international controls as will temporarily be needed to insure that
injustices are prevented or properly rectified.

Our Ongoing Responsibility

We know that millions of Americans share the anguish we
express, and endorse the alternatives we propose. If they have been silent
heretofore, we plead with them to speak up now, and pledge them our
support. If they have spoken earlier and felt no resonance of public
response, we plead with them to speak again, so that together we can
create the new ground swell of public outcry that will force a reappraisal
and a new direction.

We reaffirm our own responsibility to urge that new direction.
We pledge to lay this burning concern upon the consciences of our religious bodies, through our local congregations, our denominational agencies, our councils of churches, and our involvement in civic groups, so
that increasing pressure can be brought to bear, through the pulpit, the
public forum, the mass media, and the ballot box, upon those in public
life who make our policy decisions.

As we face a difficult and dangerous period in the history of man,
we remember that our task is not to assign blame for the past, but to
accept responsibility for the future; not to cast the stone of condemnation, but to offer the helping hand of reconciliation; not to proceed, self-
righteously and vindictively, but to walk humbly and repentantly.

We who are so deeply involved in the immensity of the present
war must have the courage to initiate the steps that will lead to peace. If
we do not take those steps, we firmly believe that God will judge us
harshly, and will hold us accountable for the horror we continue to unleash. But if we do turn about, if we seek to undo whatever measure we
can of the wrong that has been done, then we also firmly believe that as
we walk that long and hard and often discouraging road, God Himself
will be with us, to guide and chasten and sustain us, and that He will
deign to use even us in restoring some portion of the divine creation we
have so grievously misused.

8
Technology

Man's own technology forces religious questions upon him. It confronts him with the dilemma of choosing between "the safety of the given and the risk of the new." Whether through cybernation or atomic power, technology persistently compels man to ask, "For what purpose?" No turning back for answers to a nontechnological world is possible.

If these new technical devices are indeed here to stay, what priorities will man assign to them? Will their use be determined by man's present socioeconomic systems, or will they force the revision of those systems? As Robert Theobald argues, "the generalized use of the computer threatens to destroy . . . all the present rights of the individual unless we change our socioeconomic system." Yet, as Theobald continues, the only way to run the complex society of the second half of the twentieth century is with the help of the computer.

Will man and the machine be able to live without conflict side by side? Is it possible for technology and human dignity to coexist? Differing responses are made by Walter Ong and Gerald Sykes. Ong offers the hope that new techniques and tools of communication will enhance man's ability to relate to the outsider in society and to undertake social action. Sykes, however, claims that the "technolatrous" bias of modern society has resulted in the creation of the "Aztech," the contemporary man of incessant action who recognizes no delicate ethical dilemmas and experiences no painful thoughts.

Space exploration, that dramatic result of technology, offers further challenges to the values of modern man. Milan Machovec and Paul Tillich, a Marxist and a Christian theologian, respectively, present two views of the human dimensions of space exploration. Machovec sees in space exploration a possibility for the fulfillment or, more accurately, the perpetual fulfillment, of the urge by which man's being is defined. Man, says Machovec, is characterized by his urge for a sense of quest, and that urge will be satisfied by his efforts to map and control an inexhaustible universe. Those efforts will give meaning to his life. Tillich, however, would reply that quest alone is not enough, that unless it is responsibly informed by ethical values, quest is meaningless. Any quest for knowledge or control, says Tillich, must reply to the question, "For what purpose?" and the reply must be "judged in the light of the meaning of life in all its dimensions." It is in the forming of the basis for such a judgment that religion plays one of its most important roles in the technological age.

Robert Theobald

Cybernation and the Fulfillment of Man

My chief concern, as a socioeconomist, is to examine the drives which arise from the development of cybernetics and to see how they can be employed to meet our fundamental goals—rather than subvert them. I

Reprinted from *Liberation* (March 1965) by permission of the author.

Robert Theobald is a socioeconomist whose writings include *The Rich and the Poor, The Challenge of Abundance,* and *Free Men and Free Markets.*

am not interested in trying to use cybernetics to preserve our existing socioeconomic system; indeed, I intend to prove that continuation of this system will make it impossible to realize our fundamental goals. Put another way, the recruiting of cybernetics to aid in the maintenance of some of our industrial-age values will make it increasingly difficult to realize these goals.

Four fundamental drives arise from the application of cybernetics in the form of computer systems: the drive toward unlimited destructive power, the drive toward unlimited productive power, the drive to eliminate the human mind from repetitive activities, and the inherent organizational drive of the computer within a cybernetics system. . . .

. . . If we are to have a more fulfilling way of life in the cybernetics-based abundance era, we must take conscious steps to enable us to arrive at a new set of restraints and lack of restraints and a new balance between them.

Let us begin with a consideration of the drive toward unlimited destructive power: it is now generally accepted that this can only be prevented from destroying mankind if we renounce force, and even the threat of force, and that this requires that negotiation and arbitration become the means of settling disputes. In effect, nations will have to move toward world cooperation and world law. We are, at the present time, witnessing the early efforts of institutions which could become the creators and administrators of world law, but we continue to view such efforts as primarily aimed at peace-keeping. Despite the discussions at meetings and conferences, our perception of the role of world-cooperation in achieving socioeconomic advances remains very dim, for we still allow language and cultural barriers to impede the free flow of information. The physical barriers to communication are being lifted. With the aid of cybernetics, the channels are opening. Our role is to ensure that we use them, not allow ourselves to be persuaded that we should block them once again.

The drive toward unlimited productive power can result in vast benefits, both internationally and domestically, but only if we change the methods presently used to distribute rights to resources. It is, of course, impossible to determine the final pattern which will emerge but I believe that the need for three steps can already be seen:

1) The rich countries should accept an unlimited commitment to provide the poor countries of the world with all the resources they can effectively employ to help them to move into the cybernetics-based abundance era. Let me state explicitly, however, that such a commitment should not be accompanied by the right to dump unwanted surplus industrial-age products and machinery into the poor countries. Rather,

the poor countries must move as directly as possible from the agricultural era to the cybernetics era, without being forced to pass through the industrial-age process of socio-cultural and economic realignments.

2) Domestically, we should adopt the concept of an absolute constitutional right to an income through provision of Basic Economic Security. This would guarantee to every citizen of the United States, and to every person who has resided within the United States for a period of five consecutive years, the right to an income from the federal government sufficient to enable him to live with dignity. No government agency, judicial body, or other organization whatsoever should have the power to suspend or limit any payments assured by these guarantees. I believe that the best means to implement these guarantees would be to amend the Employment Act of 1946 to read: "It is the policy of the United States government either to provide job opportunities for all those seeking work, or, if jobs are not available in sufficient number, to guarantee an income of sufficient size to enable the family to live with dignity."

3) A second principle, Committed Spending, should also be introduced, which would embody the concept of the need to protect the existing middle-income group against abrupt major declines in their standard of living, for a very substantial proportion of this group will lose their jobs in the next decade. This principle is based on the premise that in the process of transition between the industrial age and the cybernetics-based abundance era, socioeconomic dislocation should be avoided wherever possible, whether caused by sudden large-scale reduction in demand or by sudden withdrawal of economic supports for valid individual and social goals. Let me remind you at this point that the validity of the classic objection, "we cannot afford it," has been destroyed by the drive toward unlimited productive power. We can afford to provide the individual with funds which will encourage and enable him to choose his own activities and thus increase his freedom, and, *at the same time*, increase, to the required extent, expenditures on community needs: particularly education, medical services, recreation facilities and conservation.

There is now general agreement that if we are to profit from the drive to eliminate the human mind from repetitive tasks we must greatly increase our emphasis on education. We have been unwilling to face up to the fact that the school and the university were designed to serve the requirements of the industrial age. We have therefore concentrated our attention on longer periods of education for more and more people, rather than on changing the educational system to make it appropriate for the cybernetics era. We must find ways to develop the creativity and to enlarge the capacity of each individual in terms of his own uniqueness.

We will have to teach people to think for themselves, rather than to absorb and then regurgitate with maximum A-level efficiency the theories of past thinkers. I believe that the best way to do this is to change our educational process from being discipline-oriented to being problem-oriented: to set up educational systems which will force people to face all the implications of each problem and to evaluate the individual's potential in terms of his ability to perceive new interconnections between aspects of the problem.

We must do this in such a way as to avoid the "new-education" emphasis on means—the smoothly-interacting group or seminar—and concentrate on ends—the kind of problems which will be studied. I think this can probably best be achieved through what we can call the two-dimensional seminar technique. Here the choice is up to the individual; he enters the system at the first level with a multiple choice of seminars; he can then go on to specialize by movement up the levels of complexity in one problem area, or he can choose to gain wider knowledge by horizontal movement, through participation in many seminars.

Education along problem-oriented lines is the prime necessity of the future and it is also the prime reason why we cannot preserve our present industrial-age values nor return to the simple values of the agricultural era. The set of values of the cybernetics era will be unique: attitudes toward time and space, production and consumption, will have to be appropriate to the realities of this era. In the future we are going to value those who can think system in all fields—not only about the problems of society but also about the individual. For example, the patient will respect his doctor on the basis of his ability to understand him as a biological system, rather than value his apparent quasi-magical techniques as in our agricultural past.

I am sure that many humanists will be shocked by my acceptance of system-thinking for they fear that man will be destroyed by the rationality implicit in system-thinking. In this view the rational is synonymous with the concept of the logical solution to any problems inherent in a task, the choice of the one best way to do something, the constant search for the efficient. Compared to any system or smoothly running organization, man's thought processes are less rational, more subject to accident and distortion. According to this thesis, it follows that man must inevitably end by acting according to the instruction of the efficient decision-making mechanisms which he himself created for his service, to carry out his wishes, to fulfil his needs. But the efficient, knowledgeable servant becomes the administrator, the teacher and thus, the master. This is the case put forward by Jacques Ellul in his book originally published in France in 1954 under the title of *La Technique*, and published in the United States under the title *The Technological Society* (New York:

Alfred A. Knopf, 1964). It is impossible not to concede the immense strength of Ellul's argument, even though it was based on the organizational efficiency drives existing before the emergence of the computer and its accelerating drive toward maximum efficiency. My acceptance of system-thinking is based on reality: on my willingness to face up to the fact that there is no way to avoid the development of computer systems in the second half of the twentieth century. Our only hope is to accept this reality and to use all of man's energy to recruit technological drives for the attainment of our fundamental goals.

Let me conclude: the fundamental effect of cybernetics is antientropic as Charles Dechert has pointed out. The increasing efficiency of organization permits greater output with less energy input. In the industrial, scarcity age, this process could only have worked to our advantage for demand exceeded supply and energy sources were always insufficient. In the cybernetics-based abundance era, however, we are being confronted with the need to place restraints on both production and the new energy sources, lest their drives destroy us. The danger of exploding production is no less real than that of destructive explosions. It is incorrect to assume that because we have presently unfulfilled global production needs, we can absorb any extra amount, and rapidly.

We are living in a world of exponential growth. But Dennis Gabor, Professor at the Imperial College of Science and Technology in London, has pointed out:

> . . . exponential curves grow to infinity only in mathematics. In the physical world they either turn round and saturate, or they break down catastrophically. It is our duty as thinking men to do our best toward a gentle saturation, instead of sustaining the exponential growth, though this faces us with very unfamiliar and distasteful problems.

For many people the most distasteful of all these problems is the fact that there is already insufficient toil to go round—that it is now necessary to allow vast numbers of people to do what *they want to do* simply because they personally believe that their activity is important. The guaranteed income proposal mentioned above recognizes this reality, and it has therefore been attacked from both ends of the political spectrum, and from every point in between, on the grounds that the proposal would promote the lazy society. For example, August Heckscher, who served as President Kennedy's special assistant for cultural affairs, declared: "The very idea of large populations doing nothing but pleasing themselves goes against the American grain," and then went on to make proposals for job allocations and income distribution which Gerard Piel has described as "instant feudalism."

We have not yet been willing to recognize the true extent of the challenge posed by the drive toward unlimited destructive power, un-limited productive power, the elimination of the human mind from repetitive tasks, the organizing drive of the computer within a cybernetics system. We have not yet been willing to recognize that we live today in the truly lazy society—a society where we allow technological trends to make our decisions for us because we have no mechanisms to allow us to control them. We have not yet been willing to recognize that man's power is now so great that the minimum requirement for the survival of the human race is individual responsibility.

Man will no longer need to toil: he must find a new role in the cybernetics era which must emerge from a new goal of self-fulfillment. He can no longer view himself as a super-animal at the center of the physical universe, nor as a super-efficient taker of decisions self-fashioned in the model of the computer. He must now view himself as a truly creative being in the image of a creative God.

Walter J. Ong

The Spiritual Meaning of Technology and Culture

In attempting to discern some of the spiritual meaning of tech-nological culture, we shall be concerned with the relation of technological culture to the media of communications as we see them developing through the course of history. This discussion attempts two things: first, to sketch the historical development of communications, and second, to suggest the relationship obtaining between our present culture and the

Reprinted from an occasional paper published by The Church Society for College Work (February 1967), *Technology and Culture in Perspective*, by permission.

Walter J. Ong is Professor of English at St. Louis University.

art of communications. In this task, we will be called upon to analyze the effect of man's increasing sophistication in communications in terms of qualitative analysis rather than, as has hitherto been the case, in terms of a quantitative analysis. We are concerned not so much with the accumulation and diffusion of knowledge as we are with the kind of knowledge communicated. Further, we are concerned with the effect of evolving stages of communications upon man's conceptual and psychic patterns.

There are basically three distinct stages through which communication has become increasingly sophisticated: the oral-aural stage; the chirographic-typographic stage; the electronic stage. Each one of these stages is marked by the distinct effect communications had upon the men living in these separate eras.

The oral-aural stage is marked by the awesome power of words. A word is a sound, a source of power, an action. When a word is taken in its primary, basic state, as a sound (as it must always be taken before writing), it is an indication of power. Unlike the object of any of the other senses, sound indicates a present use of power: something is going on. A primitive hunter can see a buffalo, smell a buffalo, touch and taste a buffalo when the buffalo is quite dead. If he hears a buffalo, he'd better watch out. Something is acting. Sound exists only when power is actively being used. This is the basis for the often noted Hebrew view of words as events. They are indeed events, even today, in their native habitat, the world of sound. You cannot stop a sound and have sound: you have then only silence.

In a completely oral culture, innocent of writing, words are sounds only and thereby of a piece with actuality. It was through words as sounds that man first forged his relationship with the universe about him. His syntheses tended to be auditory rather than visual. He made less than we do of the world as structure and more of the world as harmony—hence, the harmony of spheres found in early cosmology and philosophy. In Plato, however, we can see the movement from oral-aural concepts to visual concepts.

Next is the chirographic-typographic stage. The evolution from primitive pictographs to the invention of the alphabet can be seen as the consequence of man's increasing need for keeping records. The invention of the alphabet shows a remarkable psychological revolution. This may be seen from two facts: first, there was a remarkable time span required for man to bring himself to the invention of the alphabet—some 500,000 years; second, all alphabets now in use or ever known to have been in use can be traced to one single alphabet—namely, that carried around the Mediterranean by the Phoenecians about 1500 B.C. Other writing systems, such as Mesopotamian cuneiform or Chinese character writing, had various places of origin. The alphabet, the only system to convert sound directly into spatial equivalents, was, however, invented only once.

What could the invention of the alphabet do to sound? In the first place, sound is a time-bound phenomenon since it exists only when it is going out of existence. We cannot have, for example, the word "sophisticated" as a series of sounds present all at once. But we can have the letters present all at once. The alphabet deactivates words by pretending they are objects in space, which they are not. Modern science, when confronted with the necessity of measuring sound, was forced to the analogous process of measuring not sound but its spatial equivalents; hence, the oscillograph and oscilloscope.

This tension between time-less (written, printed) and time-bound (oral) concepts of words has had a massive effect upon man's psyche. One illustration of this phenomenon can be seen by contrasting the ways in which literate man and illiterate man seek relief from their anxieties. Literate man finds relief in various kinds of schizophrenic withdrawals from reality, but illiterate man is incapable of this type of withdrawal. Illiterate man finds his most immediate relief in unrepressed hostility. He runs amok, or goes berserk, as witness the Congolese rioters. I would suggest that Achilles' wrath in the *Iliad* may be some kind of carry-over from a pre-literate tradition.

With the invention of letterpress, alphabetic typography, came an even greater intensification of special awareness. Copernican cosmology, Newtonian physics, and the developing sophistication in the making of maps made an issue of observation. Movable type and the lock press removed words further and further from the action of speaking and brought them more and more into the realm of observation. They became objects of vision and, since type can be moved, of manipulation. Knowledge became a commodity, a kind of thing.

At this point we may make an important generalization. Vision depersonalizes; speech personalizes. The truth of this statement may be seen in a simple illustration. Seemingly, in every known human culture, to stare at a person is considered a major breach of etiquette and, if deliberate and persistent, a mark of hostility. And what is a stare but a sustained gaze without talking? In staring, one treats another person as an object. In speaking, one treats another person as a person. Sound relates to the interior dimension of man. Sight relates merely to man's exterior. Any quantitative advance seen in the transition of the oral-aural stage to the typographical stage in the development of communications must be carefully weighed in terms of the qualitative evaluation of the effect of this development upon interpersonal communication.

With the advent of the electronic stage, we find voice again coming into its own, yet in a different way. Through telephone, sound tapes, and radio we find the sound of the human voice carried through the medium of sub-visual electrons. Further, the advent of rapid transportation and communication has encouraged the direct confrontation of people. In modern technology, we have learned that sight alone does not suffice for the space age. The achievements in sonar development and in radiotelescopes serve to underscore this belief. In specific academic disciplines we find that in philosophy, logic has given way to dialogue. In theology, the form-critical approach to Scripture study has pointed man's search away from the written word and back to the oral tradition underlying that word.

The conjunction of technological culture and rapid communications has ushered in an age of simultaneity. The contemporary man on the street has a general awareness of what's happening at any given time all over the world. Further, all cultures are present with us simultaneously. History has become compressed into the present. The focus of historicism on the present does something to the human consciousness that is different from what the more antiquarian pursuit of history does. Relating events from history and prehistory demands a sense of the here and now. It relates the exterior structure of the universe to a state of mind. We are the first age in the history of mankind which has undertaken a serious academic study of itself and its place in history.

There are those who would argue that our fast-paced culture has pushed the past beyond man's immediate awareness. I would argue, to the contrary, that technological man's focus on the present keeps him in touch with his past, while, at the same time, giving him the impetus to plan for the future. The increased capability for recovering and storing mass quantities of information, as seen in such sophistications as the computer, equips man for his decision-making task in a fashion which would invite the envy of our ancestors. For a man to be truly human he must be free to choose between alternatives. Yet freedom of choice implies knowledge of consequences of available alternatives. The conjunction of modern communication with the massing of circumstantial information in electric circuitry has provided man with this knowledge, thus freeing him and making him more truly human.

Earlier we remarked on two different sets of tensions which the development of communications had created in man. For oral-aural man reality was time bound. For his counterpart in the typographical age, reality was time-less. Oral-aural man, through his dependence upon sound, had an interior orientation, whereas typographical man, with his emphasis on sight, had an exterior orientation. Technology provides the possible synthesis of these recurring tensions. We recognize in our present age the increase of personal emphasis in philosophy, theology, and ethics. We point to the intense interiorization found in contemporary art and poetry. With the recovery of sound, we find modern man emphasizing deep personal reflection more and more. This is coupled with man's increasing ability to relate to the "outsider" in society and to social action concerns. This last characteristic seems to be the hallmark of the kind of social revolution of which we are a part.

Two contemporary illustrations should serve to demonstrate vivid ways in which modern technology, through new media of communication, has enhanced man's interior through the recovery of sound. At the time of the assassination of President Kennedy, the entire country was brought into a massive personal intimacy previously unknown. This personal intimacy was brought about largely by virtue of the "on the spot" television coverage of all of the complex events happening practically simultaneously in different parts of the globe. Secondly, the installation of the "hotline" linking Moscow and the White House provides a classic example of decision making in as highly personalized a way as possible. The "hotline" reaffirms a recovered emphasis on personal decision in the midst of a culture we erroneously tend to think of as impersonal and mechanistic. Impersonalization and mechanization are persistent, but there are at least equally strong countervailing tendencies.

My thesis, then, is that much of the spiritual meaning of technological culture is found in the realm of communication. Through technology, man has recovered the dimension of sound. With the recovery of sound, man has found a new interior orientation as well as an emphasis on his time-bound nature. From these two dimensions have come man's increasing concern with personal and responsible decision making. As man exercises his decision making capabilities he affirms and reaffirms his own humanity.

Gerald Sykes
A New Salvation, A New Supernatural

Man rushes first to be saved *by* technology, and then to be saved *from* it. We Americans are front-runners in both races. The United States led the world away from small wheat fields and toward big ones, away from outhouses and toward toilets, away from the virgin forest and toward the pulp mill, away from scarcity and toward abundance, away from few loaves of bread that were nutritious and toward many loaves of bread that are not, away from the peasant and toward the factory worker, away from the child of nature and toward the quiz kid. Now a few Americans want to go, not in the other direction, but toward an intelligent use of their new advantages that permits them to find abundance in their personal lives, lives that have not been processed out of genuineness or fulfilment. It seems like a reasonable wish. Actually, it is a presumptuous wish, which may never be granted, even to the most intelligent. The many catches to progress are not so easily shaken off.

The effect of advanced technology on human beings is better observed in the United States than anywhere else, because Americans have been exposed to it more nakedly, more eagerly, more rewardedly, than anyone else. This effect becomes clear when relatively traditionless Americans are compared with the citizens of a highly traditional country, the French. Some years of residence in France have permitted me to observe a few of the differences. The question is this: What happens to people when they are highly technicized, spared much of the drudgery of the past, and given opportunities that their ancestors never dreamed of?

Reprinted from "Technology and Human Values" (An Occasional Paper on the Role of Technology in The Free Society), published by The Center for the Study of Democratic Institutions. © 1966. By permission of the publisher.

Gerald Sykes, critic and novelist, has been a member of the faculty of the School of General Studies of Columbia University.

What has already happened to the Americans? What is in the process of happening to the French?

My answer, in brief, is that most people relish their opportunities and do not ask difficult questions about them. The vast majority are as pleased and as thoughtless as a child with a candy bar. A few of them, however, look for ways to be saved from their savior. And then they, too, are offered a new salvation by the many. And most of the specially gifted few accept it. And this American drama may very well be restaged in France.

Americans have not been protected against improved technique by traditional culture; they have been uprooted, in a manner that has not yet been put into the language of ideology, by the real revolution of our time, and they have had to develop insights and resources that are quite new. There are many new ethical dilemmas in every American's life.

One of them is this: The American can now have more power than he or his ancestors ever had before—power to cure disease, to live longer, to be rich, to travel, to acquire more knowledge, to transform himself from provincial to world citizen, at least in information. But if he obtains this new power—and it is all but impossible for him, if he has talent, to avoid obtaining it—a social demand will be put upon him. He will be required (all quite impersonally, of course; no pact between Faust and Mephistopheles, or anything medieval like that) to use symbols—verbal symbols, words—in a way that his society desires. His society is committed to turnover, to production and consumption in ever increasing amounts. And words are more important now to turn over than things. Merchandising is of greater value to the economy than manufacture, which can be handed over to robots or semi-robots. Craftsmanship has become vestigial.

The gifted American, then, must learn how to merchandise his talents. His talents must be bought, or else he will "starve"—get enough to eat perhaps but share none of the prestige or excitement of the new society. Today we do not live Platonically off slave labor, or Benedictinely on a feudal farm, or Jeffersonianly next door to wilderness; we live "Madisonianly" by the sale of our wits. And our wits must be packaged attractively or they go unnoticed. Our wits express themselves in symbols, but the symbols must seem real if anyone is to pay real dollars for them. If this means that symbols must be aimed at customers, at the worst and weakest in customers, so that a steady stream of real dollars may be obtained (and it does mean just this, with mathematical precision), we begin to understand an inherent ethical catch in the new technical order, its obligation to rely on the *misuse of symbols*.

This catch is most obvious in politics and commerce, but it also exists in art and science. In academic life it usually takes discrete forms:

excessive specialization, excessive avoidance of value-judgments, and similar devices of shrewd "hedging" and unnoticed secession from the concerns of other men. These evasions of responsibility become inevitable as soon as morality becomes social, not personal. In a highly technicized society morality becomes more and more social and less and less personal. It is easier to fool society than one's inner voice, so long as that anachronism remains audible.

In the United States the man of action has more unchallenged power than his kind has had since the beginning of civilization. He can be corrected only by facts, never by tradition or by criticism. If he makes a costly mistake that can be avoided in the future by getting criticism, he puts a critic on his payroll. He knows that he needs men of thought because he gets his power now, not through action, as in the old red-handed days of blood and guts, but through words, which he uses in any way he legally can. To use them effectively, he needs the cooperation of men of thought, because he has discovered that things cannot be sold without the enhancement of ideas and the ornaments of culture. He therefore rewards men of thought when they cooperate with him, and fails to reward them when they do not. In nearly every case they cooperate, not because of coercion but because their lives, and those of their families, become more enjoyable when they do. They are admitted to the many benefits of the new prosperity—a second car, or a first wine cellar. Few of the few men of thought are immune to such privileges. Indeed, it would be unrealistic and inhuman to expect them to cling to their traditional poverty in an age that has made abundance part of its style of life. If he were alive today, Socrates would be expected to be at ease in the Hilton Hotel in Athens.

The anthropological terms "men of thought" and "men of action" are used here to describe the present struggle for power. The men of action have power, but they need the assistance of the men of thought. The men of thought resemble the Toltecs, who, archaeologists tell us, created the civilization of Mexico, which was taken away from them by a cruder, more military, more commercial tribe called the Aztecs. The word Toltec meant master craftsman, or artificer, or architect. If we add a modernizing "h" to Toltec, we get "Toltech," embodied by such men of thought as the poet, the physicist, the philosopher. If we add a modernizing "h" to Aztec, we get "Aztech," or such men of action as storekeepers, statesmen, chiefs of staff. The Aztechs have achieved unprecedented control over nature through the application of scientific methods they did not create. Like the old Aztecs, the new Aztechs merely took over ideas and skills that had been patiently produced over centuries by men of greater humanity and greater responsibility. Like the old Toltecs, the new Toltechs—the scientists and artists of our own day—must submit to the authority of a more primitive kind of man who happened to be on hand when thought, to which he had contributed nothing, produced a bonanza. His more primitive skills are needed for organization, distribution, and regularity.

The man of action, or Aztech, does not have to face delicate ethical dilemmas. He has his troubles, many more and much subtler than the man of thought, or Toltech, is willing to admit or even to contemplate. It is significant that social novels dealing sympathetically with "titans" or tycoons are no longer produced by good novelists, who on the whole have turned as narcissistic as good poets, because they are similarly preoccupied with a quest for identity in a time of drastic alienation. But the Aztech, though neglected as a subject for works of art, is not concerned with finding who he is, or with lamenting a time that has given him more undisputed power than his tribe ever had before. He has no delicate ethical dilemmas, because he has also been given—by men of thought—a philosophy called pragmatism, and it solves most of his dilemmas for him, not as Charles Peirce or William James might have expected, but on the side of an expediency that is to his taste.

He has encountered so few obstacles to his acquisition of power that he understandably holds contemporary men of thought in low esteem, except when they may help to create such things as a rival Sputnik, or a theology to shore up the church, or paintings that offer social prestige, sound investment, and tax deduction. The new prosperity, made possible in part by the thought of Toltech economists, such as John Maynard Keynes, has been so vast, so fast, so irrational—that is, dependent on mass purchasing that has been stimulated by appeals to subliminal factors—that newly rich Aztechs no longer turn to intellectual Toltechs for philosophic guidance. Thought no longer intimidates them. Nor do they hold any priesthood in awe. They have cut themselves free from the forms of salvation that they inherited from their parents and their teachers—salvation religious or salvation secular, salvation by faith or salvation by good works. They respect all these earlier forms of salvation, but they save their real enthusiasm for a new salvation, one that they invented themselves.

The new salvation is the product of a new tempo, the extraordinary speed with which successful men of action must now operate. They want to do good works, especially good works that may bring favorable publicity or stabilize the economy that made them rich. But they lack time to go properly into the nature of the good works. So they engage experts to tell them which words are good and most advisable to support. And when they receive the best advice possible, they sign a check and feel better. It is the quickest and easiest form of salvation of all: no immersions, no conversions, no sermons. You merely put your name in the right place, and you enter the newest extension of heaven. If you don't happen to be a millionaire, you can also be saved. Smaller sums will also do the job.

Every nation has its own road to salvation. The new American road is salvation by checkbook. An earlier religious book has been superseded by the ingenuity of our time. Occasionally the new salvation leads to a mistake, but ordinarily it pays off. One of its better known mistakes took place in the Bay of Pigs in Cuba. The landings by anti-Castro Cubans in the Bay of Pigs were made possible by the signing of checks. They originated in the belief that something could be got for relatively little. Long-standing habits of easily bought success entered that decision. New habits of overhasty reliance on counsellors also entered it. Some foreigners offered to restore the Caribbean to its beautiful old submissiveness. Why not let them do it? Salvation by checkbook was offered us, and we grabbed it.

Not often does it work out so badly. Usually everyone is made happy, fund-raisers, donors, and beneficiaries. It permits the donors to go back to work right away—and they have to go back right away, to make sure that they have lost nothing while they were out doing a good deed. More important, a pattern of incessant action is maintained, without the bother of painful thought. The Aztech does not have to face the swarm of doubts that might incapacitate him if he gave them the chance, doubts that might in an earlier time have led him in his middle years into a monastic life of expiation.

Milan Machovec

Philosophical and Anthropological Aspects of Space Research

. . . Neither Christianity nor Marxism has as yet developed any kind of model for a "philosophy of space research." Both positions grew out of purely worldly, that is, material and social, roots. Man in his social, practical, and ethical existence is their traditional concern—nothing more.

Nevertheless, it is self-evident that no task is so "new" that the specific spiritual tradition of this or that position would be indifferent to it. One should expect that Marxists would take a different position with regard to the "cosmic" tasks than Christians. There again one would expect the students of Jacques Maritain to take a different position from those of Karl Barth or Rudolf Bultmann; only the work of Teilhard de Chardin represents a valuable spiritual preparation. Thus one can expect that perhaps not the details, but certainly the *ultimate meaning* of space research will be defined differently by one who sees the centre of his spiritual existence in the figure of Jesus Christ and in the biblical word, and by one who sees his tasks primarily in the rationalization of social life, in overcoming the class struggle and the various forms of "alienation." Both of us are at the beginning. Therefore I wish to make only a few comments on a possible basis of a Marxist "cosmos philosophy." Hopefully this will also be interesting for a Christian reader and can encourage him to think about the same problems from his specific presuppositions.

The penetration of space, and especially the travelling to other

Reprinted from *Student World*, No. 4, 1966 (Geneva: World Student Christian Federation), by permission of the publisher. The selection consists of exerpts from *The Meaning of Life* by Milan Machovec, published in German and Czech. Translated by Harriet Wilkins.

Milan Machovec is Professor of Philosophy, Charles University, Prague.

cosmic bodies, planets which look more or less like our earth, is surely a much greater upheaval in the natural history of the earth than anything since the appearance of man. In comparison to this upheaval, all previous great social revolutions and scientific-technical discoveries in the history of man appear subordinated as only an internal affair of an only earthly preparatory stage, as a more or less quantitative matter of the simple—although always necessary—growth of the abilities of this being before it could come to a qualitative transformation, i.e., to the entrance of this being into an entirely different natural milieu. Such a far-reaching upheaval will surely have enormous effects on man himself. Therefore even the preparation alone, on the one hand, necessarily awakens many entirely new philosophical problems; on the other hand, it presents in a completely new light some of the older questions of man's philosophical self-knowledge as they have appeared in the changing dialogue of philosophical systems. This turning-point in man's history and its "conversion of nature" are so far-reaching that, even though we may not admit it today, they will certainly have a strong effect in a subtle manner on social-political, even ethical problems of man, some of which may seem quite far away.

It is incorrect to reduce the question of human entry into space to the problem of what man will do with the cosmos. For example, what mineral deposits will he find and use, or will he discover a milieu suitable for the emigration of a part of humanity to another planet, even a milieu which is sufficiently similar that he could make it livable through his own ability, by creating a proper atmosphere with the aid of chemical elements? Already this cannot be categorically excluded with regard to Mars and Venus, although it may be more possible with other planets of more distant solar systems. Such and similar questions show only one aspect of the whole matter, however. Another problem which is no less important is what the cosmos will do with man. What effects will the "open cosmos" have on "Adam's race," on the psycho-physiological and social development of his life, on his conception of values and ideals, on his evaluation of himself, on the understanding of his mission and of the historical cosmic meaning of human existence?

First, as an initial indication of the great importance of the problematic of the "cosmic epic" of the future, as a mythical Cerberus who threatens the rash intruders, stands the fact that even the first and then each subsequent, in principle new, step on other heavenly bodies could threaten the existence of earthly humanity. Each step could bring the confrontation with microbes or similar things which, when carried back to earth, could destroy all life. There could be things so foreign and unusual that "our" nature and civilization would simply not have the proper defences at the right moment; and before they had been created, it could be too late. It could be a phenomenon with which our entire medical science could fail to cope, because none of its specializations would be competent to counter this X-factor in that moment, regardless of medical science's great capacities with regard to antiseptics and prophylaxis. Although this eventuality may not be probable, it is clear that even the possibility of its occurrence must alarm the moral powers of humanity in a new way.

Further consequences result from all of this, however. The most elementary security of the human race demands not only that, in the future, landing on other planets will no longer be an object of competition between two opposed groups of people, but also that, until the landing is really possible, its realization be delayed until a world collegium of scientists of all kinds has most carefully examined the eventualities of the 'flight and return, including the most fantastic and least probable. Otherwise, the first or some subsequent step of man into space could also be the last step of all humanity. For the reasons mentioned here, entry into a foreign natural milieu of other worlds shows itself as a task of an entirely different sort from those of man's first steps into space in the 1960's. Vanity, whatever its cause, could be disastrous here. What would be the use of reaching Venus or Mars if a few years after the return of the first astronauts our planet would be forced to traverse the universe as a lifeless rock or at most a fabulous ant hill?

When we consider the reflection cast by these first tasks of man's cosmic epoch on his morality and the meaning of his existence, it even seems desirable that later, when man's flight to other planets is quite real and possible, after all the dangers of return which have been mentioned are solved, the action should be examined from other viewpoints, from the standpoint of man himself. Humanity ought not to step out into space without being morally prepared for the greatest historical upheaval, for the most demanding task imaginable. A glance at social-political relationships and the total morality profile in the life of the inhabitants of earth, however, reveals that they are extremely weak in this regard and offers little hope that man will ever be in a position to stand so high. From the standpoint of cool reason, the "conquering of the cosmos" is doubtless more nearly a task for a humanity already united. And what is the situation today? Everything seems to indicate that the landing on other planets will be exploited, among other things, as a political trump by competing social-political systems. A warning about this must be given with great seriousness, regardless of the system to which we give our sympathies, the more so because it is precisely for the sake of our common humanity that we have chosen to belong to one system or another. Has it ever been possible, however, to subordinate politicians' ambitions to cool reason? We should not resign ourselves yet. On the contrary, it is possible that precisely a "boundary fatalism" and dangers of the abyss of the scientific-technical achievements and tasks of that period could become the historical factor which would aid in overcoming the centuries-old passions of the politicians, to the abolishing of the political drive (to all humanity's advantage) as a fanatical emotional system of the assertion of the interests of human groups; it might aid, on the other hand, a really scientific leadership of human affairs to come to the fore. The events of recent years even let one see at least the bare possibility for such a hope, though little more.

In such circumstances, one thing is most to be feared: the eventuality that men will not be able to decide to open all the hidden places of all theoretical systems. There is not a single political, sociological, anthropological, or religious theory in the world which must not consider the new facts, especially the facts of such great importance as, for example, not only the first space flights, but also atomic weapons, the rise of cybernetics, the "modern man's" epidemic of psychological and nervous disorders, etc. If humanity perishes, then it will be either in consequence of rash experimentation or, more probably, of conservatism which stifles the readiness to consider critically all possible consequences of experimentation, including the remote possibilities.

It is remarkable and thought-provoking that while humanity is theoretically fully conscious of the tools of disaster created by modern science and technology, the majority still behaves practically as it was taught by centuries-old, firm religious faith; it still behaves as though man's future were guaranteed by some cosmic intelligence and plan. In view of the "open cosmos," it is more than necessary to revise critically all our basic assumptions about the questions involved in being inhabitants of earth, including those which seem to have a purely political character. For example, if in a particular form of the transition in one country or another from the system of private enterprise to the scientific direction of all production, one seeks to persevere dogmatically, one can easily fall into a pernicious faithfulness to one's own *idée fixe* which could be fatal for the reality of the social conflict on our planet and for the destiny of man in general. The lack of willingness "to risk new ways" can, in fact, become the greatest risk of all.

In such a critical self-examination, it is especially necessary from our point of view to establish, quite coolly and without illusions, that man's inner situation in the twentieth century—even when we do not consider today's major or minor purely political difficulties—is more precarious than ever, because there has never before been such a gigantic gap between the effective power of the scientific-technical means at man's disposal and his moral capability. This does not necessarily mean that men are on the average morally "worse" today than ever before. Even if they were generally somewhat better—and where should one get the standards for judgment?—than in the age when man used the bow and arrow and later the sword, this possible moral improvement is certainly much less than the difference between bow and arrow and perhaps muskets, on the one hand, and the modern destructive armaments, on the other. Apocalyptic possibilities of danger result. Those mentioned here may possibly appear too sombre or "fantastic" to many readers; but before they have clearly appeared as "real," before we will be ready to take seriously the problem of "men in space," human problems will no longer exist.

Although it may only develop within the commune of universal humanity, "after all men have become brothers," the history of the epoch of the astronauts can reactivate every phenomenon of common, older human history, because situations arising on other planets could be similar to those of the older, earthly history. If we believe in historical materialism, we can expect that the social conditions of the future epoch will gradually exclude and make antiquated such phenomena as crime, perversion, sadism, mass murder, chauvinism, and race prejudice, because the class antagonisms necessary for the development of such conditions will be abolished. This is valid, however, only for the future social epoch on our planet. We cannot predict all situations which might be presented by the conquest of other planets. Let us not fool ourselves: when these phenomena have appeared once, or better, not only once, in past history, they could develop again. Man is able to do what he has been able to do. The actual development of these phenomena has undoubtedly caused the antagonisms between the classes in society. It is also determined, however, by man's natural position as a creature closely related to beasts of prey. Sadism, cruelties, and mass murder are not only historical matters; in their previous forms they were rather the historical activization of certain natural human tendencies.

Even without consideration of the purely scientific-technical aspects, the problem of landing men on a foreign heavenly body has proved to be a matter which is questionable from so many viewpoints that one can expect even more pessimistic voices and advice to abandon the program and "not run risks." This will not succeed, however, because entry into space is not a simple matter of a player's free consideration whether or not he should take up a course which cannot be exactly foretold. Rather the entry is the result of a definite, relatively independent development of scientific-technical progress. Entry is not only made possible by this progress; in a certain sense it is even *demanded*. In spite of all the unforeseeable risks and sombre possibilities, it is in a quite other sense an act of self-preservation, the most human act possible. It threatens mankind directly with a certain risk of the hastening of its demise, its liquidation. If this entry succeeds, it can become an act of liquidation of the human demise, which could not be avoided in the far distant future if we remained only on the mother planet. The way to other planets can be a leap into the abyss. It will more likely be an act of remarkable self-preservation of mankind, a saving act aboard a sinking ship, an act of "eternalizing" human life. Let us now approach the optimistic prospects of the beginning of the cosmic epoch. These will not be of less far-reaching importance than the reservations already mentioned.

We have mentioned that the atom and the cosmos, which are both so dangerous for the very existence of mankind, were opened up before humanity's historical unification. We have indicated the enormous dangers which could result if "politics"—that is, the politics of yesterday, mistrustful, group-oriented, often even Machiavellian—would seek to saddle astronautics for itself. One only needs to think of the movement towards military use of space, among others! Nevertheless, there are quite real grounds for the hope that entry into space would bring quite different consequences. It is quite possible that even the huge proportion of hidden cosmic dangers and risks could have very positive effects on the mentality of earthly inhabitants, that it would strengthen mankind's critical sense of reality and healthy human understanding, that it might even "humanize" politics. From the standpoint of cosmic goals and human interests, the purely earthly class and other group interests of human nature could appear in a new light and seem less important, even petty. The eventuality of an atomic, bacteriological, or even cosmic death can be considered a greater danger than that of the so-called "East" to the so-called "West," and vice versa. The interest "to be or not to be" could become greater than "to have or not to have." The egotistical class interests which have maintained their position in many corners of our planet right up to the beginning of the cosmic epoch must show a willingness to submit social matters to scientific direction as a result of this breaking in of the cosmic problematic on the human mentality. They must no longer stand in the way of destiny. The "revolution" of the atomic age must take other forms than the revolution of the age of the barricades. The perspective of the classless society must no longer lead to reciprocal acts of violence in the cosmic epoch.

The beginning of the cosmic epoch surely awakens in men the conviction that our beautiful blue planet (Valentina Tiereschkow) is a kind of "homeland of mankind." When we shall use it as the starting point for extremely dangerous expeditions, we shall thereby discover that the "journey home" is appreciated with even greater tenderness, and therefore should be all the more concerned to bring about unity "at home." Regardless of his philosophical, religious, or political position, every man capable of judgment must admit that in view of the task of, let us say, colonizing Venus or Mars, or even of the confrontation with beings from foreign solar systems, it is quite absurd that his own home planet should become a battleground. It is absurd that the proud and powerful "conquerors of the cosmos" should behave insanely in their own homeland, should shoot each other at every confrontation, should burn out each other's cities, should seek to exterminate themselves. Therefore, with good reason one can expect that this diversion of attention to the cosmic problems and the beginning of the cosmic epoch of man's history will help him definitively to humanize this planet and to find a meaning for life for millions here at home. This could ultimately be the most important, perhaps even the only, result of the attempt to open the cosmic epoch of history. And yet this is not really probable, since in our time the cosmic epoch is more than a dream.

After the solution of the difficulties of entry into space, the core of the problematic, "man in space," comes into the foreground of our attention, i.e., the problem of the existence and the activity of men in space. What is man really looking for there? Entry into space is, as we have demonstrated, an enormous scientific-technical problem which places great demands not only on man's ability and intellect, but also on his morality and complex consciousness. Nonetheless, the task is quite clear from a philosophical viewpoint. It is also indisputable that this has to do with a task of a progressive character, i.e., one can construct human talent and mind-set positively on it and can develop constructive and moral human abilities on this basis. If man is able to overcome the hidden dangers of entry into space, a much more complicated philosophical problem enters the picture. The possibility of further "problems of conquest," and therefore the scientific-technical tasks, depends on the solution of this problem. The problem is what mission man has for the distant future time outside his home planet. Again this is a certain variation on our problem of the meaning of human life. In a certain sense, it is a quite new phenomenon, previously unheard of; at the same time, it is a variant of the ancient problem of Ardjunah in the Indian *Bhagavad Gita* and of the biblical prophets.

The following questions arise immediately. Will man's entry into space (we understand "entry" here in the philosophical sense not just as the first achievement, but rather as the centuries or perhaps even millennia of an epoch of expansion) be simply "expedition" or "colonization"? Will the earth always remain man's real "home"? Or is it in a historical sense only a "cradle" of these men who could also settle in other corners of the universe? If we compare the age of the astronauts with the age of overseas discovery, we will surely find many "Antarcticas"; will we also discover new "Americas"? Only one of them, one single habitable foreign planet—or one that could gradually be made habitable through human know-how—would have fantastically revolutionary effects on philosophy and the metaphysics of human existence. Most important, afterwards the presupposition of a time-bound existence of "earthly" men, as it has been presumed by both the religious and the scientific-technical world views, would lose its validity.

Even the first successes in the conquest of space—yes, even those already achieved—place the problem in a quite new light. If human life is not necessarily bound to its "cradle," to the earth, then the law of fate, of the "eternal return," would no longer be necessarily valid, because mankind, or at least a part, could even survive the destruction of the earth itself. The inexorable laws of time will also be valid for the planet which would become the "second home" of humanity, but even these need not bind man with fateful necessity. When men have adopted even the principles of movement in space and of successive settlement, when they have found a second place of refuge, they will later discover still others. The destruction of these further heavenly bodies would not have to come at the same time, i.e., if it should be possible to reach other solar systems; and because of this the temporally "unlimited" existence of mankind is theoretically possible. Even though such an "eternity" (whether cosmic or religious) is beyond our imagination, it is none the less thinkable and capable of eliminating at least those depressing elements of our world view, which up to now have seemed most inevitable and which threatened to destroy everything, the sadness of the fated future decline of man and all human values. "The decline of man" still remains a very real possibility, a much more probable eventuality; nevertheless, it ceases to be an unavoidable necessity of fate, and this has far-reaching consequences for the activity, morality, and perspectives of optimism and humanism.

Great, even fantastic, perspectives are thus opened to materialistic philosophy. (These are not only a sort of vision; rather they are something really possible, actually quite simple.) The most fantastic ideas of the mystics and the philosophers of religion are poor by comparison. It opens up for materialistic philosophy that area best characterized by the following biblical texts: "Eye hath not seen, nor ear heard . . ." "I saw a new heaven and a new earth. . ." If the cosmos is, in the final analysis, of one and the same material structure, which is materialism's fundamental assumption; if the laws of nature can be mastered by man, then man's penetration of the cosmos opens real prospects of a genuine conquest of space in the sense of man's mastery of the cosmic law. Practically it will undoubtedly have to do with only a small part of the universe. Theoretically, however, there are no longer any places in the cosmos which one can declare with absolute certainty to be unreachable, and therefore unexplorable or unconquerable through human knowledge.

Even if some galaxies travel away from us at an inconceivable speed for millions of years, there is no reason why they must be considered once for all as bright, but vanishing points in the sky. At the moment we cannot say anything definitive about their paths (they may move in circular orbits and "return" some time). We can say even less about the speed with which we will one day be able to move through the universe. Furthermore, even the possibility of conquering even a small part of the universe . . . brings quite disruptive factors into our philosophical view of the world and the meaning of human life in it. Such factors are not only pointed towards the future; rather—as the logical reconstruction of the world view in the materialistic spirit itself—they are even pointed back into the past.

From what we established previously, it is clear that it is ideologically irrelevant whether we find nothing more in the immediate universe than dead rocks or, on the other hand, a design, purposefulness, or even traces of a past design and purposeful deeds. Possible striking proofs of purposefulness in another corner of the universe could at most prove that there another "humanity" is achieving or has already achieved successes similar to those that the earthly "race of Adam" only now hopes for. However, even the grand perspectives of science on the occasion of humanity's entry into the cosmic epoch do not justify the ancient hypothesis of God. They can force religion to give up even the last remnants of the "natural" basis of the "super-natural," the "cosmic mysteries."

Another idea from the early history of philosophy now also appears in a new light. This developed at one time as a compromise between religion and materialism, or more precisely, between the belief in an absolute purposefulness of all things in the world and materialism, which was often much too clumsy and considered purposefulness an absolute error. This is the idea of the "demi-urge," i.e., not an absolute being, not a "creator," but a powerful, if not unlimited, "organizer" of a part of the universe. The idea of the "demi-urge" is remarkable for other reasons and in a quite different sense than previously. If we no longer consider purposefulness in opposition to cosmic chance; if we rather consider purposefulness as a kind of boundary occurrence of cosmic "chances"; if the "mastery" and "purposeful" direction of a part of the universe by man (i.e., the idea of the intervention in the processes already taking place on another planet) becomes a real perspective; then man can become—intentionally or unintentionally—a "demi-urge" in the future history of other planets. He can set off there a certain causal chain of biological processes; he can become their first "instigator," the "demi-urge" of another humanity of other times. This is basically realizable even today in that, for example, certain primitive forms of life are sent to other heavenly bodies. Another consequence, however, which materialism cannot exclude would be the possibility that similar acts have already taken place repeatedly in the universe, specifically in regard to our earth during the genesis and evolution of life on this planet.

Man goes into space not only to find mineral and energy reserves, not only to discover there something quite unexpected and fantastic. Primarily he goes in order to understand himself at last, in order to be able to solve definitively the greatest riddle of his own "human" nature and history through the comparison with other worlds and perhaps also with other beings. The question is: What am I really? What is man?

If it should be possible for a rational being—whether earthly man himself, a being similar to him, or a *homunculus*, an offspring of the human race, a long-term gamma-variant of life, or some "coalition" of similar beings from various planets—to master the universe, perhaps even to guide rationally the movement of heavenly bodies by utilizing the laws which govern them; if such a being learns all natural laws and knows how to control them; will it still be man? Would not the role of this being in the universe resemble more closely the religious idea of God? After the "conquest of space" and after the "fulfilment of history," will not man become God? Not at all! This perfect being which would control the universe is not all-powerful. It is distinguished from the idea of God in two ways. While it can organize the universe out of free will or make chaos out of the ordered cosmos, it cannot destroy the universe; it cannot annihilate the basic material and its internal order. On the contrary, however, it can—and this is a kind of "freedom" of this being as compared with God—it can destroy itself whenever it wishes; it can make chaos out of the elementary order of its own component parts.

For man who is still "imperfect," who is just beginning to "conquer" space, there are always tasks with which he grows, with which he develops himself positively, with which he can find a feeling of satisfaction and happiness. If he should absolutely fulfil the task of conquering space, if he should introduce anti-entropic processes into the whole universe, and if man or his successor were to behave sovereignly towards the galaxies like a billiard player towards the balls, then suicide would be his only specifically "human" possibility. If he were completely to master space, so that no tasks would remain for man, he would have to make it possible for the battle for order to begin again by arbitrarily introducing chaos. The "race of gods" would have to retire so that the "race of men" could begin anew to concern themselves with something.

Happily there is no danger that the universe could be "absolutely" conquered; that because of the "solution" of all problems there would be no problems left to tackle. To the anthropological aspect of the search for the meaning of human life, it makes no difference whether the universe is "open" or "closed." The only important thing is that practically it is "endless" for us, i.e., that it is so enormous and so varied in its offerings that it is actually inexhaustible for us. Only this is a guarantee for the real possibility of an "immortality" of the human race, which we mentioned before, for the possibility of a battle for happiness by each subsequent human generation. The foundation can always be offered by the program of the further conquest of space, which would destroy a "realizing" of the conquest. If man could assume in space the role of a "god," i.e., of an absolute master of all natural laws and phenomena, he would no longer know what to do with himstlf, just as the highly developed human understanding has never known what to do either with the idea of God or with the speculation about the content and functional meaning of an "absolutely perfect being."

The absolute man would be "inhuman," just as the "absolute being" melts into "non-being." The "master-role" of men in space—as well as here on earth—has meaning only as an ideal. It is one of the means for fulfilling the concrete battle of concrete men for the meaning of human life. But "absolute divinity" cannot be the purpose in life of a concrete being. Mankind would then no longer have a purpose! It would lose its own poverty and paradise. It would be poorer because of its attempt as a Prometheus to rise above the abyss to the stars, from temporality to eternity, from meaninglessness to the meaning of existence in the universe.

Paul Tillich

The Effects of Space Exploration on Man's
Condition and Stature

The subject under discussion has two sides; the one is the effect
of space exploration on man as such, and the other is its effect on man's
view of himself; the first requires more a report about man's condition,
the second more a valuation of man's stature in consequence of the space
exploration. But this distinction cannot be maintained when one goes into
the concrete problems which have arisen as an effect of space research
and space travel. A decisive part of man's condition, as it is caused by his
penetration into space beyond the gravitation of the earth, is his self-
evaluation on the basis of this achievement. On the other hand, its conflicting evaluations are brought out by the contrast of the negative and
positive effects of space exploration on the human condition. Therefore I
intend to deal with the problems of our subject without any sharp
demarcation between the effects of space exploration on the situation of
man, and on his view of himself.

Historical Precedents

The present situation is the result of many steps made by
Western man since the Renaissance. It would be unrealistic and would
prevent an adequate answer if the last step, however important and
unique it is, were considered in isolation from the previous steps. Many
effects, both on man himself and his view of himself, appeared long ago;
and it leads to a distortion of facts and valuations, if contemporaneous

Paul Tillich was a philosopher-theologian who before his death in 1966 was
a professor at the University of Chicago.

writers overemphasize the uniqueness of the present achievement in comparison with what has been done and thought before in the series of steps which have made the present one possible.

The Renaissance is not the rebirth of the ancient traditions as the term is often misunderstood, but it is the rebirth of Western society in all respects, religious, cultural and political with the help of the ancient sources of the Mediterranean civilization. In this process the traditions were transformed in many respects, due to the Christian background of the Renaissance. One of the most important transformations is the turn from the Greek contemplative and the medieval self-transcending ideals of life to the active, world-controlling and world-shaping ideal. This implied a high valuation of technical sciences and the beginning of that fertile interaction between pure and applied sciences which immensely contributed—and is still doing so—to the fast development of both of them. There was little of this interaction in Greece, the late ancient world and the Middle Ages; it was something new, not a repetition, but a rebirth. One may express the situation in three geometrical symbols, the circle for the fulfilment of life within the cosmos and its potentialities—as found in classic Greece; the vertical or the striving of life toward what transcends the cosmos, namely the transcendent One, the ultimate in being and meaning—as found in late antiquity and in the Middle Ages; the horizontal or the trend toward the control and transformation of the cosmos in the service of God or man—as found in the period since the Renaissance, Reformation and Enlightenment. The "discovery of the horizontal" is the first step in a development in which space exploration is the preliminary last step. Both are victories of the horizontal over the circular and the vertical line.

The transition from the vertical to the horizontal line in the determination of the "telos," the inner aim of human existence, was greatly helped by the astronomy of the Renaissance and the related "utopian" literature. The Copernican astronomy had thrown the earth out of the center of the universe—the least divine of all places—and elevated it to the dignity of a star amongst other stars. About the same time a highly influential philosopher, Nicholas of Cusa, taught the immanence of the infinite within the finite, e.g., in earth and man. This raised the significance of everything in the world by making it an expression of the divine life and it gave impetus to the expectations of a fulfilment of history on this planet. The "utopian" literature shows visions of a future which unites religious, political, economic and technical elements. This again raised the importance of technology in relation to the pure sciences far above what it was in Greece and the intermediary periods. Typical for this situation is Leonardo da Vinci who combined the anticipation of the ideal in his paintings with empirical studies of natural phenomena and with technical experiments—in which, just as today, techniques of war played a great role.

In the seventeenth century the realization of the problems, implied in these beginnings of the modern period of Western history, increased and found a characteristic expression in Pascal's confrontation of man's smallness with his greatness. He experienced with many of his contemporaries the shock of man's smallness in view of the universe of recent astronomy. At the same time, he experienced in his own work as mathematician and physicist the power of the human mind to penetrate into the calculable structures of nature, his greatness even in face of the quantitative vastness of the universe. In Pascal many problems of man's present self-interpretation are anticipated. The human predicament in its contradictory character is shown just as we see it today. And he also asked the question which is highly relevant for our problem: What has become, under the control of the horizontal line, of the vertical one, the line toward what transcends the cosmos? He answered with his famous words which contrast the "God of Abraham, Isaac and Jacob" with the "god of the philosophers." He himself was struggling to save the dimension of the ultimate, which transcends the greatness as well as the smallness of man. He did it for himself, but the development followed the horizontal line in the eighteenth-century belief in human progress; in the nineteenth-century belief in universal evolution; in the ideologies supporting the industrial, social and political revolutions of the three last centuries. There were always theological, mystical, romanticist and classicist attempts to recover the vertical line or to return to the circular world view of classical Greece. But the drive towards that which lies ahead proved to be stronger than the longing back to a world in which it is more important to look at the eternal essences of the cosmos than to anticipate a future to be created by man.

One of the shocks connected with the removal of man and his earth from the cosmic center was basically theological. Since the Biblical literature as well as its interpretation in fifteen hundred years of church history was based on a world view in which the earth was in the center of the universe, and human history the ultimate aim of the creation of the earth, and the Christ the center of human history—an urgent question arose: What about the position of man in the providential acting of God, what about the cosmic significance of the Christ in the universe as a whole? Does not the moving of the earth out of the center undercut both the central significance of man and the cosmic significance of the Christ? Is not the whole "drama of salvation" reduced to a series of events, happening on a small planet at a particular time without universal significance?

With these problems, already alive in the Western world, the age of space exploration started.

The Emotional Reaction to Space Exploration

The first reaction to the break through the gravitational field of the earth was naturally astonishment, admiration, pride, increased by the national pride of those who achieved the breakthrough, diminished but not annihilated by the feeling of national humiliation of those who could have achieved it but did not. Yet there was almost no exception to a feeling of astonishment about man's potentialities, hidden up to then, but now revealed: Man is not only able to explore transterrestrial space, he is also able to change the astronomical picture by adding something to what was given to him by nature. Admiration was particularly directed to the theoretical and technical intelligence of those who were responsible for the successful penetration of the earthly sphere, and to the moral courage of those who risked their life in actualizing what was a human potentiality and had now become real. A consequence of this admiration was the status of heroic pioneers, given to the astronauts, even to those in the enemy camp, and of bearers of esoteric wisdom, unattainable for most human beings, given to the atomic scientists. The emotional power of these reactions is very strong and not without important sociological effects. They became symbols, and thus decisive for the formation of a new ideal of human existence. The image of the man who looks down at the earth, not from heaven, but from a cosmic sphere above the earth became an object of identification and psychological elevation to innumerable people.

The same image unlocked streams of imagination about encounters inside and outside the gravitational field of the earth with nonearthly, though not heavenly (or hellish) beings. The largeness of the literature of scientific fiction, often done as a sideline by scientists themselves, preceded as well as followed the actual progress of space exploration. But it reached its full extension only after actual achievements in this direction had been attained. Its real importance is not the occasional anticipation of scientific or technical discoveries, but it is the fulfillment of the desire of man to transcend the realm of earth-bound experiences, at least in imagination. The so-called "Gothic" novel did this with the help of supranatural divine and demonic interferences in the natural processes of life, the spiritualistic novel did it through the ambiguity of psychic phenomena which appeared as neither unambiguously natural or unambiguously supranatural. Science-fiction, especially if connected with space exploration, transcends the bondage to the earth by imagining encounters with natural but transterrestrial beings. Mythological as well as psychic supranaturalism are replaced by a transterrestrial naturalism: the earth is transcended, not through something qualitatively other, but through a strange section of something qualitatively the same—the natural universe.

At this point an observation can be made which should have some restraining effect on the drive toward earth-transcending imaginations (whether they are called experiences or mere phantasy): the content of these imaginations is always a combination of elements taken from earthly experience. The "beings" whose pictures are given are either glorified (angels and heavenly saints), or vilified duplications of the human figure (demons and inmates of hell), or they are combinations of elements by which the human figure is disfigured, as in scientific fiction. This shows a definitive limit on man's possibility of escaping the bondage to his earth even in imagination. The imagined worlds are construed with parts or elements of earthly experiences, even if these experiences are religious or artistic.

The last remark leads to another basically negative group of emotional reactions to space exploration. It has somehow concretely raised man's awareness of the immensity of the universe and the spatial distances in it. Just the experience of bridging some of these distances and consequently imagining the bridging of more of them have increased the sensitivity to the actual remoteness of even the nearest solar system beyond our own. The dizziness felt by people at Pascal's time facing the empty spaces between the stars has been increased in a period in which man has pushed not only cognitively but also bodily into these spaces. His anxiety of lostness in a small corner of the universe, which has balanced pride in his controlling power since the time of the eighth Psalm, has grown with the growth of the controlling power. One of the reasons for this anxiety is the loss of the ultimate transcendent above the greatness and the smallness of man—the answer to the question of man's predicament by the Psalm as well as by Pascal. The other, more particular reason, unknown to both of them, is the fact that man can use his controlling power for self-destruction, not only of parts of mankind, but of all of it. The intimate relation of space exploration to preparation for war has thrown a deep shadow over the emotionally positive reaction to space exploration. And this shadow will not recede as long as production of weapons and space exploration are tied up with each other.

Spiritual Consequences of Space Exploration

In describing the emotional effects of space exploration and its scientific precedents we have avoided value judgments except in an implicit way. It is, however, necessary to make them explicit and to discuss some ethical problems connected with our subject.

One of the results of the flight into space and the possibility of looking down at the earth is a kind of estrangement between man and earth, an "objectification" of the earth for man, the depriving "her" of her "motherly" character, her power of giving birth, of nourishing, of embracing, of keeping for herself, of calling back to herself. She becomes a large, material body to be looked at and considered as totally calculable. The process of demythologizing the earth which started with the early philosophers and was continued ever since in the Western world has been radicalized as never before. It is too early to realize fully the spiritual consequences of this step.

The same is true of another radicalization: the flight into transterrestrial space is the greatest triumph of the horizontal line over the vertical. We have gone forward in directions which are practically limitless while the farthest distances on earth are restricted to a half-circle which, if continued, leads in a full circle back to the beginning. However, this triumph of the horizontal raises serious spiritual problems, which all come down to the basic question: "For what?" Long before the break through the gravitational field of the earth the question "for what?" had been asked with increasing seriousness and concern. It had been asked in connection with the endless production of means: machines, tools, gadgets! It had been asked in connection with the question of the meaning of life; and it had been asked whenever the ways of modern civilization in technology and business were subjected to prophetic criticism, be it in religious or in secular terms. If the question is now asked in connection with space exploration, it becomes more abstract and more urgent than before. For here the horizontal line is almost completely formalized. The aim is to go forward for the sake of going forward, endlessly without a concrete focus. Of course, one could call the desire to learn more about cosmic space and about astronomical bodies in it, a concrete aim. But this is only an accidental aspect. The desire to go ahead whatever may be encountered gives the real impetus. But just as the *exclusive* surrender to the vertical line (in scepticism) leads to the impossibility of expressing anything and acting in any direction, so also the *exclusive* surrender to the horizontal line (in what one could call "forwardism") leads to the loss of any meaningful content and to complete emptiness. The symptoms of this emptiness are already conspicuously among us in the form of indifference, cynicism and despair. And space exploration is not the means of healing it, but it may become a factor in deepening it after the first enthusiasm has evaporated and the pride in man's almost divine power (Ps. 8) has receded.

These spiritual dangers, however, should never lead to a decision to give up either the production of technical tools or the attempts to penetrate into the outer-terrestrial spaces (as the danger of radical mysticism should not lead to a rejection of the mystical element in every religious experience). For danger is not a reason to prevent life from actualizing its potentialities.

This leads to another problem, connected indirectly with our subject, the problem of the responsibility of the scientist for dangerous possibilities implied in his discoveries. The problem is as old as scholarly thought and was for millennia a source of conflict between the priestly guardians of the holy and the prophetic or philosophical critics of the traditional beliefs. Even if the sociological, political and economic causes of such conflicts are taken into account, a genuine, tragic element remains: The priest is aware of the catastrophic consequences which criticism of holy traditions can have on the spirit of many people. But neither the prophet nor the philosopher can resign from his vocation to fight for justice and truth, even if sacred beliefs must be destroyed. This is probably the earliest example of the conflict between the safety of the given and the risk of the new. The dangers connected with present scientific discoveries do not refer to the "salvation of souls" but to the very existence of mankind. But the problem itself and the tragic implications of any possible solution are the same. And the answer should be the same: Tragic consequences of the discovery and expression of truth are no reason for giving up the attempts to discover and the obligation to express truth. The danger for the soul of the believer should not keep the prophet or the reformer from pronouncing truth in the vertical dimensions; and the danger of destructive consequences from scientific discoveries (including those in social sciences and psychology) should not keep the scientist from searching for and expressing truth in the horizontal dimension. It is bad to try to avoid tragedy if the price is to avoid truth. Therefore, even if space exploration, through its military implications, increases the chances of tragedy, this would not be a reason for stopping it. But such danger would be a powerful motive to balance the horizontal by the vertical line, to receive weapons against ultimate tragedy. In other words: The answer to the tragic implication of the pursuit of the horizontal line is not to break off this pursuit but to continue it under the criteria coming from the vertical line. But, one asks, is this still a possibility? Has not the power of the horizontal drive, especially in its scientific expressions almost cut off the relation to what transcends the universe and its scientific exploration? Has not man's image of himself in all Western religions been made obsolete by the horizontal dynamics of the last five hundred years? And does not space exploration pronounce the last word in this respect?

There is no doubt that science has undercut the cosmic frame within which man has seen himself in Biblical literature and ecclesiastical teaching, namely, as the bearer of the history of salvation for the universe, as the *only* creature in whose nature God could become fully manifest, as he who will experience his own historical end as the end of the universe. Today's astronomy considers the possibility of other religiously meaningful histories in other parts of the universe, with other beings in whom God could have become fully manifest for them, with another beginning and another end, equally separated by a gap of uncounted billions of years as human history is from the beginning and the end of the universe (if such categories can be applied here at all). If space exploration is seen in this context, as the preliminary last step in a long development, one can say that it has changed tremendously the cosmic frame of man's religious self-evaluation. But one must add that it has not changed the divine-human relationship which had been experienced and symbolically expressed within this frame. Therefore one can answer the question, whether the dynamics of the horizontal have cut off the vertical, with a definite No! It is still possible for man to transcend tragedy and break through the horizontal movement with its tragic implications for the vertical and with its power to restrict. This "stature and condition" of man has not changed, although the way of its actualization must be different from that of periods in which the horizontal line had not yet shown its driving power.

Sociological Consequences of Space Exploration

While the question of the right of scientific inquiry to go ahead without considering possibly dangerous consequences was answered affirmatively, another question arises to which an answer must be given. It is the economic question, how much of the income of a nation (or of all nations) should be given to space exploration? A main argument against space exploration is the immense amount of money needed for it which, according to the critics, should be used for more important projects, such as cancer research or study of the best ways of restricting the increase of the world population. In both cases it is the conquest of bodily evils, disease and hunger, to which priority is given. This seems to be natural from the point of view of justice and *agape*. But actually it is neither natural nor was it ever real. *Agape* requires that the individual be always ready to help the sick and the poor in personal encounters as well as in social projects. And justice demands of society and its political representatives the continuous fight against the structures of evil in all its forms. But neither justice nor *agape* prohibits the use of economic power for cultural production. Otherwise no human potentiality, neither scientific nor technical, neither artistic nor ritual, neither educational nor social could ever have been actualized. But they *have* been actualized at a tremendous cost, and in their development they have produced powerful weapons against the structures of evil (mostly without intending to do so).

"Priority of needs" cannot mean that the whole cultural process should not have been started before the most immediate needs, such as conquering hunger and disease, had been satisfied. The term "priority" in the context of our problem is meaningful only in a particular situation. The question is: Which demand on the economic reserves of any social group has priority in this moment? And if a definite preference is established, the next question is: In which proportion shall economic aid be given to the preferred project in relation to other important projects? Finally it must be considered whether the rejection of one project, such as the next phase of space exploration, implies the certainty, or even a real chance, that one of the alternative projects will be accepted by the responsible authorities. It is, for example, highly improbable that the money saved by the stopping of space exploration would become available for cancer research or a restriction of the population explosion. Beyond this, all these considerations would become academic in the moment in which it is manifest that space exploration has military consequences and belongs to the realm of competition with a potential enemy. Then it has priority over against all projects without direct military importance. The decision lies in the hands of those who have knowledge of the relevant factors and the power to balance the different points of view in terms of priorities and on the basis of the actual situation. They cannot be bound by a static hierarchy of priorities. Their only criterion should be the human aim of all political decisions (which certainly transcends national power as well as scientific progress). In this they are subject to the judgment of their conscience, the criticism of their contemporaries and the later judgment of history.

But here a conflict arises which is intensified by the sociological implications of space exploration: It contributes greatly to a general trend in our period, the growth of esoteric groups who through their knowledge and their inventiveness by far surpass what can be reached even by highly learned and productive people, not to speak of the vast majority of human beings. Such elites are esoteric and exclusive, partly through natural selection, partly through public prestige, partly through skillful exercise of their power. An aristocracy of intelligence and will to power has developed in the West as well as in the East and equalized to a considerable degree the two originally opposite social and political systems. Space exploration in the democratic world strengthens the antidemocratic elements, which are present in every democratic structure. There is a tendency in the average citizen, even if he has a high standing in his profession, to consider the decisions relating to the life of the society to which he belongs as a matter of fate on which he has no influence— like the Roman subjects all over the world in the period of the Roman empire, a mood, favorable for the resurgence of religion but unfavorable for the preservation of a living democracy.

It seems strange to raise the question of the consequences of space exploration for the ideal of education. But it is pertinent to the actual situation. If only the most extraordinary mathematical and technical intelligence can reach the top of the hierarchy of space theoreticians, and if only the most extraordinary bodily and psychological fitness can reach the top of the hierarchy of practical space explorers, it is understandable that these two types of man are raised to the place of ideal types according to which every individual should be formed, though in many degrees of approximation. This demand was made in this country most urgently after the success of the first Russian "Sputnik." There was a strong reaction on the part of the humanistically minded educators and also of many students who did not want or were not able to undergo the rigors of the education which would bring them to the top of the new hierarchy.

But the question is not solved by a transitory balance between the two ways of education or by the serious attempts to combine them. The preponderance of the non-humanistic way can hardly be overcome because of the actual structure of modern society and the impact it has on the life of every individual. It drives, often unconsciously, the most gifted and ambitious members of the younger generation into an educational system which guarantees them participation in the higher echelons of the social pyramid. Education cannot resist the solid structure of a social system and its demands on every individual in it. But again, this is no reason for cutting off space exploration or the developments on which it is based. For human nature is not expressed in its full potentialities by the horizontal line. Sooner or later it will revolt against the latter's predominance. And then space exploration will be judged in the light of the meaning of life in all its dimensions.

part three
Call and
Response

9
A Call for Style

The issues examined in this book challenge man to face up to the future or default to an accidental destiny. They challenge religion to speak to modern man in a language he understands. As Samuel Miller affirms, man is a congenital believer, never abandoning faith itself, although often changing the object of his faith. Religion must furnish this will to believe with objects of faith that not only serve the human interests of man but will be as lasting as possible.

One way that religious men demonstrate the character of the object of their own faith is through the exercise of what Edward Farley calls their "piety," the expression of their faith and of their concomitant concern for the world. Farley calls for a new, "radical" piety, one which is truly reflective of the real, modern world, and which truly affects it.

Albert Camus pleads that all men, both the religious and the nonreligious, recognize "that the world needs real dialogue, that falsehood is just as much the opposite of dialogue as is silence, and that the only possible dialogue is the kind between people who remain what they are and speak their minds." The way in which men face and respond to the questions and issues of the world creates that world's style of human relations, and it is Camus' hope that that style will become the style of dialogue.

Samuel H. Miller

Man the Believer

Today the assumption is widespread that believing has fallen on evil days. Modern man has brushed the cobwebs from his mind, cast off ancient illusions, and looks now with honest realism at the world in which he lives. His sophistication is antiseptic, washing everything clean of any superstition or superfluous meaning or religious inference. Science has trained us all to be wary of overtones or exaggerations; we believe only what we can prove—the rest is sheer self-deception. This is the age of unbelief!

There is plenty of evidence to buttress such a position. For a century or more we have heard of the "death of God" in such a chorus of voices philosophical, religious and literary that only a bishop could have made a best seller out of the news—and if God is dead, what is there left for a man to believe? Moreover, the great structure of Christian dogma has fallen into ruin during the past three centuries, having been demolished by the sciences through a series of relentless attacks on all sides until the only hope of the faith is to cast off its mythological garb and assume an existential pose—so if the grand scheme of Christian truth is no longer valid, what is left for believing? And on top of all that, it is

From *Are You Nobody?*, published by John Knox Press. Reprinted from *The Christian Century* (September 23, 1964), by permission.

Before his death in 1968 Samuel Miller was Dean of Harvard Divinity School.

being assumed in many quarters that we have now reached the time
when the church is no longer necessary for religion, inasmuch as the
world has grown up and can read the signs of grace in history without
the supporting counsel of the church—churchless Christianity, it is called,
now a popular movement in Japan but with not a few followers in many
other places. The stage is swept clean, and we are ready for another
act—but what part the believer is to play in it is not plain. He would seem
to belittle more than a quaint anachronism.

That the believer is embarrassed in this modern world is rather
obvious. Both the innocence of ritual and the ritual of innocence have
been lost in the sharp teeth of our hypercritical faculties. We have probed
and penetrated, observed and analyzed, tabulated facts and gathered
data, until it seems that whatever escaped us could be scarcely more than
a shadow, perhaps no more than the shadow of our own hands, but
certainly nothing real. No one has ever put it more simply than did
Freud: If science cannot discover it, it just isn't there!

Certainly the strain on *believing* is heavier than ever before. We
have pushed the structure of relationships further in all directions; we
understand more than ever before; we will not rest content until we can
corner the obscurity, X-ray the darkness and discern the connections. We
are impatient with mystery, skeptical of anything we cannot measure or
isolate. All of which means we do not like questions framed in such a way
as to make it difficult for us to find answers; we turn the questions around
to fit the kind of answers we can find. As for the naive language of space
and power by which we once described God, it leaves us embarrassed
now, yet we find no easy substitute. The radical subtlety of religious
realities puts a new burden on believing.

But these very facts—our clear seeing, our fundamental realism,
our skeptical judgment, our loss of innocence and repudiation of credul-
ity, our mature sophistication and refusal to be taken in—all are the very
factors which make it increasingly impossible to confuse real believing
with its counterfeits. The profoundest belief comes only with the most
sophisticated minds. There is no better example of this than Søren
Kierkegaard, whose penetrating analysis of the inadequacy of Hegelian
rationalism is accompanied by the most passionate believing. Or similarly, the astute genius of a Pascal, whose clear distinctions still provide
us with profound perspectives. Or even better, the example of Christ
Jesus. Here one can only measure the most penetrating skepticism about
the contemporary convictions of his day and the amazing simplicity of a
profound faith. In our day the very factors that seem to have made this an
age of unbelief are those which support the integrity of believing. Believing has been pushed from its false premises to a frontier where the
contrast is stronger and the decision clearer.

If we continue to regard belief as a kind of variable, fluctuating with each age, rising and falling like the tide, the truth is, it seems to me, that we do not understand the situation in regard to man's believing. Believing is as much an integral factor in man as are eating and sleeping. It is intrinsic to his nature. He neither gains nor loses faith; he merely changes the object of it.

Indeed, he believes in the most outrageous things. Under the mixed signs of romanticism and reason he has believed in Utopia, in the French Revolution and in Brook Farm. Believing is as inevitable as breathing. One way or another he believes, negatively or positively; if not in heaven, then in hell; if not in God, then in fate; if not in fate, then in law; if not in law, then in aimless chance.

Under the charismatic Führer he believed in Aryan supremacy and the mass extinction of Jews. He believes in vegetarianism, reincarnation, the existence of people on other planets, ouija boards, infallible scriptures, salvation by psylocorbin drugs, free enterprise. There is little or nothing that man, even modern man in all his supposed sophistication, will not believe. Man is simply an inveterate, incurable, inevitable believer. Sometimes what he believes in makes sense, and at other times it does not. No matter: he must believe. And if not in a reality that reason points to, then in a fantasy which his reason will rationalize. Believing is the act by which he relates himself to history, the act of interpenetration, the act most human whereby he invests himself in the meaning he perceives or imposes on the stream of events which bears him down the stream of time. Nor does he hesitate to "mythologize" science, politics, race or business.

Indeed, utterly wrong, it seems to me, is the traditional notion that man begins his relation to the world and history in reason and that when reason can carry him no further and he still seeks to extend his experience he relies on faith. Believing is prior to reason: it is fundamental to it and sustains it. Man is basically a believer, and only as he is a believer is he a reasoner.

Probably the most radical problem of our time is not so much the effort to demythologize the New Testament as the far-advanced demythologizing of man himself. Those dimensions of his own being which correspond to the nature of myth in the tradition of faith have been held in contempt and have rapidly fallen into atrophy. Other levels of experience have become so favored, the traffic of idea and activity has become so channeled, the energies have been so attracted and expended in special ways that the larger perspectives and magnitudes of thought and sensibility have been evacuated and great stretches of roads and towns, once busy with life, are now empty except for the hollow echoes of ghostly memory.

Another way of saying this is to draw attention to the interesting way in which the center of believing has moved from the focused center of the church to the more generalized area of secular activity in the world. Nowhere is this more intensely and blatantly illustrated than in the sphere of politics. Believing, in its most serious sense, which has been associated traditionally with heresy and orthodoxy, is no longer bitterly contested in the religious realm; heresy and orthodoxy are not sharply discriminated, and they no longer arouse intense anger of fanaticism in the religious community. But in politics they do: tolerance and humor tend to vanish; angry citizens draw up petitions demanding the dismissal of professors who dare to sponsor a candidate of the opposite political party. As for the conflict with communism, there is no limit to either the paranoid suspicion or the fanatic hatred which it has engendered. Believing in the political arena has become the act of absolute judgment, of heresy and orthodoxy, of demonic fears and inquisitional ethics. Read in the light of older events in ages of absolutism, the political trials, confessions and manipulations take on an entirely new aspect—all the symptoms and syndromes are there but under political signs. Believing has become secularized, or politicized. It has its own *mysterium tremendum,* its own numinous aura, its own sanctity and blasphemy.

There is a great mystery in man the believer. He does not so much believe when the way is open and made easy. It is only in the pinches, when life forces him against the wall, when all the odds are against him, when there is no reason at all to believe, that he does believe. He believes when everything is against belief. One is reminded of Camus' remark about the existentialists. "It is strange," he says, "that works like those of Kafka, Kierkegaard, and Chekhov . . . completely oriented toward the Absurd and to consequences—should in the long run lead to that tremendous cry of hope." Call it hope if you will; it is faith, too. It is the cry which evinces man's freedom, his reach beyond despair, his believing—the sign and gesture of a transcendent reality in himself. Man simply cannot submit to the Absurd as the final dimension in reality; his own voice utters a word beyond the Absurd—a word of mystery, to be sure; of dignity always; and in truth the celebration of a joy that reverberates through the silences of sea and sky until creation itself gathers new meaning. Man the believer is the first Adam who discovers in his fall the negative reach of the spirit; man the believer is the second Adam who discovers in Christ the positive reach of the atonement, in which the highest and the lowest, the sublime and the common, the ultimate peace and the deepest suffering are all brought together.

Edward Farley

Requiem for a Lost Piety

The Christian faith is a "life" phenomenon. Something about the Christian faith makes it impossible for it to be excluded from the concrete levels of human decision and attitude. Or, to put it another way, faith cannot help expressing itself, set itself forth in the actual activities and attitudes of the faithful person. Thus it would be accurate to say that to the degree to which a person's concrete life is ordered, effected, oriented by the faith, to that degree he is called religious, devout, spiritual, pious, "Christian." Faith is expressed in voting, relaxing, being married, eating and drinking, attending or not attending committee meetings. Faith tends to put forth patterns of action that affect all levels of the human being: innermost attitudes; external actions, including both creative and novel actions as well as regular habitual actions; responses to things, including critical responses, joyous responses, and angry responses.

Our first reaction to this might be to remember that faith is merely an invisible and inward sort of reality, since it is a gift of God, a response to God, and also a relation to God. We cannot help also remembering that we are told that our "light" should shine before men, that those in the Kingdom are known by their fruits, and that those who claim to love God but who hate their brothers are simply liars. Faith apparently has also an outward and visible aspect. But why?

Why is the Christian faith like this? What is there about the Christian faith that makes it so all-pervasive, so concrete? The answer lies in the nature of faith itself. If faith is a situation of being laid hold of by the good news of Jesus Christ, if faith is the situation of being forgiven

From *Requiem for a Lost Piety*, by Edward Farley. The Westminster Press. Copyright © 1966, W. L. Jenkins. Used with permission of the publisher.

Edward Farley is Associate Professor of Systematic Theology at Pittsburgh Theological Seminary.

by God, we are freed to live before God, not merely in guilt or cynicism, but as his sons. Forgiveness, then, sets us free, but this freedom is freedom not *from* God's Word, but for obedience *to* God's Word. In the questions about what to do and be, faith cannot ignore God's Word.

Faith not only is something that presses into the realm of concrete acts and attitudes. Such acts and attitudes tend to fall into a pattern. In other words, not only the beliefs and doctrines of the Christian faith tend to have a unity, but the interpretation of the gospel as a clue to our being and doing also tends to have a unity. Everyone sees some things as more important than other things in the gospel. Furthermore, we tend to take one thing and make that the basic clue to what it means to live the Christian life. For some, the habits and acts of the Christian life are unified and ordered under prayer; for others, the imitation of Christ and Charles Sheldon's question, "What would Jesus do?" are decisive. For still others, the Christian life means essentially tough-minded, fist-clinched battling in the social and cultural crises of the time.

Such a pattern or unity of our acts and attitudes arises for several reasons. Because the foundation of it all is an interpretation of the gospel, that interpretation itself tends toward a pattern. If, on the one hand, we interpret the gospel as essentially a power or presence that produces certain religious feelings inside us, then our concrete living of the gospel will be a search for whatever produces those feelings. If, on the other hand, we see the gospel as a power working to transform human society, working for justice and human welfare, our concrete acts will reflect a pattern unified by that theme. . . .

Perhaps we are ready now to look again at this word "piety." I am using piety to denote *that which unifies the specific acts and attitudes of the Christian life. A person's piety is a pattern of being and doing that arises out of a specific interpretation of the gospel.* Insofar as several such patterns might conceivably be present in a person's actions, we could speak of several pieties. If a person sees all the attitudes and acts of the Christian as being unified by worship and prayer, his piety would be a *prayer* piety. If the goal is attained by self-denial, discipline, even self-punishment, then it is an *ascetic* piety. Sometimes a whole period of the church has its own "piety," as in the Middle Ages or in Colonial America. Therefore, we speak of an ascetic piety or piety of self-discipline in monastic orders, where life was organized around a personal discipline designed to bring the "flesh" and the passions under control and to order the mind toward God. Closely related would be a *mystical* piety, where life's acts and attitudes are ordered as a means to the vision of God and the contemplation of his presence. Insofar as Roman Catholicism and Protestantism have overall ways of looking at the Christian life that form patterns and unities, we can speak of Roman Catholic piety or Protestant piety. Roman Catholic piety is a sacramental piety where the sacraments, especially the Blessed Sacrament or Eucharist, are channels of grace and power to renew and purify the Christian man constantly.

It should be clear by now that piety in this sense is inevitable to faith. Insofar as faith always exists in the concrete details and acts of human life, and insofar as such are informed at all by the ground of faith, the gospel, there will be some patterns or unities in these acts, and accordingly, pieties. . . .

In its day, Protestant piety played its role, perhaps the central role, as a resource for dealing with the deepest problems of the human being: *consolation* when life falls in; *reconciliation* between individuals (such as man and wife, parents and children, quarreling friends), *reconstruction* of the weakened and distorted, such as emotional collapse, guilt, paralyzing fear; and *re-creation* of new and living perspectives and attitudes on things. . . . The real source and resource of these things, *for Protestant Christians themselves,* is no longer Protestant piety. The resourcefulness of man himself proves to be more efficient and more successful in these matters than the Christian life in the form of Protestant piety. The work of consolation, reconciliation, reconstruction, and re-creation is undertaken enthusiastically by marriage counselors, psychiatrists, artists, social workers, public school teachers, government agencies, the Peace Corps, the Job Corps, the war on poverty, in short, society tapping its own resources for the reconstitution of the human being.

This leaves the Protestant churches caught in an almost impossible dilemma. They can justify their existence by appealing to their otherworldly function, giving up any stake in man's earthly career, concerned only with "pie in the sky by and by." Or they can attempt to compete with society's endeavors, a competition that turns out to be a reproduction and imitation of those endeavors at a small and inefficient level. Or to put the dilemma another way, the church can either become the cultic fringe of the activities of culture, or it can try to become one more agency for human welfare running after society's endeavors crying, "Me too." If the former way is taken, the church and its message tend to be superfluous to the concrete problems of the human being (the griefs and disruptions and helplessness that call for consolation and reconciliation and reconstruction). If the latter way is taken, the church and its message become simply superfluous. That is, since society shows itself more able to deal with these problems through its own agencies of power and wealth, it does not need to duplicate itself in another vast institution such as the church.

However much we dwell on the "otherworldiness" of traditional Protestant piety, we must admit that in its time it did have crucial effects on human society and on human beings. It really did function to console and reconcile and reconstruct. Now it functions primarily as a verbal tradition, providing a way of *talking* about religion and mankind and values. What it does not do is to serve as the concretization of faith, a powerful resource for actual problems, an interpretive guide for decisions that count. In other words it is no longer a living *piety*.

This breakdown of Protestant piety (a concrete and detailed pattern in which faith can express itself) helps explain a great deal about the contemporary church. This is why the hymns make little sense to us and our singing of them is "vain repetition." This is why no clear pattern of "religious training" of children is available. It explains the many in college and seminary whose impulses and intentions are "Christian," but who are deeply stung by a skepticism that leaves them wondering what Christian doctrine and the Christian life are all about. . . .

Because of the collapse of traditional patterns of obedience that gave meaning to the Christian life, contemporary Christendom, like the exiled Jews, must worship the Lord in a "foreign" age and in a "foreign" land. When the Jews were taken to Babylonia, the forms and institutions that formerly gave particularity to their expressions of faith (the Temple and its cultus, the code of laws for national and economic life) were removed. The Jews were not merely exiled from a territory; they were also exiled from a religious pattern of life. In this sense we, too, live in exile. With traditional Protestant piety gone, and pseudo pieties competing for our energies and activities but unable to fill the vacuum, how can we sing the Lord's song in this foreign land?

We differ from the exiled Hebrews especially in one important respect. Our exile is in one sense permanent. We cannot go back to Protestant piety. . . . We cannot return to traditional piety simply because we cannot return to any *one* piety. The many traditions of Christendom (Greek Orthodox, Catholic, Anglican, Calvinist, sect group, African, and Asian) now live before each other in a way that makes it impossible to identify *the* Christian life with any one of them. Christendom has always been comprised of a plurality of traditions. The new feature is that, due to the shrinking of the world and increased ecumenical conversation, these traditions now live before each other and are pushed to acknowledge each other, at least as *Christian* traditions and pieties. . . .

What remains for us who live by the waters of Babylon and who would sing there the Lord's song? Is piety, in every aspect now relativized and dispersed over a pluralism of "styles" of life and "shapes" of parishes, more a matter of taste than necessity? At this point we must make some difficult distinctions. I tried to say in previous chapters that genuine piety is a real expression of Biblical faith. As such it will be an expression of some element in the gospel such as Christian freedom, Christian love, or life in the church. Insofar as every genuine piety is an expression of Biblical faith, it will have certain characteristics. In other words, there is a common, irreducible content and structure in every Christian piety, no matter how different in other respects such pieties are from each other. These common and universal marks of genuine piety should be distinguished from particular historical expressions that will vary from age to age and place to place. Perhaps this distinction is between the indispensable elements in the Christian life and the ever-changing styles or concrete patterns that arise in response to specific situations.

. . . I would submit the following as the minimum conditions and basic marks of Christian piety wherever it is found, whatever its style.

1. *Revelation as the ultimate source of piety.* Christian piety arises as a response to the demand of God, and this means the God of the Christian gospel. God and his own self-disclosure is the root and source of genuine piety. Hence, all methods are excluded that proceed merely according to what is useful, pleasurable, practical, or which limit themselves to analyses of human nature or the world. If such matters are ever included, they must in some way be measured by God's revelation.

2. *Specific and concrete directions for being and doing.* No piety is possible unless revelation provides some actual guidance about what is man's "good," what is appropriate to his individual person and society. This element in Christian ethics is what K. E. Kirk calls the element of codification or formalism, and what Edward LeRoy Long terms the casuistical element. Its traditional symbol is the Torah, or Law. In times past this formalist element has threatened to swallow up almost everything else in the Christian life. The sorts of appeals Roman Catholics have traditionally made to "natural law," and the setting forth in Protestantism of rigid and unchanging moral codes, have produced in our times a strong reaction against the whole formalist element. Some writers seem to suggest that piety can do without this element completely. What we cannot forget, however, is that after the criticisms of the formalist element are all in, after our case has been made for human freedom and creativity, after we have observed the historical relativity of this and that law, principle, and custom, we are still left with something called the *human being.* Furthermore, this human being is not merely a nothing. In spite of Jean-Paul Sartre's claim that there is no "human nature," we must observe that if there are human beings, distinguishable from beetles, clocks, and milk shakes, there will be certain things appropriate to the existence, the betterment, even the "destiny" of human beings. Laws,

codes, and the like are human attempts to portray certain "structures of appropriateness."

Even when such an element is admitted, it does not settle the question of its status, how such might function in Christian ethics, in what way we can legitimately appeal to it. At least this much is clear. Such structures are not simply synonymous with the Word of God. They have a relativity about them to the degree that one can imagine situations in which they must be bypassed. Such a qualification does not, however, eliminate structures of appropriateness from the Christian life, functioning there as guides, clues, summaries of past wisdom, etc.

3. *The condition of radical transformation.* Christian piety does not comprise the totality or the basis of life under the gospel. For Christian piety (the pattern of the Christian life) is itself the expression of a faith which is prior to it and which makes it possible. Many terms give expression to this: The Christian life proceeds from a "new birth." Good works are "fruits" of justification. The pattern or style of living called "Christian piety" is the expression of the forgiven, freed, and transformed person. In other words, the Christian life is not merely a way of being or doing that is put into effect by will power unrelated to the problem of man's fundamental helplessness and slavery to sin. The Christian life is not so much a seeking, a quest, an inquiry, or a discipline as it is a giving-expression-to, an overflowing, a consequence. Hence, joy, praise, and thanksgiving are more adequate descriptions of the direction of piety than resolution, striving, and tension.

4. *The conjunction of a contemporaneous Word and present decision.* Since the Christian life is life under a present demand of a living God, it can never be seen merely as obedience to laws fixed in the past. Hence, the typical question of Christian piety is not, What is in the law or the tradition? Rather, it is, What response must now be made to God as he speaks at the conjunction of past wisdom, the present situation, and my own decision?

5. *The context of a social and historical environment.* The Christian life is always lived in a situation that includes various human communities and environments: the world situation as a whole, the neighborhood, the place of work, the family, the church. Therefore, Christian piety can never be reduced to the individual concern of how I can be pure. Its more typical type of response is: What does so and so need? What response does this situation warrant?

6. *The demand of a rigorous discipline.* The situation of the Christian life makes heavy demands upon human capacities and powers. Living the Christian life means fighting for causes, shrewdly planning and plotting, interpreting the Christian gospel with a minimum of senti-

mentality and self-deception. This means that Christian piety does not occur apart from tough-minded intellectual labor and political-social struggle. In short, it requires some kind of self-discipline. This "rigorist" element is the grain of truth in such themes as self-examination, pilgrimage, and religious exercises. . . .

[These] six elements seem to be so integral to the Christian life that if any one is eliminated, a significant distortion is effected. When radical transformation is alone emphasized, the Christian life becomes a *pietism*, an exclusive concern with warmness of heart and religious emotions. When rigorous discipline is made prominent, the Christian life becomes a mere moralism. When the contemporaneous Word is alone stressed, the Christian life tends to become an idolatry of the contemporary, tending to ignore past wisdom and historical sources of revelation. When specific directions are embraced in isolation, the Christian life tends to generate into a petty legalism. When the present *context* of church, world, and nation rules, the Christian life tends to become a mere imitation of the secular sciences and humanistic wisdom.

Can we say anything else about what it may mean to sing the Lord's song besides stating what are the very general marks of Christian piety? Let me repeat. No one can just invent or propose a piety. Yet one further step seems possible. We can make some more specific derivations from the six elements. If they really are the general elements of the Christian life, we can be more specific in anticipating certain ways that faith will express itself at the level of fundamental attitudes. I would focus on three.

The most prominent fact in the life of the Christian is the fact of the gospel, the claim that the final word about man and the world is not a word of condemnation and despair but a word of grace and hope. The Christian is, of course, aware of evil in a radical and very terrifying sense. Yet he sees evil as taken up in the gospel, not vice versa. This means that the Christian looks upon himself and the world through a particular lens. The world is not only given by God, an expression of God's love and grace; it is still ruled by God and is the object of God's saving concern. It is even the place where God "assumed flesh." Now, these rather abstract-sounding notions are merely attempts on my part to explain a certain basic attitude that Christians have toward this world, their total environment which they have at the hands of God. The deepest and most lasting attitude toward the world is not *resentment* but gratitude. Yet this rather static language still misses the point. Because the Christian sees every event as in some way a servant of God and because he is beginning to be free from mere fear and resentment toward these events, the Christian is constantly "alert" and "sensitive" to the world. He sees the future as a realm of surprises, from which come new events, relationships, enjoyments, and tasks.

The point is not so much that the Christian is seeking *experiences* of the world. That would be the opposite of Christian piety, because the self and its experiences would be the real objects of concern rather than the world. Instead, the Christian delights naïvely, almost childishly, in the way spring came this year (not in his *experience* of it), in the wrinkled face of an old woman in the grocery store, in the complexity and mystery of the new employee. "Delight" is perhaps too strong. It seems to say that the Christian responds to every event with the same tone of feeling, which is, of course, nonsense. "Alertness," "curiosity," "wakefulness," the potential and open reception of these events and persons for what they are—would be a more accurate description of it.

While I have not worked this matter through in the way it might be done in the more complete analyses of Christian ethics, my own suspicion at present is that childlike and wakeful enjoyment and alertness to the world is the most fundamental of various attitudes of Christian self-consciousness. For it seems to be the correlate in self-consciousness (to borrow a term from Schleiermacher) of justification by faith. On the negative side, confident alertness toward the unceasing waves of events that come rolling over us drives out a fearful and anxious reception of those events, so that the dominant relation the human being has to finite things is not that of insecurity toward them and an attempt to secure himself by running away from them, or clinging to some one of them for his protection. On the positive side, grateful alertness faces onto the world of objects and events with what Tillich calls the "courage to be." The condemned, guilty, and fearful man tends also to be the paralyzed man, fearing to perceive and understand the world, fearing to act on it and in it with his whole being. Paul's description of the Christian man marching into the future, decked out with the armor of God, portrays a kind of courage that justification creates. Only when events are embraced courageously can they really be enjoyed. Accordingly, they become not mere threats to man's being but occasions of enjoying, working, understanding, creating; in short, occasions for the praise of God through the total being of man in interaction with the world.

When this is the case, the competition between selfishness and unselfishness is no longer the major issue. Alert and spontaneous enjoyment of the self and the world is not a "moral" category in the sense of an ethical principle, the consequence of a moral effort. Since it is the correlate of justification, human works do not produce it. This does not mean that "alert enjoyment" is amoral, totally beyond laws and principles. Rather, the human being, released partially, at least, from fearful and anxious reactions to the world, spontaneously expresses his true being, which is comprised in part of the structures of appropriateness that pertain to his being. Furthermore, alert enjoyment must be the fundamental source of other patterns and attitudes in the Christian life, for this is what impels, guides, and colors responsible acts, forgiveness, compassionate militance, and all the rest.

The opposite of alert enjoyment of the world is imprisonment in the self, where the only matters the person is alert to are interior matters. This is virtually to be without a world. Charles Williams' *Descent Into Hell* portrays this very phenomenon. The "descent" is really a descent into the self, with the world gradually dropping away. To use more traditional language, a person "sins" against this piety when his typical response to the world is that of boredom, finding that which God gives as his environment merely dull, uninteresting, and superfluous.

A second specific attitude of piety could be anticipated from the first. If the Christian sees his environment, his "world," as given to him by God, he will inevitably sense that it is something for which he is responsible. According to the ancient story, the created environment was given to Adam and Eve as something to enjoy, something "pleasant to the sight and good for food" and also something for which they were responsible, something "to till and keep." This responsibility in the world includes responsibility for one's own person, his body, mind, and capacities. This is an abstract way of specifying the attitude of a responsible and competent taking up of one's tasks in the world. For the Christian sees not only his own gifts and capacities but the opportunities of developing and using them in the world as well as a grace. The primary way to be a Christian carpenter is to be a skillful and competent carpenter. The same holds for housewife, lawyer, or laborer. To put it negatively, whenever all sense of responsible response to the world through competent work is lacking, we have a practical, if not theoretical, atheism. I am not talking at this point about the Horatio Alger "virtue" of labor, hard work, carrying one's load, or getting ahead. I am talking, rather, about an attitude that sees work as a responsible response to the world and a competent use of one's capacities as part of that response. A person may work very hard and still work irresponsibly. . . .

A third specific expression of Christian piety sounds like a contradiction. For want of a better name, I would call it compassionate militance. The kind of world we live in is a world of continually developing problems and challenges that come forth from our natural and social environments. This is further complicated by the fact that ours is a "bent" world, a world marred by malice, ignorance, and a network of evil. It is a world in which simply to capitulate is to turn matters over to "principalities, . . . powers, . . . the world rulers of this present darkness." The

Christian cannot be a Christian (one for whom the most prominent fact is the gospel) in such a situation without constant fighting. What is he fighting for? Not simply for religion or the church. The Christian is fighting wherever and whenever human welfare is at stake. He fights tyranny, prejudice, poverty, superstition, panic, crime, and just plain silliness. He fights in church, in the union, at the office, at the plant, in the professional association, in the bureaucracy, and in the neighborhood. He fights through teaching his children, giving money and withholding money, voting, reading the newspapers, writing letters, working for the party, and attending boring meetings. He fights in humor, shrewdness, anger, and compassionate love. He knows that sometimes he may fight on the wrong sides and in the wrong ways. These are simply the risks he must take, for fight he must. . . .

Albert Camus

The Unbeliever and Christians

Inasmuch as you have been so kind as to invite a man who does not share your convictions to come and answer the very general question that you are raising in these conversations, before telling you what I think unbelievers expect of Christians, I should like first to acknowledge your intellectual generosity by stating a few principles.

First, there is a lay pharisaism in which I shall strive not to indulge. To me a lay pharisee is the person who pretends to believe that Christianity is an easy thing and asks of the Christian, on the basis of an

Reprinted by permission of the publisher from *Resistance, Rebellion, and Death* by Albert Camus. Translated by Justin O'Brien. Copyright © 1960 by Alfred A. Knopf, Inc.

Albert Camus was a leading figure in the postwar French existentialist movement. This selection is part of a statement made at the Dominican Monastery of Latour-Maubourg in 1948.

external view of Christianity, more than he asks of himself. I believe indeed that the Christian has many obligations but that it is not up to the man who rejects them himself to recall their existence to anyone who has already accepted them. If there is anyone who can ask anything of the Christian, it is the Christian himself. The conclusion is that if I allowed myself at the end of this statement to demand of you certain duties, these could only be duties that it is essential to ask of any man today, whether he is or is not a Christian.

Secondly, I wish to declare also that, not feeling that I possess any absolute truth or any message, I shall never start from the supposition that Christian truth is illusory, but merely from the fact that I could not accept it. As an illustration of this position, I am willing to confess this: Three years ago a controversy made me argue against one among you, and not the least formidable. The fever of those years, the painful memory of two or three friends assassinated had given me the courage to do so. Yet I can assure you that, despite some excessive expressions on the part of François Mauriac, I have not ceased meditating on what he said. At the end of this reflection—and in this way I give you my opinion as to the usefulness of the dialogue between believer and unbeliever—I have come to admit to myself, and now to admit publicly here, that for the fundamentals and on the precise point of our controversy François Mauriac got the better of me.

Having said that, it will be easier for me to state my third and last principle. It is simple and obvious. I shall not try to change anything that I think or anything that you think (insofar as I can judge of it) in order to reach a reconciliation that would be agreeable to all. On the contrary, what I feel like telling you today is that the world needs real dialogue, that falsehood is just as much the opposite of dialogue as is silence, and that the only possible dialogue is the kind between people who remain what they are and speak their minds. This is tantamount to saying that the world of today needs Christians who remain Christians. The other day at the Sorbonne, speaking to a Marxist lecturer, a Catholic priest said in public that he too was anticlerical. Well, I don't like priests who are anticlerical any more than philosophies that are ashamed of themselves. Hence I shall not, as far as I am concerned, try to pass myself off as a Christian in your presence. I share with you the same revulsion from evil. But I do not share your hope, and I continue to struggle against this universe in which children suffer and die.

And why shouldn't I say here what I have written elsewhere? For a long time during those frightful years I waited for a great voice to speak up in Rome. I, an unbeliever? Precisely. For I knew that the spirit would be lost if it did not utter a cry of condemnation when faced with force. It seems that that voice did speak up. But I assure you that millions of men like me did not hear it and that at that time believers and unbelievers alike shared a solitude that continued to spread as the days went by and the executioners multiplied.

It has been explained to me since that the condemnation was indeed voiced. But that it was in the style of the encyclicals, which is not at all clear. The condemnation was voiced and it was not understood! Who could fail to feel where the true condemnation lies in this case and to see that this example by itself gives part of the reply, perhaps the whole reply, that you ask of me. What the world expects of Christians is that Christians should speak out, loud and clear, and that they should voice their condemnation in such a way that never a doubt, never the slightest doubt, could rise in the heart of the simplest man. That they should get away from abstraction and confront the blood-stained face history has taken on today. The grouping we need is a grouping of men resolved to speak out clearly and to pay up personally. When a Spanish bishop blesses political executions, he ceases to be a bishop or a Christian or even a man; he is a dog just like the one who, backed by an ideology, orders that execution without doing the dirty work himself. We are still waiting, and I am waiting, for a grouping of all those who refuse to be dogs and are resolved to pay the price that must be paid so that man can be something more than a dog.

And now, what can Christians do for us?

To begin with, give up the empty quarrels, the first of which is the quarrel about pessimism. I believe, for instance, that M. Gabriel Marcel would be well advised to leave alone certain forms of thought that fascinate him and lead him astray. M. Marcel cannot call himself a democrat and at the same time ask for a prohibition of Sartre's play. This is a position that is tiresome for everyone. What M. Marcel wants is to defend absolute values, such as modesty and man's divine truth, when the things that should be defended are the few provisional values that will allow M. Marcel to continue fighting someday, and comfortably, for those absolute values. . . .

By what right, moreover, could a Christian or a Marxist accuse me, for example, of pessimism? I was not the one to invent the misery of the human being or the terrifying formulas of divine malediction. I was not the one to shout *Nemo bonus* or the damnation of unbaptized children. I was not the one who said that man was incapable of saving himself by his own means and that in the depths of his degradation his only hope was in the grace of God. As for the famous Marxist optimism! No one has carried distrust of man further, and ultimately the economic fatalities of this universe seem more terrible than divine whims.

Christians and Communists will tell me that their optimism is based on a longer range, that it is superior to all the rest, and that God or history, according to the individual, is the satisfying end-product of their dialectic. I can indulge in the same reasoning. If Christianity is pessimistic as to man, it is optimistic as to human destiny. Well, I can say that, pessimistic as to human destiny, I am optimistic as to man. And not in the name of a humanism that always seemed to me to fall short, but in the name of an ignorance that tries to negate nothing.

This means that the words "pessimism" and "optimism" need to be clearly defined and that, until we can do so, we must pay attention to what unites us rather than to what separates us.

That, I believe, is all I had to say. We are faced with evil. And, as for me, I feel rather as Augustine did before becoming a Christian when he said: "I tried to find the source of evil and I got nowhere." But it is also true that I, and a few others, know what must be done, if not to reduce evil, at least not to add to it. Perhaps we cannot prevent this world from being a world in which children are tortured. But we can reduce the number of tortured children. And if you don't help us, who else in the world can help us do this?

Between the forces of terror and the forces of dialogue, a great unequal battle has begun. I have nothing but reasonable illusions as to the outcome of that battle. But I believe it must be fought, and I know that certain men at least have resolved to do so. I merely fear that they will occasionally feel somewhat alone, that they are in fact alone, and that after an interval of two thousand years we may see the sacrifice of Socrates repeated several times. The program for the future is either a permanent dialogue or the solemn and significant putting to death of any who have experienced dialogue. After having contributed my reply, the question that I ask Christians is this: "Will Socrates still be alone and is there nothing in him and in your doctrine that urges you to join us?"

It may be, I am well aware, that Christianity will answer negatively. Oh, not by your mouths, I am convinced. But it may be, and this is even more probable, that Christianity will insist on maintaining a compromise or else on giving its condemnations the obscure form of the encyclical. Possibly it will insist on losing once and for all the virtue of revolt and indignation that belonged to it long ago. In that case Christians will live and Christianity will die. In that case the others will in fact pay for the sacrifice. In any case such a future is not within my province to decide, despite all the hope and anguish it awakens in me. I can speak only of what I know. And what I know—which sometimes creates a deep longing in me—is that if Christians made up their minds to it, millions of voices—millions, I say—throughout the world would be added to the appeal of a handful of isolated individuals who, without any sort of affiliation, today intercede almost everywhere and ceaselessly for children and for men.

10
Religious Responses

To the spiritual demands of the modern, revolutionary world, religious men and institutions are attempting an honest and realistic response.

The Roman Catholic Church's most dramatic response came in the form of the creation of the Ecumenical Council. Pope Paul's "The Role of the Church in the Modern World," an excerpt from one of the many documents issued by the Council, exhibits a new and hopeful positive attitude toward secularism. Secularism and the modern attitudes that produced it are no longer to be relentlessly despised by the Church; they are to be examined and understood so that the Church can work for the betterment of man from within the framework of the modern world.

Robert McAfee Brown, an observer at Vatican II and a spokesman for the ecumenical movement, endorses the Council's affirmation of the modern world but warns against uncritical acceptance of that world and against ecclesiastical para-structures that compete with existing societal structures.

For some American Protestants, the idea of a union of churches raises the spectre of centralized, monolithic church government. Some of that fear, however, should be dispelled by the points made by Patrick Rodger and C. Darby Fulton in their debate over organic church union. This debate makes it clear that those interested in closer cooperation between sects shun any suggestion of a church which functions monolithically. Rodger draws attention to the ecumenical emphasis on the word "organic." The ecumenical movement, he asserts, is not working for a contrived union of formal church structures but is seeking to stimulate the natural growth from within of a sense of spiritual union. Fulton replies that creedal and theological differences make any kind of church union presently impossible, but he goes on to make a recommendation perhaps not wholly irreconcilable with Rodger's hopes. Aspire, he urges the church, not for union but for unity: "not 'one church,' but one mind, one spirit, one faith."

Charles Bolton describes a new religious phenomenon related to ecumenicism but going beyond it: "a syncretist movement aiming at the union of all those who believe in God," including both Asians and Africans. Bolton sees the current movement in this direction as an effort by the Vatican to achieve world religious dominion. Whether or not Bolton's assessment of the motives behind the Vatican's interest in non-Christian religions is accurate, the question of the relations between the major religions of the West and the East is an issue in contemporary religion and will have to be dealt with soon by religious men everywhere.

The last selections in this chapter convey the tone and direction of some of the regenerative movements active on the American religious scene. Stephen Rose, criticizing present ecclesiastical structures as wasteful, preoccupied with irrelevant housekeeping chores, and too far removed from the realities of the modern world, proposes a restructuring to create a "grass roots church," dedicated to *local* ecumenicity and equipped to cope with the concrete problems and issues of the real world. Charlotte Bunch, similarly, is dedicated to the reformation and reconstitution of religious institutions to enable them to deal uninhibitedly with the problems of a secularized world. Churchmen may be alarmed by the threat to traditional religious attitudes and methods posed by the views of Rose and Bunch, but alarm must not be allowed to cloud judgment of the possibilities contained in new approaches, for new approaches may hold the key for the future of religion. The style with which men of religion prosecute their faith, whether with vigorous confidence or in frantic fear, may determine the destiny of religion.

Pope Paul VI

The Role of the Church in the Modern World

. . . Coming forth from the eternal Father's love, founded in time by Christ the Redeemer and made one in the Holy Spirit, the Church has a saving and an eschatological purpose which can be fully attained only in the future world. But she is already present in this world, and is composed of men, that is, of members of the earthly city who have a call to form the family of God's children during the present history of the human race, and to keep increasing it until the Lord returns. United on behalf of heavenly values and enriched by them, this family has been "constituted and structured as a society in this world" by Christ, and is equipped "by appropriate means for visible and social union." Thus the Church, at once "a visible association and a spiritual community," goes forward together with humanity and experiences the same earthly lot which the world does. She serves as a leaven and as a kind of soul for human society as it is to be renewed in Christ and transformed into God's family.

That the earthly and the heavenly city penetrate each other is a fact accessible to faith alone; it remains a mystery of human history, which sin will keep in great disarray until the splendor of God's sons is fully revealed. Pursuing the saving purpose which is proper to her, the Church does not only communicate divine life to men but in some way casts the reflected light of that life over the entire earth, most of all by its healing and elevating impact on the dignity of the person, by the way in which it strengthens the seams of human society and imbues the every-day activity of men with a deeper meaning and importance. Thus

Reprinted from *Pastoral Constitution on the Church in the Modern World*, pp. 37–45, Second Vatican Council, December 7, 1965 (National Catholic Welfare Conference: Washington, D.C.). © 1965. By permission of the publisher.

383

through her individual members and her whole community, the Church believes she can contribute greatly toward making the family of man and its history more human.

In addition, the Catholic Church gladly holds in high esteem the things which other Christian Churches and ecclesiastical communities have done or are doing cooperatively by way of achieving the same goal. At the same time, she is convinced that she can be abundantly and variously helped by the world in the matter of preparing the ground for the Gospel. This help she gains from the talents and industry of individuals and from human society as a whole. The Council now sets forth certain general principles for the proper fostering of this mutual exchange and assistance in concerns which are in some way common to the world and the Church.

Modern man is on the road to a more thorough development of his own personality, and to a growing discovery and vindication of his own rights. Since it has been entrusted to the Church to reveal the mystery of God, Who is the ultimate goal of man, she opens up to man at the same time the meaning of his own existence, that is, the innermost truth about himself. The Church truly knows that only God, Whom she serves, meets the deepest longings of the human heart, which is never fully satisfied by what this world has to offer.

She also knows that man is constantly worked upon by God's Spirit, and hence can never be altogether indifferent to the problems of religion. The experience of past ages proves this, as do numerous indications in our own times. For man will always yearn to know, at least in an obscure way, what is the meaning of his life, of his activity, of his death. The very presence of the Church recalls these problems to his mind. But only God, Who created man to His own image and ransomed him from sin, provides a fully adequate answer to these questions, and this He does through what He has revealed in Christ His Son, Who became man. Whoever follows after Christ, the perfect man, becomes himself more of a man. For by His incarnation the Father's Word assumed, and sanctified through His cross and resurrection, the whole of man, body and soul, and through that totality the whole of nature created by God for man's use.

Thanks to this belief, the Church can anchor the dignity of human nature against all tides of opinion, for example those which undervalue the human body or idolize it. By no human law can the personal dignity and liberty of man be so aptly safeguarded as by the Gospel of Christ which has been entrusted to the Church. For this Gospel announces and proclaims the freedom of the sons of God, and repudiates all the bondage which ultimately results from sin (cf. Rom. 8:14–17); it has a sacred reverence for the dignity of conscience and its freedom of choice, constantly advises that all human talents be employed in God's service and men's, and, finally, commends all to the charity of all (cf. Matt. 22:39).

This agrees with the basic law of the Christian dispensation. For though the same God is Saviour and Creator, Lord of human history as well as of salvation history, in the divine arrangement itself, the rightful autonomy of the creature, and particularly of man is not withdrawn, but is rather re-established in its own dignity and strengthened in it.

The Church, therefore, by virtue of the Gospel committed to her, proclaims the rights of man; she acknowledges and greatly esteems the dynamic movements of today by which these rights are everywhere fostered. Yet these movements must be penetrated by the spirit of the Gospel and protected against any kind of false autonomy. For we are tempted to think that our personal rights are fully ensured only when we are exempt from every requirement of divine law. But this way lies not the maintenance of the dignity of the human person, but its annihilation.

The union of the human family is greatly fortified and fulfilled by the unity, founded on Christ, of the family of God's sons.

Christ, to be sure, gave His Church no proper mission in the political, economic or social order. The purpose which He set before her is a religious one. But out of this religious mission itself come a function, a light and an energy which can serve to structure and consolidate the human community according to the divine law. As a matter of fact, when circumstances of time and place produce the need, she can and indeed should initiate activities on behalf of all men, especially those designed for the needy, such as the works of mercy and similar undertakings.

The Church recognizes that worthy elements are found in today's social movements, especially an evolution toward unity, a process of wholesome socialization and of association in civic and economic realms. The promotion of unity belongs to the innermost nature of the Church, for she is, "thanks to her relationship with Christ, a sacramental sign and an instrument of intimate union with God, and of the unity of the whole human race." Thus she shows the world that an authentic union, social and external, results from a union of minds and hearts, namely from that faith and charity by which her own unity is unbreakably rooted in the Holy Spirit. For the force which the Church can inject into the modern society of man consists in that faith and charity put into vital practice, not in any external dominion exercised by merely human means.

Moreover, since in virtue of her mission and nature she is bound to no particular form of human culture, nor to any political, economic or social system, the Church by her very universality can be a very close bond between diverse human communities and nations, provided these trust her and truly acknowledge her right to true freedom in fulfilling her mission. For this reason, the Church admonishes her own sons, but also humanity as a whole, to overcome all strife between nations and races in this family spirit of God's children, and in the same way, to give internal strength to human associations which are just.

Therefore, this Council regards with great respect all the true, good and just elements inherent in the very wide variety of institutions which the human race has established for itself and constantly continues to establish. The Council affirms, moreover, that the Church is willing to assist and promote all these institutions to the extent that such a service depends on her and can be associated with her mission. She has no fiercer desire than that in pursuit of the welfare of all she may be able to develop herself freely under any kind of government which grants recognition to the basic rights of person and family, to the demands of the common good and to the free exercise of her own mission.

This Council exhorts Christians, as citizens of two cities, to strive to discharge their earthly duties conscientiously and in response to the Gospel spirit. They are mistaken who, knowing that we have here no abiding city but seek one which is to come, think that they may therefore shirk their earthly responsibilities. For they are forgetting that by the faith itself they are more obliged than ever to measure up to these duties, each according to his proper vocation. Nor, on the contrary, are they any less wide of the mark who think that religion consists in acts of worship alone and in the discharge of certain moral obligations, and who imagine they can plunge themselves into earthly affairs in such a way as to imply that these are altogether divorced from the religious life. This split between the faith which many profess and their daily lives deserves to be counted among the more serious errors of our age. Long since, the Prophets of the Old Testament fought vehemently against this scandal and even more so did Jesus Christ Himself in the New Testament threaten it with grave punishments. Therefore, let there be no false opposition between professional and social activities on the one part, and religious life on the other. The Christian who neglects his temporal duties, neglects his duties toward his neighbor and even God, and jeopardizes his eternal salvation. Christians should rather rejoice that, following the example of Christ Who worked as an artisan, they are free to exercise all their earthly activities by gathering their humane, domestic, professional, social and technical enterprises into one vital synthesis with religious values, under whose supreme direction all things are harmonized unto God's glory.

Secular duties and activities belong properly although not exclusively to laymen. Therefore acting as citizens in the world, whether individually or socially, they will observe the laws proper to each discipline, and labor to equip themselves with a genuine expertise in their various fields. They will gladly work with men seeking the same goals. Acknowledging the demands of faith and endowed with its force, they will unhesitatingly devise new enterprises, where they are appropriate, and put them into action. Laymen should also know that it is generally the function of their well-formed Christian conscience to see that the divine law is inscribed in the life of the earthly city; from priests they may look for spiritual light and nourishment. Let the layman not imagine that his pastors are always such experts, that to every problem which arises, however complicated, they can readily give him a concrete solution, or even that such is their mission. Rather, enlightened by Christian wisdom and giving close attention to the teaching authority of the Church, let the layman take on his own distinctive role.

Often enough the Christian view of things will itself suggest some specific solution in certain circumstances. Yet it happens rather frequently, and legitimately so, that with equal sincerity some of the faithful will disagree with others on a given matter. Even against the intentions of their proponents, however, solutions proposed on one side or another may be easily confused by many people with the Gospel message. Hence it is necessary for people to remember that no one is allowed in the aforementioned situations to appropriate the Church's authority for his opinion. They should always try to enlighten one another through honest discussion, preserving mutual charity and caring above all for the common good.

Since they have an active role to play in the whole life of the Church, laymen are not only bound to penetrate the world with a Christian spirit, but are also called to be witnesses to Christ in all things in the midst of human society.

Bishops, to whom is assigned the task of ruling the Church of God, should, together with their priests, so preach the news of Christ that all the earthly activities of the faithful will be bathed in the light of the Gospel. All pastors should remember too that by their daily conduct and concern they are revealing the face of the Church to the world, and men will judge the power and truth of the Christian message thereby. By their lives and speech, in union with Religious and their faithful, may they demonstrate that even now the Church, by her presence alone and by all the gifts which she contains, is an unspent fountain of those virtues which the modern world needs the most.

By unremitting study they should fit themselves to do their part in establishing dialogue with the world and with men of all shades of opinion. Above all let them take to heart the words which this Council has spoken: "Since humanity today increasingly moves toward civil, economic and social unity, it is more than ever necessary that priests, with joint concern and energy, and under the guidance of the bishops and the supreme pontiff, erase every cause of division, so that the whole human race may be led to the unity of God's family."

Although by the power of the Holy Spirit the Church will remain the faithful spouse of her Lord and will never cease to be the sign of salvation on earth, still she is very well aware that among her members, both clerical and lay, some have been unfaithful to the Spirit of God during the course of many centuries; in the present age, too, it does not escape the Church how great a distance lies between the message she offers and the human failings of those to whom the Gospel is entrusted. Whatever be the judgment of history on these defects, we ought to be conscious of them, and struggle against them energetically, lest they inflict harm on spread of the Gospel. The Church also realizes that in working out her relationship with the world she always has great need of the ripening which comes with the experience of the centuries. Led by the Holy Spirit, Mother Church unceasingly exhorts her sons "to purify and renew themselves so that the sign of Christ can shine more brightly on the face of the Church."

Just as it is in the world's interest to acknowledge the Church as a historical reality, and to recognize her good influence, so the Church herself knows how richly she has profited by the history and development of humanity.

The experience of past ages, the progress of the sciences, and the treasures hidden in the various forms of human culture, by all of which the nature of man himself is more clearly revealed and new roads to truth are opened, these profit the Church, too. For, from the beginning of her history she has learned to express the message of Christ with the help of the ideas and terminology of various philosophers, and has tried to clarify it with their wisdom, too. Her purpose has been to adapt the Gospel to the grasp of all as well as to the needs of the learned, insofar as such was appropriate. Indeed this accommodated preaching of the revealed Word ought to remain the law of all evangelization. For thus the ability to express Christ's message in its own way is developed in each nation, and at the same time there is fostered a living exchange between the Church and the diverse cultures of people. To promote such exchange, especially in our days, the Church requires the special help of those who live in the world, are versed in different institutions and specialties, and grasp their innermost significance in the eyes of both believers and unbelievers. With the help of the Holy Spirit, it is the task of the entire People of God, especially pastors and theologians, to hear, distinguish and interpret the many voices of our age, and to judge them in the light of the divine Word, so that revealed truth can always be more deeply penetrated, better understood and set forth to greater advantage.

Since the Church has a visible and social structure as a sign of her unity in Christ, she can and ought to be enriched by the development of human social life, not that there is any lack in the constitution given her by Christ, but that she can understand it more penetratingly, express it better, and adjust it more successfully to our times. Moreoever, she gratefully understands that in her community life no less than in her individual sons, she receives a variety of helps from men of every rank and condition, for whoever promotes the human community at the family level, culturally, in its economic, social and political dimensions, both nationally and internationally, such a one, according to God's design, is contributing greatly to the Church as well, to the extent that she depends on things outside herself. Indeed, the Church admits that she has greatly profited and still profits from the antagonism of those who oppose or who persecute her.

While helping the world and receiving many benefits from it, the Church has a single intention: that God's Kingdom may come, and that the salvation of the whole human race may come to pass. For every benefit which the People of God during its earthly pilgrimage can offer to the human family stems from the fact that the Church is "the universal sacrament of salvation," simultaneously manifesting and exercising the mystery of God's love for man.

For God's Word, by Whom all .things were made, was Himself made flesh so that as perfect man He might save all men and sum up all things in Himself. The Lord is the goal of human history, the focal point of the longings of history and of civilization, the center of the human race, the joy of every heart and the answer to all its yearnings. He it is Whom the Father raised from the dead, lifted on high and stationed at His right hand, making Him judge of the living and the dead. Enlivened and united in His Spirit, we journey toward the consummation of human history, one which fully accords with the counsel of God's love: "To reestablish all things in Christ, both those in the heavens and those on the earth" (Eph. 11:10).

The Lord Himself speaks: "Behold I come quickly! And my reward is with me, to render to each one according to his works. I am the Alpha and the Omega, the first and the last, the beginning and the end" (Apoc. 22.12–13).

Robert McAfee Brown

The Church Today—A Response

. . . "The Church in the Modern World" deserves, and will receive, whole volumes of commentary and critique. All that can be offered here is a sampling of reactions by one reader. As a Protestant studies this document, he finds many emphases that encourage him, and with which he can make common cause.

1. Most important is the positive attitude toward "the world" that is in evidence throughout the document. In the past, there has been much Protestant negativism toward the world and the flesh, and until very recently "secularism" was the favorite whipping boy of Catholic apologists—all of which was a denial of the goodness of creation, and much of which leaned perilously close to a kind of Manichean or Gnostic dualism. But "The Church in the Modern World" adopts an affirmative stance from the beginning. To Christians, "nothing genuinely human fails to raise an echo in their hearts" (Art. 1; cf. also Art. 3). "Man is not allowed to despise his bodily life" (Art. 14). "Men are not deterred by the Christian message from building up the world . . ." (Art. 34).

This means, among other things, a willingness on the part of the Church to learn from the world, as well as speak to the world. This may have been even clearer in earlier drafts of the document (cf. the statement, "We should listen to the voice of God . . . in the voice of the times," in the draft debated at session three), but the concern exemplified by that statement is still present in the final document, with its assertion that Christians must "recognize and understand the world in which we live" (Art. 4), and in the importance for them "of scrutinizing the signs of

"A Response," by Robert McAfee Brown, is reprinted from *The Documents of Vatican II*, published by Guild Press, America Press, Association Press, and Herder and Herder, and copyrighted 1966 by The America Press. Used by permission.

Robert McAfee Brown is Professor of Humanities at Stanford University and an observer at Vatican II.

the times and of interpreting them in the light of the gospel" (Art. 4). There are even occasional hints that the Council Fathers have listened to the gospel of Marx as well as the gospel of Mark (cf. Art. 30).

This positive view of the world has the further corollary that all men must work together for the betterment of the human lot. There is, of course, a special opportunity for Christians to work together: "The Catholic Church gladly holds in high esteem the things which other Christian Churches or ecclesial communities have done or are doing cooperatively by way of achieving the same goal" (Art. 40). What begins as statement ends as exhortation: "Wherever it seems appropriate, this activity of Catholics [of collecting and distributing aids] should be carried on in unison with other Christian brothers" (Art. 88 and cf. Art. 90).

The widening circumference of cooperative possibilities is clarified in the closing paragraphs, where various arenas of dialogue and cooperation are delineated:(a) the dialogue within the Church, recognizing lawful diversity, (b) dialogue with "those brothers and communities not yet living with us in full communion," (c) with "all who acknowledge God," (d) with those "who cultivate beautiful qualities of the human spirit, but do not yet acknowledge the Source of these qualities," and finally (e) with "those who oppress the Church and harass her in manifold ways" (Art. 92). This openness extends even to atheists, for "while rejecting atheism, root and branch, the Church sincerely professes that all men, believers and unbelievers alike, ought to work for the rightful betterment of this world in which all alike live" (Art. 21).

Another corollary of this positive attitude is reflected in a new kind of openness. There is a recognition that "new forms of art . . . may be brought into the sanctuary," that the faithful should "blend modern science and its theories and the understanding of the most recent discoveries with Christian morality and doctrine," and that teachers of theology should "try to collaborate with men well-versed in the other sciences" (Art. 62, cf. also Art. 57).

This openness is likewise exemplified by certain things the Council did *not* say. It is significant that despite strong pressures the Council did not use the document as an occasion for another wholesale condemnation of communism. It is strikingly consistent with Pope John's initial concern that the Council not issue condemnations and anathemas, that the present document, rather than engaging in anti-Communist diatribes, seeks ways in which dialogue can be fostered between men of different convictions.

2. Important also are the twin recognitions that the Church, along with all Christians, must bear a large measure of responsibility for the present plight of the world, and that rather than striving to rule in the

affairs of men, the Church must offer herself as a servant to men. The document is free of the kind of "triumphalism" that has often characterized Catholic (and also Protestant) ecclesiasticism. Rather than placing all blame on atheists, for example, for their lack of belief, the document acknowledges that "believers themselves frequently bear some responsibility for this situation" (Art. 19). Since atheism often arises in reaction to deficiencies in the "religious, moral or social life" of believers, the latter "have more than a little to do with the birth of atheism" (Art. 19).

In even more sweeping terms, lack of full fidelity to the gospel on the part of Catholics is acknowledged as an important cause of man's unhappy condition today. "The Church . . . is very well aware that among her members, both clerical and lay, some have been unfaithful to the Spirit of God during the course of many centuries. In the present age, too, it does not escape the Church how great a distance lies between the message she offers and the human failings of those to whom the gospel is entrusted" (Art. 43).

The Church, in seeking to remedy this situation, must offer herself as the servant Church. An early paragraph sets the tone for all that follows: "Inspired by no earthly ambition, the Church seeks but a solitary goal: to carry forward the work of Christ Himself under the lead of the befriending Spirit. And Christ entered this world to give witness to the truth, to rescue and not to sit in judgment, to serve and not to be served" (Art. 3).

The overall principle is given explicit content later in the document. The Church, it is asserted, "does not lodge her hope in privileges conferred by civil authority. Indeed, she stands ready to renounce the exercise of certain legitimately acquired rights, if it becomes clear that their use raises doubt about the sincerity of her witness or that new conditions of life demand some other arrangement" (Art. 76).

3. In the light of the attention focused on religious liberty at Vatican II, the buttressing given to this theme within the present document is encouraging. Because of the "growing awareness of the exalted dignity proper to the human person . . . there must be made available to all men everything necessary for leading a life truly human . . . [including] rightful freedom in matters religious too" (Art. 26). Again, "Respect and love ought to be extended also to those who think or act differently than we do in social, political, and religious matters too" (Art. 28). The specific implications of this are spelled out later on, in a guarantee of "the right of free assembly, of common action, of expressing personal opinions, and of professing a religion both privately and publicly" (Art. 73; cf. also Art. 28, with its echoing of *Pacem in Terris*).

4. The stress put upon lay activity and involvement is also important. While the Vatican Council did not achieve the full emancipa-

tion of the laity, it did register significant theological advances in the Constitution on the Church, some of which were consolidated in the Decree on the Apostolate of the Laity. But "The Church in the Modern World" may actually provide more leverage than the latter document.

If Article 43 seems almost to remove the priest from an active role in the life of the world, it at least opens the way clearly to the laity. There is an explicit denial that the seeking of a heavenly city can discharge from the Christian his responsibility to reshape the earthly one. And in this task, the layman is urged, in a crucial phrase, to "take on his own distinctive role" (Art. 43). It is even pointed out that the pastor's insights may not be distinctive or helpful, and that lay initiative, quite apart from what a pastor may suggest, is to be encouraged.

This gradual emergence of the layman, so much a theme of conciliar speeches and concerns, may turn out to be one of the most important advances registered by Vatican II, and "The Church in the Modern World" will be one of the documents most often cited in making the point.

5. One particular insight about the nature of humanity is worth underscoring. There has often been a tendency for Christians to exalt the individual and his rights in such a way that an individualist understanding of humanity emerges. "The Church in the Modern World," however, is very clear that man *qua* man must be understood in social terms. He is not an individual who becomes social; he is a being whose individuality can be understood only in and through his social relations.

"This social life," the document insists, "is not something added on to man" (Art. 25). For this reason, "Man's social nature makes it evident that the progress of the human person and the advance of society itself hinge on each other" (Art. 25). This is important not merely as an anthropological insight, but for its obvious corollaries in the field of social action; it renders untenable the frequent attempt to describe Christian ethical responsibility in purely individual terms (e.g., "religion and politics don't mix") and underscores the need for corporate human action on a large scale to help large groups of people. The interdependence of all men and societies can thus be stressed, and even the word "socialization," so often suspect in ecclesiastical circles, can be employed positively rather than pejoratively (Art. 25).

6. Space does not permit an extended analysis of the specific problems discussed in Part Two of the document. It should be noted, however, that the best emphases of the "social encyclicals" have been incorporated into the chapter on "Economic and Social Life" (Art. 63–72), and that these Articles are among the best in the entire document.

The reiteration of the rights of collective bargaining, of unionizing and of striking, are set forth unambiguously, and there are passages on the need for land reform that will be helpful to Churches in under-developed areas and parts of the world where feudal attitudes still prevail.

The material on war, while subject to much reworking within the Council, and certainly unsatisfactory to pacifists, does provide some checks on the inordinate use of power. Indeed, the fact that a small group of American bishops felt the document too sweeping in its indictment of nuclear weapons is a left-handed tribute.

It would be a less than responsible critic who simply offered praise. If the document is to be a first rather than a last word, we have an obligation to suggest areas in which further clarification is needed. Again, only a sampling of such suggestions is possible.

1. The most obvious instance of this need is in the material on marriage. The document does register one very important advance, for it goes far beyond the traditional teaching that the procreation and educa-tion of children are the primary ends of marriage. Thanks to the interven-tions of such men as Cardinals Léger and Suenens, the document stresses the importance of conjugal love. Sexual love between men and women is clearly distinguished from "the dispositions of lower forms of life" (Art. 51)—where one has a suspicion it often used to linger in the thought of earlier moral theologians. Pure conjugal love "involves the good of the whole person" (Art. 49). In such statements the lie is given to the notion that sex in marriage is evil, or only a concession to concupiscence, or valid only for procreation.

But it must also be recorded that the section is deliberately ambiguous on the relation of this insight to birth control. At many points the document only reiterates "traditional" teaching, and pessimists (at least Protestant pessimists) will be inclined to read it exclusively in such terms. Actually, in spite of strong efforts to foreclose discussion of birth control, the Council deliberately left the matter open, and thus achieved at least a modest victory. The crucial "footnote 14" (173) of the chapter on marriage not only cites the traditional teaching of *Casti Connubii*, but also cites Paul VI's speech to the papal commission on birth control, noting that a fresh examination of the problem is called for. The Protes-tant commentator cannot underscore too strongly that the matter needs resolution, since not only Roman Catholics are affected by the matter, but other persons as well, for whom the denial of birth control information to non-Catholics desiring to have it constitutes a serious moral as well as social problem.

2. Having registered appreciation for the document's positive approach to the world, a caveat must now be entered. There is a danger that in the laudable desire to affirm the world, the document may affirm it too uncritically.

Although proper in the context in which it is cited, the statement that "the Church knows that her message is in harmony with the most secret desires of the human heart" (Art. 21), illustrates a temptation throughout the document to assume that the gospel crowns the life of natural man, rather than being, as well, a challenge to, and judgment upon, that life. The document minimizes the degree to which the gospel is also a scandal and a stumbling-block, by which men can be offended as well as uplifted. (At a number of the press conferences in Rome, one could detect a desire on the part of defenders of the *schema* to explain controversial portions in such a way that they would not seem "offensive.") The making of common cause with others must not be achieved at the price of blunting the uniqueness and distinctiveness of the Christian message.

In subsequent Catholic reflection upon this problem, then, it can be hoped that the brief references to the relationship of eschatology and ethics (cf. Art. 39) will be further developed. Similarly, although the final version is more realistic about man's sin than were earlier drafts, there needs to be more recognition of the pervasiveness of sin in men and human institutions, so that the hopes raised by the tone of the document will not be unnecessarily dimmed by the hard realities of the world. The ongoing power of evil is a theme to which more attention could have been given. If this be Protestant pessimism, it is at least a pessimism we have learned from Scripture and tradition as well as from the daily newspaper.

3. After urging Catholics to cooperate with all men, the document then suggests "that some agency of the universal Church be set up for the world-wide promotion of justice for the poor and of Christ's kind of love for them. The role of such an organization will be to stimulate the Catholic community to foster progress in needy regions, and social justice on the international scene" (Art. 90). Although the article itself does not clarify precisely what the nature of such an organization would be, post-conciliar discussion has clarified the need for such an organization within the Catholic Church. Just as there are various structures within the Church to implement concern for the liturgy, for ecumenism, and the like, so there is need for a structure that can implement the thrust of the present document, and that can, indeed, go beyond the specifics of the document as new occasions in the future demand new responses from the Church. Without such a structure, there is a danger that the ideas of the document will not easily be translatable into action.

The caveat to be entered is that care must be taken to ensure that the Catholic Church does not in the process develop autonomous structures parallel to, and competing with, already existing structures that are seeking to alleviate poverty, hunger, illiteracy, and other ills of mankind.

The purpose of Article 90 must be to provide structural means of ensuring that Catholics are thrust more clearly into common cooperation with all other men of good will. If the organization proposed can achieve that end, it will represent a notable implementation of the spirit of The Church in the World Today.

While hoping that the ongoing debate will point to further areas needing development and clarification, it must be stressed in conclusion that the document contains so many opportunities for ecumenical social involvement that it will be as important to implement the document's strong points as to improve its weak ones.

Patrick C. Rodger

Organic Church Union: Yes

Few expressions have been more widely misunderstood than "organic union." The phrase has been taken to mean "contrived union" or "union artificially imposed from above." Yet the dictionary definition of the word "organic" is plain: "of the bodily organs, affecting the structure of an organ, having vital organs." Nor do we need to rest our case simply upon etymology, for the New Testament itself gives the fullest interpretation of "organic," in a way that must surely command the obedience and stimulate the action of Christians today. Thus St. Paul, in a famous passage, describes vividly and succinctly his vision of the Church: "Rather, speaking the truth in love, we are to grow up in every way into him who is the head, into Christ, from whom the whole body, joined and

"Organic Church Union: Are Churchmen Ready? Yes" by Patrick C. Rodger. From *Christianity Today* (November 5, 1965), Volume X, No. 3, pages 4, 6, 7, by permission.

Patrick C. Rodger is a priest of the Episcopal Church in Scotland and Executive Secretary of the Faith and Order Department of the World Council of Churches.

knit together by every joint with which it is supplied, when each part is working properly, makes bodily growth and upbuilds itself in love" (Eph. 4:15, 16).

The analogy of the human body takes us so far: growth is something *spontaneous*, "from the inside"—it is not to be forced. And again, growth is a slow and steady process *into* something, into the stature of the full-grown man. But St. Paul's use of his metaphor overflows its analogical use and needs to be taken with the whole of that great epistle of his. For the unity he describes is that appropriate to a spiritual fellowship: a unity in truth and love. The walls of hostility are broken down in Jesus Christ, the old nature is put away, the old incompatibles (Greek-Jew, male-female, black-white) find themselves reconciled by the Cross, and men are "renewed in the spirit of their minds."

No antithesis, then, could be more false to the letter and the spirit of the Scriptures than the common modern antithesis between "spiritual unity" and "organic union." There is no scriptural warrant (and this conviction has been an ecumenical spur to many) for the idea that "spiritual unity" implies indifference to external forms. And much of the present quest for "organic union," which extends over so many continents and churches today, is precisely this: to find the external forms appropriate to the unity of spirit into which the good hand of God has been leading them more and more. This necessarily implies the humdrum (yet often difficult and painful) process of institutional reorganization; but the latter can only be regarded as worthwhile if there is a spiritual imperative underneath. The basic question is: "Is the Church itself a part of the Gospel? And if so, a Church divided, or indifferent to unity? Or a Church *visibly* witnessing to the power of Christ, which alone makes men 'to be of one mind in a house'?"

The origin of the modern expression "organic unity" is hard to trace. The earliest use of it we can discover, referring to the union of churches, is in the Declaration of the South India Church (1907), where the uniting churches declare that they "have determined for the glory of God to unite organically into one body." The phrase was used at the Edinburgh Missionary Conference of 1910, and it is found in an interesting publication of 1912: *Messages of the Men and Religion Movement*, Volume IV, *Christian Unity; Missions* (Association Press, New York). In the report of the Commission on Christian Unity, of which William Jennings Bryan was a member, it was stated that unity, at least in the mission field, should lead to "a virtual union of Protestantism and an organic union of our Protestant denominations" and would involve the adoption of "an ecumenical creed in which all the essential truths of Christianity shall be confessed" (p. 59).

One may trace the development of this concept in the ecumenical movement down to the most recent and perhaps the most celebrated expression of it, the so-called New Delhi Statement on Unity, which was issued from the Third Assembly of the World Council of Churches in 1961:

> We believe that the unity which is both God's will and his gift to his Church is being made visible as all in each place who are baptized into Jesus Christ and confess him as Lord and Saviour are brought by the Holy Spirit into one fully committed fellowship, holding the one apostolic faith, preaching the one Gospel, breaking the one bread, joining in common prayer, and having a corporate life reaching out in witness and service to all and who at the same time are united with the whole Christian fellowship in all places and all ages in such wise that ministry and members are accepted by all, and that all can act and speak together as occasion requires for the tasks to which God calls his people.

One thing immediately strikes us in that statement (to which a remarkably wide range of churchmen, from Orthodox to Salvationists and Friends, subscribed), namely, that it spells out "organic union" very plainly in terms of "all in each place." A question mark is set, not only against ill-feeling or competition between fellow Christians, but also against any form of institutional separation that is accepted as normal or permanent. For if we truly enjoy that spiritual unity which we claim to have as brothers in God's household, where is its visible, nay *local*, manifestation?

At the same time, it is perfectly clear that the New Delhi Statement still leaves open a thousand questions. The way in which "organic union" is to be achieved is still a matter of intense discussion. It could not be otherwise, since the World Council of Churches "cannot and should not be based on any one particular conception of the Church. It does not prejudge the ecclesiological program" (statement by the WCC Central Committee, Toronto, 1950). For if New Delhi revealed a fairly wide consensus on the *marks* of unity, the member churches are still far from agreement on the authentic form of that unity or the conditions which must be fulfilled in order to recover it. It would therefore be truer to say that the WCC creates a climate, or an opening, for the growth of organic union, than that it "promotes" such union, especially if the latter be understood in the sense of "administrative unification." It should be remembered that the New Delhi report explicitly rejects union that would lead to "uniformity in organization, rite or expression," and this rejection of the idea of "a single centralized administrative authority" was reiterated by the WCC Executive Committee at Odessa in 1964.

What, then, of the concept of "organic union" as it affects church union negotiations now in progress? At present there are more than forty separate negotiations, involving churches in six continents. Most of them cross the lines of denominational family and ecclesiastical polity. They seek to bring together Episcopal, Methodist, Presbyterian, and Congregational traditions, and in most cases (as in Nigeria, Ghana, and Ceylon) to create a united church within the framework of a single country. In nearly every scheme of union, it is intended that the united churches shall be in communion with one another and with the denominations from which they sprang—the New Delhi Statement's reference to "a ministry and members . . . accepted by all" is taken with great seriousness. "Organic union" therefore implies unification (often gained by slow and painful degrees) in faith, worship, discipline, and organization—and at least an openness to wider union, under the sign of "one holy catholic and apostolic Church" in which Christians of many different traditions profess their belief.

The very number of such prospective unions poses a question: What will be the relation between all in one place (country or nation) and all in *every* place? Is not the universality of the Church in danger of being swallowed up by a hundred nationalisms and provincialisms? No one can answer this question (though we may observe that this is the very contrary of the oft-discussed danger of "the one super-Church"). Professor Werner Küppers, an Old Catholic theologian, has indicated one line of approach to an answer, which combines the principle of self-government with that of conciliar consultation. He refers in particular to the way in which the various autocephalous (self-governing) Orthodox churches gather periodically in council to discuss matters of faith and practice. May this be the pattern for the "united churches" of the future? Already in the Report of the Second World Conference on Faith and Order, at Edinburgh in 1937, the need for "some permanent organ of conference and counsel" was noted (p. 253). Since that day, the need has begun to be filled in many different ways. Apart from the establishment of the World Council of Churches itself, there have been the assemblies or synods within denominational families (Frankfurt, Helsinki, Toronto, and so on) and the continuing life of such groups as joint missionary societies, national councils of churches, and associations of evangelicals. The overlapping relationships of all these groups raise many problems of ecclesiology, which have hardly yet received systematic study. How are they to be regarded as partners within the one Body of Christ, rather than as competing claimants for the time and loyalty of their members? One thing seems clear, at least: the fellowship which such groups, whether of a worldwide or interconfessional character, have engendered does *not* appear to have destroyed within the churches the desire for "organic union," with full fellowship in Word and Sacrament and full recognition of ministry and members. Rather, it often seems to afford a necessary stage of preparation; for if we do not know one another, how can we love one another?

We have already suggested, as the most powerful motive for seeking "organic union," that the churches cannot witness to the fullness of Christian truth unless they are trying to give visible and ordered expression to their unity in Christ. But the converse is also true: a genuine, as opposed to a spurious, unity. Those who take part in the ecumenical movement have long been accustomed to gibes about the "lowest common denominator" approach—and they ought constantly to assess what truth there may be in such criticisms. But it has been a basic principle of the Faith and Order movement since 1910 that if we have to "give up" parts of Christ's truth in order to unite with one another, such a unity is not worth seeking. "Organic union" grows around the backbone of truth. It is if "we walk in the light, as he is in the light" that we "have fellowship one with another" (I John 1:7). We can also say (though this should hardly be news in the year 1965!) that it is only as we engage in honest and open conversation with one another that we discover how partial has often been our own apprehension of the truth as it is in Christ. There are facets of our own traditions, previously hidden from our eyes by a kind of provincial myopia, that the exigencies of studying "organic union" bring to light. And when we delve into these traditions of ours, again and again we together strike the bedrock of the Tradition of the whole Church, which is Jesus Christ himself, "handed over" to the death of the Cross, "handed down" in the *paradosis* of Christian history and experience.

To sum up:

1. "Organic union," by dictionary definition and by scriptural doctrine, refers to the healthy state of Christ's body, in which human diversities are at once included and reconciled. To use the phrase as a synonym for "institutional amalgamation" argues a poverty-stricken theology, and also fails to take account of the living experience of united, or uniting, churches across the world.

2. "Organic union" has never been promoted by the World Council of Churches or its agencies, in the sense that a single method of unification, based upon a single doctrine of the Church, has been recommended as a panacea. As we have seen, the responsibility for action rests squarely with the churches themselves, in their various national and denominational situations. But such a declaration as the New Delhi Statement presses upon all churches (not excluding the Orthodox or the Roman Catholics) the question: "How does your church today measure up to the stature of Christ's Body, as it is described, for example, in Ephesians 4?" (The same question evidently applies to all councils, federations, or other associations of Christians, which may by some be

regarded as satisfactory alternatives to "organic union." They do not escape the questioning of the New Testament.)

3. "Organic union" cannot afford to be indifferent either to the claims of truth or to the claims of holiness. For it is the Body of Christ that we are discussing, and in that Body *alone* unity, truth, and holiness cohere and give life to the members. Church history plainly indicates that indifference to either of the two latter aspects of the Body can only lead to a unity which, sooner or later, falls apart. This is why ecumenical work is at once so costly and so worthwhile.

C. Darby Fulton
Organic Church Union: No

Most Christians are friendly to the ecumenical ideal in principle. If there could be one church, honoring to Christ, united in faith and fellowship, the fervent hopes of many hearts would be fulfilled.

At the same time, many Christians feel that any outward, structural, or organic "union" that does not rest upon an inner unity of belief and conviction is likely to be a snare. And the posture of this article is that such a unity does not exist today in sufficient measure to give reality to the "one church" idea. Further, any attempt to force an organic union (with majorities coercing minorities) might result in resentment and even open rebellion, with the last state being worse than the first.

It will probably be agreed that the greatest obstacle to union lies in our theological differences—that is, in the area of faith. Here the

"Organic Church Union: Are Churchmen Ready? No!" by C. Darby Fulton. From *Christianity Today* (November 5, 1965), Volume X, No. 3, pp. 5, 7, 8, by permission.

C. Darby Fulton has served as a missionary to Japan and was from 1932 until his retirement in 1961 Executive Secretary of the Board of World Missions of the Presbyterian Church, U.S.

cleavages are wide and deep. The common vocabulary of Christian conversation tends to obscure them, but they are there. Traditional language continues to be used with little change but with widely divergent meanings. It can no longer be assumed that such words as "atonement," "redemption," and "reconciliation" are being employed in their primary and familiar biblical meaning. To one Christian "reconciliation" is a precious word, full of the deepest spiritual meaning, assuring the believer that he is at peace with God, that the estrangement of sin has been ended through the work of Christ, and that he is received into full fellowship with the Heavenly Father. As used by another, the word has little of such content and refers mainly to human relations, the breaking down of those barriers of class, nationality, culture, language, and race that separate men and engender misunderstandings between them. And there is no article of the Christian faith that is not a battleground for conflicting views as irreconcilable as opposites. Is the Bible the authentic and infallible Word of God, or is it a mixture of wisdom and error from which the truth must be separated by careful rational examination? Is the essence of the Gospel soteriology or sociology? And what of the person of Christ, the nature of salvation, the meaning of the Atonement, the life everlasting? In all these, the differences are overwhelming. Such differing views are not nuances of the same position. They are often completely antithetical, so that it strains the meaning of the word "Christian" to include them all in the one category. This is not to say at this point who may be right or wrong. It is rather to remind us of the magnitude of the gulf that separates us and to emphasize the untimeliness of the "one church" idea in the present situation.

To see how vitally the question of church union is related to matters of faith, one need only review the experience of certain communions that have been involved in union negotiations. In case after case, even among churches of the same theological tradition, overtures for union have been defeated on the primary ground of doctrinal divergencies, or of varying trends toward liberalism or conservatism. And even when such mergers have been successfully concluded, they have frequently left behind them dissident minorities large or small that have continued as separate bodies. If this happens with closely related denominations, how much greater the difficulties that must be encountered in any proposal for a single inclusive church!

It is difficult to escape the feeling that the advocates of one church are approaching the matter from the wrong end. One faith must come first; then one church may follow. There can be no genuine unity until the basis for unity is laid. Christian faith is grounded in the Bible. This is the norm. The shocking erosion of faith, so widespread in the Church today, is the sure result when men doubt the Word of God and join the secular confusion. And this sweeps away the very foundation on which any real unity can be built. The parable of our own national life illustrates the point. Our nation is established upon the broad principles of her Constitution, which provides the basis for unity. The Constitution is the contract or agreement by which the citizens of the United States propose to order their lives as a people, and which they are sworn to uphold. Any perversion of the Constitution or any habit of disregarding its clear provisions would threaten the solidarity of the nation, and might lead to confusion and anarchy. Similarly, nothing can more easily destroy the essential fraternity and oneness in the Church than vagueness or disagreement on the cardinal principles of faith. The divisions within Protestantism are in large measure the result of doctrinal aberrations of one kind of another, whether of modernism on the one hand or of narrow obscurantism on the other. The responsibility for this disunity must be laid more at the feet of those who advocate another gospel than at the feet of those who decline to join in a retreat from biblical faith.

Most of the insistent demands for one church come from the side of theological liberalism. Ironically, this very liberalism stands as the greatest single obstacle to union, making the unity effort suspect in the eyes of those who see it as a movement of compromise or of varying shades of unbelief. Thus the question of union itself has been, and continues to be, a chief cause of strife and disunity within many denominations.

Another deterrent to "one church" is the fear of ecclesiastical power. Monopolism, whether in business, government, or religion, easily becomes the instrument of abuse. The totalitarian church is as much to be dreaded as the totalitarian state—possibly more, for the monopolistic church extends its control over the hearts and consciences of men as well as over their political structures and social institutions. Millions of people still remember the lessons of history. They cannot erase easily from their minds the record of era after era, nation after nation, in which the church became the symbol of oppression, exercising dominance over every sphere of life, subjecting even the state to its decrees, ruling the consciences of men, and destroying human freedom. Examples are many, but one will suffice. In Mexico earlier in this century, the "one church" with its totalitarian power owned three-fourths of the land, controlled the banks and the national economy, directed public education, managed elections, and virtually ran the country while it underwent moral and spiritual decline. A revolution was necessary to wrest the nation from ecclesiastical oppression and restore freedom to the people.

Although we do not have one church in our country, the dangers of concentrated power are apparent in trends that have currently made the National Council of Churches a controversial subject in many denominations. Highly significant has been the impression created that the council speaks as the voice of Protestantism. Its pronouncements on almost every conceivable subject, many of which seem only remotely related to the Church's primary spiritual mission and message, have aroused the deep concern of thousands of evangelicals. Anyone who so desires may obtain from the central office of the NCC a list of all pronouncements, statements of policy, and resolutions issued since the council's organization fifteen years ago. A quick glance at these will reveal the alarming extent to which they are weighted with political, economic, and social issues, and how little there is of redemptive, evangelical content. They do not differ materially from the statements of secular organizations that speak in these fields except that they bear a Christian label. Many of them seem tantamount to partisan lobbying, whether so intended or not. There is a persistent emphasis on a largely secularized Christianity that is little more than a baptized humanism, devoid of grace and spiritual power. A preoccupation with social relevance appears to have led to a serious neglect of the Gospel of faith and salvation. To this extent there has been a distortion of the Christian message. It would be tragic indeed if in seeking to make her message relevant to contemporary life the Church lost her relevance to God, to Christ, and to the salvation of men.

It is doubtful whether the National Council of Churches has made any notable contribution to the cause of real Christian unity. If its Division of Overseas Ministries may be taken as an example, it would be difficult to find one significant service that was not already being performed by the former Foreign Missions Conference of North America and other agencies of cooperation before the council came into being. Actually, the formation of the council radically reduced the number of boards and societies engaged in cooperative planning and action in their overseas ministries.

These problems, apparent enough in the case of the National Council, would be greatly intensified if there were one church. The concentration of power within a single organization always presents a temptation to overbearing authority. In the case of the Church, as experience has shown, the power is manifested in the application of pressures through lobbying and manipulation in political and public issues, and in the final suppression of individual conscience and freedom.

As long as there is liberty to exist as distinct ecclesiastical bodies in which we find a congenial spiritual adjustment, to which we can yield our full loyalty and through which we can work in happy cooperation with others of like faith in sister denominations, why should we surrender that privilege? What is to be gained? Are the unions of churches more effective in leading men to Christ? Does the spiritual birthrate rise? Does

Christian liberality flourish when churches. unite? Are consciences free that are forced to bend to compromise? And what reality would there be to an organic union that harbored every kind of creedal and theological disunity? How long could it possibly last?

There is no particular virtue in union itself; everything depends upon the purposes for which the union exists. There can be union in unbelief. Yet some persons seem to feel that to be divided is itself a cardinal sin. They speak of denominations as the "scandal" of Christianity. We are told that the non-Christian world is confused by our many sects, and that this hinders its acceptance of our faith. The point, we believe, has been greatly overplayed. Christianity offers nothing novel in this respect. Every religious system has similar, and even wider, divergencies. The pattern is familiar all over the world.

The real "scandal" is not in the plurality of churches. Rather, it is in the disaffections in faith and doctrine that have made divisions inevitable. Was the Protestant Reformation a mistake? Were Luther, Calvin, Huss, and Zwingli irresponsible dissidents who splintered the Church and doomed it to perpetual division? Or were they courageous voices who challenged the evils of the day and called the Church to remembrance of her true role in the Gospel?

It is not "one church" that we need, but one faith; not union, but true Christian unity. The fact is more important than the form. And it is not something that we can have merely by voting it, or by desiring it. Christian unity is more than the sentimental "togetherness" about which we hear so much today. It is more than a spirit of sanctified camaraderie, more than a cup of coffee between Sunday school and church. It is not just a collegiate exuberance such as we express when we sing, "The more we get together, the happier we will be." It is more than a mood or attitude, more than an outflowing of good will. Christian unity rests on real substance. It has definite and objective content. It derives from certain roots of common loyalty, of common acceptance of truth, and of mutual purpose and commitment. The *koinonia* is not something apart from the *kerygma*. The fellowship is *in the Gospel* and its proclamation.

Here, then, is something to which the Church can aspire—not "one church," but one mind, one spirit, one faith. Let her give herself and all her energies to the fortifying of those foundations of her unity which Paul describes in that magnificent trilogy, "One Lord, one faith, one baptism." If she pursues these goals with all her heart and soul and mind, perhaps that other ideal of "one church" will not always elude her.

Charles A. Bolton

Beyond the Ecumenical: Pan-Deism?

A new phenomenon in religion is becoming more prominent as each year passes. It is a syncretist movement aiming at the union of all those who believe in God. This phenomenon goes far beyond the so-called ecumenical movement, which strives to unify all those who call themselves Christian. Before the Roman church took the ecumenical movement seriously, she generally alluded to it disparagingly as pan-Protestantism. The new movement is blessed by some of the hierarchs of the Roman church as the *pro Deo* (for God) movement.

To promote to the full the objective of this new trend, the Vatican has set up . . . a Secretariat for Non-Christian Religions. This new establishment, which will operate in Rome under the direction of Paolo Cardinal Marella as another arm of the Curia, parallels the Secretariat for Christian Unity.

It is interesting to note in this connection the changing vocabulary of the Vatican. Some recent popes have made much use of the terms *Il Padre Commune* ("The Common Father") and *La Casa del Padre Commune* ("The Father's House"—the Vatican) in their appeals to bring Christians back home. In establishing this new activity, the Pope now describes Rome as the *Patria Commune,* the "Common Fatherland" for all believers. However difficult it may be for Muslims, Buddhists, and Jews to regard Rome as their "common fatherland," the idea is that the new secretariat will make them feel that they now "belong." It seemed as though Paul VI was reaching beyond the history of the papacy and the Roman church to the universality of the old Roman Empire embracing

Reprinted by permission of the publisher from *Christianity Today* (October 23, 1964), Vol. IX, No. 2.

Charles A. Bolton is Professor of Modern Languages at Houghton College, Houghton, New York.

many nations when he said: "By the institution of this organism, no pilgrim will henceforth be a stranger in Rome, where the Church, faithful to her history and her catholic faith, shall always be the 'common fatherland.'"

The activities of the *pro Deo* group, which no doubt paved the way for the new secretariat, seem to have been chiefly confined to organizing international banquets, called *agapes* or love-feasts, thereby changing the character of the meetings of the early Christians, which were certainly closed to non-Christians.

Fraternizing with the East

To those familiar with the history of Roman Catholic missions in recent centuries, the idea of fraternization with oriental religions is not completely new. Throughout the seventeenth century and well into the eighteenth a bitter controversy raged between certain Jesuit missionaries and their opponents about what is sometimes called "Chinese rites." In fact, the desire to transform Catholicism into an oriental cult, though within certain limits, began with the Jesuit missionary De Nobili early in the seventeenth century. He assumed the saffron robe of the monk, observed Brahmanic rites and fasts, and tried to be as much like a Brahman as possible. In China the Jesuit missionaries later attempted to use similar methods in order to make themselves as completely oriental as possible.

Despite fierce opposition, the methods of De Nobili were approved for a time. But all these attempts to "naturalize" Roman missions in the East were finally suppressed by a bull of Pope Benedict XIV, *Omnium Sollicitudinem*, in 1744. After this decree, the Roman missions in the East were destined to become like so many Latin colonies planted on foreign soil. This has often been deplored in modern times, and no doubt the recent Vatican approach may be seen as a return to the "assimilation" attempts of previous centuries.

Evangelicals do not always realize how spiritually satisfying to some Roman Catholic intellectuals is the idea of assimilating and adapting all human cultures—and to some extent all religions—inside one vast theocratic Roman Catholic Church. Karl Adam in his *Spirit of Catholicism* has tried to show how much this is a part of the modern Roman *Weltanschauung*.

An increased impetus in this direction comes from a growing consciousness that the Catholic-Protestant divisions seem to be lessening and that many world cultures are still outside the range of Catholicism, especially of a Catholicism identified with Western culture. Some have begun to ask if African and Asiatic cultures might have something in their philosophy, theology, and mysticism, as well as in the less difficult fields of music and art, that might be included under the name "Catholic." Certain Roman apologists might boldly assert that these cultures "belong" to the Catholic idea.

Teilhard de Chardin, chiefly through his posthumous book, *The Phenomenon of Man*, has become the prophet of a new evolutionary outlook, centering the climax of world development in the formation of a new creation in Christ. This would also imply for some—among them, no doubt, Arnold Toynbee with his synthesis of world history—the idea of a convergence of religions, however repellent this might seem to many.

I first came upon this extension of ecumenism into pan-deism among some Roman Catholic scholars interested primarily in the "reunion of the churches," Roman, Orthodox, Anglican. This was just before Pius XI brought out his encyclical, *Mortalium Animos* (1928), which was seemingly directed against the World Council of Churches and the ecumenical movement generally. These were condemned as "pan-Protestantism." Yet even then a number of Roman scholars had already made public the idea that the Church Catholic is "Jewish, is Moslem, is Buddhist, is Taoist." The idea behind this was the concept of a true catholic or universal order of religion that must be able to include the highest aspirations and achievements of all religions and cultures. It was felt that the same ecumenical spirit that sought to bring together the historically separated Christian churches should be able to reach out to the religions of Asia, of Africa through Islam, and to the Jewish diaspora.

An obvious bond with Jews and Muslims through the Old Testament was recognized. The "Our Father" of the Christian was also the God of the Jews and the Allah of the Muslims. It was explained that to unite with Hindus and Buddhists, Christians should explore the hidden reality—the "ultimate reality," the infinite, the absolute, the everlasting, the all-pervading spirit that marks the religious experience of the Orient. Many felt that Western culture has lost the sense of a living and inspiring presence in intimate religious experience and "knowing," because this is not regarded as something for the ordinary believer but is rather the privilege of an esoteric few, called "mystics." Some religious observers in the Roman church have believed that just as contact with non-Roman churches might have a salutary and broadening influence on many Roman Catholics, so also for people of Western culture, contact with the religious experience of the East might lead to the vitalizing effects of the "inner light" and the "inner presence," which seem so essential a part of the oriental religious outlook.

Surprisingly, some have seriously declared that this universal outreach should include even atheists, on the plea that many so-called atheists are in reality seekers after God in their own perverse way.

What is the Goal?

We may perhaps ask what is the ultimate aim of the Curia in promoting the pan-deist movement. Undoubtedly, certain Roman Catholic thinkers have a sincere desire to promote greater unity and peace in the world. Such thinkers envisage ecumenism as a fulfillment of Christ's prayer, "That they all may be one." Their beliefs and education convince them that unity implies submission to one authority, and this submission is taken to be a divine mandate to include everybody in the one sheepfold of the pope. The same thinkers accept as a natural prerogative Rome's promotion of world unity by any religious means whatever. Thus they do not necessarily discern in Rome's ecumenism and pan-deism a project for world dominion. Yet this danger certainly exists.

Evangelicals should remember that the bull of Pope Boniface VIII, *Unam Sanctam*, still exists and is generally taught as an infallible utterance in Roman seminaries. In this bull the pope proclaimed that to attain salvation every soul must be subject to the Roman pontif. He also promulgated the doctrine of the "two swords"—the spiritual and the temporal—by which he affirmed that the pope as vicar of Christ had supreme power not only in religion but in all things temporal.

Evangelicals should also remember that Paul VI was crowned in June, 1963, with the same symbolical emblem of dominion invented by Boniface VIII, and with the admonition (in Latin): "Remember that thou art the ruler of kings and the father of princes."

And finally, evangelicals should not forget that the basic justification for the world ambitions of the papacy as interpreted by the Curia is still a misinterpretation of Jeremiah 1:10: "See, I have this day set thee over the nations and over the kingdoms, to root out, and to pull down, and to destroy, and to throw down, to build, and to plant."

On August 6, 1964, Paul VI published his first encyclical, *Ecclesiam Suam*. Several passages in this lengthy message confirm all that has been outlined above about Vatican approaches to the great non-Christian religions. The following is the most relevant:

> Then we see another circle around us. This too is vast in its extent, yet it is not too far away from us. It is made up of the men who above all adore the one, supreme God whom we too adore. We refer to the children, worthy of our affection and respect, of the Hebrew people. They are faithful to the religion which we call that of the Old Testament. Then there are the adorers of God according to the conception of monotheism, especially the Moslem religion, deserving of our admiration for all that is true and good in their worship of God. Then there are also the followers of the great Afro-Asian religions. . . .

Stephen C. Rose

The Grass Roots Church

1. DENOMINATION. We [the Editors of Renewal] believe that denominationalism is obsolete, both theologically and in terms of the capacity of denominations to organize the Church in the most effective and obedient manner. We believe that participants in a renewal movement must openly express their willingness to forsake denominational loyalty at every point that such loyalty impedes the ecumenical witness of the Church, particularly at the local and metropolitan level. Denominationalism is theologically obsolete because it denies to all Church members the total theological resources of all the denominations, forcing upon individual Church members an intolerable choice of modes of worship and an equally intolerable allegiance to a fragment of the total Church. The denominations are structurally obsolete because they have turned into national bureaucracies, removed from local situations, which, by their very nature, impede the development of the Church's mission at the local level. We feel that the merger of denominations "at the top" is of value only if there is a radical transformation of the combined denominations to provide resources for local, ecumenical witness. While we appreciate the creative leadership at the top in many denominations, we see this leadership continually thwarted by the institutional demands of denominational self-preservation. Thus we have little hope in renewal movements aimed at restoring the life of individual denominations. Such movements are too easily domesticated. We advocate, as an alternative, the formation of a pan-denominational grass roots organization of all persons, clergy and lay, who wish to fight for the Church structure which we shall propose.

Reprinted from *Renewal*, February 1966 (Chicago Missionary Society, Chicago), by permission of the publisher.

Stephen C. Rose is an editor of *Renewal*.

2. THE THREE FUNCTIONS OF THE CHURCH. We believe that the Church has three tasks: Chaplaincy (the proclamation of the Biblical insight into the human situation); teaching (the integration of this Biblical insight with the realities of the contemporary world); and abandonment (the self-giving of the Church to the world). Chaplaincy refers to the priestly, liturgical, pastoral ministry of the Church. It is the ministry which today's seminaries claim to be preparing ministers to undertake. But the structure of today's Church leaves the clergyman with virtually no time to realize this essential ministry. Teaching has been utterly short-changed by the denominationally-organized Church, despite the massive investment of funds in sometimes creative study materials, and the almost wasteful investment of local congregations in under-staffed and under-utilized educational facilities. The ministry of teaching requires specialized personnel, around-the-week facilities, and recognition by the Church-at-large as one of the Church's three essential tasks. Today the burden of teaching falls on ministers who already have too many responsibilities. The Church in its present structure offers virtually no training to adults. And the moribund quality of the instruction given to youth is partially attested to by the vast numbers of young persons who become disenchanted with the Church as soon as they leave home. The present understanding of the ministry and the present structure of the Church makes a teaching ministry virtually impossible. Abandonment refers primarily to the Church's ministry to the world. It embraces specialized ministries aimed at making urban life more human, involvement of Christians in the social struggle, and the style of life that ought to become the distinguishing mark of individual Christians and the Church as an institution. Today the presently structured Church is so caught up in institutional maintenance that it cannot perform the ministries of teaching and chaplaincy. And, with the current, utterly inefficient emphasis on the denominational local congregation, virtually no funds exist to support specialized ministries of any sort. When a congregation cannot support the ministries of chaplaincy, teaching and abandonment, it is both theologically and structurally irrelevant.

3. GOALS FOR THE RENEWAL MOVEMENT. The renewal movement should draw its theological rationale from St. Paul's missionary methods as outlined particularly in the First Letter To The Corinthians, chapters 12 and 13. Briefly St. Paul advocates that the Church is the Body of Christ. He states that the Body is made up of many parts, each one playing a specific function. In other words, he sees specialization—the division of responsibilities so that each function of the Church can be implemented—as essential to a healthy body. The absurdity of today's structure is revealed by the fact that we have lumped nearly every one of

the tasks that Paul outlines into the job description of the contemporary minister. This has led to a situation in which as many as two-thirds of the students in some seminaries indicate they cannot accept the present definition of the ordained ministry. The restructured Church will be based on a differentiation of function, on a recognition that some are called to preach, some to be prophets, some to be helpers, some to administrate, some to teach.

St. Paul also emphasizes, throughout his writings, that the local Church is the primary expression of the Body of Christ. If the local Church is not equipped properly, then it becomes irrelevant and incomprehensible. We can translate his concern into modern terms by saying that what must take place is a restructuring of the Church at the grass roots.

Another goal of the renewal movement will be the recovery of the total Biblical understanding of the human situation. This means in our day that theology must be freed from the academic confines of the seminary and developed in the context of the active engagement of the Church in the world. In particular this means a recovery of the depths of the Old Testament, which at the dawn of Church history was the worship resource of the Church. God is not to be seen as having retired to some celestial lounging place after the advent of Christ, but rather as the brooding, active, argumentative, cajoling One who reveals Himself in history. Theologically, this means that we must become Jews in spirit before we can become Christians.

4. SPECIFICS. Since today's local denominational congregation can scarcely perform the functions which the Church is called to implement, we must arrive at a totally new understanding of the local congregation, based on a total restructuring of the Church at the local level. Since virtually no single congregation can support all three ministries—chaplaincy, teaching, and abandonment—we suggest the following elements of a new structure. First, local churches must band together to form cooperative ministries. Within a given cooperative ministry a single facility would be used for the ministry of chaplaincy. It would conduct services designed to offer the Church member the full range of Christian worship throughout the week, from the Episcopal liturgy to the silent meetings of the Quakers. Assuming that ten present-day congregations were involved in the cooperative ministry, possibly three facilities which now house congregations would be adapted for the teaching ministry of the restructured Church. They would be staffed by ministers and trained laymen who see their mission as teaching. In particular every neighborhood would have a full-time facility for the training of adult laymen. The remaining buildings would be sold unless they could be easily adapted to

the ministries of abandonment: i.e., direct service to specific unmet needs in the community. (In no case should Church ministries of abandonment repeat what the secular world is already doing. They should aim at the unmet needs.) Each neighborhood would have a full-time center for pastoral counseling.

Theological seminaries would be called to restructure as follows. They would train men and women for specific ministries within the restructured Church. Some would be trained to preach, some to teach, some to counsel. The seminaries would also open their doors to the laity in the following way: The seminaries would agree to support the cooperative ministry concept by offering ten intern-year students and one professor to any cooperative ministry on an annual basis. In return, the given community would send ten laymen to the seminary. This would bridge the chasm which now exists between the seminary and the Church at large. Certain seminaries would be designated as centers of advanced theological study and students inclined toward teaching careers could transfer to these centers if they felt called to do so.

Denominations would be called to restructure in the following manner. The bulk of current denominational expenditures are used for servicing the needs of local denominational congregations. This includes funding new church development projects, producing curriculum at the national level, and the support of local congregations that are unable to support themselves. We believe that all of these functions should be turned over, as much as possible, to the metropolitan and regional structures of the several denominations. This would include the transfer of church extension funds, funds for educational programs, and all other funds now used for the maintenance of local denominational programs. The denominations should, before turning these funds over, elicit an agreement that the local denominational units will use these funds on an ecumenical basis with other local denominational units. The basic principle informing the use of these transferred funds should be the priority of the cooperative ministry concept. We are calling here for the decentralization of approximately 90 per cent of current national programs conducted by denominations. We recommend that the national denominations see themselves in the future as research and development agencies serving the whole ecumenical Church. In particular we urge that endowments and other funds that could not legally be removed from the jurisdiction of national denominations be seen in the future as seed money for creative experimentation in areas that are beyond the purview of the proposed cooperative ministries. Denominations, shorn of many current institutional functions, would be free to concentrate on pilot projects, *ad hoc* experimentation, and on creative ecumenical projects that would still be needed on the national and international level.

The original purpose of denominations was to do what no single congregation could do for itself. Our proposal assumes that functions once carried out by denominations can most fruitfully be returned to the local level. We feel that the future of the denominations lies in experimentation, research and development, and in serving the needs of a Church that would be truly ecumenical at its base.

We feel, in addition, that the distinctive theological contributions of individual denominations will be enhanced, rather than eliminated, in our proposed cooperative ministry structure. The worship of the cooperative ministry, in particular, would provide room for all legitimate traditions, because it would bring all the current resources of the denominations into a central worship facility serving the local neighborhood. We feel strongly that genuine dialogue at the local level is preferable to the creation of a routinized "ecumenical" theology forced upon the local churches from the upper echelons of Protestantism.

Thus our impatience with denominationalism is impatience with its present form and structure. We wish to free denominations for service, not to eliminate them.

Church membership would be redefined. One would become a member of the cooperative ministry and then, from year to year, would elect membership in one of the specialized ministries. Thus membership would refer both to confession of faith and mission in the world. The combining of present Church budgets at the local level would be more than enough to finance the cooperative ministries. Indeed, over half the funds would be available for outreach ministries, such as community organization.

The cooperative ministries would be the basis of the renewed Church. Essentially, the Church would then be organized along viable geographical lines. Since the metropolis is rapidly becoming the primary geographical unit in this country, any "superstructure" needed to support the local ministries or to carry on programs within the total area, would be metropolitan and ecumenical, rather than national and denominational. Thus, we would come to refer to the Church in Chicago; the Church in New York; the Church in Boston, etc.

Within the metropolitan framework and the cooperative ministry structure, the number of ordained ministers needed would diminish by about half. Indeed ordination would be reserved only to those with specific preaching and sacramental responsibilities. Thus as many as half of today's ministers would become laymen and an equal number of future seminary graduates would be laymen. This suggests that, with the emphasis on local and metropolitan training centers, the laity would become the prophetic arm of the Church. Laymen would regard the ministries of chaplaincy and teaching as fundamental resources and the ministry of abandonment as the fundamental expression of their faith in the world.

5. BEGINNING POINTS. . . . Ministers in local areas should meet and publish their own "bill of rights" to indicate that they are no longer content with the job description of the clergymen in the presently structured denominational Church.

Seminary students should consider the possibility of learning a "second skill" so that they will have an alternative to the ministry as it is presently defined, pending basic structural change.

Seminary faculties should initiate concrete debate on the role that seminaries can play in a cooperative, grass-roots renewal movement.

The National Council of Churches should immediately consider means by which it can influence the denominations to decentralize and provide support for the cooperative ministry concept.

Laymen should initiate discussions of the cooperative ministry concept with their ministers.

Associate pastors and assistant pastors in local congregations should be freed of institutional responsibility to work with a special committee of laymen to determine prospects for a cooperative ministry in their area.

6. CONCLUSION. . . . Let our motto for the moment be, "The ecumenical movement must be local; the Body of Christ must incorporate specifically defined functions; and the renewed Church must be as faithful to the Biblical reality that brings it into being as to the world that calls it into service." Above all, let us begin to substitute concrete, positive proposals for the carping and back-biting that characterizes our existence in the outmoded denominational Church structure.

Harold H. Viehman
Charlotte Bunch

The University Christian Movement:
An Exchange of Letters

November 22, 1966

Dear Miss Bunch:

I was among the friends of the University Christian Movement who listened with admiration and thanksgiving . . . you unfolded UCM hopes and plans to the Advisory Council, in the New York meeting on November 9 [1966].

In my responsibility as Secretary of the United Presbyterian Division of Higher Education, I recognize three responsibilities: (1) to attempt to understand the UCM and the goals and aspirations of those of you who are called to leadership in these formative days; (2) to discover ways of interpreting the UCM to the United Presbyterian Church in the U.S.A.; (3) to find ways by which the work and mission of the UCM may be aided and abetted by the United Presbyterian Church. In short, to learn how to aid without meddling.

In the course of the evening with the Advisory Council, I made extensive notes on what I thought I was hearing from . . . you. To facilitate a more accurate representation of UCM, I write this letter, submitting my interpretation of what I heard to your scrutiny and corroboration or correction. I would be deeply indebted to you, and greatly aided in my own work, if you would take the time to review my observations, and give me the benefit of your own corrective insights. I recognize that my

From "An Exchange of Letters Interpreting the Goals and Perspectives of U.C.M. Leaders," by Harold H. Viehman and Charlotte Bunch. Reprinted by permission.

own terminology may be strange to you and you may not recognize the UCM in these characterizations. Your comments on this point would also be appreciated.

As the two of you spoke, I began to make notes that distinguished that to which you would have UCM adhere, from some contrasting possibilities. In my language, that which you would "eschew" in favor of another development.

Here, then, for your scrutiny, is my list of UCM "Eschews":

1. In UCM—you would eschew the separation of Christians from non-Christians or non-confessing persons, being convinced that there is a wide company of students and faculty with whom you are engaged in a searching involvement in the world. Another way of stating this—in UCM you would eschew the sacred-secular dichotomy.

2. In UCM—you would eschew much of the piety found in most church circles to affirm a strong faith and to live in the real advent—the true expectation that God is breaking through meaningfully in the lives of students and faculty in these days in quite unpredictable ways.

3. In UCM—you would eschew bondage to political and organizational forms so familiar to students (and especially Christian student fellowships) in order that you may insist that structures become, once again, instrumental to emerging insights, purposes and programs.

4. In UCM—you would eschew captivity to categories of thought that reduce the real to the measurable and observable, in order that you might search out and reaffirm the deeper covenants of mankind.

5. In UCM—you would eschew internationalism in order that you might affirm the necessity of the world of mankind. In this you recognize fully the divergencies which mark men in this world—divergencies of cultural, political and creedal experience and loyalty—but you will insist that they be appropriated because of the riches they represent, rather than be allowed to shackle and separate men with the traditional institutional forms in which they are found.

6. In UCM—you would eschew easy acceptance of the limitations upon learning imposed by conventional patterns of higher education in favor of a reappraisal of education in the search for truly liberating knowledge in this century.

7. In UCM—you would eschew dogmatic, ordered, doctrinal, a priori theology—in favor of developing theological formulations that are attendant upon life struggle.

8. In UCM—you would eschew the use of history as the source of norms for life, and would affirm only its instrumental value as you seek to devise new patterns in an age of widespread and fast moving change.

9. In UCM—you would eschew an evolutionary approach to the institutions of culture, including, of course, the church, in favor of creating the new and necessary institutions required to live meaningfully today.

In summary, this is what I thought I heard. I heard also the frustration that these affirmations bring as one seeks to incarnate these insights while being faced also with the necessity of living decisively in this decade where issues are presented to you on the basis of assumptions and understandings which you seek to change. Vietnam is a good example of just such a dilemma demanding decisive treatment.

If I understand you, however, I can only applaud the courage and integrity involved in your leadership and pray that God will abundantly bless the University Christian Movement.

Sincerely yours,

Harold H. Viehman, Secretary
General Division of Higher Education
The United Presbyterian Church in
the United States of America

January 15, 1967

Dear Mr. Viehman:

Thank you for your response to the Advisory Council meeting of the University Christian Movement. Your perception of what we are trying to convey was quite keen. After reading your letter over closely, . . . I find that [I am] in basic agreement with what you have understood and stated as UCM eschews.

One of our central dilemmas is indeed that of finding ways to express and live out our understandings when they are constantly defined by old modes of thinking and acting; as you put it, "where issues are presented to you on the basis of assumptions and understandings which

you seek to change." This dilemma is key both in trying to work out new modes of response to issues so presented and in communication, where language alone seems to be "used up" as a medium of communication. It might, therefore, be most helpful for you in interpreting UCM if I elaborate on some of that to which we would have UCM adhere to take the place of the assumptions and understandings underlying the "eschews."

Although each of your points differs, I have put them together into four main groupings:

1., 2., and 7. Each of these refers accurately to our nature as a "Christian" movement. Our conviction that faith and theology today are being renewed, in quite unpredictable ways, through involvement in and with the secular, not in Christian ghettos of pietism, grows out of our experience in the 1960's. For example, while religious creeds and formulations often seemed far-removed from the lives and problems of most people, many of us saw the spirit and living theology of the freedom movement blow fresh air into people's lives—and into the churches and universities. Thus, the UCM, as with many students, is interested in exploring how Christian insights and values apply today, but we find that such insights have more meaning when they are consciously developed within the life around us and not in the abstract. In our theological reflection, then, non-confessing persons, who share in this struggle for a more human society, are naturally part of the community seeking to understand itself in this world.

3. and 9. Structurally, the UCM is indeed trying to discover ways that structures can be made to enable rather than predetermine directions and movement. This does not necessarily mean (as number 9 might imply) that we opt only for the creation of new institutions in place of the old. We recognize that creating those "institutions required to live meaningfully today" involves us not only in creating anew or transforming the old but also in finding non-organizational forms of responding to human needs and insights. Even in the creation of the UCM, situations change so fast that we must have constant flexibility in order to avoid new bondage, yet, the line between flexibility and chaos is often difficult to draw in seeking to be both responsive to an ever changing world and effective in an over-institutionalized society.

4., 6., and 8. Numbers 4 and 6 clearly capture the need today to recover the sense of the wholeness of man, and particularly the role of education in liberating the whole man. Process '67 will, of course, focus on this question and attempt to find new patterns of education—of developing means to cope with vast amounts of information, of relating

values to decision-making and issues-definition, and finally of linking action to knowledge. Within this process the role of history and the insights it provides are key. Certainly history is to us instrumental, not normative (no. 8), but this defines its use and does not diminish its importance. (After all, I was a history major!)

5. This is perhaps the most perplexing problem within the life of UCM—internationalization that is neither absorption nor paralyzing diversity. We would embrace the description you gave of a pluralism that appropriates diversity but does not demand consensus in order to move forward, but we must confess great difficulty in making this a reality.

There should perhaps be at least one final point in your description of UCM. We "eschew" the notion of "lowest-common-denominator ecumenism" and the demand for consensus in order to move. We adhere, rather, to the need for some common vision and trust that allows us to act out our diversity as a movement with some sense of common identity and hope that we are "ecumenically" together in our search for a better life for all men.

As you can tell, I found your nine eschews quite insightful into our hopes and frustrations. This response is necessarily too brief as it will take continuing UCM experience and conversation together to understand further what issues will emerge as we seek to change basic understandings and assumptions. I hope, therefore, that we can have further conversation about the things to which we "adhere"—about the movement we of the UCM hope we are building. Thank you for your thoughtful response, and I hope we shall be in touch in the future.

Peace,

Charlotte Bunch, President
University Christian Movement

Index of Authors